Fanny and Adelaide

FANNY
&
ADELAIDE

 The Lives of the
Remarkable Kemble Sisters

ANN BLAINEY

Ivan R. Dee

CHICAGO 2001

FANNY AND ADELAIDE. Copyright © 2001 by Ann Blainey. All rights reserved, including the right to reproduce this book or portions thereof in any form. For information, address: Ivan R. Dee, Publisher, 1332 North Halsted Street, Chicago 60622. Manufactured in the United States of America and printed on acid-free paper.

Library of Congress Cataloging-in-Publication Data:
Blainey, Ann, 1935–
    Fanny and Adelaide: the lives of the remarkable Kemble sisters / Ann Blainey.
      p. cm.
    Includes bibliographical references and index.
    ISBN 1-56663-372-9 (alk. paper)
     1. Kemble, Fanny, 1809–1893. 2. Actors—Great Britain—Biography.
3. Plantation owners' spouses—Georgia—Biography. 4. Kemble, Adelaide.
5. Singers—Great Britain—Biography. I. Title.

PN2598.K4 B58 2001
792'.028'092—dc21
[B]   00-050440

For Adelaide Lubbock

Contents

Preface

THIS IS A DOUBLE BIOGRAPHY of the remarkable Kemble sisters. It would be hard to find, in European civilization in the last two centuries, two sisters who achieved more success across the arts and professions. Born in 1809 into a celebrated theatrical family, Fanny Kemble was the most famous English-speaking actress of her day before she left the stage to marry the Philadelphia slave-holder Pierce Butler. For more than sixty years she was seldom out of the public eye, acting in plays, writing books, reading Shakespeare in front of large audiences, and fighting for the abolition of slavery. Her searing intellect and indomitable personality made people love her or hate her. No one could ignore her.

Her sister Adelaide, five years her junior, ranks among the finest of English-born opera singers. Making her debut in Venice in the exacting role of Norma—and singing nothing but a leading role thereafter—she won acclaim across Italy and at two brilliant seasons at London's Covent Garden before marrying the rich Edward Sartoris.

It seemed logical to combine the two lives of the Kemble sisters in one book. Both Fanny and Adelaide were launched in the theatre in an extraordinary way and instantly became stars. Even when for a decade and a half they lived on opposite sides of the Atlantic Ocean, they remained in touch and contrived to come together for long periods. They were rivals as well as intimate friends: opposite sides of the same coin. They were also promoters of the status of women before that cause was fashionable. Long after their professional careers were over they were artistically alive and capable of captivating celebrated individuals who were a generation younger. In her old age, Fanny's admirer was the novelist Henry James while Adelaide's devoted friend was the painter Frederic Leighton.

The idea of writing double lives was spurred by the discovery of large bundles of long-lost Kemble letters. The main sequence was written by

< ix >

Adelaide Kemble to the family of Count Thun in Bohemia between 1838 and 1879: in fading ink the letters reveal Adelaide's innermost feelings for her parents and sister, and for the love of her life, Francis Thun.

I should add that no life of Adelaide has previously been attempted. And the seven or more biographies of Fanny Kemble have not adequately explored the intimate relationship between the sisters, the alternations of envy and affection on Fanny's part, and the dynamics of the extraordinary Kemble family. Past biographers have not fully understood the low social status of women in the theatre of the time, and how that humble status affected and spurred Fanny. Nor have they realized that much of Fanny's distinctive outlook—especially on women's rights and slavery—sprang from her upbringing in theatrical circles where an independent life for a woman was normal.

Some time after my book had entered the publishing process, I heard of the publication of Catherine Clinton's book, *Fanny Kemble's Civil Wars*. I read it eagerly and with pleasure. I soon realized that our respective books did not often emphasize the same episodes or phases of Fanny's life: indeed, a large section of Dr. Clinton's book has to do with Fanny's daughters. And she touches only in passing on the life of Adelaide, who occupies half my book. So, to a surprising degree, we cover different ground.

My view of Fanny's personality and motivation sometimes differs from that depicted by Dr. Clinton. I see Fanny as a complex character, to some extent an image of her actress mother, whose depressive and tempestuous nature she largely inherited. I also see Fanny with the help of Adelaide's observations. Fanny censored much of her surviving correspondence, and new insights were waiting in the 220 or more candid family letters that I have been the first biographer to read and use.

This cache of lost Kemble letters had come into the possession of Adelaide Kemble's great-granddaughter, Adelaide Lubbock, who stored them in a trunk in the cellar of her house in Kent, England. She presented me with these bundles, unread for so long, and in her last year encouraged me to write this book. I dedicate the book to her.

A. B.

Melbourne, Australia
January 2001

Fanny and Adelaide

1

God Almighty's Nobility

In 1815, not long before the battle of Waterloo, the French actor Talma called at a house near Covent Garden in the heart of London. At the front door he was received, not by the well-known actor he was calling upon, but by the actor's daughter, a precocious child of five. When the girl asked who he was, Talma declared in a resonant voice that he was a tragic actor and a celebrated one. "So is my uncle," the child replied, "and so is my father."

The small girl was Fanny Kemble, who was herself to win great fame as an actress. More than sixty years later she remembered—or claimed to remember—how she told the Frenchman on the doorstep, not only how famous were her relatives, but how exasperating was her newborn sister, Adelaide. Fanny announced that Adelaide had the touch of the tragic actress, because she cried all day long. This reminiscence about her sister's trying behavior was probably a mirror of Fanny's own emotions. While it is highly unlikely that, at the age of five, she likened her bawling baby sister to a would-be actress, her story reveals what she thought about this interloper in her nursery. Though Fanny loved her sister, she also saw her as a competitor—which Adelaide proved to be. Adelaide Kemble was to become the finest English opera singer of her time.

The sisters were born into one of the most remarkable families of the British stage. Their grandparents, most of their uncles and aunts, and many of their cousins were actors. The largest share of the family's fame, however, rested on three who were head and shoulders above the rest: John Philip Kemble, the girls' uncle; Charles Kemble, their father; and Sarah Siddons, their aunt.

Leigh Hunt, the critic and essayist, who knew and observed the family closely, was one of many who looked on these three Kembles with a respect approaching awe. On stage they were incomparable artists. In drawing

< 3 >

rooms they were polished guests, the equals in manners and education of a duke or duchess. Hunt called them "God Almighty's nobility," and he was quick to point out that they were welcomed into the best circles of English society.

That the Kembles were so welcomed was extraordinary because the stage was then a disreputable profession, and the Kembles sprang from the lowest rung of the theatrical ladder. In the public mind, actors stood on three rungs. There were those at the top, who played in the best London theatres and were sometimes acceptable in society; those in the middle, who acted in the provinces in established companies and were respected within the profession but socially unacceptable outside it; and those at the bottom, who roamed the countryside in disreputable troupes, performing in inns and barns. The great Kembles were born into one of these raffish strolling troupes, which placed them, in the social hierarchy of the time, only a notch above tramps and performing bears.

Roger Kemble, the father of John Philip, Sarah, and Charles and grandfather of Fanny and Adelaide, was a Hereford barber. In 1752, at the age of thirty-one, he joined a strolling troupe, having fallen in love with one of its actresses. Onstage he had few theatrical skills, but offstage he was adept at playing the gentleman. Meeting him in old age, the theatrical biographer James Boaden declared that Roger Kemble looked and spoke like a seventeenth-century bishop, and that "his countenance excited reverence beyond any that I have ever seen."

Roger Kemble had grown up believing that he was descended from a distinguished Catholic family, the Kembles of Wiltshire and Herefordshire, who numbered among their ranks the Blessed John Kemble, a Catholic priest martyred in 1678 and beatified by the pope. Roger believed passionately in his aristocratic, sainted ancestry. A large part of his gentlemanly bearing derived from this belief, and his children's air of good breeding was similarly colored by it. The family was deeply disappointed when, years later, the Royal College of Arms was unable to verify the Kembles' aristocratic background.

Roger did not stay long with his first troupe. After a few months he joined another, where he fell in love with the manager's daughter, a strong-willed, handsome girl named Sarah Ward. Roger proposed marriage and was accepted, but Sarah's father withheld his consent. A convert to Methodism—which condemned Catholics and actors—John Ward refused to have a papist actor as a son-in-law. For almost a year the deadlock continued. In 1753, while the troupe was playing in Cirencester, Sarah defied her father and married Roger. When Ward heard what she had done, he is supposed to have told her: "Well at least you haven't disobeyed me by marrying an actor; the devil himself couldn't make an actor out of your husband."

Sarah Kemble was never backward in doing as she pleased. When James Boaden met her in her old age, he was equally struck by her strength of character and her forceful conversation and referred to her as the "old lioness." Conversation was a talent that Sarah passed down to her grandchildren, especially to Fanny.

On John Ward's death, Roger inherited the company, but it was Sarah who ran it. A demanding woman, she expected the best from her employees and her children, eight of whom survived infancy. Though it was usual for children from theatrical families to follow in their parents' footsteps, this was far from Sarah's aim. She considered the life too hard and too risky. The troupe was almost continually on the road—a night here and a night there, and then on with the wagons to the next town. Companies of actors were required by law to perform in licensed theatres. Since strolling players acted only in unlicensed venues, they risked fines or imprisonment at every performance. Sarah wanted something better for her children. As she trudged in the wake of the wagons, she vowed she would educate and elevate her offspring. But beggars could not be choosers. The troupe was continually short of players, and all eight of Sarah's children appeared on stage when they were young. The eldest two were exceptionally talented, as even their mother was forced to admit.

In resolving to educate her children, Sarah Kemble eventually had her way. Somehow money was found to send the eldest son, John Philip, to school: first to a Catholic school in Staffordshire, and then, like his namesake, the Blessed John, to the celebrated English Catholic college in Douai, France. His father hoped that the boy would become a priest, but John Philip was willful. At nineteen he ran off to join a band of actors. So outstanding was his talent that within eight years he was a leading player at the foremost theatres in London and on his way to becoming, in Byron's phrase, the "most supernatural" of actors.

The eldest daughter, Sarah, was sent to a girls' school in Worcester, leaving at sixteen to become a lady's companion. It was hoped she would make a satisfactory marriage; but being her mother's daughter, she had a mind of her own. At eighteen she insisted in quick succession on becoming an actress and marrying a mediocre actor named William Siddons. Two years later, when she was twenty and heavily pregnant, she was spotted in a

Cheltenham theatre by a London talent scout. Sarah was playing Rosalind in *As You Like It*, which required her to dress as a boy. The sight of her "big belly" poking through her doublet at first so tickled the scout that he hardly noticed her acting. But after a few scenes he ceased to see her belly. By the next post he wrote to David Garrick, the celebrated actor-manager at the Theatre Royal in London's Drury Lane, to announce that he had found a potential star.

Sarah Siddons rushed to join Garrick's company, but the work demanded more skill than she had so far acquired. Defeated, she retired to the provinces. Seven years later she returned to Drury Lane, transformed. On October 10, 1782, she made her second London debut, playing Isabella in *The Fatal Marriage*. The performance made theatrical history. For more than three hours, Mrs. Siddons's mesmeric face and superb voice held the audience spellbound. She projected innocence, despair, and madness with electrifying intensity. Spectators were bathed in tears. One woman, desperately trying to hold back sobs, fell into a convulsion and "stayed in that miserable state for a considerable time after the curtain dropt."

Within months a Siddons cult was sweeping the country. Vast crowds were prepared to wait all day outside the theatre in the hope of buying a ticket. Each night giant waves of emotion surged back and forth between actress and audience. The effect was addictive. Once seen, Sarah Siddons had to be seen over and over again.

Writers and painters could not stop singing her praises. Samuel Johnson called her a "prodigious fine woman." Joshua Reynolds signed his portrait of Sarah on the edge of her gown, saying that he wanted to go "down to posterity on the hem of her garment." The essayist Willam Hazlitt was so carried away by her Lady Macbeth that he wrote: "It seemed almost as if a being of a superior order had dropped from a higher sphere to awe the world with the majesty of her appearance. Power was seated on her brow, passion emanated from her breast as from a shrine; she was tragedy personified." For thirty years, Sarah Siddons was queen of the British stage and the popular imagination. Wrote one rapturous observer: "Were a Wild Indian to ask me, What was like a queen? I would have bade him look at Mrs. Siddons."

The youngest of Mrs. Siddons's brothers was Charles, the father of Fanny and Adelaide. Twenty years younger than Sarah, he was born in 1775, just as his sister was beginning her phenomenal career. Like John Philip, Charles was packed off to school at Douai. On returning home he was found a respectable post as a clerk. Though he longed to act, Charles seemed to have no talent. A tall, skinny youth, he was so awkward it seemed he would trip over his feet every time he stepped on stage.

Refusing to accept his family's warnings, Charles joined a troupe. A year later, at the age of eighteen, he applied for work at the Theatre Royal at Drury Lane, where his brother, John Philip, was the powerful actor-manager and his sister, Sarah Siddons, the leading lady. Though his acting initially verged on hopeless, the performers absorbed him into their company; and over the following ten years he disciplined his gawky arms and legs to reveal a "fine majestic figure" capable of performing with flair in leading roles. As Leigh Hunt put it, Charles was the "nearest approach to Shakespeare's gentleman, and to heroes of romance."

At the Drury Lane theatre Charles Kemble met his future wife: a delightful dark-haired, dark-eyed actress a year older than himself named Marie Thérèse De Camp. Marie Thérèse claimed to have aristocratic blood: she maintained that her great-grandfather was the French Marquis de Fleury. More relevant, she sprang from a French theatrical family in the service of the Austrian empress, Maria Theresa, who was reputedly her godmother and was certainly her namesake. Marie Thérèse's father, George De Camp, was a flute player at the imperial court theatre in Vienna, where her uncle was ballet master and her aunt, Simonet, was a well-known dancer.

At the age of two Marie Thérèse moved from Vienna to London, where her father found work in the theatre orchestra at Drury Lane. By the age of six, she was dressed in tights and spangles and playing a cupid at the opera house. By the age of eight, in pink satin breeches and a powdered wig, she was performing in French plays in a juvenile troupe managed by a Monsieur de Texier. By the time she was nine, her father was dead, and her stage earnings were helping to support two little sisters and a younger brother.

Her mother became the housekeeper to a nobleman, and it was in his house that Marie Thérèse, known as the "little French fairy," first danced before the Prince of Wales—the future King George IV—and his unofficial wife, Maria Fitzherbert. Thereafter, according to her elder daughter, Marie Thérèse became one of their favorites, and was "fondled and petted and played with, passing whole days in Mrs. Fitzherbert's drawing room." Occasionally the prince would place her "under a huge glass bell, made to cover some large group of precious Dresden china." There her small figure and flashing face produced a "more beautiful effect than the costly work of art."

A girlhood passed in theatrical circles and among the more profligate of the aristocracy could have been corrupting, but Marie Thérèse was determined to retain her respectability. Her younger daughter would later marvel that her mother passed through the "two worst extremities of society" yet "remained honourable in deed, and uncontaminated in thought." This was not to say that Marie Thérèse was priggish or cold. On the contrary, she was highly emotional. Desperate for security and love, she was prone to tantrums and jealousy. Both her daughters later testified that hers was a "passionate, vehement, susceptible and suffering nature."

At the age of eighteen, Marie Thérèse appeared at the Haymarket Theatre in a novel version of *The Beggar's Opera* in which men and women exchanged roles. Her dancing, her soprano voice, and her superb legs clad in tight male breeches caused a sensation. Leigh Hunt praised her "beautiful figure, fine large dark eyes, and elevated features, fuller of spirit than softness but still capable of expressing great tenderness." As a singer, dancer, and actress combined, she had few rivals in England.

Soon after *The Beggar's Opera*, Marie Thérèse met Charles Kemble. She is said to have fallen in love with him on sight, but he did not respond. She tried to arouse his affection, displaying the "wildest and most passionate love," but their natures were poles apart. Charles, according to his younger daughter, was a "mild and gently amiable person of cultivated tastes and refined habits—with a great deal of natural tenderness, but a man of the world without one particle of romance or passion—and utterly incapable of answering and comprehending a nature" such as Marie Thérèse's. He could take his pick of women and had no wish to settle down. Nevertheless Marie Thérèse persisted and eventually won him over. In 1800 they became engaged.

The engagement displeased Charles's older brother and mentor, John Philip, who was said to be "violent against it." No reason was given, but the cause may be guessed. Five years before, in January, 1795, a drunken and amorous John Philip had forced his way into Marie Thérèse's dressing room. She had called for help and been rescued—some say by her brother, some say by Charles. On January 27, readers of the London *Times* were intrigued to see a formal announcement signed by John Philip Kemble apologizing for his "improper and unjustifiable behavior" toward a woman of irreproachable character. Why he so freely confessed his sin is not known, but one imagines that pressure was brought to bear by the De Camp brothers. If so, it is not difficult to see why he disliked the idea of Charles marrying a De Camp.

When the engagement was announced, John Philip declared that he would not support the marriage until Charles turned thirty. He seems to have believed that the couple would not be prepared to wait another five years. Marie Thérèse, however, would not capitulate. She told a confidante that she could "never form an idea of being happy with any other man." On July 2, 1806, after nearly six years of delays and deferments, Marie Thérèse and Charles were married at St. George's Church in Bloomsbury. As might have been predicted, they did not live happily ever after.

In her new life Marie Thérèse was utterly absorbed in her husband, but he was less so in her. Marriage failed to curb his wandering eye. Charles was "run after in the most shameless way by many of our fine ladies," wrote his younger daughter, so "you may imagine what her jealous sufferings were." Deeply wounded by her husband's infidelity, especially since she herself had waited so long and faithfully to marry him, Marie Thérèse grew possessive, cruel-tongued, and addicted to tantrums. Year after year she tried to wrest from Charles the love and reassurance that her passionate nature craved and from which his calmer and less committed nature shrank. When she died an obituarist close to the family observed that she was well cast as the jealous, tempestuous Lucy Lockit in *The Beggar's Opera*. Noting that Marie Thérèse was "excellent company," he regretted that her tongue was so often "barbed." Even her elder daughter, who took a most charitable view of her mother, conceded that Marie Thérèse possessed a "savage rather than a civilized nature."

Outsiders seldom saw Marie Thérèse's tantrums and tirades. To them she appeared to be a most entertaining woman: shrewd and amusing, generous by nature, polished in manner, and with a striking turn of phrase. This was the more remarkable since French, not English, was her native tongue. Her elder daughter maintained that she spoke English with "more originality and vivacity than any Englishwoman I have ever known."

Outsiders also commented on Marie Thérèse's independent will, though independence was not rare in women of the stage. In theatrical culture they were expected to negotiate their own salaries, look after their own money, and even manage their own theatres. This degree of emancipation was a century or so ahead of women's gains in other professions. Marie Thérèse took power and independence as her due, a belief that she passed on to her daughters.

She had no intention of giving up her career after marriage. It was accepted that actresses should perform throughout pregnancy and give birth, as it were, between performances. Marie Thérèse's son, John Mitchell, was born a bare nine months after the marriage. Probably he was not her first child. Decades later, her elder daughter, Fanny, set out to chronicle the family history and recorded that Marie Thérèse's eldest child was a boy called Philip, who had died in earliest infancy. She did not realize that she was thereby revealing that Philip must have been illegitimate.

By the time John Mitchell was born, Sarah Siddons, John Philip, and Charles Kemble were acting exclusively at the Theatre Royal at Covent Garden. John Philip had bought a one-sixth share in that theatre for twenty-three thousand pounds. The sum was colossal, but John Philip considered that the theatre was an incomparable asset.

The theatre's power came from its partial monopoly of the "legitimate" drama. Back in the time of Charles II, playwrights had been among the most vocal critics of the king and his ministers. To curb their voices, Parliament resolved that all theatres should be licensed. Licenses were restricted to two in London—at Covent Garden and Drury Lane—and a few in Ireland, Scotland, and the provinces. Over the years, ways were found to evade this law, and by the Kembles' time scores of unlicensed theatres were putting on plays, thanks to a legal loophole whereby performances containing singing and dancing could be legally classed as concerts. These upstart theatres irritated the monopolists but had failed to dint their power.

In London the theatres in Covent Garden and Drury Lane reigned supreme, and of the two, Covent Garden was the more splendid. Set in the magnificent market square designed by the famous architect Inigo Jones, it seemed more like a temple than a playhouse: a temple dedicated to Melpomene, the Greek muse of tragedy, and to Sarah Siddons, her high priestess. To approach the theatre doors, playgoers pushed through a press of bodies: women selling oranges, little boys hawking playbills, garishly dressed prostitutes, and a crowd of loiterers. Inside they found a world of magic. A great horseshoe of galleries soared to the roof, holding close to three thousand people. In a time when private houses were dimly lighted, the brightness inside the theatre seemed miraculous. It came from rows of mirror-backed crystal chandeliers hanging from the front of the boxes. Once those myriad candles were lit, the radiance was as dazzling as noonday sunshine. When the curtain rose and powerful footlights shed their rays over the stage, the theatre seemed like a vast temple of light.

In the top galleries, tucked under the roof like pigeons in a loft, roosted the poorest and most demanding spectators. Even before the play began, they would shout and throw orange peels on the people beneath. Once the performance began, their voices were seldom silent, calling out for encores and yelling abuse when an actor annoyed them. Below, in the boxes, sat the sedate people of rank and fashion: gentlemen in exquisitely tied neckcloths and ladies in low-cut evening dresses, their white shoulders and jeweled necklaces glowing in the candlelight. On the ground floor, known as the pit, women of the middle classes rubbed shoulders with gentlemen of any rank. Most wore street clothes, and all sat on hard wooden benches without backs.

Performances began at half-past six, but only those in the galleries and pit arrived on time—unless Mrs. Siddons, whose very presence demanded punctuality, was appearing. The boxes began to fill at about eight, and gentlemen who had dined at their clubs arrived around ten. Having missed the main play, they were in time for the frivolous afterpiece, which went on until well past midnight. They preferred to see a cheeky actress bare her ankles in *The Day after the Wedding* rather than to sit through three solid hours of *Hamlet*. Halfway through the evening, any empty seats were sold cheaply; the incoming raggle-taggle contained its quota of "nymphs," who loitered in the foyers looking for business. Many a bibulous clubman, titillated by the sight of his favorite on stage, left after midnight on the arm of a prostitute.

The theatre at Covent Garden was not only a moving cameo of London life but the Kembles' home and the basis of their fame and income—their lifeblood. On September 20, 1808, in the darkness of the early morning, the theatre was struck by disaster. A piece of wadding, discharged from a musket during the play, quietly smoldered in a recess of the stage and then burst into flame. Within minutes the building was ablaze, and a brisk breeze sent showers of sparks down the adjoining streets and across the wide market square. Householders and servants, awakened by the crackle of flames and the smell of smoke, rushed from their beds. Seizing buckets of water, they pounced on the glowing cinders that fell on their roofs and into their yards. But in the deserted alleyways there was no one to pounce, and many sparks turned into full-scale conflagrations.

At the first alarm, a messenger sped to the Phoenix Insurance Company to summon its fire engines. But when the engines arrived, no water pipe could be found. After frantic searching, the hoses were at last connected, and with jets spraying, the firemen broke through the great door of the theatre. They were too late. As they burst through the doorway, the roof crashed down, burying them in masonry. Those not killed by the fall were scalded to death by the steam of the hoses. When rescuers cleared away the rubble, eleven charred corpses were uncovered, the flesh, "literally peeled off the bone."

The theatre had been the repository of priceless treasures. John

Philip's large collection of plays had gone up in flames. So had musical scores by Handel and Arne, of which there were no other copies. The expensive organ Handel had left to the theatre—the one used for his oratorios—was burned to ashes. Mrs. Siddons's costly stage costumes had perished, and so had acres of expensive scenery. To add to the disaster, the building was insured for only about one-quarter of its value.

Next morning John Philip Kemble held court in his elegant house in the newly built district of Bloomsbury. Though they were in a state of shock, the Kembles were not blind to the drama and gained some comfort from exploiting it. The scene in John Philip's bedroom, where family and friends were gathered, was highly theatrical. Charles sat on the sofa, his face and garments black from the fire: he had just come from sifting through the wreckage. John Philip stood before his dressing table mirror "totally absorbed, and yet at intervals attempting to shave himself," wrote one observer. "His mind was raised rather than dejected, and his imagination distended." From time to time he would lay down his razor and lift his arms in sweeping gestures, declaiming in his mighty voice that all was lost—the theatre, the library, the music, the scenery. Only the coat of arms of England remained, proudly emblazoned over the theatre's blackened doorway. When James Boaden entered the room, Mrs. John Philip jumped from her seat and cried out in a voice of anguish: "Oh Mr. Boaden, we are totally ruined."

Patrons came to the Kembles' aid. The Duke of Northumberland donated ten thousand pounds toward rebuilding the theatre, and the public raised another fifty thousand. Three months after the fire, there was sufficient capital to begin rebuilding, and John Philip devised a stone-laying ceremony worthy of the occasion. It invoked Masonic rituals and starred the Prince of Wales, who adored displaying himself in public and could always be trusted to give a memorable performance.

On the last day of 1808, vast crowds braved the morning rain to assemble in the Covent Garden marketplace for what promised to be a splendid spectacle. Elegant ladies and gentlemen looked down from covered grandstands, and spectators thronged the sidewalks. The Prince of Wales, magnificently dressed as a Grand Master of the Freemasons, paraded with his entourage down a green-carpeted platform, to the accompaniment of military bands and a twenty-one-gun salute. Standing before the foundation stone, he delicately grasped a silver trowel, and with theatrical flair, spread cement across the stone's surface, like a chef icing a giant cake. That done, ropes and pulleys majestically lowered the three-ton stone down into its cavity. To signify that the stone was correctly laid, the prince struck it three times with a silver mallet. Finally, like a high priest of old, he raised three cups filled with corn, wine, and oil, and scattered their contents over the stone—performing his duties, so onlookers said, with a histrionic talent that rivaled that of the Kembles. John Philip, splendid in Masonic uniform, stood exultantly beside his prince, while Mrs. Siddons, decked in flowing black ostrich feathers, looked on and the massed bands played "Rule, Britannia." Never in the history of England had a family of the theatre stood so high as the Kembles on that glorious day.

With four massive Doric columns at the entrance, and friezes and statues around the walls, the completed theatre was a splendid neoclassical edifice. The architect Robert Smirke—who later designed the even grander British Museum—made little attempt to keep within his budget. Nor did John Philip, who called for crystal chandeliers and solid mahogany doors. The building in the end carried a debt exceeding twenty thousand pounds, and John Philip Kemble, as manager and shareholder, bore a substantial portion of that debt. As the proprietors desperately needed to raise revenue, they decided to abolish the cheap gallery on the second-highest level and replace it with expensive private boxes. In one sweep the number of cheap seats was reduced by more than half. The proprietors also added a surcharge to every ticket in the house.

For some years it had been the contention of lower- and middle-class playgoers that London's only two licensed theatres were abusing their power. When Covent Garden raised its prices, the allegation seemed proven beyond doubt. The disgruntled occupants of the pit found allies in the now-diminished gallery. Their combined protest fell on the head of John Philip Kemble.

On September 18, 1809, the opening night of the rebuilt theatre, well-trained demonstrators crowded into the pit and gallery. As soon as John Philip Kemble appeared on stage, they called aloud for him to restore the old price. The rest of the performance was a dumb show, for not one word could be heard. At the end of the play, the mob refused to go home and began drumming on the floor and yelling for the management. John Philip, desperate to clear the theatre, sent for two magistrates to read the Riot Act, but this only provoked violence. The rioters began to smash the seats and, with shouts of "Dowse the glims," to shatter the precious chandeliers. It was not until police arrived to arrest the ringleaders that the crowd dispersed.

From then on, for sixty-six nights, the rioters came to each perfor-

mance with the tools of their trade hidden beneath their clothing, including rattles, bells, and banners. One night they managed to smuggle a live
pig into the gallery, and its squeals added a high-pitched descant to the
protest. The moment a Kemble appeared on stage, the cacophony would
begin. There would be an opening "yell of clamor and execration," and
then the bells would jingle and the horns would hoot. As the din increased,
the Old Price dance would commence: thousands of feet and sticks stamp-
ing on the floorboards reverberating to the chant: "O.P.! O.P.!" Outside the
theatre, Mrs. Siddons's carriage was manhandled, and back in quiet
Bloomsbury, the windows of John Philip's house were broken. Mrs. John
Philip, in fear of her life, kept a ladder under her window so that she could
escape through the garden if the house was attacked.

＊   Inside the theatre, appeals to reason were futile, as were attempts to
arrest the guilty. Using trained prize fighters to search the spectators as they
entered the theatre achieved little. In the end, after the longest disturbance
in English theatrical history, John Philip Kemble capitulated. Having
opened the theatre's balance sheets and books to public scrutiny, he met
the rioters' terms by lowering the prices. That evening the protesters signaled their success by raising a banner in the pit. It bore the stark inscription, "We are satisfied."

At the start of the Old Price riots, Marie Thérèse was seven months
pregnant. When John Philip decreed that an opera should be staged instead
of a play in the hope of drowning the clamor, Marie Thérèse agreed to sing.
To appear in front of a banging, whistling mob would have required strong
willpower of any performer; in advanced pregnancy it took extraordinary
courage. Marie Thérèse marched on stage as Lucy in *The Beggar's Opera* and
weathered the apple-cores and shouts of abuse. Just over two months later,
on November 27, 1809, she gave birth in Newman Street, London, to the
first of her daughters, Frances Anne, known as Fanny.

In years to come, friends of the family would wonder whether those
prenatal events contributed to Fanny Kemble's combative nature, but it is
more likely that her willfulness was inherited from her forceful mother and
grandmother. On the other hand, Fanny's high level of anxiety may well be
related to the events of 1809 and their sequel. The rebuilding of the theatre
and the damage caused by the Old Price riots left the Kembles in serious
debt. For the next twenty-five years their lives would be punctuated by financial crises. Fanny and Adelaide grew up in a climate of worry, which
probably left a permanent mark.

From infancy Fanny had an untamable talent for naughtiness, enlivened by a strong sense of the dramatic and a capacity for speaking up. One early incident reflected all these qualities. Fanny was seated on the lap of Mrs. Siddons and about to be chastised for a misdemeanor. She halted her aunt in mid-sentence by raising her gaze and piping with almost studied innocence: "What beautiful eyes you have." Aunt Siddons laughed and let her go without punishment.

The incident took place at Westbourne Green on the outskirts of London, where Sarah Siddons and Charles Kemble were briefly neighbors. It was there that Fanny's brother Henry, the second son, was born when Fanny was nearly four years old. From this rural suburb Fanny was sent away to a boarding school in Bath run by her aunt, a former actress. Her departure for a distant school soon after Henry's birth was prompted by her naughtiness. "I suppose," the adult Fanny recalled, "in human annals there never existed a more troublesome little brat than I was for the first few years after my appearance on this earthly stage."

Fanny's favorite memories of her year at boarding school centered on theatrical events, for she was already attuned to the world of the theatre. She rejoiced in visits to the mansion of Claverton Park, where Fanny and her cousins were sometimes taken to play. In later life, she vividly recalled its puppet theatre, where the son of their host used small wooden puppets to act out Shakespearean dramas. "These," Fanny recalled, "were the first plays I ever saw." She remembered also the thrill of acting in her aunt's drawing room. The youngest girl in the school, she was cast as the child in Sheridan's *Pizarro*. At one point in the play, her strong young cousin, John Twiss, would run across the room holding her aloft in one hand. It was her first taste of theatrical applause, and she loved it.

By her fifth birthday, Fanny was back in London, living with her parents in a tall, narrow building called Covent Garden Chambers, close to the family's theatre. There Fanny's younger sister, Adelaide, was born. The day and month of Adelaide's birth—February 13—are documented in the family's later letters. The year is far from certain, being recorded in her obituaries as 1814 and 1815 and on her death certificate as 1816. As the birth seems not to have been registered, the most relevant document is the baptismal register of St. James's Church in the London suburb of Paddington. It affirms that Adelaide Kemble was baptized there on November 24, 1815. As it was the policy of the church to baptize children soon after they were born, it seems likely that Adelaide was born in that year. This supposition appears to be endorsed by Fanny's autobiography, *Records of a Girlhood*. In it she wrote that in August 1830, Adelaide was in her sixteenth year. It seems safe, then, to assume that Adelaide was born on February 13, 1815.

Fanny vividly recalled her sister's birth, joining it in her mind with the visit of the French actor Talma. She also remembered her sister's capacity for gaining attention. A willful, passionate child herself, constantly craving notice, she did not take kindly to any rival in the nursery, as her emotional outbursts after her brother Henry's birth bore witness. At least her first rival had been a boy, and she had retained the distinction of being the only girl in the family. The arrival of yet another baby—and a female into the bargain—provoked even wilder tantrums.

Marie Thérèse made no attempt to look after her babies in person. As she continued to appear regularly on stage, she was excused from the duties of mothering and in particular of breast feeding. After her younger daughter's birth she performed less frequently, but she did not alter her habits. "She was prevented," commented Adelaide, "by her profession from fulfilling those first natural and dear duties that bond mothers to their children—she suckled none of us." Adelaide wondered whether "this may in some sort account for her utter want of *tenderness* towards us." In the end, Adelaide was forced to conclude that Marie Thérèse gave little affection to her children because she was more of a wife than a mother: "all her affections were swallowed up in her engrossing feeling for my father." Marie Thérèse had little left for her children, and she was only too glad to leave the mothering to someone else.

That "someone else" was Marie Thérèse's second sister, Adelaide, known to the children as Aunt Dall. Like most of her family, Dall had gone on the stage in her youth, joining a company run by Charles Kemble's brother Stephen. There she fell hopelessly in love with a Yorkshire squire who did not return her affections. In the sad aftermath, she came to live with her sister. From that time on—which was soon after Fanny's birth—Dall became, in Fanny's words, the "good Angel of the home," devoting her life to her sister's children and assuming the role, if not the title, of mother. Fanny called her "the happiest human being I have ever known" and marveled that she could spend each day "in a serene, unclouded, unvarying atmosphere of cheerfullness." Adelaide called her "the most unselfish person I have ever known."

As well as tending the children, Dall did her best to protect them from their turbulent mother. Timid little Adelaide shrank from Marie Thérèse. Dall shielded her from her mother's tirades and attempted to build up her confidence. Aggressive Fanny constantly confronted her mother in the hope of gaining the attention she craved. Dall was always ready with reassuring words when Fanny's confrontations failed. Serene and loving, Dall provided the ballast without which that theatrical household would have floated away on a tide of self-assertion and emotion. Without her the children's lives, in all probability, would have been shipwrecked.

In the eighteen months following Adelaide's birth, Fanny became almost uncontrollable. She was constantly at loggerheads with her mother, at war with her brothers, and resentful of her baby sister. Unable to endure her tantrums, her parents packed her off to school again, this time across the English Channel to Boulogne on the French coast, a fashionable place for the education of English daughters. While her parents' decision no doubt restored peace to the household, Fanny regarded it as harsh.

Only a child of monumental placidity could cope with the ordeal Fanny faced in Boulogne, and at seven years old she was far from placid. Classes were conducted solely in French, and when Fanny arrived she could speak no more than a few words of the language. She spent her first months in a pitiable state of disorientation and isolation, crying nightly into her pillow. She lacked even the comfort of another child of her own age, for she was the youngest in the school. As the miserable days passed, she felt totally abandoned.

Once she began to master the French language and feel more in control of her life, she stifled her misery, grew a tough outer shell, and rebelled. Whereas she had initially been overemotional, impulsive, and combative, she became angry and defiant. She recalled how she displayed an "audacious contempt for all authority" and a "cheerful indifference to all punishment."

Her rebellion swiftly brought her into conflict with the headmistress, a sallow and grim disciplinarian named Madame Faudier, who believed that girls must be forced into submission and that wickedness must be forcibly driven out. Fanny was frequently punished, usually by being locked in a confined space—a common punishment at that time. Sometimes she was imprisoned in a dark cellar, where she crouched on the top step, as near as possible to the crack of light beneath the door, too terrified to put her foot on the bottom step for fear she might somehow plunge into an abyss. Thus, with her arms clasped tight about her knees, she would weep "in a martyrdom of fear," she herself recalled. But even though she quaked with fright, nothing could stifle her defiant spirit. One day she was locked in a garret from which a trap door led onto the roof. When a passerby reported to her teachers that a child was skipping exultantly about the roof, Fanny's headmistress exclaimed in exasperated French: "it must be that little devil of a Kemble."

When such chastisements failed to find their mark, Madame Faudier decided on a punishment that went beyond the practices even of those harsh days. She ordered that Fanny be taken to a public execution, so that she could see firsthand the ultimate punishment for disobedience. A few days later, quivering with trepidation, Fanny set out in a teacher's custody for the town square. By some fortunate chance, they arrived too late to see the actual guillotining. Fanny was never sure whether this was intentional on the teacher's part or merely accidental. They did arrive in time, however, to see the ghastly machine, with its tall posts and crossbar, and to witness a sad-looking man cleaning the blade. The horrific sight sank deep into Fanny's already fevered imagination. Thereafter, for many months, she suffered "every conceivable form of terror," whether sleeping or waking.

FANNY ENDURED almost two years in Boulogne, without a holiday at home or a visit from a relative to lighten her wretchedness. Her parents seem to have believed that total separation was necessary to tame her and that the taming process needed time. It was not until the summer before her ninth birthday that Fanny saw England and her family again. She was as untamed as ever and, if anything, more adept at naughtiness.

The family had moved to a house beside open fields, not five miles from the theatre at Covent Garden. Confronted by the present-day sprawl of the city, one forgets how small an area one million Londoners occupied in 1818. Present-day suburbs such as Hampstead and Highgate were country villages, and beyond Marylebone and Paddington, the haymakers swung their scythes. On the western side of London, the city ended at Tyburn, the infamous site of public executions in the previous century. From there the high road ran to Bayswater, bordered on one side by the "untidy ravelled-looking selvage" of Hyde Park and Kensington Gardens, and on the other by open land. About a mile down the road, a lane led off to a gentle rise, on which stood the Kembles' cottage. The rise was called Craven Hill, and to Fanny—just released from the prison of Boulogne—it was one of the sweetest places on earth.

The Kembles occupied a small terrace house, one of a row of twelve cottages whose balconies and verandas were entwined with honeysuckle. Around the houses stretched nursery gardens ablaze with blooms, and cool green meadows spotted with cows. Only a meadow and the high road separated the Kembles from the gates of Kensington Gardens, where, like little

Miss Muffet, the children could buy halfpenny bowls of curds and whey. Since Marie Thérèse was performing only intermittently, she threw her energies into fitting up the house and, with a very small outlay, added comfort and elegance to every room she touched.

Fanny returned to an unfamiliar household. Notwithstanding Craven Hill's nearness to the theatre, her father no longer lived full time with his family, occupying rooms in London for part of each week. Fanny's brothers were at school: Henry, who was six, at a local school, and John, who was eleven, at Dr. Richardson's Academy at Clapham, on the other side of the city. Adelaide was a baby no longer. She had grown into a shy little four-year-old who regarded her older sister with awe. This reassured Fanny, who graciously allowed the little girl to trail after her as she roamed the lanes of Craven Hill. One imagines them wandering happily down the grassy pathways: both dark-eyed and dark-haired, Fanny chubby and short for her age, Adelaide tall and willowy for hers. They are dressed in straw hats and simple, high-waisted gowns. Adelaide's skirt finishes at the knee to reveal, as was the custom of the time, a pair of frilly, ankle-length pantalettes.

At holiday time, Fanny's brothers returned home, and the sisters' lives became exciting. John took over their holiday activities. He taught his young brother and sister how to color and cut out "printed sheets of small figures, representing all the characters of certain popular plays," which he had bought at a London toyshop. The colored figures became cardboard puppets for the plays they performed inside their toy theatre. Fanny and Aunt Dall ran up a blue silk curtain for the theatre, while John, who was keen on chemistry, improvised footlights as well as a miniature explosion to simulate the blowing up of a mill. This entertainment was their special delight during holidays, absorbing them hour after hour.

In the following year, John insisted that they should take the bold step of becoming real actors. Searching through his parents' library, he found a play with four main characters, so that even little Adelaide could play a principal part. *Amoroso, King of Little Britain* was not easy to stage, for there were songs as well as words. But the rehearsals went so well that the children invited some of their parents' friends to watch the performance. The adult audience included John Liston, who had played the part of Amoroso on the real stage; Charles Mathews, the gifted comic actor; and Charles Young, a stalwart member of the Covent Garden company and a favorite of the younger Kembles. These adult actors and their wives and children, along with Charles and Marie Thérèse, made up the amused and expectant audience on the first night of *Amoroso*.

Fanny's and Adelaide's debut upon the stage was an event of importance in their lives. It appears to have gone off well. "We contrived to
speak the words, and even to sing the songs," wrote Fanny, "much to our
own satisfaction." There can be little doubt that shy, little Adelaide was
quietly pleased by the prolonged applause. There can be even less doubt
that exhibitionist Fanny was jubilant and could not wait for her next appearance.

While the children were playing at theatre, Marie Thérèse prepared to
leave the real stage. At forty-five she was still handsome, with an expressive face and a graceful walk, but her small waist and the slender legs that
had once thrilled audiences had disappeared. Marie Thérèse was fat to the
point of obesity. For a long time, refusing to acknowledge her size, she continued to play the parts of sprightly young girls, for she hated the idea of
portraying matronly women. Finally she bowed to the inevitable, and in
June 1819 prepared for her farewell appearance.

To retire was no easy decision, for Marie Thérèse had been part of
the theatre since the age of six. To quit completely was like withdrawing
from a drug. Retirement also removed her from the Covent Garden company, one of the vital bonds which tied her to her husband. Though she
never ceased to fear he might be straying, she could keep an eye on him
while she acted with the company. Without Covent Garden, she suffered
from jealousy in the extreme. Underemployed and overimaginative, she
rampaged around the cottage, soothing her feelings by rearranging the furniture, a remedy she would resort to whenever her agitation got the better
of her. Fanny would remember her father's "piteous aspect" as he arrived
home at the weekends to find everything moved from its last position for
the umpteenth time. Instead of offering the praise which his wife craved,
he would exclaim, "Why bless my soul! what has happened to the room
again!"

Marie Thérèse's irritability fell often on the children, especially on rebellious Fanny. "My mother's intensely nervous organization, acute percep-
tions, and exacting taste made her in everything most keenly alive to our
faults and deficiencies," Fanny later observed. Whenever the children behaved stupidly, their mother would say emphatically: "I hate a fool." The
"unsparing severity" of the phrase, wrote Fanny, "has remained almost like
a cut with a lash across my memory." Fanny eventually realized that she and
her older brother John "were endowed with such robust self-esteem and
elastic conceit as not only defied repression, but, unfortunately for us, could
never be effectually snubbed; with my sister and my younger brother the

case was entirely different." In response to their mother's verbal lashing, Fanny and John became recalcitrant, while the other two children retreated, quaking.

Adelaide, her sister's temperamental opposite, avoided her mother as much as possible and hid away inside herself. Her solace was Aunt Dall, who tried to persuade her to regard her mother with more confidence. As Adelaide herself would see in future years, both she and her mother had hearts which usually overflowed with love. If only, she sighed later, they could have found a way to make contact with one another.

When Fanny wrote her reminiscences late in life, she colored her childhood with a happy, tomboy glow. There can be little doubt, however, that, under her mother's lashing tongue, even magical Craven Hill turned sour for her. An adventurous and independent child, she writhed under her mother's strictness and impossibly high standards. Though she tried to appear tough and indifferent, she hated being reproved, punished, or derided whenever she tried to decide or do anything for herself. She also resented the affection and sympathy that Aunt Dall lavished on Adelaide. A curious anecdote lifts the veil on her unhappiness and lays open the resentment that she felt as a child toward her sister. Fanny recorded that while at Craven Hill she decided to do away with Adelaide once and for all. She had been told that the berries from the privet bush contained a deadly poison. One day she stealthily picked some and placed them in Adelaide's way. She hoped that her sister would eat them and die.

After hours of picturing Adelaide's death throes—sometimes with pleasure, sometimes with horror—Fanny decided to heed her conscience and avert the tragedy. Sick with anxiety and guilt, she ran to Aunt Dall and confessed all. Adelaide was saved, though it is doubtful if she was ever in real danger, since she was a cautious child and had also been warned about the dangers of the privet bush.

One morning, not long after this episode, Fanny's feelings of resentment boiled up into rebellion. She and her aunt and sister were wandering through the summer meadows when an argument broke out between Dall and Fanny. As it grew in force, her aunt lost her usual serenity and ordered Fanny back to the house. Instead of obeying, Fanny made off in the opposite direction, toward Tyburn. She had made up her mind that she would run away to London and go on the stage.

In fact she ran no further than the cottage of a neighbor, where she was "ignominiously captured" an hour or so later. Both incidents show how troubled and unmanageable she was: "I had become a tragically desperate young person," she later remarked. Her running away shows how, even at the age of ten or eleven, her thoughts were focused on becoming an actress.

Fanny's ambition was scarcely surprising. As far back as she could remember, she had heard thrilling stories of the theatre and had longed to be part of it. While she was still in the nursery, Charles Young taught her how to imitate her Aunt Siddons's famous sleep-walking scene from *Macbeth*. Under Young's instruction, Fanny would stand in the middle of the nursery floor, fold her fat little arms, and pull down her mouth and eyebrows in a "portentous frown." Then she would lisp: "My handth are of oo color." Young would laugh so affectionately that she felt like a real actress.

In June 1819, a year or so before Fanny's attempt to run away, Sarah Siddons had emerged from seven years' retirement to play the role of Lady Randolph in John Home's play *Douglas*. So great was the public anticipation of this extraordinary event—Mrs. Siddons was to play for one night only—that from early morning people thronged Covent Garden, hoping for admission when the doors opened late in the afternoon. Caught up in the excitement, Fanny wanted desperately to see the play. She cried and pleaded with her father, reminding him that she had never seen her aunt on stage. But he told her that it was impossible—there was not a spare seat in the house. To prove his point he led her out into the square to see for herself the milling crowd.

Fanny, strong-willed and persuasive, ultimately had her way. When the curtain rose she was there, all eyes and ears and nerves. Though later in life she remembered few details of her aunt's performance, she never forgot the great roar—"Siddons!"—which arose from the audience when the solemn figure in black appeared before them. As Fanny sat in that hushed theatre, experiencing the blast of emotion which Mrs. Siddons projected—strong enough to make women faint and men weep—there seems little doubt that she conceived a longing to become an actress herself.

But for the time being her ambition was thwarted. At the end of the summer, 1821, she was packed off to another school in France.

2

The Little Devil of a Kemble

The little devil of a Kemble discovered, to her relief, that her second French school was far more agreeable than her first. Her new head-mistress, a kindly Englishwoman named Frances Rowden, bore no resemblance to grim Madame Faudier. Before coming to Paris to open her school for *jeunes demoiselles* in an old stone house off the Champs Elysées, Mrs. Rowden had taught at a fashionable girls' school in London. There she had charge of three future writers—Mary Russell Mitford, Letitia Landon, and Lady Caroline Lamb. Having coped with their turbulent schooldays, she had little difficulty in managing Fanny.

Mrs. Rowden loved performers. John Philip Kemble's portrait graced her parlor, and she recruited her music and dancing masters from the Covent Garden theatre orchestra and the French opera ballet. A convert to Evangelicalism, among her favorite stars were eminent preachers. Three times a Sunday—and sometimes on weekdays—her pupils marched in a long line to the British embassy chapel or to a French Protestant church. Afterward they were required to set down in writing a summary of the sermon they had heard.

Far from resenting the rituals and those long sermons, during which she dared not doze for a second, Fanny came to enjoy them. Like Adelaide and her brothers, she had been raised not in the Catholic faith of her father but in the Swiss Protestant faith of her mother, and at home she was used to the customs of "average English Protestants of decent respectability." The family prayed in the morning, said grace at meals, and attended church on Sundays. At Mrs. Rowden's, Fanny discovered a type of religion where prayer was equated with excitement and the Bible was the rule of life.

She also discovered in herself a liking for preaching, and became so clever at memorizing the sermons that her schoolfellows used to wheedle her into penning their summaries as well as her own. Most rewarding, she

< 23 >

loved the thrilling prose of the King James Bible, "the noblest words the world possesses or ever will possess." Later Fanny wrote: "An intimate knowledge of the Bible has always seemed to me the greatest benefit I derived from my school training." For the rest of her days she would thank her school for uncovering and encouraging her natural piety.

It was at Mrs. Rowden's, too, that Fanny discovered just how well she could act. Assigned the role of Hermione in the school's production of Racine's *Andromaque*, she threw herself with enthusiasm into learning and rehearsing her part. When, on the opening night, she made her entrance before the audience of parents and friends, her talent was unmistakable. "I electrified the audience, my companions, and, still more, myself," she recalled. She was therefore astonished and hurt when Mrs. Rowden commented: "Ah my dear, I don't think your parents need ever anticipate your going on the stage; you would make but a poor actress."

Fanny had every reason to feel surprise and anger at Mrs. Rowden's comment, although she already had an inkling of what might have provoked it. Charles Kemble desired something more respectable for his daughter than a life on the stage. Mrs. Rowden was simply obeying his wishes in discouraging her star pupil. With those dismissive words came Fanny's first intimation of how the world despised actresses.

In time Fanny came to accept Mrs. Rowden's verdict because she revered her headmistress. A dignified figure, unfailingly kind to her pupils, Mrs. Rowden did not antagonize. It was difficult for Fanny to feel more than passing animosity toward her, or, indeed, toward anyone in the school. She liked most of her teachers, and one mistress she adored. Young, vivacious, and intelligent, Mademoiselle Descuillés preferred rewarding to punishing her pupils, and ruled them through charm. It was the perfect formula for dispelling Fanny's aggression.

The girls at Mrs. Rowden's followed a strict routine, rising early and studying until mid-afternoon. On sunny afternoons they played in the courtyard behind the schoolroom, dropping stones into a deep well and running till they heard the splash. It was a soothing life. As the months passed, Fanny learned to curb her rebellious nature and impulsive tongue and to live in reasonable harmony with her French and English classmates—though to live comfortably in close proximity to others would never be one of her conspicuous virtues. On the academic side the school was less rewarding. The curriculum was far too ladylike to satisfy Fanny's vigorous intelligence or thirst for knowledge. Nevertheless, she did acquire some skills. The sewing classes where she learned to cut out dresses she would bless all her life. The dancing class brought unfailing pleasure; Fanny had a passion for dancing. She liked the dancing master, whom she described as a "dapper, dried-up, wizen-faced, beak-nosed old man in brown wig" who played the violin and made faces when they missed their steps. She also showed a special skill in languages. Like her sister too, she had a gift for mimicry—"a sort of mocking-bird specialty," she called it—which neither of her brothers shared.

She excelled in literature and on her own impulse dipped into history, novels, and poetry, especially the novels of Sir Walter Scott and the poetry of Lord Byron, who were then at the height of their fame. Fanny wept when she heard of Byron's death. She devoured his poems, "quivering with excitement," until she realized how wicked his life had been. One night in the dormitory her conscience, sharpened by all those hours of sermons, impelled her to seize the book of poems and thrust it inside the mattress of her neighbor's bed. She never recovered the book, though she eventually recovered her enthusiasm for Byron.

As in her previous schooldays in France, Fanny was not sent home for holidays. Instead, she stayed in the houses of French friends at vacation time. Occasionally—all too rarely—her father visited her, agreeably surprised, each time he came, at how she was growing up. He enjoyed taking her about Paris with him, seeing the city afresh through her eyes. One can imagine them, arm in arm, sauntering down the dusty paths of the Bois de Boulogne (as unkempt in those days as a briar patch) or entering a crowded theatre on the boulevard. He is an imposing figure, more than six feet tall, handsome and dashing in a wide-shouldered coat and tapering trousers; Fanny barely reaches his shoulder. She wears a smooth, high-waisted gown and high-crowned bonnet, beneath which her young face glows with eagerness. Those short-lived excursions shone in her memory as "pleasant days of joyous *camaraderie* and *flânerie!*—in which everything being new to me, was almost as good as new to my indulgent companion."

When the time came to leave school and return to England, Fanny was very much improved. Aged nearly sixteen, she was well-mannered, poised, and attractive. She saw herself as a very pretty-looking girl, with "fine eyes, teeth and hair, a clear vivid complexion and rather good features."

Despite this self-assessment, Fanny had not inherited the true Kemble looks. Her famous aunt, uncle, and father were tall and stately, with imposing Roman noses, noble foreheads, and long arms capable of impressive gestures. Fanny had a small nose and a stocky body, although her waist was small. She was barely five feet tall, and she slouched until Marie Thérèse put her in a back brace and arranged for her to receive posture lessons from a sergeant in the Foot Guards. Thereafter, though she grew no taller, she learned to walk, by her own account, with a "flat back, well-placed shoulders, an erect head, upright carriage and resolute step," which made her seem slimmer and taller. Fanny's hands and feet were also rather too large for her body, a defect in an age when tiny feet and fine hands were among the hallmarks of female beauty. But in one important respect, even as a teenager, Fanny was a true Kemble. Her face was wonderfully mobile and expressive.

While Fanny was living in Paris, her family had scattered. Her mother, aunt, and sister spent most of each summer in a rented cottage in the Surrey village of Weybridge, a straggle of houses dotted around a common about twenty miles to the southwest of London. Her brothers were at a boarding school run by a Dr. Malkin about ninety miles to the north in the historic town of Bury St. Edmunds. Her father continued to live in London, close to the theatre, and there, each winter, Marie Thérèse, Adelaide, and Dall joined him.

It was to Eastlands Cottage on the edge of the Weybridge common that Fanny traveled on her long-awaited return to England in the summer of 1825. The journey took three hours from London and, sitting on top of the coach with her father, she could have wept with embarrassment. She was wearing an outsize straw hat, like a giant cartwheel, which she had bought in London to replace her bonnet, which had blown away as they crossed the English Channel. The straw hat, in a style which had not yet penetrated the rural backwaters, provoked stares in every village they passed. To make matters worse, she was worried that she might not recognize her mother, her anxiety presumably aroused by the prospect of a difficult reunion. But when Fanny stepped down from the coach, her spirits suddenly lifted. She removed her hat and sank thankfully into her mother's arms.

Fanny was about to enter a more harmonious phase of her relationship with her mother. The maturity she acquired at Mrs. Rowden's school seems to have included an insight into her mother's nature. In *Records of a Girlhood*, Fanny described her mother as "frank, fearless, generous and unworldly." No one can doubt that she meant those words. In later life she spoke so favorably of her mother and was so careful in excising every critical reference to Marie Thérèse in her published letters that biographers and historians have been inclined to assume that theirs was always a loving relationship.

Fanny's appreciation of her mother's virtues seems to have stemmed from their reunion at Weybridge. By that time Fanny was mature enough to applaud her mother's honesty and to view her mother's failings with kindness. Most important, Fanny was normally strong enough to withstand her mother's often cruel frankness. Marie Thérèse noticed the difference; she went so far as to say that her elder girl, who had been in childhood "quite unmanageable," was "altered and reformed in disposition."

It was fortunate that Fanny had acquired this inner strength, because the atmosphere inside the little stone cottage at Weybridge was volatile. Marie Thérèse was liable to erupt into sharp-tongued outbursts at any moment. Sensibly, she did her best to keep busy by cooking, making batches of jam from the fruit that grew in the garden, and even producing wine from the small black grapes that grew over the back wall of the house. She fished at all hours and in all weathers in the river Wey, finding the act of sitting for long stretches by the riverside soothing to her nerves. On these expeditions, she insisted that her daughters carry her basket and rods and set up her stool. Fanny became a convert to fishing, whereas Adelaide, who hated baiting the hook with the worm, came to dread these outings.

When their mother became impossible, both girls found relief in the common and its pine woods: "beautiful rambling and scrambling ground." Adelaide loved the "wild purple swell of the common." When her mother's scolding tongue drove her out of the house, she would lie beneath the trees, looking up at the clouds, smelling the scents of fresh earth and crushed pine needles, and listening to the hum of the bees in the heather. When she looked back on her childhood, she considered that these were her happiest hours. In the open air she could think her own thoughts and dream her own dreams.

With her brothers and Fanny away at school, Adelaide had grown accustomed to her own company and was usually happiest when alone, but at times she felt lonely. After Fanny came home, her loneliness was banished. Though five and a half years separated them, the sisters were at last old enough to enjoy one another's company; Fanny's long absence in Paris meant that they met again almost as strangers, the memories of past grievances faded.

Thanks to the social skills learned from Mrs. Rowden, Fanny was quickly able to win her sister's confidence. Soon they were inseparable. Dressed in long cloaks and stout boots, they made excursions down the country lanes, accompanied by their big Newfoundland dog and a small terrier. Back in the cottage, they read novels and poetry to one another, played duets on the piano, and visited the neighbors: the path to the house next door was worn bare by the pressure of their feet. When John and Henry came home from school, the girls joined in games of cricket—but only to field, because the boys would never let them bat. The girls came to dread the blow of the hard ball on their shins and fingers and thought it cruel to be relegated always to the inferior position of fielding. Basking in her sister's admiration, Fanny forgot to feel jealous; and when their mother scolded them, or when arguments arose with their brothers, Fanny stood up for Adelaide, thereby earning an even larger share of her sister's devotion. Within a very few months, Adelaide was expressing her gratitude to "dear, dear Fan" and relying on her sister almost as much as she did on Aunt Dall.

IN THE SUMMER of 1826—Fanny's second summer at Weybridge—Adelaide caught smallpox. This was particularly disturbing to Marie Thérèse, who had ensured that all the Kemble children were vaccinated in infancy. But the practice of vaccination was new and little understood. Physicians did not know, to quote Fanny's words, "that the power of the vaccine dies out of the system by degrees, and requires renewing to ensure safety." Too often only partial immunity was conferred by vaccination—or none at all.

After Adelaide became ill, Marie Thérèse lost all faith in vaccination. In her view—a view that was common at the time—the best protection was a mild dose of the disease itself. So when Adelaide's smallpox proved to be unusually mild, leaving only a scar on her nose, Marie Thérèse decreed that Fanny must deliberately try to catch the disease from Adelaide.

Fanny, having been sent to London at the onset of Adelaide's illness, was summoned back and exposed to the contagion. In less than three weeks she was burning with fever, covered in watery blisters, and fighting for her life. Though a local doctor was summoned at once, there was little he could do: the only hope lay in careful nursing. Day and night in the darkened bedroom, Marie Thérèse and Aunt Dall stood watch by Fanny's bed, forgetting their own fear as they worked to save her. They spooned water and opium into her swollen mouth, changed her sweat-soaked sheets and nightgown, and sponged the blisters, which began to fill with stinking pus. On nights when Fanny's temperature soared, they had difficulty quieting her, so restlessly did she toss. She babbled strange words, saw visions, and imagined herself in terrifying places.

After two weeks of fever and delirium, Fanny's temperature dropped, and the blisters began to form scabs. She survived, but her face was permanently pockmarked.

When Fanny described the episode in her memoirs, she was careful not to blame her mother. But she did let slip a strange remark. The small-pox, besides leaving pits on her face, rendered—in her own words—"my complexion thick and muddy and my features heavy and coarse, leaving me so moderate a share of good looks as quite to warrant my mother's satisfaction in saying when I went on the stage, 'Well my dear, they cannot say we have brought you out to exhibit your beauty.'"

Given her part in the events which caused her daughter's illness, Marie Thérèse's remark seems particularly cruel. Its inclusion in Fanny's memoirs suggests that Fanny may have been inviting her readers to pass a judgment against her mother that she could not bear to pass herself.

Fanny tried to make light of the smallpox in her later writings—and her biographers have made light of it also—but no girl, not even one as resilient and combative as Fanny, could easily override the shock of a disfigured face. She had gone to her sick bed a pretty girl, and she had emerged a month later with marked and coarsened features. Even conceding that this was an era of pockmarks, she must have found the experience shattering. She was only sixteen, highly charged by nature, and at the height of adolescence, when emotion runs high and self-esteem often runs low. Though outwardly she shrugged off her pitted face, the blow to her self-confidence must have been crushing, and the aftershock must have continued for months, if not years.

How one wishes that Fanny had not censored her published letters so carefully. In the absence of firm evidence, the closest one can come to understanding her pain is to notice the asides in her girlhood letters: "Nature has certainly not been as favorable to me as might have been wished," she confided to a friend in the second year after her illness. In another letter, she said regretfully that she suffered from a "want of good looks." After her illness, Fanny became reclusive. "I can't help fancying," she wrote defiantly in 1827, "that hours spent in my own room reading and writing are better employed than if devoted to people and things in which I feel no interest whatsoever, and do not know how to pretend to the contrary."

Fanny's face was virtually her dowry, for no daughter of Charles Kemble could hope to bring to marriage either money or social position outside the theatrical profession. Believing that her looks were blighted, Fanny must have begun to wonder how she would fare in the marriage market. Though once again she has left behind little evidence of her feelings, a clear connection would seem to exist between the disfigurement of her face and her decision, made soon afterward, that she would never marry. One cannot push this connection too far, because she believed that her decision was based rationally on an estimation of her character. But it does seem possible that a girl who knew that her face was permanently marked and her bargaining power was diminished would, consciously or unconsciously, have forsworn marriage.

A year and a half after catching smallpox, and soon after her eighteenth birthday, Fanny concluded that her outspoken and unfettered nature would never permit her to marry happily. "I am not patient of restraint or submissive to authority," she wrote in February 1828: "I do not think that I am fit to marry, to make an obedient wife or an affectionate mother. . . . I think I should be unhappy and the cause of unhappiness to others if I were to marry." The prospect of spinsterhood did not frighten her. She had grown up to believe that it was natural for women to pursue and manage careers of their own. Her actress aunts and cousins followed a theatrical career, which was, in her view, no less satisfying than the life of their married sisters. In fact she was beginning to consider that marriage was a mundane option that would not suit her mentally or emotionally. "My imagination is paramount with me," she wrote, "and would disqualify me, I think, for the every-day, matter-of-fact cares and duties of the mistress of a household and the head of a family." Her goal was "independence of mind and body," which, she had come to believe, was "the greatest desideratum of life."

While Fanny was lamenting her lost looks and pining for independence, Marie Thérèse decided that she had to overcome her daughter's self-absorption. Refusing to listen to Fanny's objections, Marie Thérèse bundled her off on a round of visits.

One of Fanny's first visits was to Bannisters, a rambling house built on the site of an old monastery close to the town of Southampton. There kind and clever Mrs. Fitzhugh, who had many times comforted Mrs. Siddons in adversity, dispensed hospitality and help to any Kemble in need. Sensing Fanny's unhappiness, Mrs. Fitzhugh drew the girl into her family circle and encouraged a friendship with her daughter Emily, a subdued little creature who resembled a greyhound. Though there was a wide difference in their temperaments, Fanny took a liking to Emily at once, recognizing the same loyal and generous nature that she saw in her mother.

Fanny would always feel at home in the tranquil Fitzhugh household, which provided her with the stability lacking in her own. "Sweet Bannisters!" she would exclaim later in life, "to me forever a refuge of consolation and sympathy in seasons of trial and sorrow, of unfailing kindly welcome and devoted constant affection." She would lie in a hammock under the cedars on the lawn and feast her eyes on the exquisitely tended garden. She also took intense pleasure in the refined taste of the house, for which she praised Mr. Fitzhugh. A member of Parliament for Tiverton, he was a lover of Greece and Rome, with a fine collection of antique busts in his hallway and a series of Italian scenes—volcanoes, seaports, ruined temples— painted by his own hand, on the walls of his oval drawing room. The only room Fanny did not like was the dining room, where a life-sized portrait of Mrs. Siddons glowered at the diners.

Fanny was scarcely back from Bannisters when she and her mother set out again. This time they went to Heath Farm near Watford, about fifteen miles northwest of London, where her aunt, Mrs. John Philip Kemble, was living out her widowhood on an estate called Cassiobury Park, which belonged to her late husband's patron, the Earl of Essex. Also invited to Heath Farm that spring were Mrs. Siddons, her daughter, Cecilia, and an old friend of the Kemble and Siddons families named Harriet St. Leger.

Fanny was captivated by her very first glimpse of Harriet St. Leger. This well-born Anglo-Irish spinster, nearly twice Fanny's age, looked unlike any woman Fanny had seen before. Harriet's face was white and delicate, and her chestnut hair curled charmingly, but she had such a distrust of feminine frippery that she insisted on wearing mannish clothes and adopting masculine ways. She draped her lanky body in eccentric black coats and skirts, thrust her feet into men's boots, and spent her days in rural tasks and what she termed "metaphysical reasoning." Of her life in the Irish countryside, she wrote: "I cut down trees, I play with my dog, I dig, I carry potatoes to the donkeys, I listen to the music of the mind." It was Harriet's metaphysical reasoning that endeared her to Fanny, who deemed her a "Plato in petticoats."

During those first intoxicating days of friendship, Fanny learned, under Harriet's tutelage, to cast off stifling, ladylike behavior and sample the simple world of the senses. With Harriet beside her, she discarded her bonnet and tramped across Lord Essex's park, singing at the top of her lungs. When she and Harriet came to a stream that flowed between banks of flowering hawthorn, Fanny pulled off her boots and stockings and bathed her feet in the brown water. The cool caress of the water and heavy scent of the blossoms made a wonderfully sensuous combination. When pangs of hunger began to trouble them, she and Harriet stopped at a roadside alehouse and ate laborers' lunches of coarse bread, sharp cheese, and brown beer. Such hoydenish behavior would have given Fanny's aunt and mother apoplexy, had they known of it. But Fanny and Harriet exulted in their freedom. At night in Fanny's bedroom in the old farmhouse, they sat up until the candle burned out, talking about literature, theology, history, philosophy, and poetry. Never in her carefully chaperoned existence had Fanny dreamed of such rich intellectual excitement. It made her determined to seek a bolder and more stimulating life for herself.

After two visits in close succession to Heath Farm, "dearest Hal" became Fanny's closest friend. Though they rarely saw one another—Harriet lived in romantic Ardgillan Castle, set high above the sea in Ireland—their friendship was sufficiently grounded for them to correspond regularly over a long span of years, and to confide in one another without restraint on topics ranging from God and politics to botany and household management. Fanny is at her most attractive in those letters: speculative, compassionate, boundlessly eager, sharply observant, and never lacking a forceful opinion. At the end of her life, Fanny saw fit to publish her part of the correspondence, and much of what is now known of her comes from those candid letters. In light of Harriet's temperament and life, some have wondered if this was a lesbian relationship. But there is nothing to suggest that it was more than a heartfelt friendship—on Fanny's part, at any rate.

As Fanny moved more into society, she came to sense the curious social position which her family occupied. The three great Kembles, because of their fame, manners, education, and Mrs. Siddons's much-publicized chastity, were often invited into "good society"—that is, to the drawing rooms of those with aristocratic connections. Indeed, it was said of Mrs. Siddons that "perhaps no actress before or since, ever possessed an equal intimacy with fashionable life." Lesser members of the Kemble clan, however, were not so welcome. Fanny later claimed that her mother was personally disinclined to seek friendships in high society, but the likely reason for the absence of such friendships was that Marie Thérèse was not famous enough to live down her actress past—particularly her appearance on stage in tight male breeches. The complexity of determining where she was and was not welcome was an unpalatable aspect of Fanny's young life, to be endured until her own fame provided her with uncontested entry to the highest circles.

One host who eagerly welcomed the entire Kemble family was the lawyer Basil Montagu. His father was the Earl of Sandwich, and his mother was Martha Ray, an actress who was later murdered by a love-crazed clergyman outside the stage door at Covent Garden. Though the earl had not married the actress, he had raised Basil Montagu as his son, sending him to Cambridge University before encouraging him to study law.

True to his theatrical ancestry, Basil Montagu adored books and the theatre and formed ties with many celebrated performers and men of letters, including Hazlitt, Lamb, and Coleridge. His third wife, Anna Dorothea, shared his tastes and was more than happy to play the role of literary hostess. Fanny described her as "queen-like, gentle, soothing, measured, prettily royal." Mrs. Montagu held a "daily court of culture and politeness" at her London house at 25 Bedford Square, where she always dressed in the same eccentric style: a long-sleeved gown of grey, black, or purple satin, with a lace half-bodice fitting up to the neck like a medieval wimple and a picturesque cap on her auburn hair. Fanny admired Mrs. Montagu's disregard of fashion almost as much as she admired her talent for hospitality and her powers of conversation.

In running her influential salon—a mixture, it was said, of a "hotel and a Parnassus"—Mrs. Montagu was helped by the daughter of her first marriage, Anne Procter, an intelligent, warm-hearted girl, who possessed what Fanny described as a "special mastery over her own language." That mastery included the gift of sarcasm, which rendered—in Fanny's words— "the tongue she spoke in and the tongue she spoke with two of the most formidable weapons any woman was ever armed with." In later life Anne Procter was nicknamed Our Lady Bitterness.

Anne Procter's husband—described by Thomas Carlyle as a "pretty little fellow, bodily and spiritually"—was another talent who brought magic to the salon. A sweet-tempered man as well as a lively talker, Bryan Waller Procter was an eminent lawyer, poet, and playwright. His tragedy *Mirandola*, written under the pen name of Barry Cornwall, contained a leading part for Charles Kemble and brought both actor and author considerable success when it was put on at Covent Garden. Many threads drew the families together, and the Procters were soon numbered among the Kembles' closest friends.

Fanny, at age eighteen, made another influential friendship at Mrs. Montagu's Parnassus. Anna Jameson was a forceful ex-governess of thirty-four, of whom Thomas Carlyle has left a memorable description. "Ach Gott!" he wrote: "A little, hard, brown, redhaired, freckled, fierce-eyed, square-mouthed woman; shrewd, harsh, cockney-irrational." The redhaired young woman was also an author, having recently published a sentimental novel called *The Diary of an Ennuyée*. The book made her something of a literary lioness.

Anna's book validated Fanny's desire for independence, and it was a thrill for Fanny to meet an author who had so decisively carved her own path through life. "I like her very much," she wrote to Harriet St. Leger, "she is extremely clever; I wish I knew her better." As the months passed, Fanny's wish came true. A close and friendly relationship was established, fueled on Fanny's part by hero worship, and on Anna's part by the chance to know the most famous family of the theatre. This certainly was the con-clusion reached by Fanny's parents, who suspected Anna of opportunism and insisted that Fanny refuse many of her invitations. Fortunately, they did not ask her to give up Anna entirely; if they had done so, Fanny might have defied them. Anna Jameson was far too attractive a role model for Fanny to relinquish easily.

While adolescent Fanny yearned for a life of her own, young Adelaide was studying her lessons under the loving eyes of Aunt Dall. Unlike Fanny, who believed ardently in female education, Adelaide thought it fortunate that she was never sent to school. Shakespeare and Milton, she main-tained, "have given me far pleasanter thoughts than the many accomplish-ments now taught."

A clear division was already forming between the sisters' talents; it was visible in the music lessons given them by their mother. Fanny sang in a contralto voice, more robust than Adelaide's but not as sweet or flexible. She sang without real aptitude, employing more dramatic expression than musicality. Her excuse was that she was put off by her mother's perfection-ism and impatience. "I sang out of tune," Fanny claimed, "and played false chords oftener, from sheer apprehension of her agonized exclamations." Adelaide, though far more sensitive to criticism, shone at her music lessons. Fanny has left a charming picture of Adelaide at a music lesson, standing beside the pianoforte in their mother's sitting-room: a thin, shy, serious girl of eleven with large brown eyes and long brown hair, singing "Oh, There's a Mountain Palm" in a "clear, high, sweet, true, little voice," her expression "touching" and "full of pathos."

Marie Thérèse had studied singing under Francesco Lanza, the Neapolitan master. Consequently she judged Adelaide's singing with a soundly based confidence. What she heard in those early lessons convinced her that her younger daughter had great promise.

In those days a singer began serious training at a much younger age than today; the danger to an immature voice was not fully appreciated. It may have been at a relatively tender age that Adelaide commenced lessons with her parents' old friend John Braham, the Jewish-English tenor. Ade-laide never forgot her first sight of him in a Handel oratorio: a "thick-set man with a light brown wig all over his eyes," who took in breaths with a noticeable swelling of his chest and a shrug of his shoulders. To Adelaide he would always be the greatest singer in England and among the finest in the world.

While Adelaide was beginning her serious training, the older Kembles were swimming in perilous financial waters. On his retirement in 1820, John Philip Kemble had made over his one-sixth share in the Theatre Royal at Covent Garden to his brother Charles. Since the shareholders were personally responsible for the debts incurred in rebuilding the theatre, it was a gift Charles would have been wiser to refuse. In years to come his family would refer to the theatre as the "poisoned chalice" and "fatal mill-stone."

When Charles acquired his share, he nursed an ambition that ulti-mately ruined him. He was inspired by the belief that the powerful theatres at Drury Lane and Covent Garden should not only train actors but also perpetuate the great British repertoire. In essence, his dream was to found a national theatre. He persuaded two of his fellow shareholders to join him in leasing the theatre, with himself as its manager. Four years later, Charles and his partners became involved in costly and unfortunate litigation.

Almost always an optimist, Charles Kemble hoped he could pay his way out of debts and lawyers' fees with a brilliant box-office success, and in 1824 such a success seemed to be at hand. That year, thrusting aside the British drama, he boldly staged a German opera, *Der Freischütz*. Packing the house for fifty-two performances, the opera earned urgently needed money. When the season was over, Charles decided to commission a new opera from the same composer. He offered Carl Maria von Weber the very large sum of one thousand pounds to write an opera expressly for the theatre at Covent Garden. In 1825, Charles and his conductor, Sir George Smart, traveled to Germany to meet Weber and speed the negotiations. The deal was clinched with expressions of hope and goodwill on both sides and Weber's firm promise that he and his manuscript would be in England by the following year.

Fanny and Adelaide awaited Weber's arrival in London with excite-ment. Though they had never seen him in person, both girls were wildly in love with his music. Adelaide could sing almost everything he had written, and Fanny was so smitten that she wore his engraved portrait in a black silk bag around her neck. Deep was their shock when the long-awaited day dawned in March 1826, and instead of the romantic hero they were expect-ing, an invalid limped into their London drawing room. Hollow-cheeked, bulging-eyed, hook-nosed, crooked-shouldered—more like a corpse than a man—Weber's consumptive appearance sent their spirits plummeting. But the moment he spoke, they were consoled. He was charm itself, and his sallies, delivered in French, were irresistibly amusing. Marie Thérèse particularly liked him, while he praised her as "a plump cosy woman of the greatest friendliness."

Sir George Smart, noticing the girls' chagrin, was at pains to put them at ease. He took Fanny by the hand, escorted her to Weber, and assured the composer—to quote Fanny's words—"that I and all the young girls in England were head over ears in love with him." Conscious that she was wearing Weber's portrait round her neck, Fanny began to blush, finally managing to blurt out how much she loved his music. Looking at her intently, Weber generously disparaged himself. "Ah, my music!" he told her, "it is always my music, but never myself!"

Rehearsals for the new opera, Oberon, were long and painstaking. It soon became clear that this opera would be extremely difficult to stage and to sing. The libretto, by the Kembles' friend James Robertson Planché, was written as an English pantomime, with some parts sung and some parts spoken. Weber did not like the style. As rehearsals progressed, he frequently altered the music and often disagreed with the singers over how a speech or a song should be performed.

Fanny recorded how frail Weber, who had less than three months to live, drove himself unsparingly. The Scottish soprano Mary Ann Paton sang divinely but acted badly, causing her exasperated father to exclaim, "That woman's an inspired idiot." John Braham, with his heaving chest and noble voice, acted and sang brilliantly. Adelaide, unfortunately, has left behind no record, but one wonders if she did not nourish a small hope that one day she would sing as divinely as Mary Ann Paton—and act with far more flair.

There were endless troubles with the elaborate stage effects. A storm, a vision, and a shipwreck had to be simulated. The lighting—which in those days was crude—had to reproduce twilight, starlight, and moonlight, not to mention a sunset. An army of scene painters worked overtime to create Oberon's Bower with a Distant View of Bagdad, a Ravine amongst the Rocks of a Desolate Island, and a Perforated Cavern on the Beach. Battalions of seamstresses were employed to sew the costumes, using bolt upon bolt of silk and gauze. Was Charles asking too much of his company? Had he overreached himself? Such thoughts must have raced through his head as the opening night drew near. He had sunk a great deal of money into Oberon. If it failed, he would be near ruin.

On the opening night—April 12, 1826—a painfully anxious Charles entered his box, wondering what the evening would bring. Miss Paton muffed her lines, just as she had in rehearsal, and Weber, who was conducting, felt so ill that it seemed doubtful he would last out the performance.

Nonetheless, by the end of the evening, Charles was euphoric. Even without thunderous applause, he felt that *Oberon* was a success—even more, that *Oberon* would be his salvation! The ravishing melodies and sensuous orchestral colors coaxed from the orchestra by poor, dying Weber proclaimed the opera a masterpiece. Adelaide agreed. The lilting song of the mermaids at the end of the second act was one of the most enchanting melodies she had ever heard. She and Dall could not help humming it as they sat in the box. In fact Dall would adopt the music as a type of good-luck charm, singing it to herself whenever she felt ill or sad.

Everyone in the family expected the opera to run for months. Next day the critics damned it. *Oberon*'s season was short. Far from rescuing Charles, the opera pushed him into near-ruinous debt.

As the months passed, the debt began to bite. By October 1827 the theatre's affairs were in crisis. Fanny explained to Harriet St. Leger that her father was "liable at any time to be called upon for twenty-seven thousand pounds; which, for a man who cannot raise five thousand, is not a pleasant predicament." Charles negotiated with his creditors and managed to stave off the immediate threat of arrest, but this did not lessen his fears of imprisonment for debt at a later time, if the creditors proved obstinate.

The financial crisis called for sacrifices. The pretty Weybridge cottage was given up, and the London house exchanged for a cheaper one. The family ceased to buy new clothes and walked through the muddy London streets rather than spend money on hackney coaches. Some sacrifices, however, Charles refused to make. The sum spent on his sons' education equaled more than half his income, but he decided that John, a highly promising scholar at Trinity College, Cambridge, must continue his studies. Even the less promising Henry, though he was taken from his country boarding school, was enrolled as a day boy at the elite Westminster School in London.

Charles was less indulgent of his wife and daughters. On them fell the brunt of the hardships. They packed up and moved house, and they wore "faded, threadbare and dyed frocks." Fanny felt so deprived that when she found a sovereign wedged at the back of a drawer in her desk one day, she became ecstatic.

Marie Thérèse, always prone to worry and sensitive to the slightest tinge of tension in the atmosphere, suffered an undiagnosed illness, which persisted through most of the autumn of 1827. Her sight and hearing were mysteriously impaired. She was unable to read, work, or do much of anything and spent her days immersed in her husband's troubles. Fanny and Adelaide, though they did not become ill, were caught up in the tension and turmoil. "My whole thoughts," wrote Fanny to Harriet, "are taken up with our circumstances."

Her father's debts focused Fanny's mind on her own future. Those days her ambition leaned toward writing, and the more she examined the literary life, the more she saw in its favor. Over the past few years, she had learned just how impossible it was for a true lady to appear on stage, for ladies were, by definition, modest creatures who shunned the limelight. Writing, on the other hand, was a profession that could be carried on privately: various well-bred women had sat at home over the past hundred years and written books without incurring the least social stigma. Above all, since Fanny's aims were primarily financial, there was money to be made from a successful play or book. She knew very well that the popular author Mary Russell Mitford—one of Mrs. Rowden's former pupils—had recently made two hundred pounds from her successful play *Foscari*. Besides, playwriting was in Fanny's blood. Her parents, uncles, and aunts were continually adapting the plays of others and sometimes wrote plays of their own.

On one of her trips to Heath Farm, Fanny had begun to write a novel on the subject of Françoise de Foix, a heroine of sixteenth-century France. The manuscript had lain on her desk for months, half finished. Now she took it up and began to transform it into a play, lacing it with jealousy, treason, and lust—surprising themes, some contemporaries said, for a girl of seventeen, but Fanny was never afraid of shocking.

Early in October 1827 the Kembles moved into a house at Buckingham Gate, Westminster. The house had little to commend it: it was so narrow that it had no more than two small rooms on each floor, with stairs so steep that Adelaide was afraid of falling down them. But it was cheap, near Henry's school, and—best of all, in the opinion of the girls—almost opposite St. James's Park, a flowery meadow with trees and paths, where on Sundays the fashionably dressed families of clerks and shopkeepers paraded their peg-top trousers and flowered hats. After church Adelaide and Fanny, in their worn shoes and shabby dresses, would stroll down Birdcage Walk toward Buckingham Palace and into the park to mingle with the Sunday crowd—wishing all the while that they, too, could be fashionable.

Soon after moving, Fanny finished her play, beginning the last act at six in the evening and completing it by half-past eleven. Next morning she read it aloud to her parents. They were astounded. "Ah my dear mother," Fanny exulted. "Oh, how she looked at me!" In their depressed mood, the Kemble parents leaped on the play as a heaven-sent blessing, quickly foreseeing that to stage a work by a girl so young, and a Kemble into the bargain, would bring immense publicity and a handsome profit. If "it succeeds," Charles exclaimed—and he did not see why, with discreet reworking, it would not—"I shall be the happiest man alive."

While she was eager to make money, Fanny's dreams went a good deal further than her father's. What she truly wanted was to see her play in print: "to make a name for myself as a writer is the aim of my ambition," she told Harriet. Fanny's brother John was of the same mind, and he supported her wish that the play, which was now called *Francis I*, should be published before it was acted.

Charles and Marie Thérèse always paid attention to John's opinions—possibly too much attention. His tutor's glowing reports from Cambridge, his impressive oratory, his membership in the elite Cambridge social and debating society called the Apostles, and his friendship with young men of potential eminence seemed the only ray of sunshine in those dark times for the family. Toward the end of 1827, however, the Kembles' hopes for John began to fade. He was becoming a radical, and the Kembles listened with fear as he started to worship the utilitarian political philosophers Jeremy Bentham and James Mill, regurgitating their radical ideas with what Fanny called a "sort of frenzy." She complained that whenever they passed Bentham's or Mill's houses, which were not far from Buckingham Gate, John fell into such paroxysms of adulation that she imagined they were passing "the shrines of some beneficent powers." Worse, John was so caught up in his own affairs that he gave not a thought to the effort his family was making to keep him at university. Even Charles began to wonder if the disproportionate share of his income spent on his elder son's education was worth the sacrifice.

While John had long been the focus of his parents' hopes—they even imagined him as a future Lord Chancellor of England—Fanny was held in lower esteem. She had been so unmanageable in childhood that she was considered a liability. Suddenly the positions were reversing. Fanny's remarkable career was about to begin.

3

"Heaven Smiles on You, My Child"

In February 1828, Fanny caught measles. As her temperature soared, her mind was so disturbed that she could not bear to look in a mirror for fear of seeing ghosts. Aunt Dall nursed her devotedly through the fever and the storms of weeping that lasted many weeks after the fever subsided. Fanny's depression was understandable. Within the space of eighteen months she had almost died of smallpox, been ill with measles, suffered the shock of a pockmarked face, and been worried to distraction by the ruin facing her father. As Dall wisely put it, Fanny was worn out in body and mind.

Her father's financial crisis lay heavily on Fanny, as it did on the whole family. For the first time in her life, she seriously considered becoming an actress. Half abandoning her earlier hope of becoming a writer—plans to stage or publish her play seemed to have stalled—she was fast beginning to revive her childhood dream and to believe that a life on the stage was the surest and quickest solution to her own ambitions and her father's poverty. Fanny began to take stock of her talent, the advantages of being a Kemble with a ready-made theatrical company to support her, and her father's belief that a fine fortune was to be made in the theatre by any young woman of talent.

Fanny also weighed the warnings, and they were ominous. She knew that the public, which was happy enough to enjoy itself at plays, looked down on the actors who performed in them. The *Encyclopaedia Britannica* expressed the prevailing attitude in an article written twelve years before Fanny's birth. Discussing the high salaries paid to stage performers, it concluded that "the exorbitant rewards of players, opera singers, opera-dancers, etc., are founded upon these two principles: the rarity and beauty of the talents, and the discredit of employing them in this manner." The term *dis-*

< 40 >

credit applied particularly to women. At a time when modesty was praised as a female virtue, an actress was considered by many to be the very symbol of immodesty, little better than a prostitute.

Fanny insisted in old age that she never heard the "subtle evils" of the theatrical calling discussed during her girlhood; but she appears, on the evidence of her letters, to have absorbed the concept, and perhaps even to have agreed with it. The idea of appearing on stage, violating "womanly dignity and decorum in thus becoming the gaze of every eye," was already distasteful to her. Whether she was aware of the opinion that actors were artificers who lived outside the bounds of honest society one does not know. Later in life she seems partly to have agreed with it. Though proud of her family's fame, Fanny accepted, even at eighteen, that acting was a dubious profession that a young girl "entered at her peril."

When she looked at the lives of her relatives, she became even more uneasy. In the task of manufacturing emotions on stage, it seemed to her that a performer became emotionally over-stimulated. The elation gained from applause combined with the stimulation gained from acting produced an unhealthy euphoria from which it took hours, maybe days, to recover. Fanny concluded that the combination of emotion, excitement, and admiration was like a drug. It "interferes with every other study, and breaks the threads of every other occupation," wrote Fanny, "and produces mental habits which, even if distasteful at first, gradually become paramount to all others, and, in due time inveterate; and besides perpetually stimulating one's personal vanity and desire for admiration and applause, directs whatever ambition one has to the least exalted of aims, the production of evanescent effects and transitory emotion."

Fanny saw only too vividly how withdrawal from acting could affect an actress. She watched Mrs. Siddons pass her nineteen years of retirement in a "deadness and indifference to everything." Cut off from the one activity which could give her emotional life, her aunt flickered briefly to life only in the evening, when she would sigh that this was the hour when she usually left for the theatre. Fanny began to foresee a similar fate for herself. Of all the unwelcome consequences of a stage career, addiction to acting probably worried her the most. She believed she might easily succumb.

While these fears carried weight, the prospect of fame, fortune, and independence eventually won out. Later Fanny insisted that the theatrical profession had always been hateful to her and that her adoption of it was "absolutely an act of duty and conformity to the will of my parents, strengthened by my own conviction that I was bound to help them by every means in my power." But this is not the message conveyed in her letters. In 1828 and 1829 she wrote with increasing enthusiasm about the rewards of acting and even defended the profession to Harriet St. Leger. In the twelve months of self-debate which led up to her decision to become an actress, her father's need for money undoubtedly tipped the balance, but her personal feelings were not so heavily weighted against the theatre as she would later have people believe.

While Fanny's parents would have preferred to see her lead a conventional life, they did not consider it a sin for a girl to follow their calling. In their opinion, to tread the boards and proclaim the words of England's great dramatists was a noble profession. The hazards lay in prostitute-ridden theatres, licentious greenrooms, and squalid theatrical lodgings. If an actress avoided such places and lived a pure life, then, they believed, she could escape the loss of morals and reputation.

The Kembles well knew that, to achieve an impeccable lifestyle, an actress or singer needed total control of her working conditions from her very first day on the stage. She might even have to attempt the almost impossible feat of starting at the top of her profession. Only under those circumstances were the elder Kembles prepared to allow their daughters to act in a theatre. In careers rarely paralleled in theatrical history, the Kemble girls commenced at the top and remained at the top; neither ever acted or sang in anything but a leading role.

One fortunate circumstance reassured Marie Thérèse and Charles. If Fanny were to act solely within the Kemble company, she could be protected and chaperoned. Fanny wrote to Harriet St. Leger: "My father is now proprietor and manager of the theatre, and those certainly are favorable circumstances for my entering on a career which is one of great labor and some exposure, at the best, to a woman, and where a young girl cannot be too prudent of herself, nor her protectors too careful of her." Even so, no amount of chaperoning could remove all the dangers, and neither Marie Thérèse nor Charles wished to commit a daughter to a risky future unless it proved absolutely necessary.

Nor was Fanny herself quite ready to embark on a career. Still suffering the effects of measles, her nerves were fragile, her imagination fevered, and her temper easily ignited. "My life at home at this time," she wrote of herself, "became difficult and troublesome, and unsatisfactory to myself and others. . . . I was vehement and excitable, violently impulsive, and with a wild, ill regulated imagination." She made scenes and provoked quarrels that, in a household already distracted by worry, proved unendurable. As soon as she was well enough, she was packed off to Edinburgh to stay with the widow and children of Mrs. Siddons's eldest son, Harry.

To escape from the tension and gloom of home was welcome. To join a household as calm and loving as that of her Edinburgh cousins was bliss. Fanny's aggression faded, and her jangled nerves were calmed in that unrestrained environment. Mrs. Harry Siddons, the former Harriet Murray, had much in common with Fanny's French schoolmistress, Madame Descuillés; she ruled through charm rather than command. Harriet never scolded, nagged, or lost her temper; her son Harry and daughters Lizzy and Sally were almost as sweet-tempered as she. Perhaps for the first time in her life, Fanny found herself treated like a woman and not a child. Whereas in London the Kemble girls were chaperoned wherever they went, Harriet often allowed Fanny to roam about Edinburgh unescorted. It was a joy to answer to no one. Years later Fanny would say that she loved Edinburgh because it was there that for the first time she discovered how it felt to be alone.

Everything about the city delighted her. Edinburgh was small, friendly, and safe to walk in. The crooked lanes and crowded medieval houses of the Old Town seemed magical. To a girl nourished on Sir Walter Scott, every turn brought to mind a novel or poem. In the New Town, where her cousins lived, the spacious Georgian squares, with their central gardens and rows of symmetrical houses, breathed order and serenity. Fanny was not surprised that Edinburgh was considered one of the most beautiful cities in Europe.

Edinburgh was also close to the sea, which was a never-failing pleasure. From Harriet's first-floor balcony, Fanny could see the blue waters of the Forth and, after dark, the flickering light of the Inchkeith lighthouse. On summer mornings she would rise early and hurry to the beach at Porto Bello and swim before breakfast. On summer afternoons she would travel as far as the fishing village of Newhaven and talk to the fishwives who walked through the streets with bare white feet and heavy baskets, shouting their melancholy cry, "Caller haddie." In Edinburgh Fanny found herself maturing in a way impossible in the strictly regulated atmosphere of her parents' home.

Warmly welcomed by her cousins, she was also embraced by their network of friends. Before her marriage, Harriet had been a leading actress at Covent Garden, and in her widowhood she had become the manager of the Edinburgh Theatre: playgoers in Scotland referred to her proudly as "*our* Mrs. Siddons." As Harriet knew many of Edinburgh's artists and writers, Fanny was able to meet first-class minds and talents.

Fanny was especially drawn to four men—all under forty—who were frequent callers at the Siddons's house. All had come from lowly beginnings, all had risen by reason of their talents, and all brimmed with intellectual excitement. The oldest were the Combe brothers—George, a lawyer, and Andrew, a physician—fanatical amateur phrenologists who believed that the bony bumps on the skull revealed a person's character. The other two in the quartet were Lawrence Macdonald, a sculptor who had studied in Rome and was about to be elected to the Scottish Academy, and Robert Chambers, an author who had risen to become one of Edinburgh's leading booksellers. His books on Scottish traditions delighted Sir Walter Scott, who "wondered where the boy got all his information."

Fanny loved the company of these fascinating men, and Harriet appears to have let her go about with them almost at will. Fanny was allowed to drive alone with Andrew Combe in an open gig while he visited his patients. (When Marie Thérèse heard of this unchaperoned "gigging," she was scandalized.) Fanny also became a regular guest at the Combes' house in Northumberland Street, where she heard discussion of all the great political and governmental questions of the day. She had long wanted a deeper knowledge of those topics, and the talk was exactly what she craved.

Drifting contentedly through the summer and winter, Fanny began to worship Harriet. Each afternoon when they dined at home, Fanny would go to a myrtle tree in the garden and pick a sprig of leaves, then present the sprig to Harriet, who would arrange it neatly in the sash of her dress. At bedtime Fanny would quietly retrieve the sprig and place it reverently in a drawer, treasuring the dried-out leaves as though they were relics. She regarded her cousin as little short of a saint. Harriet gave the lie to all the objections that were generally leveled against actresses. Conspicuously modest, virtuous, and level-headed, she gave Fanny hope for her own future on the stage.

In July 1829, after scarcely twelve months in Edinburgh, Fanny returned to the gloom of her London home, a gloom deepened by the memory of what she had left behind. Her father's affairs were in crisis, and her mother was near collapse. The atmosphere inside the cramped little house in Buckingham Gate was close to intolerable.

Charles was unable to pay the theatre's taxes. He owed the awesome sums of 896 pounds to St. Paul's parish and 600 pounds to the collectors of revenue. Distress warrants for the taxes had already been issued, and Charles daily expected the bailiffs to take possession of the theatre. Early in

August he set out on a month's theatrical tour of Ireland, not daring to wonder if the theatre would be his when he returned.

One afternoon in August, just before Charles's expected return, Marie Thérèse walked past the theatre at Covent Garden and saw bills of sale nailed to the door. Overcome by emotion, she barely managed to reach home. Staggering through the front door, she collapsed into a chair and called out tearfully to her daughters: "Oh, it has come at last, our property is to be sold." Sick with terror, Fanny tried to comfort her mother, then dashed upstairs to write to her father. She begged him to allow her to earn money, but she stopped short of offering to be an actress.

When Fanny and her mother felt calmer, they talked more sensibly about the future. Marie Thérèse knew that Charles had set various schemes in motion to raise money, but she also knew that, even if they succeeded, the theatre might soon be seized again. To operate Covent Garden successfully, he needed much more than a loan—he needed a star. Marie Thérèse looked at her daughter speculatively and began to question her. She knew that Fanny had considered going on the stage the year before: was she still of the same mind? Did she believe she could succeed? When Fanny stammered that she did not know, Marie Thérèse pulled a volume of Shakespeare from the shelf and asked her to recite a speech.

Fanny and her parents later cultivated the belief that, at the time of this audition, she had never received an acting lesson. This story implied that she had been brought up to be a lady, a picture they were always at pains to project. It also made the success of Fanny's debut the more astonishing. However, the claim that she was a novice was an exaggeration. Even if one ignores those drawing-room theatricals in which the children regularly took part at home, Fanny and Adelaide had picked up a wealth of stagecraft just by watching and listening to their family and friends. As Fanny once confessed, she and her sister had spent their youth "hearing the stage and acting constantly, tastefully and thoughtfully discussed" and had acquired "just notions on the subject of acting" from an early age.

On that fateful day in August 1829, Fanny recited one of Portia's speeches from *The Merchant of Venice*. Marie Thérèse was impressed but not convinced. She suggested Fanny should learn by heart an emotional speech from *Romeo and Juliet* and recite it for her father when he returned from Ireland. A few days later Fanny stood in the drawing room at Buckingham Gate and declaimed Juliet's lines in front of both her parents. Her nervousness was acute, and she was even more unnerved when neither Charles nor

Marie Thérèse would comment on her performance in front of her. Running to the staircase, she sat on a step and burst into tears.

TWO DAYS LATER Charles took her to the empty stage at Covent Garden. As Fanny recalled the event: "In that twilight space, as it were, with only my father's voice coming to me from where he stood hardly distinguishable in the gloom, in those poetical utterances of pathetic passion I was seized with the great spirit of the thing; my voice resounded through the great vault above and before me, and, completely carried away by the inspiration of the wonderful play, I acted Juliet as I do not believe I ever acted it again."

It was this ability to be "seized with the great spirit of the thing" that convinced Fanny's father that she could act. From that moment neither he, nor the friend he had hidden in the theatre to help him assess his daughter's talent, felt any doubt about her ultimate success. Seizing the idea of launching her at the very top, Charles announced that she would appear as Juliet as soon as the theatre reopened.

Fanny accepted his decision. She had known for more than a year that a theatrical career was her probable fate, and part of her actively willed it. But fear also stares out of the letter she sent to Harriet: "I am going on the stage," she wrote. "It is a very serious trial to look forward to, and I wish it were over." It was a serious trial indeed: if the play failed, her father might lose his theatre and go to debtors' prison. Fanny was also conscious of what she was risking, mentally and emotionally, by entering the world of the theatre. "I wish to assure you," she told Harriet, "that I have not embraced this course without due dread of its dangers, and a firm determination to watch over, as far as in me lies, its effect on my mind."

Fortunately Fanny thrived on adventure. Caught up in the excitement of the challenge, she flung herself into her part, trying to absorb in three weeks what normally took years to learn. Every morning she rehearsed Juliet at the theatre with her father, and every afternoon she rehearsed Juliet at home with her mother. In the evenings there were family discussions and debates, fittings for costumes, and more memorizing and study.

To gain maximum publicity for Fanny's debut, the Kemble parents decided to make this a family production. Marie Thérèse, though she had not acted for ten years, decided to return, as Lady Capulet, for the opening night. Charles, who was considered one of the greatest Romeos of all time, decided that it might be indelicate for him to play his daughter's lover, and chose instead to play Mercutio. This left them with a Romeo to find. In a flash of inspiration they decided to audition their younger son, sixteen-year-old Henry, knowing that Fanny and her brother as the starcrossed lovers were likely to create a sensation. But though Henry looked the part—he was so handsome, Fanny wrote, that he "might be called beautiful"—he turned out to be an untheatrical Kemble. Knowing how hopeless he was, he clowned about the stage, flapping his arms and crowing like a rooster, reducing his mother and sister to giggles. Charles, desperate for a Romeo, was obliged to engage William Abbot, though both he and Fanny knew that the choice was a poor one. As Fanny plaintively put it, Mr. Abbot was hopelessly unromantic and "old enough to be my father."

On October 5, 1829, seven weeks before her twentieth birthday, Fanny made her debut. In the morning she read, played the piano, and walked in the park, channeling her thoughts to everyday things, a routine she would always follow in times of stress. In the afternoon she rested so as to be fresh for the performance, which started at six-thirty. Well before six she and her mother drove to the theatre through a brilliant autumn sunset, which prompted Marie Thérèse to say, "Heaven smiles on you, my child."

At the theatre Aunt Dall took charge, exuding calm and order. Sending Marie Thérèse away, she dressed Fanny in Juliet's white satin gown. Then aunt and niece waited quietly in the dressing room, Fanny sitting rigidly in her seat for fear of creasing her long train. "There I sat," Fanny remembered, "ready for execution, with the palms of my hands pressed convulsively together and the tears I in vain endeavored to repress welling up into my eyes and brimming slowly over, down my rouged cheeks." Again and again Dall was forced to take out the rouge pot and retouch Fanny's cheeks.

When at last the call-boy announced "Miss Kemble to the stage," Fanny leaped to her feet, but her aunt calmly took her by the hand and led her to the wings. There they waited, Fanny almost fainting in Dall's arms. When Fanny's cue came she could not move—her limbs felt turned to stone. But resourceful Aunt Dall gave a gentle push and sent Fanny forward.

She ran straight across the stage, not daring to pause, look, or think. She scarcely heard the shout of welcome that rose from the throats of the audience. Instead she stood "like a terrified creature at bay, confronting the huge theatre of gazing human beings." When she opened her mouth her parched voice came out in little more than a whisper, and she could not imagine that one word she uttered during the whole scene could have been audible. Mercifully the scene was short, and she had little to say. In the next she had more lines, but she was better composed. And in the next—

the balcony scene—she triumphed. To quote her own words: "I was Juliet; the passion I was uttering sending hot waves of blushes all over my neck and shoulders, while the poetry sounded like music to me, as I spoke it, with no consciousness of anything before me, utterly transported into the imaginary existence of the play. After this, I did not return to myself till all was over."

As the final curtain fell, the audience exploded. Flowers were pelted down from the galleries and boxes, storms of applause and wild shouts erupted from the pit, and the entire building vibrated as hundreds of feet stamped on the wooden floor. On stage, the Kemble parents wept for happiness, and in the family box, Adelaide clapped and cried, beside herself with joy.

Next day the critics ratified the audience's verdict. Thomas Noon Talfourd, one of the most eminent reviewers, wrote that Fanny trod the boards as though she had studied and practiced the art of acting for years. Knowledgeable Leigh Hunt, never easy to please, declared that there was "no part of her performance" that he would wish to see altered.

Once Fanny became a star, her daily life altered beyond recognition. On the one hand, she was London's newest sensation, the talk of the day, a second Sarah Siddons. On the other, she was a hard-working actress. On performance days she kept to an almost Spartan routine. Her morning passed in study or rehearsal. At midday she dined on a mutton chop. In the afternoon she walked in the park, rested, and played the piano. In the evening she left for the theatre early; after she had dressed and made up, she waited in her dressing room, stitching at tapestry to calm her nerves. Called on stage, she would rise and walk to the wings, with her aunt carrying her train, ready to arrange it in becoming folds before she swept out to face the audience. When Fanny returned, Dall would fold up the train again, wrap her niece in a shawl, and escort her back to the dressing room. The sequence was repeated night after night. Fanny was always chaperoned and did not visit the greenroom. A young actress could all too easily lose her reputation, and the Kemble family was taking no chances.

Sometimes Adelaide came to the theatre with her sister, treasuring the visits as highlights in an otherwise dull existence. For the past eighteen months, life had been unkind to Adelaide. Fanny's going to Scotland had been a blow to her, and her father's worries and her mother's tantrums had caused her to retreat even further into herself. With Fanny's return, Adelaide looked forward to happier times, but these did not eventuate. Once Fanny began to act, Adelaide could feel her sister slipping away from her.

What was worse, she could feel Aunt Dall slipping away, as well. So crucial did Dall become to Fanny's career—as chaperone, dresser, and general factotum—that she had scarcely any time left for Adelaide. The poor child had never felt so alone.

On those evenings when Adelaide went to the theatre, she amused herself in Fanny's dressing room and then seated herself in a box in a corner of the wings to watch her sister act. The bustle of backstage thrilled her. She regarded the visits as wonderful treats, but Fanny did not always see them so. Adelaide had the habit of singing to herself, not quite under her breath, and the sound irritated Fanny. She grumbled that she was nervous enough without a fifteen-year-old sister making her more so. Though she continued to feel love and concern for Adelaide, Fanny was too caught up in her own life to understand the depth of Adelaide's loneliness.

Fanny had an extraordinary capacity to make money. On the nights when she played Juliet, the theatre's earnings often rose as high as five hundred pounds and seldom fell below four hundred. Suddenly the Kembles had spending money. In a rush of enthusiasm, they threw away their threadbare suits and dresses and bought new wardrobes, horses for riding, and a smart carriage. Within months the family moved to John Philip Kemble's former home in Great Russell Street, a three-story brick house next to the British Museum, set amid the dignified affluence of Bloomsbury. There Fanny furnished a spacious suite of her own, all glowing colors and flowers, as "pretty a bower of elegant comfort as any young spinster need have desired."

Most of Fanny's new wealth was lavished on dresses, shoes, gloves, and hats. Sometimes Adelaide went with her to the dressmaker and milliner, and together they chose gowns with stylish full sleeves and gathered skirts, and smart bonnets trimmed with feathers and bows. Fanny had a passion for beautiful dresses and wore them on stage and off. Her stage costumes were made by Madame Devy, the most fashionable dressmaker in London, and she exulted in dresses like the one she wore in *The Merchant of Venice*. It was made from shimmering pink and white shot silk—like strawberries and cream, she wrote—with an underskirt of pale blue satin, brocaded in silver. Her shoes were trimmed with jeweled roses. "I was *so* enchanted with my fine shoes," she told Harriet St. Leger.

The young Kembles indulged in expensive pastimes. The boys enrolled at Angelo's Fencing and Boxing Academy—the most exclusive school of its sort in London—where one of their partners was the future king of Hanover. The girls went to Captain Fozzard's Riding Academy, where the future Queen Victoria—"a very unaffected, bright-looking girl"—was a fellow pupil. Fanny shone at her riding lessons. She scarcely turned a hair when Old Fozzard—as she cheekily called her instructor—insisted that she sit on the horse without reins or stirrups, "often as not sitting left-sided on the saddle," for ladies in those days never rode astride. Even with her hands held behind her back, she seldom fell off. Her balance was excellent, and she kept her seat when the horse jumped, plunged, or reared. Adelaide, on the other hand, was frightened of horses and hated entering the ring when the captain put his riders through their paces. She was so scared that she begged Fanny to go with her to her riding lessons. Dressed identically in dark-brown riding habits and red velvet waistcoats, they looked "like two nice little robin red-breasts on horseback."

Such was Fanny's fame, and so untarnished was her reputation, that society's doors opened to her in the same way that they had once opened to her legendary aunt. "I was sought and petted," she wrote, "and caressed by persons of conventional and real distinction, and every night that I did not act I might, if my parents had thought it prudent to let me do so, have passed in all the gaiety of the fashionable world and the great London season." As it was, at fashionable dinners, dances, and concerts, her animated, intelligent, and increasingly self-possessed figure was to be seen. She described a typical ten days in her hectic life: "a dinner party at the Mayows tomorrow; an evening party on Monday; Tuesday, the opera; Wednesday I act." And so it continued through the week, with two more performances at the theatre, an evening party at home, two more dinners, a dance at the Fitzhughs, "and sundry dissipations looming in the horizon."

Fanny had an enormous capacity for enjoying herself. She quickly learned that any happy activity, especially physical activity, dispersed the stress that came from acting. She never felt happier and healthier than when dancing her feet off till daylight. When invited to a ball, she was always expected to bring a chaperone, and she often brought her father, because he flirted all night with the ladies and never told her when to go home. She liked a night of dancing to end with a morning canter on horseback in fashionable Hyde Park. Riding cured her headaches, her side-aches, and her fits of exhaustion better than any medicine.

The best tonic of all was Harriet St. Leger's visits to London. She came first in December 1830, sleeping in the room next to Fanny's at Great Russell Street. "It is a very small roost, dear Harriet," Fanny enthused, "but it is the only spare room in our house, and although it is three stories up, it is next to mine, and I hope the good neighborhood will atone for some deficiency." In the warmth of Harriet's sympathy, Fanny could feel herself relaxing. When Harriet returned to Ireland shortly before Christmas, she took Adelaide with her, and Fanny missed them both from the very moment of departure. "I stood in the dining room listening to your carriage wheels until I believe they were only rolling in my imagination," she told Harriet. "You cannot fancy how doleful our breakfast was."

It was an enormous relief to have Harriet nearby, even if only for a few weeks. Notwithstanding her outward confidence, there were times when Fanny felt scared out of her wits, and Harriet was virtually the only person to whom she could fully unburden herself. Fanny was suffering from culture shock. One day she had been an insignificant schoolgirl, the next she was hurled into a social and artistic life for which she had had scarcely any preparation. Every day brought new experiences, many of them exhilarating, but a number of them terrifying. Only by exerting every ounce of willpower did she manage to keep her composure. The specter of failure never left her. On the eve of one particularly difficult performance, she confided to Harriet that she felt "like some hunted creature driven to bay." When the play was over, Fanny collapsed onto the dressing room floor, "with only strength enough left to cry." Next day she felt a pain in her side all day long. "A stumble at starting," she told Harriet, "would have been bad enough, and might have bruised me; but a fall from the height to which I have been raised might break my neck, or at any rate cripple me for life."

Nor could Fanny overcome her misgivings about acting. Having concluded that success on the stage was like an addictive drug, she never stopped fretting in case "admiration and applause, and the excitement springing therefrom, may become *necessary* to me." She even went so far as to include in her daily prayers the hope that she "might be defended from the evil influence" of acting. Though she had craved attention all her life, she began to resent being obliged to exhibit herself in public. It had been amusing to see women eating off plates with her face painted on them, and gentlemen swathing their necks in scarves covered with pictures of her head—the nineteenth-century equivalent of today's souvenir mugs and T-shirts. But when she was stared at, every time she went to a party, she took exception. She trembled before "the violence done (as it seems to me) to womanly dignity and decorum in thus becoming the gaze of every eye and the theme of every tongue." One winter's evening she went to a party at the home of the poet Thomas Campbell. The rooms were so packed that if "one stood up one was squeezed to death, and if one sat down one was stifled." For the whole night she was "stared at from head to foot by everyone that could pass within staring distance of me." It was most disagreeable, an ordeal that intensified when a guest spilled coffee on her dress.

The elder Kembles understood the hazards of fame and advised her to keep to as simple and disciplined a routine as possible, advice which was not always followed. Fanny's parents assured her that a simple life would provide a refuge when the outside world became too much for her. The elder Kembles knew that it was dangerous to believe one's own publicity.

Fanny's father was only mildly concerned by her fears: his real interest lay in her blossoming talent. He saw that she was changing from a girl who acted solely out of instinct to one who was consciously learning her craft. After two months—during which time she played Juliet in more than thirty performances—Charles decided that Fanny was ready to take over Mrs. Siddons's repertoire. He began to present her in a stream of Mrs. Siddons's former roles, starting with Belvidera in Otway's *Venice Preserved* in December 1829.

Fanny was not entirely happy with her father's decision. Many of the parts went against her taste. The role of Mrs. Haller in Kotzebue's *The Stranger* she really disliked: "such mawkish sentiment, and such prosaic, commonplace language seem to me alike difficult to feel and to deliver." Struggling to succeed in the part, she began to wish that she had had a normal stage apprenticeship. Worse, since Mrs. Haller was one of Mrs. Siddons's greatest roles, she knew that she would be judged against her aunt. There was no way, as a mere beginner, Fanny could hope to match her aunt's skill, and she was only too aware of it. She did not suppose that there could "ever be a shadow of comparison between her and myself, even when years may have corrected all that is at present crude and imperfect in my efforts." Charles knew that a fortune could be made by presenting Fanny as a second Sarah Siddons, and he was gambling that her natural talent would carry her through. But doing so placed a crushing burden on Fanny's shoulders. One suspects that some of her later hatred of acting came from Charles's insistence that she step into the shoes of a legend.

There were sharp contrasts in the way in which Fanny and her aunt approached their work. Except for Shakespearean roles, the Siddons repertoire consisted of melodramatic showcases that suited her majestic, declamatory style of acting. The plots were unconvincing, the characters were overwritten, and the parts' appeal lay in the virtuosity of the actress's performance. To Fanny—raised at a time when theatrical taste was shifting in favor of naturalness—most of the women she was called on to depict seemed shallow and posturing. She marveled at the genius with which her aunt had fleshed out her unreal heroines and "clothed so meagre a part in such magnificent preparations."

Nonetheless Fanny was able to make the imaginative leap and succeed in acting right inside her character's skin. Like Mrs. Siddons she acquired, through a combination of instinct, intellect, and practice, the elusive art of the successful actress: the art of living emotionally inside a character and yet remaining sufficiently detached to fulfill the technical demands of the stage. Fanny described the process as the "combined operation of one's faculties, so to speak, in diametrically opposite directions." By way of example, she explained to Harriet how she went about performing a scene from *The Gamester*: "In my last scene as Mrs. Beverley, while I was half dead with crying, in the midst of the *real* grief, created by an entirely *unreal* cause, I perceived that my tears were falling like rain all over my silk dress and spoiling it; and I calculated and measured most accurately the space that my father would require to fall in and moved myself and my train accordingly."

Sometimes Fanny's acting reached new heights, and then Marie Thérèse—who saw almost every one of her performances—would embrace her and declare that she acted more persuasively than any girl of her age. Sometimes, when Fanny was emotionally slack or artistically slipshod, her mother would tell her that she was not fit to be seen. And Fanny would also tell herself that she was not fit to be seen. As the months passed she became her own severest critic. She called her performance as Queen Katharine in Shakespeare's *Henry VIII* "a schoolgirl's performance, tame, feeble and ineffective." She even went so far as to attack her father for insisting that she play the role.

Comparisons were constantly made between Fanny and Mrs. Siddons, sometimes to Fanny's detriment. Her aunt was of classic face and stature, while Fanny was stocky and not handsome, though her face was animated and expressive. Mrs. Siddons was the complete mistress of her craft; whatever the scene, she took endless pains and was always in control. Fanny, by her own admission, was often careless. The attention to minor details and finishing touches, the hallmarks of Kemble acting, were not for her, partly from lack of apprenticeship and partly because she was bored by stage procedures and rituals. In big scenes, however, her imagination soared, and her inborn talent triumphed. "On great occasions she is always great," wrote one rapturous critic, "and her spirit then fills the whole house."

At best Fanny's style conveyed intelligence, originality, and a radiant energy. But in emotional power she could never equal Sarah Siddons, whose impassioned voice, according to James Boaden, "in its wild shriek, absolutely harrows up the soul." Nor could Fanny shine in comedy, where timing and stagecraft were crucial. She admitted, after her first performance as Lady Teazle in *The School for Scandal*, that she "was as flat as a lady amateur." On the other hand, as the theatregoing diarists Charles Greville and Crabb Robinson pointed out, there were moments when Fanny in her youth projected a passion that almost matched her famous aunt in her prime. That inborn passion would soon elevate Fanny to the ranks of the finest British actresses.

4

"Everything Is Winter"

By her twenty-first birthday, in November 1830, Fanny had already gained fame and independence—those qualities she had once called the greatest desideratum of life. Her rise had been so rapid that she could scarcely believe it. She was thankful that she had saved her father's theatre, and she adored having admirers and parties, riding lessons and fine clothes, but fame and fortune often seemed unreal, and her fears were liable to surface when she least expected them. On the opening night of *Venice Preserved*, she suffered a panic attack during the mad scene. She had no sooner uttered Belvidera's last demented shriek than she was struck by uncontrollable terror and could not stop screaming. She fled from the stage, ran past the back of the scene, and—in her own words—"was pursuing my way, perfectly unconscious of what I was doing, down the stairs that led out into the street, when I was captured and brought back to my dressing room and my senses." It was some time before Fanny was able to pull herself together, and even longer before she could put the incident out of her mind. It greatly magnified her belief in the unhealthiness of acting. She said to Anna Jameson soon afterward, "I dare not feel all I *could* feel. I must watch myself."

When the London theatres went into recess for the summer of 1830, Charles, Fanny, and faithful Aunt Dall set out on a theatrical tour of England, Ireland, and Scotland. Fanny was apprehensive about the tour. She was uneasy at leaving Covent Garden, believing that London playgoers had a respect for Charles and goodwill toward herself that neither would find elsewhere. She was also daunted by the prospect of endless rehearsals with local actors. Once the tour was underway, however, her fears quickly subsided, and she was delighted to find how much she enjoyed herself.

Wherever the Kembles acted, the leading citizens were agog to meet Fanny. As Fanny and her father rode down Edinburgh's Princes Street in June 1830, Fanny's favorite novelist, Sir Walter Scott, was walking along

< 55 >

the footpath. At the sight of her, he stopped her father's horse and asked to be introduced. They met next day for breakfast, and Sir Walter's conversation delighted Fanny. Scott said to her: "You appear to be a very good horsewoman, which is a great merit in the eyes of a Border-man." This praise of her riding, uttered in so homely a way, pleased her even more than Sir Walter's observation that he had seen nothing to compare with her acting since Mrs. Siddons.

Scottish playgoers were notoriously undemonstrative—even Sarah Siddons found them so. When her passionate declamation met no response in Scotland, Mrs. Siddons used to turn away from the audience and mutter, "Stupid people, stupid people!" Performing at Edinburgh's Theatre Royal, Fanny was similarly disturbed by what she referred to as "deathlike stillness" of her listeners. Had it not been for the reassurances of Mrs. Harry Siddons and the Combes, she might have felt a failure. As it was, Fanny spent every spare moment with her cousins and their friends, riding again with Andrew Combe in his gig and sitting for a bust in Lawrence Macdonald's studio.

Ireland was a different matter. Its audiences were wildly enthusiastic. After Fanny's first appearance in Dublin, a couple of hundred men escorted her carriage back to the hotel, shouting like mad and struggling to catch a glimpse of her face through the carriage window.

When performances finished in Dublin, Fanny drove eighteen miles along the coast to the picturesque seaport of Skerries, where a treat awaited her. Close by was Ardgillan Castle, set high on a promontory above the surging waves, with the Morne Mountains fading purple in the distance. There, for a few precious days, she was reunited with Harriet St. Leger. "An angel's visit," Fanny called it, "perfectly lovely." She felt as free and happy as a bird. The two women sat in the sun on a grassy knoll, listening to the wind on the sea, and discussing, in Fanny's words, "things quite beyond ourselves till we were well nigh beside ourselves."

Back in England in September, the Kembles played in Liverpool, Birmingham, and Manchester and inspected the industrial North. Stirred by the factories and iron works, Fanny felt an instant attraction to that miraculous invention, the railway. The line between Manchester and Liverpool was almost completed. Fanny marveled at the long, deep tunnels and admired the "snorting little animal" of an engine, just like a little mare, with pistons for legs, wheels for feet and coals for oats. She "felt rather inclined to pat it." She was also enchanted by the engine's creator, George Stephenson, with whom, she told Harriet, she had fallen "most horribly in love." As the train steamed onward, she sat close beside him. "You can't imagine how strange it seemed to be journeying on thus," she wrote, "without any visible cause of progress other than the magical machine, with its flying white breath and rhythmical, unvarying pace." Stephenson explained how the engine worked and was intrigued by Fanny's quick understanding. He said he could "make a famous engineer of me," she told Harriet proudly. This praise especially pleased her because she feared that her mind might have atrophied from so much acting.

On September 15, 1830, Fanny and her parents joined a glittering assemblage invited to make the first journey on the railway. She was standing nearby when a leading politician, William Huskisson, strolled across the tracks to become the first railway fatality in recorded history. Fanny's shocked account is still a classic piece of reporting:

> Lord Wilton, Count Batthyany, Count Matuscenitz and Mr. Huskisson among the rest were standing talking in the middle of the road, when an engine on the other line, which was parading up and down merely to show its speed, was seen coming down upon them like lightning. The most active of those in peril sprang back into their seats: Lord Wilton saved his life only by rushing behind the duke's carriage, and Count Matuscenitz had but just leaped into it, with the engine all but touching his heels as he did so; while poor Mr. Huskisson, less active from the effects of age and ill health, bewildered, too, by cries of "Stop the engine! Clear the track!" that resounded on all sides, completely lost his head, looked helplessly to the right and left, and was instantaneously prostrated by the fatal machine, which dashed down like a thunderbolt upon him, and passed over his leg, smashing and mangling it in the most horrible way. (Lady Wilton said she distinctly heard the crushing of the bone.) So terrible was the effect of the appalling accident that, except that ghastly "crushing" and poor Mr. Huskisson's piercing shriek, not a sound was heard or a word uttered among the immediate spectators of the catastrophe.

At the time of the accident, the Kembles were staying at Heaton Hall, the country house of Lord and Lady Wilton, five miles outside Manchester. Lady Wilton's mother was an anomaly—one of the few professional actresses who had married an aristocrat. The invitation to Fanny and her parents to stay at Heaton Hall would seem to have owed a good deal to this unusual link, though Lord Wilton was himself an amateur organist and known to be theatrically minded. He did not demur when the Kembles appeared at dinner in medieval costume, since they had to drive immediately afterward to Manchester for their performance. Fanny wore a fetching outfit in black satin and velvet, which won her many compliments; these lessened her embarrassment at being dressed so strangely at the dinner table.

Fanny was used by then to exalted society, but she was nonetheless aware of the honor conferred on her by a visit to Heaton. Lady Wilton was extremely kind, Fanny wrote, "Petting me almost like a spoiled child, dressing me in her own exquisite riding-habit and mounting me on her own favorite horse." Fanny's parents shared her pride and pleasure in the notice bestowed on her by her social superiors.

Fanny could not help noticing that the entire house party was vastly superior to the Kembles in social rank. Their fellow guests included the formidable political hostess Lady Harriet Baring, two society beauties, an Austrian count and countess, Lord Francis Egerton, and Mr. Henry Greville. These last two accomplished and charming young men set the seal on Fanny's success.

Lord Francis Egerton was the younger son of the Duke of Sutherland. At thirty-one he was already a privy councillor and member of Parliament and had recently held the offices of Chief Secretary for Ireland and Secretary at War. More important to Fanny, he was the author of two books of poems and an early translation of Goethe's *Faust*, which had gained him something of a literary reputation. Fanny was instantly attracted to him. She told Harriet: "He is a young man of a great deal of talent, with a charming, gentle manner, and a very handsome, sweet face."

Henry Greville was Lord Francis's brother-in-law and equally well-born, being the grandson of the Duke of Portland. Cosmopolitan in outlook and fluent in European languages, he had been brought up in Brussels and was fond of recounting how, as a boy of thirteen, he had accompanied the Duke of Wellington to the Duchess of Richmond's famous ball on the eve of Waterloo. He adored the stage, especially Italian opera, and was reputed to be the best amateur singer in London society. Given his theatrical tastes, it was not surprising that he monopolized Fanny. She returned his kindness with enthusiasm, judging him a "natural exquisite" who nevertheless remained "perfectly simple and unaffected."

The visit to Heaton Hall gave Fanny a taste for the grand life, and no wonder. The magnificent mansion, designed sixty years before by the famous architect James Wyatt, contained room after room of exquisite Italian plasterwork, fine pictures, and furnishings. The beauty and luxury of the house and the clever talk of the guests brought Fanny intense pleasure and a growing sense of her own worth. Henceforth her letters and memoirs would be spiced with grand names and houses, not simply out of snobbery but to convince herself that she was more than just an actress. Acceptance by high society had become a vital source of her self-esteem.

Fanny's friendship with Henry Greville and Lord Francis Egerton grew after the Kembles left Heaton. At the theatre and at fashionable parties during the London winter season, she was always delighted when they sought her out. In the spring of 1831, the friendship was strengthened when she received an invitation from Lord Francis that very much excited her, though it was motivated by business as well as pleasure. Lord Francis had translated two French plays, one by Alexandre Dumas, the other by Victor Hugo, and he was keen to see his work performed. Using Fanny as a go-between, he hoped that Charles Kemble would accept his work for Covent Garden.

Charles was so pleased with the Dumas play that he agreed to take it, staging it the following year with Fanny in the title role of Katharine of Cleves. The translation of Hugo's play, *Hernani*, was not accepted, and this left Lord Francis with the task of finding another place for his work. Elaborate amateur theatricals were then the fashion, and he settled on the idea of putting on his work at his father's London mansion, Bridgewater House. He planned that his male friends should be the actors but, since he drew the line at permitting his wife and her friends to act in public, he sought professional actresses. It was no surprise that his first choice was Fanny.

Fanny was delighted to receive the invitation. And so, it would seem, was her father, because he rearranged her schedule so that she could accept it. The offer was doubly attractive because the early rehearsals were to be at the Egertons' country home, Oatlands, close to the village of Weybridge. A royal Tudor hunting lodge converted into a fine Georgian house, Oatlands boasted extensive gardens, a quaint grotto, and a royal dogs' cemetery. Fanny had seen it many times during her Weybridge days, and she longed to stay there.

She was also pleased to be diverted from worries that had been torturing her for longer than she cared to remember. Over the last three years her brother John had been causing the Kembles untold anxiety. In 1828 he abandoned his study of law at the Inner Temple, saying that he wanted to enter the Church of England. In 1829—the year of Fanny's debut—his unorthodox views caused him to fail his theology examination for his Bachelor of Arts degree at Cambridge. Disgusted by the university's conservatism, he decided to go to Germany to study the more liberal theology of certain Lutherans. His friend Alfred Tennyson urged him on with a stirring sonnet:

My hope and heart is with thee—thou wilt be
A latter Luther and a soldier priest
To scare the church-harpies from the master's feast;
Our dusted velvets have much need of thee.

Early in 1830 John returned from Germany, passed his examination at Cambridge, and commenced his studies for ordination as a Church of England clergyman. On hearing that he was at last settled, the Kemble family uttered prayers of thanks. Then, suddenly, in September 1830 came the astonishing news that John was in Gibraltar, in circumstances that filled his family with fear.

It seemed that John and his friends from the Cambridge Apostles' Conversazione Society had met a Spanish emigré named General Torrijos and decided to join him in a plot to overthrow King Ferdinand VII of Spain. While Arthur Hallam and Alfred Tennyson went off to the Pyrenees to meet conspirators from the north, John Kemble and Richard Trench—the future Archbishop of Dublin—sailed to Gibraltar, where they drank and debated like schoolboys and laid plans to run guns across the sea to Spain.

Throughout the early months of 1831 the family waited anxiously for news. Rumors were rife, some saying John was safe in Gibraltar, some that he was locked away in a Spanish prison. Marie Thérèse was greatly distressed by the rumor that John was in prison: "It has broken her down," Fanny informed Harriet. In March, Richard Trench returned to London with news that John was safe but that he refused to leave General Torrijos. "Heaven knows what plans he has formed for the future!" wrote Fanny in despair. On April 2, John's twenty-fourth birthday, the Kemble girls and their mother gazed at a pencil sketch of his face and feared that they would never see him again.

Six weeks later, with all their anxieties still focused on John, Fanny and her mother set out for rehearsals at Weybridge. It was May 18 and the height of spring. The sun caressed their backs in the open carriage, and "hawthorn lay thick and fragrant on every hedge, like snow that winter had forgotten to melt." Intoxicated by her surroundings, Fanny began to throw off her cares and look forward to the days ahead. She had already met Lord Francis's wife, a woman of sweet, pious character and calm, classical beauty. Lady Francis Egerton represented everything Fanny most admired in a woman. Her ladyship standing with her babe in her arms and her handsome husband beside her was one of the most charming pictures Fanny had ever seen. She regarded them with something close to religious awe, comparing them to the Holy Family.

The house party was assembling as the Kembles arrived. It included half a dozen young men who were to be the actors—Henry Greville among them—and a small, sharp-faced politician named Lord John Russell. The architect of a controversial bill to reform the House of Commons that was then being debated, Lord John took no part in the play. He said he preferred acting in Parliament. He was nevertheless forced to perform at the dinner table, because the Egertons opposed reform and, in Fanny's words, "led him rather a hard life."

At rehearsals next morning one young man, Augustus Craven, impressed Fanny: his acting was the best she had ever seen in an amateur. He was also strikingly handsome and dashing. Fanny, initially surprised by all his talents, reminded herself that good looks and a passion for the theatre ran in his family. His aunt, Louisa Brunton, had been a professional actress before she married the seventh Baron Craven. His grandmother had written plays for Covent Garden and had been a popular amateur actress. A liberated woman, Elizabeth Craven had also scandalized society by deserting her husband, the sixth Baron Craven, and living with a German nobleman, the Margrave of Anspach. Eccentric, stylish, witty, and beautiful, the flamboyant Elizabeth had swept all before her to become one of the best-known women in London. Some of her flair had descended to Augustus, and Fanny found it irresistible.

Fanny's three days at Oatlands flashed by in a continuous round of activity. She revisited Eastland Cottage and rode with her hosts over the gorse-covered countryside, snatching leaves and blossoms to carry back to Adelaide as souvenirs. Between times she chatted with the guests, sang duets with her hostess, and rehearsed *Hernani*. Augustus Craven and she were playing Hernani and Dona Sol, the lovers. She had never felt so happy in a part.

Returning to London on May 21, Fanny and her mother found the household turned upside down. John had returned home. Fanny, more relieved than she could say, dreamed that night that John was about to come home, and then awoke to the delicious knowledge that he was there. Next morning Adelaide was due to take her First Communion at the Swiss Reformed Church. Almost as devout as Fanny, Adelaide had been keyed up for weeks and expected her family to share her sense of awe. But John's homecoming overshadowed Adelaide's long-awaited day; and as they knelt in church that Sunday morning, the prayer in all the Kembles' hearts was one of thanks for John's return.

Fanny happily resumed work on *Hernani*. She had not known that rehearsals could be so much fun. Lord Francis's young male friends adored making fools of themselves and roared with laughter whenever they mixed up their lines. They relied on the prompter for every other line. Once a stage messenger stood "stuttering, sputtering, madly ejaculating and gesticulating, but not one articulate word could he get out. I thought I should have exploded with laughter," Fanny told her diary. After the dress rehearsal, the Egertons arranged a sumptuous supper, at which Fanny's health was toasted. Overcome by unaccustomed shyness, she collapsed in her chair, "as red and as limp as a skein of scarlet wool."

Lord Francis and his friends gave three performances in the long gallery of Bridgewater House, where a temporary theatre had been built. The audience consisted of the finest society in London, who applauded with the enthusiasm of a Covent Garden gallery. On the final night the cast performed in front of "all the grandeurs in England"—Queen Adelaide, the Duke and Duchess of Gloucester, the Duke and Duchess of Cumberland, Princess Elizabeth, Prince Leopold, the Duke of Brunswick. Fanny was so nervous she could scarcely stand or control her voice. When Lady Francis took her to meet Queen Adelaide, the consort of William IV, Fanny almost fainted.

In the middle of June, between performances at Covent Garden, Fanny agreed to spend six more days at Oatlands. Her father and mother came, as well, and they rode, boated, and fished in the river. Fanny and the younger guests listened to "terrific ghost stories till one o'clock in the morning." Fanny and her hostess, by that time on intimate terms, sat in a private sitting room and read each other extracts from their diaries. In the evening, in front of the guests, Fanny and Augustus Craven acted scenes from Racine's *Andromaque* and Scribe's *Les Premières Amours*. Through a chance remark Fanny discovered that he had been at school in Paris at the same time as she: they had even met in those far-off days at a young people's party, to which she had worn a white muslin dress with a flaming-red sash. It seemed to be a magical coincidence.

In Augustus's company everything seemed magical, and Fanny floated through the heady days on a wave of happiness. Often of an evening she felt so ecstatic that she was unable to sit quietly in the drawing room with the ladies. She would hurry out into the garden, down the winding shrubbery paths till she came to a small lake with a rustic pavilion, and beside it a circle of cedar trees, their roots embedded in tall foxgloves. "The place seemed peopled with spirits," she told Harriet. Lingering there for half an hour, she gave herself up to an "invisible presence" before returning to the conversation of the drawing room.

Back in London Fanny showed signs of strain and complained of feeling deathly tired. She blamed late nights, new acting roles, and the burning of the candle at both ends, but the truth was that she had fallen in love. For years Fanny's biographers have guessed at her feelings, not knowing for certain either whom she loved or how much she loved him. Describing the incident in *Records of a Girlhood*, Fanny was discreet; she spoke simply of "an ephemeral love" and then closed the subject. Fortunately, in a letter just discovered, Adelaide was not bound by the same discretion. Fanny, she wrote, was in love with Augustus Craven, and they were engaged to be married.

Fanny had every reason to fall in love with Augustus; he combined great personal charm with an ability to give her a permanent place in that aristocratic world that had begun to mean so much to her. To add to his attraction, he did not seem put off by her lack of beauty, her disreputable profession, or her free spirit. On the contrary, as the grandson of the liberated Elizabeth, he seemed to favor free spirits. Swept away by her feelings, Fanny abandoned her decision never to marry. She now saw herself, like Lady Francis, walking on the lofty stage of aristocratic life, with a husband and child at her side.

Not having taken marriage seriously, Fanny had acquired little worldly wisdom concerning courtship. Her experience had largely been confined to a gaggle of young men, nicknamed the "bodyguard," who worshipped her across the footlights or stood in safe clusters around the stage door. One of those stage-door followers was young Augustus Fitzclarence, the illegitimate son of King William IV and the actress Mrs. Jordan. Fanny was embarrassed when, meeting him at a ball, he began to criticize his royal father. From then on she gave him little encouragement.

Fanny also had sentimental friendships with some of her elder. brother's companions. Edward Fitzgerald, Alfred Tennyson, and William Thackeray—names that stand today at the height of English literature—had all been a little in love with her at one time or another. Tennyson had written a poem to her, but he, like her other young admirers, had not dared to approach too close.

One of the most determined of all Fanny's suitors was the elderly portrait painter Thomas Lawrence, who had a special—even sinister—reason to adore her. Thirty years before, when Lawrence was twenty-eight and Sarah Siddons was forty-two, the artist and the actress had fallen in love. Mrs. Siddons, a woman of strict respectability, had kept him at a distance; whereupon Lawrence turned his attention to her daughters, indulging in a cruel courtship of each in turn. First he became engaged to Sarah's elder daughter, Sally. Then, when her younger sister Maria arrived home from school, he jilted Sally and became engaged to Maria. At this stage, to quote Fanny's words, "Violent scenes of the most painful emotion, for which the cause was inexplicable and incomprehensible, took place repeatedly between himself and Mrs. Siddons."

Within months of her engagement, Maria Siddons became ill with tuberculosis. As she lay dying, Lawrence began to court her sister again. Painfully wounded by his betrayal, Maria extracted a promise from Sally that she would never marry Thomas Lawrence. In those days a deathbed oath was held to be binding, so Sally was denied all hope of possessing the man she loved.

During Fanny's first season, in the winter of 1829–1830, Lawrence became obsessed with her. Night after night he came to the theatre to watch her act. He began to write page upon page of detailed criticism of her performances and repeatedly approached Charles for permission to paint her portrait. Knowing the tragic history of the Siddons girls, Charles was reluctant, but he was eventually worn down, permitting the sittings so long as Marie Thérèse was present as a chaperone. But no chaperone could deter Lawrence—his every brush stroke was a caress.

Fanny soon glimpsed the volcanic feelings that lay beneath the artist's silken manner, and she quickly realized that he saw her as a combination of Mrs. Siddons and her two dead daughters. Before starting his life-sized portrait of her as Juliet, he sketched her head and upper body in pencil. "What strikes you?" he asked Marie Thérèse about the sketch. "It is very like Maria," answered Fanny's mother. Lawrence then fell into a paroxysm of emotion, and, to quote Fanny's words, "became so agitated as to be barely able to speak; and at last, with a violent effort said, 'Oh, she is very like her; she is very like them all.'" Lawrence died soon after this incident, and Fanny admitted that she felt relieved. She was afraid she might have fallen in love with him and ended up as "the fourth member of our family whose life he would have disturbed and embittered."

With so bizarre an experience behind her, Fanny was not entirely ignorant of courtship, but her knowledge of the marriage market was less than that of most young women of her day. She failed to understand that Augustus's proposal was too good to be true. He was virtually out of her reach, for only in exceptional circumstances did aristocrats of her time marry professional actresses. A shrewd observer of high society had only to run down a list of such wives—the Countess of Derby, Lady Becher, Lady Thurlow, the Duchess of St. Albans, Lady Craven—to realize that all the husbands were rich and powerful and able to insist with a fair measure of success that their wives should be accepted by society. Young Augustus Craven was neither rich nor powerful and was financially dependent on his father.

There was one strong factor in the lovers' favor, and on that, presumably, they were gambling. Louisa Brunton, a lesser actress than the Kembles, had married Augustus's uncle about the time of Fanny's birth. As Louisa Brunton had succeeded in becoming a Craven, so, surely, might Fanny. Without that precedent, one supposes that Augustus would never have proposed, and Fanny and her family would not have dared to take his proposal seriously.

The precedent of Louisa Brunton partially explains the confidence and eagerness with which the Kemble family encouraged the attachment. At Oatlands, Charles and Marie Thérèse went out of their way to encourage the courtship, even though they thereby placed their own financial future in jeopardy. No respectable husband of that day would allow his wife to appear on a public stage; if Fanny married Augustus, she would be obliged to abandon her career and terminate those earnings on which the Kembles depended. Three years later, when Fanny proposed marrying a man of lesser social worth, her father opposed the match on the grounds that the Kembles' theatrical income would thereby be reduced. Charles and Marie Thérèse can only have believed that marriage with a Craven was within the bounds of possibility, and that it would repay them in social prestige what it lost them in financial reward.

Fanny herself showed a quiet determination in the courtship. The day after the final performance of *Hernani*, she was so exhausted that she stayed in bed, and Anna Jameson came to sit with her. The two began to discuss marriage. "I said," Fanny wrote in her diary, "I thought if one did not expect too much one might secure a reasonably fair amount of happiness, though of course the risk one ran was immense." The statement was tactless, because Anna was unhappily married, her husband having in effect abandoned her when he decided to become a judge on the island of Dominica. Fanny would never forget the look of pain that passed across Anna's face during the conversation. Nevertheless Fanny's remark showed how her mind was working. Fanny had made up her mind to marry.

As the weeks passed, and no public engagement seemed imminent, the strain frayed Fanny's nerves. When Anna probed the subject, Fanny silenced her abruptly. When Harriet referred to her as Juliet, she snapped that she was no Juliet, except for two lines that she could quote with "entire self application":

> I have no joy of this contract to-night;
> It is too rash, too unadvised, too sudden.

The couple was still hoping for Augustus's father's permission to marry, and for the financial settlement without which Augustus could not support a wife or even himself. To their dismay, it was not forthcoming, and the reason was almost certainly Fanny's profession. Though Keppel Craven was the eccentric son of an even more eccentric mother, he would tolerate only strict respectability in a daughter-in-law. Three years later, he withheld his consent when Augustus proposed marrying an impeccably born Frenchwoman who was also a Roman Catholic. On that occasion, armed with his fiancée's aristocratic ancestry, the son was able to fight the father's prejudice against Catholics, successfully wresting parental consent and a settlement of seventeen thousand pounds. Fanny had neither a fortune nor aristocratic relatives. Augustus was without defense against his father, and there was nothing he could do to persuade him.

As the weeks passed, Fanny's spirits sank lower and lower. Aunt Dall, fooled by neither love nor titles and long since reconciled to spinsterhood, tried to inject some common sense into her niece. As a woman of the theatre, she saw what Fanny stood to lose by marrying. She begged Fanny to count her blessings and let her man go his way: "While you remain single and choose to work, your fortune is an independent and ample one; as soon as you marry, there's no such thing. Your position in society . . . is both a pleasanter and more distinguished one than your birth or real station entitles you to; but that also is the result of your professional exertions, and might, and probably would alter for the worse if you left the stage."

Fanny was forced to admit the truth of her aunt's logic: "it seems," she wrote sadly, "that I have fortune and fame (such as it is)—positive real advantages, which I cannot give with myself, and which I cease to own when I give myself away, which certainly makes marrying any one or any one marrying me rather a solemn consideration; for I lose everything, and my marryee gains nothing in a worldly point of view." Augustus would have lost prospective wealth by marrying her; and Fanny probably would have gained only a precarious position in society. There was only one solution—the couple must part.

The parting was agonizing. Fanny later wrote about the pain and its depressing aftermath, during which it seemed that her "very life blood must pour away." Though Fanny was deeply unhappy, she does not seem to have felt ill will toward her beloved. They were fate's victims—or so she seems to have concluded—and neither could fight the laws of society. What she did blame was her profession. This episode confirmed her worst fears. After the failure of her love affair, Fanny's ambivalence toward acting was deeper than ever.

Four months later, Lady Francis Egerton begged the Kembles to revisit Oatlands. Recalling her former happiness there, Fanny cried bitterly when the invitation arrived and could not make up her mind whether to accept or not. When her father's illness caused her to refuse, she felt such relief that she realized the reunion would have been unendurable. She wrote in her diary: "Everything is winter now, within and without me; and when I was last there it was summer, in my heart and over all the earth."

The autumn and winter brought Fanny other losses. Sixteen-year-old Adelaide had been unhappy from the time Fanny began to act; she missed her sister's company and Aunt Dall's loving care. Her days seemed to pass in dull lessons and music practice, jokes with her brother Henry, and an occasional visit to the country. Often she moped about the house, not knowing what to do with herself.

At first Marie Thérèse considered hiring a governess, and Fanny took up the idea enthusiastically, writing long letters on the subject to Anna Jameson. She had strong ideas about what type of woman they should employ. They needed someone capable of calming Adelaide's nerves and fostering her reasoning powers—the Kembles were all too excitable and irrational, in Fanny's view. If no such woman could be found, then Adelaide would be better off alone. Her sister was a little jewel, Fanny told Anna forcefully, "and it will be a sin if she is marred in the cutting and polishing."

Though Marie Thérèse searched for months, no suitable candidate came forth. In the end Adelaide's musical talent offered a solution. On the evening of August 22, 1831, Charles's old friend Adolphe Nourrit was to dine with the Kembles at Great Russell Street. Magnetic and melancholic,

Nourrit was the leading tenor at the Paris Opera, and Adelaide was agog to meet him. At the same time she was scared, because she guessed that she was facing a musical test.

After dinner Nourrit sang for his host and hostess, his exquisite top notes floating across the lamp-lit room. As the applause died away he turned to Adelaide, gracefully inviting her to take his place. Nervously she stood beside the piano and sang her best aria—then waited for the response. It was more enthusiastic than she had dared to hope. Nourrit was so pleased that he invited her to join him in a duet. Fanny, "frightened to death for self and sister," played the accompaniment and stumbled over the keys.

Charles eagerly accepted Nouritt's high opinion of his daughter's voice, and plans were quickly laid. Just more than a month later, while Adelaide was still elated after singing with the great tenor, she and her mother traveled to Paris, where Adelaide was enrolled as a student of Professor Giulio Bordogni of the Paris Conservatoire.

Fanny felt her sister's loss, as did the rest of the family. But by far the most far-reaching losses of 1831 were financial. By the middle of the year the box-office earnings were down, and debt was again accumulating. The reasons were not hard to fathom. Fanny had been overexposed to the public and had become less of a drawing card. Also, the minor theatres were defying the monopoly of London's two major theatres and had begun to perform a repertoire similar to that of the Covent Garden. The competition was eating away at the profits.

Charles and his fellow proprietors initiated lawsuits against the proprietors of the minor theatres, who shrugged off the prosecutions, reassured that public opinion was on their side. Meanwhile the debts mounted at Covent Garden. "I do not know," wrote Fanny despairingly, "and I do not believe any one knows, the real state of terrible involvement in which this miserable concern is wrapped."

Charles's dream of maintaining a vigorous national theatre had become an obsession. "It is pitiful," wrote Fanny, "to see how my father still clings to that theatre." She expressed utter exasperation at his folly: "If I had twenty or a hundred thousand pounds, not one farthing would I give to the redeeming of that fatal millstone, which cannot be raised, but will infallibly drag everything tied to it down to the level of its own destruction."

By November 1831, Charles was exhausted and ailing. His ten-year lease on the theatre had just expired, and though he renewed it for another year, he did so in the knowledge that he faced a hard financial struggle. By the middle of the month he was almost too weak and feverish to leave his bed. It was painful for Fanny "to see him drag himself about, and hear his feeble voice."

Attended by two doctors, who bled him and applied mustard plasters to his side, Charles rallied slightly. However, in December he developed a cough and began to spit blood, at which the doctors shook their heads and diagnosed inflammation of the lungs. Fanny felt as if she was turning to stone when she heard their diagnosis. Her father was so ill that on some nights when she left for the theatre, she wondered if he would be alive when she came home again.

Neither Fanny nor her mother was capable of coping with so serious an illness. Marie Thérèse returned to her old nervous habit of constantly rearranging the furniture; and Fanny could not enter her father's sickroom without crying. At the height of their anxiety, she and Henry lay on the sofa in her bedroom and "cried together almost through the whole afternoon." Only Dall stayed calm enough to nurse the patient. "Night and day she has watched and waited on him," reported Fanny. "She is invaluable to us all, and every day adds to her claims upon our love and gratitude." Meanwhile Fanny was obliged to continue acting in a theatre that was half full. "No words can describe what I have suffered at that dreadful theatre," she wrote to Harriet.

Charles defied his doctors' pessimism. Six days before Christmas, 1831, he was declared out of danger, and thereafter he steadily gained strength. As he lay in his convalescent bed, he reviewed his financial situation. He could see only one hope, and that was to give up his theatre's lease and act in the United States for two years. He had received a generous offer from Stephen Price, a former lessee of the theatre at Drury Lane, who was then at the Park Theatre in New York. By accepting Price's offer, Charles believed he could make enough to pay off the debt, reclaim the Covent Garden theatre, and save something for his old age.

Fanny was aghast at the plan. Though Charles was barely out of convalescence, she told him plainly that she would not take one voluntary step toward America. She preferred to dispense with the house, the horses, and the carriage, and let the whole family retire to Europe and live cheaply. Anything would be better, in Fanny's view, than being "obliged to separate and go off to that dreadful America!" The argument reached a climax one afternoon in March 1832, when Charles collapsed and cried out dramatically, "Good God what will become of us all!" Fanny, "cold as stone," could only say, "God help us all!" She knew at that moment that no matter what she said, they would sail for America.

On Friday, June 22, 1832, Fanny made her last professional appearance on that Covent Garden stage, which had long nourished—and was now ruining—the Kembles. The play was Sheridan Knowles's *The Hunchback*. Julia was a role that Fanny had always enjoyed playing; but as her father led her offstage, she cried so bitterly that she could scarcely speak to the many friends who had come backstage to say goodbye.

Father and daughter now prepared to tour theatres in England and Scotland for one month before embarking for America. Their preparations included an agonizing series of family farewells. In London they said goodbye to Adelaide, who had returned from France expressly to see them before they left. Fanny was more distressed than she had imagined by this parting. She had missed her sister when only the short distance of the English Channel separated them: how much worse would be the wider separation of the Atlantic Ocean.

In London they also said farewell to Henry, while John traveled with them as far as Greenwich and waved goodbye as their ship sailed down the Thames. The parting from Marie Thérèse was the saddest of all, and they left it to the last. Fanny called it "a tearing away and wrenching asunder." Her mother sailed with them as far as Edinburgh, and when Marie Thérèse took her final leave of them on July 8, all three were beside themselves with grief. Slowly her mother's London-bound ship sailed along the Forth, within sight of their windows. Fanny sat near her father in their lodgings, with a book in her hand, "not reading but listening to his stifled sobbing."

When father, daughter, and faithful Aunt Dall reached Liverpool, their port of embarkation for America, an agony surfaced in Fanny that she had thought was safely locked away. Its cause was presumably a letter of farewell from Augustus Craven. Though she deleted most of the references to him from her published reminiscences, she allowed this last shadowy expression to remain: "I did not think," she wrote, "there was another day in store for me as this. I thought all was past and over, and had forgotten the last drop in the bitter cup."

Fortunately, Harriet St. Leger was to come to Liverpool to see them off. During these wretched months, Fanny had come to rely more and more on Harriet. "Good friends are like the shrubs and trees that grow on a steep ascent," Fanny told her. "We unconsciously grasp and lean upon them for support and assistance on our way."

Harriet arrived in Liverpool, clutching a portrait of herself for Fanny to remember her by and insisting that "if anything should go ill," she should at once be summoned across the Atlantic. She begged Fanny to look on America as an exciting adventure. And if Fanny could not lose herself in adventure, Harriet advised, then she should try to forget her own distress by cheering her father. Fanny knew that this was common sense, but she found the task easier said than done. "When one's own heart is all but frozen," she told Harriet, "one knows not where to find warmth to impart to those who are shivering with misery beside one."

On August 1, 1832, Fanny folded the last theatrical costume into the last of the twenty-one trunks that were to sail with them and made her final farewells. Weeping copiously, she assured her Liverpool friends that she was leaving them against her will and that she would not be happy until she returned. As she spoke, she clutched a bunch of carnations to her breast, vowing that she would keep them until she stood again on English soil. Down at the docks her mood lifted briefly, because Harriet had come to see them off. But Fanny's spirits sank again when she boarded the ship and entered the cramped cabin. Unpacking her diary, she made a dramatic entry: "Here I am," she wrote, "on board the *Pacific*, bound for America, having left home, and all the world behind."

5

A Genteel Slave-owner

The voyage to America took one month, and the weather was as up and down as Fanny's moods. On days when the sailing ship was tossed about by the waves, she did not dare to eat a meal in public, in case she became too nauseous. Instead she ate in her tiny cabin, with Dall as her companion. For ten days she lay mostly on her bunk, while the ship pitched, bounced, reeled, and shuddered, and waves banged against the skylight and seeped into the cabin. Poor Dall was more seasick than Fanny, and heartsick as well. It hurt Fanny's conscience to think of her aunt leaving the comforts of home, not to mention her dear Adelaide, "to come wandering to the ends of the earth after me."

When the sea calmed and the sun shone, Fanny sat on deck in the shade of a canvas awning, embroidering a cover for her Bible and reading a life of Byron. Determined to be cheerful, she threw herself into the social routine of shipboard life. She was soon the life and soul of the dances, charades, card games, and concerts with which the travelers filled the hours they spent at sea. One evening she and a male passenger sang through an entire book of Moore's Irish Melodies. On another she read aloud from Anna Jameson's *Characteristics of Women*, which had just been published in London and was dedicated to her. On Sunday afternoons, when the church bell rang, she accompanied Charles on deck for services under the canvas awning. Fanny was deeply impressed by this gathering of strangers, alone on the silent sea, and united only by their dependence on God. That night she wrote in her diary: "I felt more of the excitement of prayer than I have known for many a day—and 'twas good—oh! very, very good."

Fanny exulted in the snowy crests of foam against the ship's sides, and the glittering spray around the prow. What moved her most, however, was the aurora borealis, those atmospheric lights sometimes seen in northern latitudes. They "rushed like sheeted ghosts along the sky," she wrote, and

< 72 >

"made heaven and earth appear like one vast world of flame." Fanny considered that the journey was worthwhile for this sight alone.

Just out of view of the American coast, she befriended a little bird that had fallen on to the deck. She made a cage out of a basket and fed it with seed, but the next day it died. "Poor little creature!" she mourned. "How very much more I do love all things than men and women." Love was on her mind, and Augustus Craven was never far from her thoughts. Before long her pent-up unhappiness flowed onto paper.

Tis all in vain, it may not last,
The sickly sunlight dies away,
And thick clouds that veil the past,
Roll darkly o'er my present day.

Have I not flung them off and striven
To seek some dawning hope in vain;
Have I not been forever driven
Back to the bitter past again?

Fanny's moods were volatile. On September 3, 1832, when the ship approached New York, her spirits rose, and by the time the ship anchored off Staten Island, she was close to euphoria. When fellow passengers begged her to join their farewell party, she drank everybody's health and did not go to bed until two o'clock in the morning.

Next day she, Charles, and Dall were up at six, ready to board the steamboat for the ride to the shore through fog and rain. As they approached the dock, the other passengers strained their eyes to make out the buildings, but Fanny kept hers downcast. "I could not endure to lift my eyes to the strange land," she wrote, "and even had I done so, was crying too bitterly to see anything."

When Fanny finally brought herself to look, the sight of New York pleased her: she thought that the city's brightly painted houses, with their green venetian shutters, looked continental. She was also surprised by the city's size and vigor. Though Fanny knew that New York was the largest city in America, with a population racing toward a quarter of a million, she was unprepared for the bustle and swagger in the streets, the smoking chimneys of the many factories, and the sight of the produce arriving from the fast-multiplying farms in the interior.

As the days passed, Fanny's enthusiasm faded. Everything about her hosts attracted her criticism. She thought their clothes were showy, their manners too familiar, their flowers vulgar, and their carriages uncomfortable. Most of all, she objected to the behavior of the young girls. "Society is entirely led by chits," she wrote in her diary. New York's upper class had "neither elegance, refinement, nor the propriety which belongs to ours; but is a noisy, rackety, vulgar congregation of flirting boys and girls, alike without style or decorum."

This was a harsh judgment, but there was no doubt in Fanny's mind that the standards of upper-class England were far above those of America. Since she herself had risen high above her station through a hard-won command of the nuances of good society, she took pride in delivering her criticisms and spoke them aloud more often than was tactful.

Thirteen days after the Kembles' arrival in New York, Charles opened as Hamlet in the Park Theatre, appearing without his daughter. He had decided that they should make their debuts separately. Sitting with Dall in a box on opening night, Fanny ached with anxiety for her father. When his performance was followed by prolonged applause, she was thankful, though she could not help thinking that London playgoers would have risen to their feet and waved their hats and handkerchiefs. She was happier when she heard that her father's reception, by New York's standards, was wildly enthusiastic.

On the following night she prepared to make her own debut. Fanny had chosen to play Bianca in Millman's *Fazio*, sensing that she needed a part in which she could succeed under any circumstances. As it happened, her caution was well founded; rehearsals with the local actors had gone poorly. On opening night her leading man botched his lines, but she managed to override him. Fanny's skills as an actress had improved steadily over the past three years, and she was approaching the height of her powers. American theatregoers were astonished at the ease and brilliance of her performance. Philip Hone, the politician and diarist, wrote that he had never seen "an audience so moved, astonished, and delighted. Her display of the strong feelings which belong to the part was great beyond description, and the expression of her wonderful face would have been a rich treat if her tongue had uttered no sound."

After less than a month in New York, the Kembles began their acting tour of the northern states. Setting out at six on the morning of October 8, 1832, they boarded a steamboat, then a coach, and ten hours later limped, exhausted, into Philadelphia. Every few weeks thereafter, during a span of more than six months, they swayed in stagecoaches, steamboats, and railway trains to Baltimore, Washington, Boston, and New York—and then retraced their route to play parts of the circuit again. In almost every theatre where they acted, huge crowds waited for tickets, and houses were quickly sold out. Fanny recorded that there was such a mad scuffle at the box office in Philadelphia that one man was injured, while another made forty dollars by scalping tickets.

On reaching Washington, the Kembles were delighted to discover that their reputation had preceded them. The tiny theatre was crammed with the city's celebrities, including Justice Joseph Story of the Supreme Court and John Marshall, the Chief Justice. On opening night Fanny reduced the audience to tears, and the eminent judges wept with the rest. Justice Story declared, "I only thank God that I am alive in the same era as such a woman."

The Kembles were puzzled by Washington. The city seemed to be nothing but a collection of lonely buildings dotted in vast empty spaces, not at all like a nation's capital. It was the "strangest thing by way of a town that can be fancied," wrote Fanny in her diary: "a red-brick image of futurity, where nothing *is*, but all things are to *be*."

The starkness of Washington's streets did not make the Kembles any less eager to visit those marvelous buildings that *had* been completed, or any less keen to meet the distinguished people who inhabited them. Fanny was taken on a crisp January day to the Capitol, marble-white against the blue winter sky. She was thrilled to hear a speech by the golden-voiced lawyer and statesman Daniel Webster, but she was even more intrigued to see the bevy of ladies in their pink, blue, and yellow bonnets crowd the galleries and interrupt the speeches with nods and whispers. They made such a tremendous bustle, wrote Fanny, that Daniel Webster almost faltered in his oratory.

Three days later Fanny and Charles were taken to call on President Andrew Jackson at the White House. Fanny was impressed by his imposing figure: "tall and thin, but erect and dignified—a good specimen of a fine old well-battered soldier." The president spoke at length against "scribbling ladies," denouncing one in particular, to whom he attributed "the whole of the present southern disturbances." As a lady scribbler herself, Fanny felt her temper rising, but she kept it firmly in check. That evening when she described the meeting in her diary, she added a sardonic postscript. "Truly," she wrote, "if this be true, the lady must have scribbled to some purpose."

In April Fanny, Charles, and Dall arrived in Boston and settled into the Tremont House—perhaps America's best hotel—conveniently situated opposite the Tremont Theatre. From their bedroom windows they could see the jostling crowds at the box office and the hordes of Harvard University students who came to worship Fanny. Fanny thought Boston "one of the pleasantest towns imaginable." She loved the Charles River and the handsome streets, lined with solid granite houses and flowering chestnut trees. "I am enchanted with it," she wrote happily. "It bears more resemblance to an English city than any we have yet seen."

Knowing the Kembles were to play in Boston, Sir Charles Vaughan, the British minister to Washington, had entrusted them with letters of introduction to some of the leading residents. Charles quickly delivered a letter to George Ticknor, the Harvard professor of *belles lettres*. At once the proudest doors of Cambridge and Beacon Hill swung open to them. It was a remarkable response, because those doors did not open readily, and rarely to actors. The Kembles were judged an exception, and Boston high society found its judgment vindicated. Anna Quincy, the daughter of the president of Harvard, echoed many voices when she wrote that in private life Charles was very much the gentleman, and Fanny was very little the actress. Both made a very agreeable impression.

One night, at dinner in one of those grand houses, Fanny sat between John Quincy Adams, the former president of the United States, and the eloquent Daniel Webster. Thrilled to be placed between such great men, she was not so pleased by the conversation. When Adams announced that "Othello was disgusting, King Lear ludicrous, and Romeo and Juliet childish nonsense," Fanny told her diary that she had to bite her water glass to keep from flying at him.

She probably would have been happier to sit between two women, because female conversation in Boston society often reveled in books and theatre. The intellectual skills of Boston women did not surprise her. In this most English of American cities—where the Common reminded her of Green Park, and Beacon Street recalled Park Lane—Fanny recognized that "mental cultivation" was as much valued as wealth or birth. She was inclined to think that she could live happily in Boston.

In every city in which Fanny played, she found herself copied by other young women. She wore an unusual peaked riding hat, rather like a jockey's—a parting gift from Lady Francis Egerton—and saw it reproduced on hundreds of American heads. Her habit of riding a horse for exercise each day was imitated by numerous young ladies. Fanny's opinions—usually the more tactful ones—were widely quoted at society parties. Unfortunately some of her less tactful opinions also circulated. In Philadelphia, a pamphlet was passed around describing a private conversation in which

Fanny allegedly spoke derisively of America and Americans. To halt the gossip, Charles felt obliged to step in front of the curtain before one performance and persuade the audience that the rumors circulating about his daughter were false. Luckily his hearers accepted his assurances, and Fanny made her entrance to tremendous applause.

Though the tour was an unprecedented success and brought money, glowing reviews, and many compliments, it also had its disadvantages. The unremitting travel, packing, and unpacking, along with the constant tutoring of local actors, gave the Kembles little time to pause and refresh themselves. Fanny complained in a letter to Anna Jameson, "We never remain a month in any one place, and we are scarce off our knees from putting things into drawers than we are down on them again to take them out and put them back into trunks." The schedule of plays was equally grueling: "I am going to act tomorrow in *The Hunchback*," she wrote to Harriet, "Thursday, Mrs. Beverley; Friday, Lady Townley; Saturday, Juliet; Monday, Julia again; and Tuesday, Bizarre in *The Inconstant*; which ends our engagement here. This is pretty hard work, is it not? besides always one, and sometimes two rehearsals of a morning."

Fanny was depressed by the prospect of continuing this demanding routine for two years in order to raise enough money to liberate her family and save the theatre at Covent Garden. How wretched it was, she told her English correspondents, "to look along my future years, and think that they will be devoted to labor that I dislike and despise." Her tired mind was beginning to paint her father as a tyrant who worked her for his own gain. She lamented to Harriet: "I do not think that during my father's life I shall ever leave the stage."

Even one day's respite from the treadmill was welcome. Among the families who entertained them were numerous young folk, and Fanny could scarcely believe the freedom with which the unmarried girls were permitted to go about unchaperoned. Not only did young girls walk on the street by themselves (of which Fanny only mildly disapproved, since she had done so herself in Edinburgh), but they also went into society unchaperoned. She criticized the practice, and yet, as the months passed, she grew to accept it. It was foolish to force middle-aged Dall to go on horseback rides, walks, and picnics, struggling to keep pace, when no American expected it. Eventually Fanny even rode alone with a man.

Young men in the large American cities were only too eager to pay homage to her, but at first she did not encourage them. She thought her new admirers too forward. "A shy man," she wrote, "is not to be met with in these latitudes." Fanny snubbed several young men, and they promptly complained about her behavior. Her style tended to confuse her American male admirers. For no matter how often the Kembles mixed in good society, they never lost their theatricality. Being Kembles, they did not simply speak or move: they declaimed and struck poses. Mrs. Siddons employed Shakespearean tones even when ordering a simple glass of beer.

Fanny described her ancestry in terms of two distinct strands. The Kembles, she said, were theatrical and artificial—what today would proba- bly be called affected. The De Camps, on the other hand, were emotional and dramatic—what today would probably be called temperamental. Fanny maintained that she took after the De Camps and was essentially dramatic, but in fact she and Adelaide were capable of being both tempera- mental and affected. In English circles this usually caused no uneasiness. It was expected of them—they were Kembles—it was part of their attrac- tion.

In America, Fanny's theatrical manner was not so acceptable. She held herself aloof and was not afraid of contradicting and showing annoy- ance when she believed a companion was becoming too pushy. She was particularly hard on eligible young men, one of whom wondered aloud whether she really preferred married men, so unkind did she seem to bach- elors. Nevertheless, in time, two bachelors won her confidence.

One was Edward Biddle, a member of a leading Philadelphia family, whose presence was more than welcome, since Philadelphia had not ac- cepted the Kembles as warmly as other American cities. Philadelphians valued good birth above all else; and in Philadelphia, actors, without ex- ception, were judged to be lowborn. Young Mr. Biddle, heir to a banking fortune, disregarded this judgment, and being so well-born himself, con- ferred a grace on the Kembles that caused others to follow where he led. He became so smitten with Fanny that he gave her an ornate workbox, a pres- ent so expensive that it sparked a quarrel between Fanny and her father when he ordered her to give it back.

In time Edward Biddle was displaced by a "pretty-spoken, *genteel* youth" named Pierce Butler. He was slight and short, and his face, though pleasant, was not exciting. A portrait of him as a young man shows thick, dark hair and sideburns, sloping, doglike eyes, a long nose, and a petulant mouth. He rode well and played the flute well, and his manner was charm- ing, especially with women. But he could also be sullen and vindictive when crossed; and he was inclined to be lazy, preferring idleness to the practice of law, for which he had been trained. Coming from a rich and powerful family, he expected to do as he pleased. As one acquaintance said of him, "he had the perfect amiability of a selfish man."

On an October Saturday in Philadelphia, Pierce drank tea with the Kembles, offered to go riding with Fanny, and let slip that he was very rich—which made him, Fanny supposed, a great man "in spite of his inches." With studied indifference she accepted Pierce's overtures, probably sensing that such a man about town would be challenged rather than chastened by her nonchalance. Her tactics proved sound. Everything about her appeared to challenge him. Her fame, her intellect, her independence, and her forthrightness all aroused his spirit of competition. Not that he admired those qualities in a woman—but other people admired them, and he yearned to possess their possessor. Fanny was a glittering prize that Pierce was determined to win.

Fanny thought that Pierce, too, was something of a prize. Even by English standards, he was well connected. Though his father was plain Dr. James Mease of Philadelphia, his great-grandfather on his mother's side had been an Irish baronet: a lesser member of a distinguished family of Butlers, headed by the Earl of Ormonde, which for more than five centuries had produced well-known diplomats, soldiers, and courtiers. The baronet's third son, Major Pierce Butler—Pierce's grandfather—had come to America with a British regiment, entered the American Senate, and married a Charleston heiress named Middleton. The heiress's surviving fortune was destined for Pierce. In fact he had recently changed his surname from Mease to Butler so that he could eventually succeed to the estate. On the death of his maiden aunt, Pierce stood to inherit several houses in Philadelphia and two of America's richest rice and cotton plantations, worked by a large labor force of slaves.

Pierce began to court Fanny. For weeks he sent her bouquets of flowers, signing himself simply "a Friend." Given that they were in Philadelphia, Fanny and Dall at first thought the sender must be a Quaker. But it was all a part of love's game. By the time Pierce revealed himself as Fanny's flower-cavalier, he was a regular visitor, and his subterfuge lent spice to the courtship. Augustus Craven's ghost retreated, and Fanny's diary subtly reflected the change in her feelings. The countryside, which had always inspired her, took on idyllic hues that she could not wait to describe. The sky, she noticed, had an "earnest color that is lovely and solemn to look at," and the stars were more vivid than she had ever seen.

Fanny was slowly falling in love. But she still remembered the pain of loving Augustus, and the memory made her wary. One of her new friends in

Philadelphia was a married woman who tried to persuade Fanny that she should marry. Fanny shied away from such advice. She said that she would accept death more thankfully than she would accept marriage.

Though Pierce must have sensed the barriers, he took pains to keep up his courtship. On the Kembles' second visit to Philadelphia in January 1833, he appeared regularly with horses for their daily ride. Though Fanny and Dall normally were conscientious observers of the Sabbath, they surprised themselves and shocked the churchgoing passersby by riding on a winter's Sunday morning through the streets to Laurel Hill, where they halted by the river. While Aunt Dall tactfully withdrew, Pierce and Fanny wandered alone. Fanny's description catches the excitement of the moment:

> I ran down to the waterside. The ice had melted from the river, in whose still waters the shores, and trees, and bridge lay mirrored with beautiful and fairy-like distinctness. The long icicles under the rocky brow beneath which we stood had not melted away, though the warm sun was shining brilliantly on them, and making the granite slab on which we stood sparkle like a pavement of diamonds. I called to the echo, and sang to it scales up and scales down and every manner of musical discourse I could think of, during which interesting amusement I nearly as possible slipped my footing into the river.

Needless to say, Pierce Butler's arms were waiting to save her from falling, with a grasp that no doubt ended in an embrace.

Wherever the Kembles traveled on their busy circuit, Pierce followed. By the time they reached Boston in the spring of 1833, he was Fanny's acknowledged escort. That May, they rode unchaperoned by the "bright, boundless sea, smooth as sapphire." Sometimes they also rode to the nearby town of Cambridge, and beyond it to Mt. Auburn Cemetery, still surely one of the most beautiful burial grounds in the world. A lonely garden, it was carpeted in spring with purple and white blossoms, its sparse gravestones gleaming white from among groves of trees. Mt. Auburn made a perfect place for lovers' rambles. It is not known exactly where Pierce declared his love, but possibly it was at Mt. Auburn, because the cemetery remained a place of significance to Fanny in the months to come.

Late in June 1833, the Kembles boarded a river steamer for Albany, intending to make their way to Canada. At West Point they stopped for several days to visit a distant kinsman, Gouverneur Kemble, at his house on the banks of the majestic Hudson River. Reboarding the steamer, they were joined by an English traveler. He was "taller, straighter, and broader than most men," Fanny wrote, with a wild, scarred face as "dark as a Moor's," a gentle voice, and toil-worn hands on which he wore strange rings made of elephant hair. Fanny, who wanted no unbidden company, was at first annoyed and then enchanted by him. Within hours she was expressing her pleasure that he would accompany them as far as the Canadian border.

The newcomer was Edward John Trelawny, author and adventurer, once the friend of the dead poets Shelley and Byron, and, like Byron, a freedom fighter in Greece. Two years earlier he had published a swashbuckling autobiography, *The Adventures of a Younger Son*, which made him a literary lion on both sides of the Atlantic. Twice married and twice divorced—his second wife was a Greek brigand's daughter—Trelawny was interested in a third marriage, though Fanny did not then know it. He had already proposed unsuccessfully to Shelley's widow and also to her stepsister, Byron's ex-mistress, Claire Clairmont. When Trelawny saw Fanny, his pulse quickened. He liked spirited, literary women, and here was one after his own heart.

It is more than possible that Charles, well-versed in affairs of the heart, was becoming anxious about Fanny and Pierce, and invited Trelawny to join their party so that Trelawny could divert Fanny's affections. If this were so, he almost succeeded. When Pierce Butler joined the party in Utica a few days later, he was annoyed to see a new rival and vexed that this upstart adventurer did not immediately recognize his prior claim. From the very first moment, the two men circled one another like a pair of wary animals.

Over the following days a number of well-bred skirmishes took place as each man tried to assert his superiority. Though Pierce was by no means unintelligent or uneducated, Trelawny had twice his intellect and twice his education—and was also twice his size. As they sat in coaches and steamers and halted at roadside inns, he conversed with Fanny on a wide swath of topics, from Oliver Cromwell to Lord Byron, only too aware that Pierce would be left behind.

A born performer, Trelawny could not resist showing off, and Fanny could not help responding. As they trundled in a coach over bumpy hills toward Auburn, Trelawny declaimed passages from Byron's *Childe Harold's Pilgrimage*, roaring like a tiger. Fanny was riveted—his style reminded her of the great actor Edmund Kean. As they battled a deafening storm on the way to Geneva, Trelawny pulled out a pencil and paper and wrote an eloquent description of the attributes of God according to Mohammed. Fanny did not know whether he had made it up or quoted it, but that did not matter. His sense of theatre was superb.

As the travelers neared the great waterfalls of Niagara, Trelawny was well ahead of Pierce in the contest for Fanny's favor. Having been to Niagara before, he was able to describe the sight so vividly that even before they saw the column of white mist rising above the cataract and heard the roar of the water, she was aching with longing to see it. The instant they were close enough, she leaped out of the carriage and raced toward the rapids, with Trelawny running after her, crying, "Go on, go on, don't stop!"

Trelawny "seized me by the arm," Fanny told Harriet later. "I could not speak and I could hardly breathe; I felt as if I had an iron band across my breast." Locked together in a half embrace, the two stood in shared rapture on the edge of the precipice, staring down toward what seemed like the watery mouth of hell. "I looked and listened," Fanny continued, "till the wild excitement of the scene took such possession of me that, but for the strong arm that held me back, I really think I should have let myself slide down into the gulf. It was long before I could utter, and as I began to draw my breath I could only gasp out 'O God! O God!' "

The wild excitement that took possession of Fanny on the brink of the ravine owed as much, one suspects, to Trelawny's close-pressed body as to the tumultuous sight they were viewing. The memory never left her, and she would always recollect her first view of Niagara as one of the most thrilling incidents of her life.

Trelawny said goodbye to the Kembles soon afterward, and Fanny mourned his loss. Few had ever stirred her as much as he, and there was no denying that Pierce seemed dull by comparison. Pierce was a person of little cultivation and no brilliancy of intellect, she wrote to the Combes in Scotland. And yet, as she admitted to herself, this did not necessarily disqualify him as a husband. Two years before, in London, she had decided she did not want a husband with a brilliant intellect. She had written in her diary: "A well-assorted marriage, as the French say, seems to me like a well-arranged duet for four hands; the treble, the woman, has all the brilliance and melodious part, but the whole government of the piece, the harmony, is with the bass, which really leads and sustains the whole composition and keeps it steady, and without which the treble for the most part *runs to tune* merely, and wants depth, dignity, and real musical importance." What she needed was a solid, wealthy, and socially prominent husband, prepared to give her the background and support she needed, not one with a brilliance that might eclipse her own.

Pierce appeared to have stability, social prominence, and wealth. He also had "strong natural sense," Fanny wrote, an amiable temperament, and gentlemanly and thoughtful ways. She had been charmed by his sensitivity when he produced silver forks from his pocket to substitute for the rough tableware placed in front of them in the roadside taverns. Such careful attention seemed to indicate a generous nature and a desire to protect her from the roughness of life.

Marriage was on her mind for the rest of the journey. It appeared to offer a means of escape—maybe the only means—from the captive role she felt she was playing in her father's plans. Pierce had the power to rescue her and to give her security and respectability. And, unlike Augustus, he seemed to be attainable, because she could not imagine, in this land where the social attitudes of England seemed barely to have infiltrated, that any American family would consider someone as celebrated as herself to be an unsuitable bride.

In Fanny's mind, the practical drawbacks of living in America also seemed to be dwindling. She had ceased to class the American people as uncivilized. She was reconciled to her surroundings, having found "many things to like much, and a few people to love." All in all, Fanny was inclined to believe that marriage to Pierce would give her the best chance of happiness she might ever be offered.

Watching her increasing attachment to Pierce, her father and aunt grew fearful. Having at first encouraged Pierce's attentions, believing that they would weaken the painful memory of Craven, they now worried that Fanny might actually marry Pierce. They could foresee little but unhappiness in such a marriage, but they were not sure how to send Pierce away.

The Kembles moved on to Montreal and Quebec, and by late autumn they were back in New York. By then Fanny's mind was made up. She spoke openly of marrying Pierce Butler and making her home in America.

Charles did not take the announcement calmly. Besides losing his daughter to a husband in a foreign land, he was losing his main commercial asset. Once she married, Fanny would quit the stage, but—as Charles and she well knew—at least another year of touring was needed to clear his debts. Moreover, the sum of Fanny's American earnings—around thirty-five thousand dollars—would, on her marriage, go by law to her husband and be lost to her family. Charles was only too aware that he was watching his theatre, and the nest egg for his old age, slip out of his grasp. He demanded that Fanny should continue touring and ultimately return to England with him. Her response was to throw up her chin and answer defiantly that she and Pierce Butler would marry.

In the midst of this argument, Aunt Dall fell ill. The extent of her illness was at first difficult to assess. The previous year, the Kembles had been involved in a minor accident on the way to Niagara. Outside Rochester their coach had tipped on its side and struck Aunt Dall a blow to the forehead. Wet towels and plasters had been applied, and she had gone on her way, to all appearances little harmed. But as the months passed, Dall showed distressing symptoms that suggested an injury to the spine. By April 1834, when the Kembles were playing in Boston, Dall was experiencing violent spasms, and the lower part of her body was paralyzed.

Through the first three weeks of April, Fanny nursed her aunt all day and then hurried home from the theatre to sit by her side through the night. "This is my first lonely watching by a sickbed," she told Anna Jameson, "and I feel deeply the sadness and awfulness of the office." She was beginning to learn, she wrote, "what care and sorrow really are." Fanny relinquished her plan to stay in America with Pierce. Her thoughts at that moment centered on England. She longed for her mother, Adelaide, and her brothers—and the safety of home.

Dall's condition worsened, and the doctors gave up hope. On April 24 Fanny sent the tragic announcement to Harriet St. Leger. "She is dead," Fanny wrote. "She died in my arms, and I closed her eyes. . . . It has been a dreadful shock though it was not unexpected; but there is no preparation for the sense of desolation which oppresses me, and which is beyond words." Fanny chose the most beautiful burial place she could find. "We have buried dear Dall in a lonely, lovely place in Mt. Auburn Cemetery," she told Harriet, "where Pierce and I used to go and sit together last spring, in the early time of our intimacy. I wished her to lie there, for life and love and youth and death have their trysting place at the grave."

In her grief Fanny turned to Pierce. Seeing her rudderless, he seized his chance and pressed for an immediate marriage. From that moment, a tug of war took place between Charles and Pierce for possession of Fanny. Tying together the snippets of evidence, one can reconstruct Charles's tactics as he grasped whatever weapon or argument came to hand. First and foremost, he explained patiently to Fanny the moral and financial obligations she owed her family. At least another year's work was needed to ensure their financial future. Charles argued that if Pierce loved her, he would be prepared to wait for her. It was a cunning argument, because privately Charles was almost certainly ready to wager that Pierce would not be willing to wait a whole year.

During those wretched weeks Fanny's allegiance swung like a pendulum between her fiancé and her family. Pierce, however, had an unmatchable asset: Fanny was in love and as headstrong in her love as she could be in her hatreds. Pierce also had the makings of a shrewd psychologist and knew exactly when to make concessions. As Charles was adamant that Fanny's accumulated earnings belonged to the Kemble family, Pierce encouraged her to sign over her savings to her father. By so insisting, Pierce cannily removed one of Charles's chief objections to the marriage.

Shrewdest of all, Pierce pretended to accept the plan that Fanny would leave with her father for England late in June. As Charles jubilantly booked the passage and announced to friends that he was returning with his daughter to resuscitate the British drama, Pierce played his trump card, and the Kembles found themselves outsmarted. Pierce extracted the promise that before sailing, Fanny would become his wife. After a brief honeymoon he would allow her to sail to England without him. He would wait patiently for her to return to him after she had completed the theatrical season she had promised her father.

Only a shocked and bereft girl, out of touch with reality, could have believed that, once married, Pierce would keep his word and let her visit England without him. But Fanny not only believed him; she rejoiced at his unselfishness in offering such a proposal. She declared that a honeymoon of "seventeen happy days snatched on the very brink of bitterness and parting" was the least recompense she could make to one who "has followed my footsteps for a whole year."

On Saturday, June 7, 1834, Pierce and Fanny were married at Christ Church, Philadelphia, by Bishop White. Fanny wept through most of the ceremony and swooned at the end of it. Next day, on the steamer and train to New York—where the Kembles were to give the first of their farewell performances—the bride is said to have cried most of the way. Playing on those tears, Pierce persuaded her to remain in America with him rather than return temporarily to England. Less than a month later, Charles sailed home alone.

When the announcement of the wedding reached Fanny's family in England, it provoked, in the words of brother John, "much righteous indignation." Marie Thérèse was furious, and Adelaide was downcast—she had been counting on Fanny's return in July. Adelaide also wondered about

Fanny's husband. It was disconcerting to think of her sister surrendering her independence to any man, let alone to someone unknown to them. "It seems strange to think," Adelaide wrote, "that her movements and my happiness should depend on a person of whose existence I have no definite idea."

Among the personal details that Fanny conveyed in her letters home, there was almost certainly no mention of Pierce's most potent attraction—his sexuality. Nothing could dim its magnetism: after eight years of miserable marriage, Fanny would nonetheless write to him: "I cannot behold you without emotion: my heart still answers to your voice, my blood in my veins to your footsteps." In those early months of wedded life, sexuality would seem to have been the key ingredient in the relationship, and it can have been no surprise that within two months of the ceremony Fanny found herself pregnant.

The onset of pregnancy plunged her into depression. Not unnaturally, she blamed her bodily condition for her mood, but even without the hormonal changes of motherhood, Fanny's circumstances were enough to push her toward a nervous breakdown. She was still mourning Dall, who had been closer to her than her own mother. She had parted from her father with strained feelings. Worst of all, she was desperate for emotional and intellectual excitement.

For the past five years she had feared becoming addicted to acting, and after her marriage she learned the extent of her addiction. The withdrawal was painful. She and Pierce were staying with Pierce's brother John and his wife while their own house was being refurbished, and Fanny felt like an outcast. She had nothing in common with Pierce's family and was well aware that most of its members regarded her as a lowborn English interloper. Nor did she have much in common with Pierce himself, apart from sex—and that, as she was beginning to discover, was an inadequate substitute for mental stimulation. She missed her father and Dall, the excitement of the theatre, and the intelligent and admiring circle that permanently revolved around the Kembles.

Shut up day after day with her dull, unsympathetic in-laws, Fanny was consumed by boredom and irritation. She preferred her animals. "My pets are a horse, a bird, and a black squirrel," she wrote to Anna Jameson, "and I do not see exactly what more a reasonable woman could desire. Human companionship, indeed, at present, I have not much of." In the same vein, she added, "you can have no idea—none—none—of the intellectual dearth and drought in which I am existing at present."

To fight off her low mood, Fanny turned to work. Fortunately she had a project in hand. The previous year, only too aware of what she and her family owed Dall, she decided to make her aunt a gift of money. Knowing that the money she earned from acting belonged to her father, she decided to finance the gift by writing a book. In England and America there was a buoyant market for travel books, the more candid the better. The diary she kept of her American travels—candid in the extreme—cried out for publication. Dall's death had not diminished Fanny's will to publish or her desire to achieve. In fact she was sensible enough to know that a healthy dose of achievement was the only answer to her boredom and depression.

Pierce insisted on reading the diary in manuscript, and he was appalled by its tone. Fanny had written without thought of publication, and page after page was dotted with tactless criticism of America and its inhabitants. The fact that her severity was often softened by a charming energy and naïveté, interlaced with passages of brilliant description, did not lessen his dismay.

Pierce had been brought up to believe that men were superior to women and that wives were subject to a husband's will. As he was fond of explaining to Fanny, the church, society, and the law reinforced his views, for women surrendered their property and many of their rights to their husbands on marriage, and the marriage ceremony made the wife vow to obey her husband. Drawing on this authority, Pierce told Fanny that it would be madness to publish her manuscript. He insisted that she either cancel the contract she had signed with the Philadelphia publishers Carey and Lea, or, failing that, make extensive alterations, which he would personally supervise. Pierce was shocked that she did not immediately obey him. On the contrary, she wept and raged and refused to listen. "Every sentence, even word, that I wished to alter," Pierce remembered later, "was stoutly defended, and my suggestions made her very angry."

So, with the marriage less than six months old and a child on the way, Fanny and Pierce discovered each other's true view of the obligations of a marriage. That they were incompatible was an understatement, for while Pierce believed that his wife was duty bound to obey him, Fanny was prepared to obey only her own conscience and her own judgment.

How was it possible that Pierce, after eighteen months' close acquaintance, could have been so foolish as to commit himself to a woman whose idea of marriage differed so radically from his own? Fanny was outspoken to a fault, and it is inconceivable that she attempted to hide her views prior to her marriage. The answer to this riddle must lie partly in Pierce's combative nature. Fanny was a prize worth gaining, a highly strung filly awaiting his subduing hand. That he was so sure he could tame her is more puzzling. The most persuasive explanation of their basic misunderstanding seems to lie in the cultures from which they sprang. Fanny had been brought up in the unusual world of the English theatre, where, whether married or single, women were the acknowledged mistresses of their own words and actions. Pierce had grown up in America, where—as Fanny had noted with surprise—girls were expected to be spirited and independent when single but docile and dependent when married. Ignorant of the implications of Fanny's atypical English upbringing, Pierce seems to have believed that she would follow the conventional path and turn into an obedient wife.

As Fanny's pregnancy developed, the Butlers' quarrels became bitter. They centered on what Fanny called her "useless existence" and on Pierce's refusal to allow her the freedom that would make her life more satisfying. After one such quarrel, in November 1835, when she was three months pregnant, Fanny packed her clothes, arranged for the care of her pet bird, and walked into the winter darkness. She was away for three hours, returning late at night. She went straight to her room, and in Pierce's words, "threw herself on the bed, and lay there all night without undressing. She did not speak to me or I to her." The next day brought recriminations, tears, and a reconciliation of sorts. Pierce refused to take the incident too seriously and regarded it as a girlish and romantic cry for help. In those early months of wedlock, Fanny often begged to be allowed to return to her family in England. Of this behavior Pierce wrote, "I looked on these as merely perverse fancies, to be dispelled by the birth of her child."

Five months before the baby's birth, *Journal*, by Frances Anne Butler, appeared in print. Its pages bore rows of asterisks where Pierce's veto had prevailed; but it contained enough gunpowder to blow its author to notoriety. "The city is in an uproar," wrote Fanny's friend Catharine Sedgwick. "Nothing else is talked of." A young critic writing for the *Southern Literary Messenger*, later identified as Edgar Allan Poe, summed up what most readers felt about Fanny's "sturdy prejudices, her hasty opinions, and her ingenuous sarcasms." In the verdict of most, the book was a farrago of ignorance and impudence, written by a cocksure girl who had repaid the kindness of her American hosts with arrogance and ingratitude, and who had failed to see that the United States was a remarkable example of that independence of spirit for which the Kembles, in the British Isles, saw themselves as flag wavers.

While Pierce made self-righteous remarks, Fanny steeled herself against the onslaught. She shrugged off the reviewers' attacks, describing them flippantly to the English publisher John Murray as the "wrath of the natives." She may even have welcomed the notoriety as an antidote to boredom. What she could not so easily shrug off was the animosity she aroused in a public that had once worshipped her; nor could she ignore the distress of those who had once been her friends. Everywhere she saw reminders of the ill will she had generated. Lampoons of her book reached the bookshops. Once she picked up a copy of *Outlines Illustrative of the Journal of F-A-K*—and found herself gazing at cruel drawings of scenes from her *Journal.*

Even Pierce was ridiculed. His ineffectual control of his wife was a gift to the wits and the scandalmongers. "Fierce Cutler, husband of the diarist Fanny Thimble Cutler," was featured in a book called *My Conscience! Journal of Fanny Thimble Cutler.* Proud Pierce had become the butt of jokes. How his patrician relatives must have hated Fanny and wished that they could blast her out of existence.

The book roused a storm among the English relatives, too, when it appeared in a London edition published by John Murray. Charles and Marie Thérèse were appalled by what they called the mixture of vulgarity and sublimity on nearly every page. Marie Thérèse said that she "was divided between admiration and disgust, threw it down six times, and as often picked it up." Even Adelaide was perturbed and wished that dearest Fan had not exposed herself to such bitter attacks.

When the uproar was just beginning, Fanny and Pierce moved into a home of their own on the rural fringes of Philadelphia, close to the village of Branchtown, about six miles from the center of the city. Though the house was grandly called Butler Place, and Pierce referred to it as his country seat, it was just a plain, smallish, two-story stone house with verandas in the front and dormer windows in the roof. Fanny called it a "second-rate English farmhouse"—it was part of a working farm of about 300 acres that belonged to Pierce's maiden aunt. Under the terms of the late Major Butler's will, the farm and house were to pass to Pierce on his aunt's death, along with the major's other properties.

Now that she possessed a house of her own, Fanny threw herself into the role of housewife, "engaging servants," as she told Harriet St. Leger, "ordering china, glass, and furniture, choosing carpets, curtains and house linen, and devoutly studying all the time Dr. Kitchener's 'Housekeepers Manual and Cook's Oracle.'" Aiming valiantly at self-improvement, she mapped out a course of study and asked for divine aid in achieving it. She studied dairy farming and bookkeeping, with very little success, and learned to deal with unruly farmhands, snakes, and spiders.

A sense of the nearness of God was one of her chief supports in those dreary months. Each morning and evening she prayed, read the Bible, and took stock of her soul. It was the beginning of the serious development of a side of her nature that she had first discovered at school, and which a friend would later call her "great and fervent piety," the "most distinguishing stamp of her character." At Butler Place Fanny's piety sustained her. Her desire to succeed in the station to which God had called her gave energy to her practical efforts. Yet her loneliness and mental stagnation remained pitiful. "I have no friends, no intimates and no society," she wrote to Harriet. In those last weeks of pregnancy, Fanny felt utterly alone.

On the morning of May 28, 1835, the baby was born. She was named Sarah, after Fanny's aunt, Sarah Siddons, and after Pierce's mother, Sarah Mease. Fanny was flooded with maternal love the first instant she saw her baby and was overcome with tenderness when the little creature sucked at her breast. Fifty years later she would still remember "that blessed year of nursing a child."

Fanny's joy was mixed with pain. Her new responsibilities lay heavily on her. Sunk in the debility and depression that sometimes follow child-birth, she lacked the strength to bear her cares. She had always been fearless with horses, but sitting in the carriage and hearing the horse kick out unexpectedly, she felt an unaccustomed pang of terror, knowing her child, so vulnerable to harm, was there beside her: "though I did not lose my wits at all," she told Harriet, "and neither uttered sound nor gave sign of my terror, after getting her safely out of the carriage and alighting myself I shook from head to foot, for the first time in my life, with fear."

Little Sarah bound Fanny to Pierce, for she knew that he would never give up his daughter, and legally he could not be made to do so. If she were to go back to her own family, she would have to leave the child behind. As Fanny sank further into depression, this fact loomed large in her mind.

In the quarrels with Pierce during her pregnancy, Fanny had spoken many times of her longing to return to her single life. As she struggled in the depths of depression, the urge to escape became so overwhelming that she was prepared to do anything to achieve it—even to leave her child. She argued with a pitiable logic that it was better for her to go before the child was old enough to suffer grief at being abandoned by her mother, and before she herself had bonded too intimately with her child. "If you procure a healthy nurse for the baby she will not suffer," she told Pierce, "and provided she is fed she will not fret after me. Had I died when she was born you must have taken this measure, and my parting from her now will be to her as though she has never known me, and to me far less miserable than at any future time."

Fanny did not leave. As she returned to health, her depression lifted, and, as the months passed, she came to love the child more fiercely and protectively. After Sarah's birth, Fanny became aware that the child was a hostage to fortune, and—more frightening—a hostage to Pierce Butler, as well.

6

An Enchanted Bohemian Castle

During those years when Fanny held center stage, Adelaide played in the shadows. She did not seem to mind, because she genuinely adored her sister. Without any prompting she would say to friends: "Fanny is a thousand times nobler, better, and more useful and *dearer* than I am."

Fanny was grateful for the adoration. She loved her little sister—even if she sometimes seemed to forget her existence—and she always tried to have Adelaide's good at heart. Still, Fanny's love had its own terms. She could not tolerate the possibility that the younger girl might eclipse her. Adelaide's talent as a musician disturbed Fanny, because she knew that her own musical ability was poor by comparison. Her piano-playing, in her own words, had not progressed beyond "that empirical and contemptible sort which goes no further than the end of boarding-school young ladies' fingers." And her singing was worse. When asked to sing in company, her hands grew cold, her face grew hot, her voice grew husky, and her notes were flat. Adelaide, on the other hand, usually earned universal approval.

Fanny blamed her mother for her backwardness. "I think my progress was really retarded," she wrote, "by the excessive impatience with which her excellent ear endured my unsuccessful musical attempts." While this was no doubt partly true, the greater blame lay with Fanny herself. She became impatient with subjects that needed long and painstaking study. For much the same reason, she never managed to master the subtlest points of acting.

On Christmas Day, 1831, Fanny had been asked to sing in front of her parents in the Kemble drawing room. It was one of those occasions when, to quote her own words: "I feel like a wretch, and I sing like a wretch, and I make all my hearers wretched." Knowing she had done badly, she waited for her mother's usual disapproval. This time Marie Thérèse took pity on her, and along with the criticism Fanny had expected, Marie Thérèse threw in a

< 92 >

snippet of praise. She said that Fanny's voice was stronger than Adelaide's—which may well have been true, since Fanny's voice, like everything else about her, was decidedly robust.

That night, when Fanny wrote in her diary, she included her mother's unusually reassuring praise. She also added that she was sorry that her sister's voice had grown so thin. But it is doubtful if Fanny really was sorry. On the contrary, she was probably secretly relieved, because she appears to have clung to this scrap of praise like a life raft.

Ever afterward the strength of a singer's voice was of prime importance to her. She entertained the belief that a voice was meant to convey emotion rather than to show skill, and that a loud voice and dramatic ability—the two qualities she possessed—counted for more than beauty of tone or technical facility. She began to ignore her mother's critical remarks and to sing confidently in public. She also criticized Adelaide's technically proficient and lighter style of singing.

Fanny need not have felt threatened by Adelaide, because at this stage of her life, the younger girl was incapable of offering a threat to anyone. Adelaide was a web of adolescent uncertainty and contradictions. At times she was so shy in company that she could barely speak; at other times it was difficult to persuade her to be quiet. She had spent her childhood adoring her brother John and had absorbed some of his revolutionary idealism, which sat strangely with her shyness and her sheltered, ladylike upbringing. She did not care if she shocked her mother's friends with revolutionary pronouncements; in fact, she rather enjoyed doing so and took no notice of parental expostulations to hold her tongue. Adelaide also had a quick temper and was as forceful and theatrical in expressing it as any member of her family. In fact, she was theatrical altogether, and she loved to declaim and to act.

Her brother John's friend Alfred Tennyson, later the poet laureate, remembered Adelaide copying out his poem "The Sisters" and "raving about it at intervals in the most Siddonian tone." Her brother's friend William Thackeray, the future novelist, also remembered "Miss Tot," as her brothers called her, spouting poetry and singing with her guitar. Thackeray said that she was sweet, shy, clever, and affectionate. He also added that she was no beauty, which was probably an understatement. At sixteen she was growing so quickly that she looked like a beanstalk.

In October 1831 Adelaide traveled with her mother to Paris to become a pupil of Professor Giulio Bordogni at the conservatoire. It had been arranged that she should live with Mrs. Lavinia Forster, the widow of the late chaplain to the British embassy in Paris. Mrs. Forster was the daughter of Thomas Banks, the first English neoclassical sculptor, and the mother-in-law of Baron Henri de Triqueti, an eminent French sculptor. She herself was a leading hostess in circles devoted to music and art, and she numbered Chopin, Ingres, and Delacroix among her friends. Sensitive, sweet-natured, and delightful in appearance, Mrs. Forster charmed Adelaide on sight. She was "so *pretty*," wrote Adelaide admiringly, "with a pink and white complexion and clear, grey eyes which were always so tender and so kind."

Having raised three daughters of her own, Mrs. Forster was a relaxed guardian. Adelaide was allowed to explore the city, and she never tired of the ancient, narrow streets lined with wine shops and silk merchants, cafés and barbers. There were no footpaths in the old parts, and the press of people, carts, and carriages made the roads dangerous, but the risk of accident only heightened Adelaide's sense of adventure. She also loved the newer sections of the city: the wide and airy streets near the boulevards, with their handsome freestone houses, towering six or seven stories above the passersby. Just as Fanny had blossomed in the freedom of Edinburgh, Adelaide bloomed in the freedom of Paris.

TO STUDY UNDER BORDOGNI proved to be a stroke of luck. A professor at the conservatoire since 1820, he had taught many successful singers, including two celebrated sopranos, Henriette Sontag and Laure Cinti-Damoreau. Besides being a teacher, he was a leading tenor at the Théâtre-Italien, where his perfectly placed voice and elegant style delighted the composer Rossini, who wrote roles especially for him. On stage and off, Bordogni cut a dashing figure and knew how to charm his public. Adelaide looked forward to her lessons. In later life she was fond of saying that whatever skill she had in singing she had learned during those "three years of patience and labor" with "dear Bordogni."

It was Bordogni's task to teach Adelaide the finer points of the *bel canto* method of singing—the art of floating the voice on the breath—and Adelaide's apprenticeship was as exacting as that of any Olympic athlete. The foundation of the skill was breath control; Adelaide was required to develop strong respiratory muscles to support and control her breathing, a powerful lung capacity, and a finely tuned coordination of muscles, breath, tone, and pitch. These, along with the usual aural and mental skills of a first-class musician, formed the heart of the technique.

In the first half of the nineteenth century, a first-class *bel canto* technique was essential for any singer of substance. Once mastered, the technique could extend the vocal range, produce a seamless tone up and down the scale, and provide a flexibility and technical virtuosity that other methods of singing have seldom matched. That Adelaide achieved mastery cannot be doubted, because the critics agreed, once she made her debut, that her voice bore the hallmarks of thorough and intelligent training. Her natural voice was mezzo-soprano, capable of singing between the middle and high ranges. She was fortunate, because a mezzo-soprano, trained upward and downward to cover a span exceeding two octaves, was the fashionable voice of the time. That she achieved this range without loss of quality is testified by some of the leading opera writers of her day. The distinguished English critic Henry Chorley described her voice as "originally limited" but "moulded, rendered flexible, and extended in compass, by study and incessant practice, till it became capable of every inflexion, of every possible brilliancy."

Training in Paris offered abundant opportunities, for now that the widely popular Rossini was living in France and writing for the Parisian stage, the city rivaled—some said it surpassed—Milan, Naples, and Venice as the opera center of Europe. The greatest voices sang there, and Adelaide had the thrill of hearing them. It was no wonder that she blossomed.

Then, suddenly, the stimulus was cut off. In the summer of 1832 she was brought home from Paris by her brother John so that she could say goodbye to Fanny, her father, and aunt before they sailed for America. At the time she did not regret leaving Paris. Cholera was raging in the crowded tenements, and many Parisians judged it wiser to leave the capital for the summer. Moreover, since Louis Philippe's coming to the throne two years before, political tension had been simmering throughout France. Riots broke out in June, just as Adelaide was leaving the city. All in all, it seemed a wise time to depart.

As soon as her father and Fanny sailed to America, Adelaide's mood changed. Cholera and riots were forgotten; she ached to be back with Mrs. Forster. Shut up in Great Russell Street with her mother, it was impossible for Adelaide to maintain her newfound independence, for she was treated like a disobedient child. When she finally regained the safety of Paris, she was weak with relief and vowed she would never live with her mother again. It was therefore a terrible blow to receive a letter the following year ordering her to come home. Marie Thérèse had become ill and depressed, and the family had decided that Adelaide must return to care for her.

Managing to postpone her return as long as possible, Adelaide did not reach London until the start of 1834. There she found herself trapped in her old restricted life. At the age of nineteen she was expected to live in constant proximity to her mother, without Aunt Dall as a buffer to protect her. She was even expected to sleep in the same room as her mother. Describing this phase of her life she wrote, "It was intolerable; I was *never* alone."

The quarrels became so bitter that Marie Thérèse decided that her daughter had been spoiled and needed a stern system of reeducation. Looking back on that wretched time, Adelaide felt that she had been the subject of "all kinds of experiments." Rather than effecting a change, the experiments only roused her stubbornness. Somehow she resurrected the old steady, unloving mood from her childhood and employed it as armor against her mother's assaults.

Through the early months of 1834, the quarrels between mother and daughter intensified. Both Adelaide and her mother longed to love and be loved but were unable to find a path to walk in peace and affection. Then came the shattering news of Aunt Dall's death, followed by the distressing announcement of Fanny's marriage.

Aunt Dall's death was a shock and a loss, of a magnitude completely new to Adelaide. Her aunt was the person she loved most, and the person to whom she looked to shield her from her mother. The knowledge that Dall was dead was almost like Adelaide's own death warrant. Grief-stricken and despairing, she slipped into a state of lassitude. "I went through all I had to do like one in a heavy sleep," she remembered. "My faculties were all numbed and the only mental sensation left to me was that of an utter hopelessness that seemed to become a part of my very being and to chill and thicken the blood in my veins."

To Adelaide's wretched eyes, there seemed no help in sight, for all the family members on whom she had once relied were scattered or lost to her. Dall was dead, and Fanny was planning to spend her life in America. Even her brothers, who might have helped her, were following paths far distant from her own. Henry, now a soldier, was with his regiment in Ireland, and John rarely came to see her.

Adelaide's misery in those middle months of 1834 was almost unbearable, made worse by the fact that she dared not express it openly. Too afraid of her mother's lashing tongue to ask for sympathy, Adelaide pushed her fears inward. She suffered from migraines and fainting fits. To keep herself from breaking down, she began counting the days until her father's return from America, pinning her happiness on his arrival. But when Charles arrived in August 1834, he proved a bitter disappointment. He was broken in spirit, poor in health, and lamenting the loss of his beloved Covent Garden.

Marie Thérèse was overjoyed to have her husband back, clinging to him with a possessive pleasure that soon turned her joy to pain. Charles had never been able to satisfy her raging need to love and be loved. He "was very sincerely attached to her," wrote Adelaide, "but his calm northern temperament *could* not possibly satisfy the burning ocean of Southern blood that seemed to flow in her veins." Marie Thérèse "bought the bitter joy of his presence with such storms of suffering" that she "was only at peace when away from him and full of sad longing." Her life became "a torment to her," and to everyone else.

Unable to cope with Marie Thérèse's moods, and probably afraid of rousing her jealousy by favoring Adelaide, Charles refused to acknowledge that his wife and daughter were distressed: "to this day," Adelaide later wrote bitterly, "my father who passed the three last years of my suffering under the same roof with me, has no idea of what I endured." His indifference to her unhappiness seemed a deliberate avoidance of responsibility, and one for which she could never fully forgive him.

By the end of 1834 Adelaide was suffering daily fainting spells, and a sense of futility had taken over her life. Looking back she would remember: "My courage was not gone but all hope was—I had none left—and my health was going very fast in consequence of the incessant pressure on my nerves." By the final months of the year, her illness had become so acute that her father and other relatives were forced to take action. A family council was called, during which it was decided to separate Adelaide from her mother. Charles's late sister, the actress Elizabeth Whitlock, had left him a cottage at the village of Addlestone, near Chertsey in Surrey, and Marie Thérèse was persuaded to live there. Adelaide's relief at the separation was intense, and she wrote to Harriet St. Leger: "I do not think she will ever live with us again. We are all happier apart—The quiet I am now enjoying is heaven to me."

The one pleasure in Adelaide's life during those dismal years was her music. Thanks to faithful practice and continuing lessons, her voice was shooting up from the roots that Bordogni had carefully planted. Her new teacher was probably John Braham, the singer with the swelling chest, and she also learned, for a time, from the visiting Italian bass, Giovanni Cartagenova. Adelaide was beginning to discover her worth as a singer and to indulge in quiet dreams of achieving an independence through the opera to match Fanny's achievements in the theatre.

At this period, it was Adelaide's voice—not her appearance or her personality—which was her potential asset. Later she would become imposing and statuesque, like her aunt Sarah Siddons, but at twenty she looked as unprepossessing as her father had in his youth. Adelaide was tall and skinny; her arms and legs splayed awkwardly, she had the Roman beak of the Kembles, and she paid little attention to her dress. She looked like a cross between an ugly duckling and a young scarecrow. Her finest features were her eyes: large, dark, and liquid like her mother's, and capable, when lit up, of delivering her plain face into beauty.

In May 1835 Adelaide was ready to make her public debut—as an unpaid amateur—at a concert of ancient music, a London series under royal patronage. In the days leading up to the concert, she became extremely anxious, for she had none of Fanny's combativeness and was only too aware of her own shortcomings. She felt cheered when the orchestra, seeing her slight, girlish figure standing before them, spontaneously broke into applause during the rehearsal. The reassuring memory carried her through to the day of the performance.

Adelaide sang two songs by Handel for her debut: "In Sweetest Harmony," from *Saul*, and "Hide Me from Day," from *Il Pensieroso*. Her first song began without an accompaniment, a challenge even for an experienced singer, but Adelaide conquered her fears and made a success of her debut. The *Morning Post* noted that she survived the opening test marvelously, singing with "infinite spirit and effect" and correct intonation. The newspaper's final judgment must have given her heart: "Her voice is a soprano of very good compass and quality, her enunciation is articulate despite an occasional lisp. She must practise her shake until it becomes close and certain, and she will be a valuable acquisition to the concert room." She sang so impressively at that first concert that Queen Adelaide summoned Marie Thérèse to the royal box to congratulate her on her daughter's performance.

Next day Adelaide looked back modestly on her debut. "Dear Hal," she wrote to Harriet St. Leger: "I have succeeded as well as heart could wish—and though I ache all over this morning I am inwardly very happy . . . I know you won't think me the vainest person on earth."

Charles had moved his household to 11 Park Place, a pretty little cul-de-sac off fashionable St. James's Street. Adelaide chose the attic for her room, and she would stand for hours under the sloping roof, gazing out across the trees of nearby Green Park to the rooftops beyond. Secure in her attic, she felt eager for life. Notwithstanding her shyness, she enjoyed playing hostess at her father's soireés or visiting the houses of Fanny's fashionable friends.

For a time her mother's harsh tongue had sapped her confidence and made it difficult for Adelaide to form friendships; but now, when she went to parties at the homes of the Egertons, Grevilles, or Procters, she was astonished at how successfully she mixed, especially with the men. She began to think of marriage, although few of the young men she met came up to her standards. Very often a young man's word or action showed "worldliness or littleness of feeling," in Adelaide's opinion, and in an instant his attraction was gone.

According to Adelaide's later account of her youth, only three young men earned her wholehearted approval, and all three were in some way debarred to her. Possibly she believed that they were socially beyond her, which was understandable in light of her sister's broken romance with Augustus Craven. More likely the attachments—if they existed at all—were her private fantasies.

Adelaide's most enthusiastic caller was Henry Greville. Though he was now an attaché at the British embassy in Paris, he never missed seeing Adelaide on his trips to London. They were an unlikely combination—polished man about town and gauche girl—but they built up a close friendship based on their love of singing and often performed duets together at society soireés. Henry also brought gossip, being an acknowledged "authority in all matters of fashion both in Paris and London, and a universal favorite, especially with women, in the highest society of both capitals." Adelaide listened, spellbound, to his tales of the Paris Opera, where the principal singers were his close friends.

When amateur theatricals were put on at Bridgewater House in 1836, Adelaide was invited to take part. Henry acted opposite her, and the memory of Fanny and Augustus must have crossed her mind often. This time, however, the attachment did not blossom into courtship. Adelaide and Henry remained, in Adelaide's words, only "intimate and enduring" friends. Whether she recognized his homosexuality one cannot know.

On one visit, Henry brought with him a stunningly handsome Italian nobleman. He was the Cavaliere di Candia, the son of an aristocratic Sardinian family, who had come to Paris as a political exile after supporting the Young Italy Party in its campaign to liberate and unify the Italian states. Adelaide was enchanted by his good looks, affectionate nature, and his temper, which she called the "sweetest temper in the world." Her enchantment was complete when she heard him sing: his tenor voice was like an angel's. When he later wrote that he had adopted the stage name of Mario and was taking lessons from Bordogni in the hope of becoming a professional performer, she was glad because it was the choice she would have made herself.

Another caller was Trelawny, who came almost as soon as he returned to England from America. On those early visits he spoke almost exclusively of Fanny. One wonders if the Kembles had heard Anna Jameson's opinion: that if Trelawny loved anyone, it was Fanny Kemble—"who appears to be his ideal of womankind." Adelaide accepted Trelawny at face value. She saw him as a corsair, stepping out of the pages of Byron's poem, and everything about him thrilled her. She frequently took his part when well-meaning outsiders disparaged him. When her mother's friends the Mayows tried to warn her about him, she retorted: "They are incorrigible Tories and think people of any other persuasion are only fit to burn at the stake."

Adelaide's brief excursions into society were the high points in an otherwise dull existence. Often, for days, she saw no one but her father, and he was anything but lively. The daytime silence of the house depressed her, and she preferred the more natural quiet of the night. After her father was in bed, she would go from one room to another, finding peace and contentment for an hour or two. She never ceased to miss Fanny and longed for a letter from Philadelphia. Knowing nothing of the Butlers' marital troubles—Fanny kept them hidden—Adelaide was puzzled by the sparseness of her sister's letters. She had no inkling that Fanny's reticence sprang from the fact that there were numerous topics about which she dared not write.

In October 1836 a long-awaited letter from Fanny announced that she was about to visit England with her daughter Sarah. One month later Fanny's ship approached Liverpool after a stormy passage of twenty-eight days. In winds so fierce that Fanny despaired of surviving, she had knelt beside her nursemaid, prayed for deliverance, and tried to calm everyone's nerves by singing every song she could recall.

The sisters met at Park Place; and when Adelaide clasped Fanny in her arms, she believed that neither of them had ever been so ecstatic. Fanny looked radiant. She seemed, wrote Adelaide, to be "younger, and healthier, and happier than when I knew her before—and her spirits are untiring, wonderful! I sit in amazement at seeing anyone so happy for so long a time together." Adelaide blessed the absent Pierce Butler for making her sister so happy. Not for a moment did she suspect that Fanny's radiance was a reflection of her sister's temporary escape from her American captivity.

In the following months Adelaide floated on a cloud of contentment. The happiest times, she told friends, were "when walking alone with my dearest Fan (which we do every day for about an hour—sometimes in the enclosure of St. James's Park and sometimes in Kensington gardens) and at night when we go to bed." Fanny shared her sister's attic bedroom, and what bliss it was for the two of them to brush their hair at bedtime and chat as they had done in girlhood. Sometimes they were joined by toddling Sarah: "there is the exquisite happiness in the dim doziness of the morning," wrote Adelaide, "when I am neither asleep nor awake—in hearing the sound of little feet round my bed, and feeling little hands upon me, and hearing my name called by a sweet young voice." Fanny's child, Adelaide continued, "is very fair, with a determined expression and brows and eyes like my father. We all dote upon her—She is my father's recreation, my mother's delight and occupation, and I feel as tho' I could lay down my life for her."

As the weeks passed, the sisters were drawn into a whirlwind of activity. "We are out morning, noon, and night," wrote Adelaide. "The hours and days appear to have lost their forms, their distinct clearcut lines have curved, quivered and melted into each other—and whole weeks fly together in a bustle that is quite bewildering." Fanny was intent on renewing old acquaintances, and she pulled Adelaide in her wake. Fanny was sorry that Harriet St. Leger and Anna Jameson were not in England, but the Procters, the Egertons, and the Fitzhughs were in town and could hardly wait to see her again.

Charles Kemble was determined to show Fanny off. On one memorable spring evening, the white-haired banker-poet Samuel Rogers sat on an ottoman in the drawing room at Park Place, training his cold, blue eyes on the pretty women. Next to him lounged Corsair Trelawny, a "ruffian-looking man, with wild mustache, shaggy eyebrows, and orbs beneath them that have the gimlet properties beyond any I have yet encountered." These were the words of thirteen-year-old Frances Appleton, whose family was known to Fanny from Boston. "The treat of the evening," continued the awestruck teenager, "beside gazing at 'lions,' was the delicious singing of Miss Kemble whose voice has more music in it than almost any amateur singer's I remember. She sings with great ease and spirit, and her intelligent face lights up into fine expressions, quite inspired. Mrs. Butler's rich bass

voice ascends, as second, delightfully." The following week Frances Appleton was again at Park Place, where she heard Charles Kemble read several
scenes from Hamlet. To an impressionable American girl, the Kembles were
almost magical.

That witty, fashionable, and artistic London reopened its doors to
Fanny was balm to her heart and a welcome antidote to the slights she had
received in Philadelphia. In the days when Fanny was famous, she had been
invited to the highly fashionable breakfasts given by Samuel Rogers at his
lavish house in St. James's Square. With joy, Fanny again took her place at
his breakfast table. Acid-tongued old Rogers liked lively young women and
was delighted to have her back, especially married and Americanized.

Rogers's set embraced London's most brilliant society, and Fanny was
proud to be among its youngest members. Years later she realized how many
of her London friends could be traced back to Rogers's gatherings. Through
him she met the Whig statesman Lord Lansdowne, a man of vast wealth
and fine taste. She also met Mary and Agnes Berry, sisters in their late seventies who had once been the belles of literary London. They held an exclusive salon in Curzon Street, and Fanny felt honored to be among their
guests.

At Rogers's breakfasts, Fanny met the witty clergyman Sydney Smith,
whom she at first criticized, believing that a man of God should not dine in
fashionable circles nor write for the Edinburgh Review. Later Fanny came to
adore him. They shared the joke that she was suffering delusions and did
not really have a husband in America. "Oh, but the Baby," Fanny would
exclaim. "The ludicrous look with which my reverend tormentor received
this overwhelming testimony of mine," she wrote, "threw the whole party
into convulsions."

At Rogers's table, Fanny met the famous hostess Lady Holland, whose
circle of writers, wits, and statesmen was the admiration of Europe. Fanny
liked quiet Lord Holland, but Lady Holland's well-known rudeness sick-
ened her from the start. Seated next to her ladyship at dinner and commanded to talk, Fanny's tongue became stubbornly quiet. Adelaide joined
the party later and was mortified when she picked up a handkerchief that
Lady Holland had apparently dropped on purpose. Instead of giving a gracious response, Lady Holland said, "Ah! I thought you'd do it," which made
Adelaide long to throw the handkerchief down again.

In this feast of visiting, the sisters dined out one evening in a party
that included Augustus Craven and the pretty French Catholic girl he had
eventually married. Fanny carried the meeting off with aplomb, saying that

she had no reason to avoid Augustus's wife. As the evening progressed, Fanny and Adelaide became increasingly charmed by Pauline Craven, whom they found sensitive and generous. With Augustus, they had more difficulty.

As 1836 drew to a close, one event stood out. Charles Kemble, poor in health and wretched at the thought that he would never again control his beloved Covent Garden, decided to leave the stage. For his farewell, he chose to play the role of Benedick in Shakespeare's *Much Ado About Nothing*, and on the morning of December 23, huge crowds gathered in the Covent Garden marketplace, hoping to gain entrance to the historic performance. By curtain time there was such a clamor for places that spectators were allowed to sit in the orchestra pit, while musicians perched on the stage. Those who had seats never forgot the night. For ten minutes, with one voice, the audience shouted the magic name of Kemble. To Charles's daughters, sitting together in a box, it was not only an emotional gathering but an emphatic confirmation of the Kembles' special place in English society.

Without the stimulus and excitement of acting, Charles Kemble sank into chronic ill health. Fanny diagnosed Charles's condition in the light of her own experience: "What a dangerous pursuit that is," she wrote, "which weans one from all other resources and interests, and leaves one dependent upon public exhibition for the necessary stimulus of one's existence." Fanny saw in her father's decline the fate she had once feared for herself. "I am thankful," she continued, "that I was removed from the stage before its excitements became necessary to me." She was deluding herself, but at that moment, filled with the joy of London, she did not need the stage.

As the weeks passed, Charles's health grew worse. He complained of a pain in his side and walked at a snail's pace. Neither the pills prescribed by his doctors nor the potions he took on his own brought the slightest improvement. Sunk in depression, he began to seem like a very old man.

Charles accused his doctors of stupidity, but he was not being fair to them. The cause of his illness was stones in the bladder, for which there was no known cure. The best palliative was said to be the waters of a hot saline spring at Carlsbad in Austrian Bohemia, about a hundred miles northwest of Prague. When his doctors suggested a visit to Carlsbad and a course of the waters, Charles cheered up immediately. Carlsbad was one of the most fashionable spa resorts in Europe, dedicated as much to the pursuit of pleasure as the pursuit of health. He would have set out instantly if he had been able.

Two months before retiring from the stage, Charles had been appointed to the government sinecure of examiner of plays. His daughters were delighted by the salary, which was four hundred pounds annually, and they were heartened by the enthusiasm with which he busied himself. The unforeseen obstacle to visiting Carlsbad was that Charles, as a government employee, could not leave England until official permission had been granted. Nor could he set out without a traveling companion, because sometimes he was in too much pain to walk. Normally Adelaide would have jumped at the chance to go with him, but she was reluctant to leave Fanny alone in England. And Fanny, who would have loved to visit Europe, was waiting for Pierce to arrive, to take her and Sarah back to America.

Their father's dilemma filled the sisters' minds for weeks and seemed to have no solution. In the end Charles broke the impasse by ordering Adelaide to go with him. Meanwhile Fanny would wait for Pierce's ship to dock, then bring her husband and daughter to join them in Carlsbad. According to Charles's optimistic calculation, the family would be reunited within four weeks.

In July 1837 Charles, Adelaide, and her maid set out from the channel port of Calais. Their journey in the horse-drawn coach was painfully slow, because they stopped at numerous towns to give Charles the chance to rest. One of their wayside stops was at the historic town of Weimar in the quiet hills of north Germany. There in the street Charles was recognized by Johann Hummel, the famous pianist. Hummel invited the Kembles to his house, and throughout one evening their host played, Adelaide sang, and Mrs. Hummel beamed with pleasure at the presence of such exciting guests. The Hummels were "amiable, simple, cordial people," Adelaide wrote to Fanny, and could not have been more welcoming. This chance meeting raised the travelers' spirits. It confirmed their belief that Charles could visit any city in France, Germany, or Italy and immediately be recognized and welcomed by those "worth knowing."

From the cobbled streets of Weimar, where Adelaide made a short pilgrimage to kneel at the graves of Goethe and Schiller, a jolting coach carried the travelers over roads that were often "no better than the channel in a mountain torrent." Rough roads, however, could not check Adelaide's growing excitement. She fell in love at first sight with the deep, narrow valley of Carlsbad, where they arrived on August 19. She admired the craggy hillsides covered with pine trees, the elegant stone buildings, and the curving stream that tumbled swiftly through the valley. It was the type of romantic landscape of which she dreamed.

Once they had settled into their lodgings, Charles was examined by a doctor, who declared that his ailment was "very curious" but far from incurable. Next morning at seven o'clock, on doctor's orders, Charles and Adelaide set out for the colonnaded arcade where a geyser of hot water shot high into the air, just as it does to this day. Pushing through the crowd of fashionable invalids, Charles took up one of the long-handled ladles and extracted a steaming cupful from the geyser. The highly mineralized water tasted unpleasant, but he managed to drink three cups. After seven visits, he showed signs of improvement. As his symptoms receded, he seemed more content, but his long silences made Adelaide wish for Fanny's presence: "We are very happy together but *so* silent!" she wrote to her sister. "We want you and the child sadly to talk and make us talk."

Soon Adelaide had few hours in which to feel lonely. News that she was a promising soprano reached the burgomaster, who invited her to sing at a charity concert. To serve as her accompanist he suggested Josef Dessauer, a name which threw her into transports of pleasure, because she had known Dessauer in Paris.

To know Dessauer was not necessarily to love him. Many people thought him a tiresome hypochondriac, and Adelaide herself admitted he was a "little, pale, miserable-looking mortal" who worried constantly about his health. He was also capable of an eccentric, childlike charm that had won her heart in her student days. Along with his other friends, Adelaide had laughed aloud at his curious leaps of imagination and quaint ways of expression. Richard Wagner later recalled that in one of these flights of fancy, Dessauer soberly reported that "he had seen his own head lying beside his bed that morning."

No one could doubt Dessauer's skill as a musician and composer. His work was admired by Chopin, Liszt, and Wagner, and his songs are still sung today. When the burgomaster announced that Monsieur Dessauer was proposing to compose a song for her, Adelaide exclaimed, "I am in *delight*."

Adelaide's concert was to be held in the Bohemian Hall, an impressive stone building facing the grassy square. Along with the geyser, the hall was the hub of town life, for once the daily water-taking was over, the fashionable sufferers demanded amusement. They promenaded through the streets, gossiped, paid calls—and went to concerts. From Beethoven down, many major artists had played at the Bohemian Hall, and Carlsbad audiences were as discriminating as any in London or Paris. Realizing the test that lay ahead of her, Adelaide grew frightened; and her fears were not allayed when, on the very day of the concert, she received a letter from Fanny announcing that the Butlers would not be coming to Europe. Pierce was due to speak at a political convention in Pennsylvania in October and insisted on taking his family home without delay.

Adelaide wept with disappointment when she read the letter. By evening when she was about to go on stage, she was in such a state of nerves that she was scarcely able to control her voice. "I sang Felice Donzella," she told Fanny, referring to a song by Dessauer that they both knew, "and it was very fortunate that I did, for any song of less emotion I must have broken down in. As it was I believe the effect was rather increased by my own agitation, and I was led back to my seat in an agony of crying with compliments and congratulations and shouts of applause."

Adelaide's concert was a triumph and led to a handful of social invitations. Though it was late in the season, the town could still muster an impressive roll call of European nobility, and Adelaide reported that "everyone of importance" was "most kind and civil" to her. Count Chotek, the viceroy of Bohemia, who was among the spectators, invited the Kembles to Prague to stay in the viceroy's palace. Other gilded doors seemed about to open to Adelaide. Though she could not then know it, her European career as a singer was brilliantly launched.

Carlsbad smiled on father and daughter. Charles drank and bathed in the waters, adhered to a strict diet, and took moderate exercise. His pains receded. To Adelaide's relief he took a liking to Dessauer, and soon all three were inseparable. She and Dessauer were frequently invited to perform together, and neither seemed able to get enough of the other's company. In those weeks Adelaide came to love the quaint little musician, but it was the love of a young girl for a kind and talented uncle. He was, as she informed Fanny, "a most amusing companion, he plays divinely on the piano, sings without any voice but with a great deal of expression, and accompanies me *divinely!* as I never was and never will be accompanied again."

There seems little doubt that Dessauer fell in love with Adelaide: years later a close friend called him her "faithful knight and follower." If Adelaide did not recognize his feelings, she certainly should have, because he gave her signs enough. While they were rehearsing together he composed for her "the most exquisite little serenade in the world." It perfectly expressed, she told Fanny, "the fullness of happiness of a man whose love has prospered—it is delicious!"

After a month of treatment, Charles and Adelaide moved to Prague, where Dessauer joined them: this was his home town, and he was eager to be their guide. Seen through his eyes, Prague took on a magical hue, and Adelaide reveled in the fine old arches and gateways and the curving streets, with their air of culture and learning. The city was then hosting an international gathering of learned men. To Adelaide's surprise, "the philosophers alone amounted to over five hundred (think of there being so much philosophy extant)," she wrote excitedly.

The viceroy, who was the Kembles' host, arranged a concert for the wise men in the great hall of the castle, and Adelaide agreed to sing, accompanied by the conservatoire orchestra. After spending a long time choosing her program, she sang popular arias by Rossini and a piece from Bellini's I Puritani, which had just premiered in Paris. She ended with songs by Dessauer, which he himself accompanied at the piano. A few days later she gave a similar concert to help the Sisters of Charity. Both times the audiences responded enthusiastically. "My success," she informed Fanny, "was complete."

Adelaide's triumph was not confined to the concert platform. As the days passed, she and her father were astonished by the warmth of their welcome from high-born Bohemia. That an English actor and his daughter should be treated as equals in so proud and formal a society amazed them, and they could scarcely believe that they had found such favor. As their visit neared its end, an unexpected meeting confirmed their social success. Just after noon on September 26, 1837, Adelaide and her father arrived at the house of the viceroy's sister, the Princess Clary, and were introduced to a man and wife who were about to leave. The man's melancholy face made an immediate impression on Adelaide: she decided that he looked like a "fine old portrait of a knight of the middle ages."

The striking face belonged to Count Franz Anton von Thun-Hohenstein, and Adelaide did not err in saying that he seemed melancholy. The face that looks out of his portrait, with its unusually long sideburns, drooping mustache, and heavy, lidded eyes, is filled with sadness. Count Thun had little cause for unhappiness—he was the head of one of the richest and most powerful families of the Austrian nobility. His family had come to Vienna from the Tyrol in the early seventeenth century, and the first of his distinguished ancestors, Christoph Simon von Thun, had been the master of household to Rudolph II and Ferdinand II. Since then, the Thuns had been field marshals, bishops, regional governors, prominent courtiers, and patrons of the arts. In 1783 Mozart had dedicated his Linz Symphony to

Count Johann Joseph von Thun-Hohenstein in gratitude for his patronage. The family had acquired vast estates, mansions in Prague and Vienna, and a handsome castle on the Elbe River in Bohemia. Count Thun was a skilled musician. Having heard Adelaide sing at the great hall of the castle, he could not leave without offering words of praise. For days to come, his sensitive comments and sincere manner lingered in her memory.

It so happened that the viceroy's sister, the Princess Clary, owned a castle at Teplitz, a pretty German-speaking spa town eighty miles to the west, not far from the present border between the Czech Republic and eastern Germany. In its own way Teplitz was as well known as Carlsbad. Its spring waters reputedly cured gunshot wounds, and the armies of Austria, Saxony, and Prussia maintained bathhouses there for wounded and sick soldiers. A course of its waters was also considered a fitting finish to the treatment at Carlsbad. Praising the unique quality of the spa, Princess Clary urged Charles and his party to join her in Teplitz and was delighted when she received an immediate acceptance.

In the castle at Teplitz, Adelaide and her father lived with the Clary family for almost three weeks, and Count Thun and his gentle countess came daily to call on them. Though Adelaide's shyness normally precluded quick friendships, the Thuns, as she called them, for she did not use the suffix *Hohenstein*, almost instantly became her friends. "I sometimes wonder at myself for having felt so drawn towards you in so short a time," she wrote afterward. "I like so few people and with such difficulty." She marveled at their fluency in English—for their native tongue was German—and at their sympathetic choice of topics that always interested her.

This mutual sympathy was not so surprising, for the Thuns were devoted to the arts and accustomed to lengthy discussions with writers, musicians, and intellectuals. Writers came to their castle at Tetschen—today called Decin—on the banks of the Elbe not far from Teplitz, attracted by the count's fine library and his wide knowledge of Bohemian folklore. Painters came to sketch the wild landscape surrounding the castle, which was admired throughout the German-speaking world. It was not unusual for musicians who performed in the Bohemian spa towns to end their tour with a private concert at Tetschen. In this way, a few years earlier, Frederic Chopin, the Polish pianist, had been invited to stay with the Thuns, whose children he had once taught in Paris. On the night of September 15, 1835, Chopin slept at the castle, accompanied by his parents, whom the count had been thoughtful enough to invite. While at Tetschen, Chopin composed a "Tetschener Waltz," which he dedicated to one of Count Thun's daughters.

All through her lonely adolescence, Adelaide had consoled herself with dreams of a companion whose soul was in harmony with her own. She imagined an ideal man—a father rather than a lover—with the mental gifts of her own father but also with the sympathy and dependability that she and her mother had failed to find in Charles. She believed that she had found her ideal man in the count—so rich and powerful and at the same time "simple, honest and warmhearted" and "free of the prejudices of birth." Eventually Adelaide realized that she loved Count Thun "as I love no one else."

Her attachment to the Thuns was so intense that she could scarcely drag herself away from Teplitz. In Dresden, her next stop, where she had been engaged in advance to sing, her thoughts ran constantly to the count and countess. They had invited the Kembles and Dessauer to stay with them as soon as Adelaide's engagements in Dresden were completed, and the invitation loomed large in her imagination.

On October 16, 1837, the Kemble party left Dresden for the Thuns' castle. The road followed the river Elbe upstream, through tall cliffs and gorges, past dark pine woods and towers set on crags, and over dramatic torrents. It was a landscape to delight a disciple of the romantic movement, and Adelaide observed it with poetic fervor, declaring that its beauty surpassed Carlsbad and Teplitz.

As evening approached, the Kembles' coach rounded a bend in the road, and Adelaide suddenly saw the Thuns' home, soaring from a cliff of rock beside the wide, fast-flowing river. It was everyone's dream of a castle—white walls rising from a rocky base, a red-tiled roof gleaming in the setting sun, and a slender clock tower steepled toward heaven. Behind, forming the perfect backdrop, rose the hills and low mountains of Bohemia, "with an eternal blue vapor upon them like the bloom on a fine plum." Even today, shabby and abandoned, the castle generates a thrill. In 1837, the sight must have been breathtaking.

As the Kembles' coach drove up the long, covered causeway toward the gates, Count Thun came to meet them, a gracious act that was not lost on his guests. Indeed Adelaide and her father could scarcely believe the kindness and simple courtesy with which they were greeted by every member of the family.

In future years Adelaide would remember almost every minute of her

visit to Tetschen: the happiest fortnight, she was fond of saying, in her entire life. Progressive parents who, within certain bounds, followed the romantic notion of free expression for children, the count and countess
imposed few restrictions at home. "I did nothing here," Adelaide wrote,
"but run like a mad woman bonnetless among the hills, write out English
poetry for Francis, the eldest son, sing what I liked and when I liked, and
love everybody and things around me." Four of the five Thun children—
Francis, Leopold, Josephine, and Anna—were at home. Josephine, the eldest girl, usually called Yuza, was almost Adelaide's age and became her
particular friend. Francis, the eldest boy, five years older than Adelaide,
won her confidence with "a thousand little looks of sympathy and words of
comfort." They were "the most affectionate truehearted creatures in the
world," she told Fanny, adding: "Oh dear Fan, if any Germans come in your
way be kind to them for the sake of those who received me with such affection—who made their home mine, and who treated me as their child."

On her bonnetless excursions among the Tetschen hills, Adelaide's
readiest companion was Francis, who was "very handsome, very good, very
refined." His likeness to his father drew her to him. He had that same romantic medieval look, but without his father's melancholy. A dreamer, an
idealist, he looked like a knight errant. Adelaide could imagine him slaying
dragons and saving maidens in distress.

It is not certain whether Francis was drawn to Adelaide's unconven-
tional looks, but he was certainly drawn to her radicalism. The future
Count Thun was a radical himself, and he was not used to finding friends of
his parents ready to agree with him. Hitherto acquainted only with the
well-bred, unopinionated female friends of his sisters, he was overwhelmed
by the ardor of this young woman. He and Adelaide would sit side by side
on the Bohemian hillsides, lost to the world, earnestly righting the wrongs
of society. Hearing them pontificating, Countess Chotek and Count Thun
shook their heads and smiled tolerantly. They affectionately nicknamed
Adelaide the Demon of Revolt.

It was plain to observers that Adelaide and Francis had a special affin-
ity. Francis "has become," she told Fanny in a careful understatement, "a
very great friend of mine." She sensed, however, a hesitation in his manner,
for sometimes he was tender and sometimes he was reserved. "He is a little
like Hamlet," she told Fanny; "he has trouble making up his mind."

How close Adelaide felt to the entire family can be gauged by her impulsive decision to open her heart to them. In a storm of tears, she confided
her life history to the count and countess. As she herself would put it later,

"the ice that for so long had been bound coldly and tightly around my heart melted away in water through my eyes." She held little back: her unhappiness, loneliness, and uncertainty poured out with a histrionic Kemble fervor. If the Thuns were dismayed, they did not show it. They listened, they advised, and they showed her affection. At last she was surrounded by a large, loving family. For the first time in her life, she told them when she left the castle, "I knew what it was to feel like a child. . . . I seem to find at Tetschen what I have been looking for, for so long—I never felt so loved and so loving, I never felt so childlike before."

Tetschen would always be Adelaide's enchanted castle: the "home more to me than ever my own was": the place she always returned to in her thoughts. Those fifteen days in a setting of beauty and wealth cemented her attachment to the father of her dreams, and to his son. Adelaide had fallen irrevocably in love with the heir to the magic castle, and she longed to marry him. That there were serpents in the landscape she sensed only dimly: her memory of the fate of Fanny and Augustus Craven had grown dim. "Here," she told Fanny, "I found all I wanted."

7

The Girl in the
Black Cassock Dress

The Thuns were now Adelaide's source of emotional warmth. "I have
lived all my days in the shade," she told them by letter soon after she
left them, "and life seems to have turned its sunny side towards me only
during the happy fifteen days I passed among you." Without their love,
Adelaide believed that she would wither like a plant deprived of sunshine.
When she left their presence, it felt like a form of death.

There had been little Adelaide could do to postpone the leave-taking.
Now that his health was improving, her father was impatient to be on his
way. Having seen Adelaide's success in the spa towns, Charles was more optimistic about her chances in the professional theatre. Though he was still
reluctant to consign a daughter to the stage, he was less reluctant than he
had been ten years before. What concerned him was his own lack of musical contacts. If Adelaide were to sing professionally, she would need influential friends to help her. On Dessauer's advice, Charles resolved to return
to England by way of Leipzig and Brussels, where he hoped to enlist musical
patrons.

Charles chose Leipzig because a strong potential ally lived there. Over
the past ten years, the brilliant young composer Felix Mendelssohn had
traveled twice to London, and in the course of those visits, he had come to
know the Kembles well. What was more, Mendelssohn had recently become director of Leipzig's popular Gewandhaus concerts and was already
employing a young English soprano named Clara Novello. Charles did not
see why Mendelssohn should not give equal support to Adelaide.

When the Kembles drove into Leipzig on November 6, 1837, the
weather had turned wintry. Snow covered the crooked streets and high,

< 112 >

pitched roofs. Adelaide, however, had no eyes for the quaint houses, or even for the famous Gewandhaus, a smallish hall, painted yellow, where the audience sat on benches arranged like those in an omnibus. Adelaide's only thought was on a miserable toothache that had plagued her all day. As they pulled up at the Hotel de Russie, she longed for warmth and bed.

Also staying at their hotel were the Novellos: father Vincent Novello, a well-known London organist, mother Mary Novello, and daughter Clara, who had sung in Leipzig four days earlier under Mendelssohn's patronage. As they caught sight of Adelaide, the Novellos were united in their dismay, for here was a possible rival to Clara. Their anxiety lent spite to their tongues. Clara and her mother began to scribble entries in their diaries that when read alongside Adelaide's letters, paint a curious vignette.

Conscious of Clara's blond prettiness, the Novellos were slightly reassured by Adelaide's plainness. Clara wrote in her diary that Adelaide looked "like an Abbé in her black cassock dress—hair brushed away from a thin face. All nose." Taking heart, the Novellos decided that Adelaide might not pose such a threat after all and softened their attitude a little. Mrs. Novello, who, despite her pushiness, had a motherly heart, decided to be kind. Since Adelaide was alone in her room all day while her father was out in the town, Mrs. Novello sent Clara to sit with her. The visit was not a success. Clara returned to her mother, brimming with complaints that Adelaide had subjected her to "a lecturing discourse."

What the Novellos do not seem to have understood—for Adelaide presumably chose not to tell them—was that she was in pain. "All yesterday and yesternight and this morning I have been dying of the toothache," she wrote to Countess Thun, "and being unable to endure with a patient spirit any more torture, have just sent for a dentist." At the best of times Adelaide found strangers difficult: in her present plight, Clara's visit must have seemed as painful as the toothache.

Later that week Felix Mendelssohn gave a reception in the Kembles' honor, at which Charles read from Shakespeare and Adelaide sang. Sitting among the guests were Mrs. Novello and Clara. They endured Charles's performance because he was famous, but when Adelaide, during the reading, flung herself theatrically at her father's feet, they seethed with quiet indignation. Adelaide's singing vexed them even more. Later Clara gained a gloating satisfaction from hearing—or claiming to hear—Mendelssohn's wife say that Adelaide's singing was so loud and abrasive that it almost broke the windows. No pupil of Bordogni's sang abrasively, and one can fairly safely assume that the courteous Frau Mendelssohn would never have been so indiscreet. The remark was almost certainly a fabrication and tells us more about Clara's jealousy than about Adelaide's voice.

Adelaide was far more generous in spirit than her critics. The day after Mendelssohn's reception, she wrote to Fanny: "I spent an evening very pleasantly with Mendelssohn, who is delightful." And she wrote touchingly to the Thuns about Clara: "There is here at present a young English concertsinger who is meeting with great success . . . her voice is *exquisite!* not so strong as mine, but far sweeter and lovelier—every note is perfect! but for all that I *forbid* you to like it as well as mine."

Mendelssohn was gracious in his hospitality and praised Adelaide's singing, but he declined to give any firm promise of help. Disappointed but not downhearted, Charles decided to leave Leipzig and make for Brussels. There he planned to visit the widow and younger daughter of the late Manuel Garcia, who for years had been Europe's leading tenor and was also the father of surely the most remarkable family in operatic history. His daughters became two of the finest sopranos of all time. His son became a teacher so seminal that most celebrated singers in opera today are said to trace their technical ancestry back to Manuel Garcia the younger.

Garcia's elder daughter, the brilliant Maria Malibran, had died ten months previously of septicemia. Aged only twenty-eight, she had been mourned by fifty thousand fans, who lined the streets of Manchester to watch her funeral pass by. The younger daughter, Pauline, who was about to make her debut, was expected to become as exceptional a singer as her sister. Charles was aware of the glory to be gained through a connection with the family. He probably also knew that the Garcias were helping Clara Novello.

Since Malibran had been dead less than a year, the family in Brussels was still in mourning; but Madame Garcia set aside two evenings so that Pauline and Adelaide could sing together. How would the sixteen-year-old Pauline sound? Musical Europe was speculating, and the Kembles were among the first outsiders to find out. From her young lips came the Garcia voice, disciplined by her father and brother—not free of imperfections, as Adelaide admitted, but glowing with potential. "A magnificent voice," Adelaide wrote to the Thuns, "precisely the same as her sister's and will I think sing as well." Adelaide and Pauline sang a duet together, and Adelaide was amazed at how well their voices combined. It was as if they had been in the constant habit of practicing with each other. "I *wish* you had been there," she told the Thuns, "you would have enjoyed it so."

Singing with Pauline, who was so soon to make her professional debut, focused Adelaide's mind on her own future. While singing in Carlsbad and Prague, she had dreamed of becoming a prima donna, but in Tetschen her hopes had turned toward becoming Francis's wife. Should she become an opera singer, or should she wait in the hope of marrying a count of the Austrian Empire? While Adelaide was staying at Tetschen, she had confided that very question to Count Thun, tactfully avoiding any mention of his son. Should she go on the stage, she asked him, or should she hope to marry a rich and well-born man? The count's answer had been cautious. He did venture to say that the stage was a dangerous step and one he would be sorry to see her take. On the other hand, if her father willed it, then she must obey. The count secured her promise that she would tell him before making a final decision.

The Kembles returned from Brussels to the lonely house at Park Place. In the gloom of foggy January days, when Adelaide could scarcely see the trees in the park from her windows, she tried to order her thoughts. She had been brought up to think that an independent career was desirable, and that a career on the stage, in carefully arranged circumstances, could be honorable. On the other hand, both she and Fanny had learned from the outside world that women who displayed themselves for money were likely to be condemned.

As Adelaide tried, in those weeks, to reconcile the divergent viewpoints, she came closer to her family's view of the profession than to Fanny's. Because Fanny had come to acting without an apprenticeship, she saw stagecraft as an easily learned skill that was basically degrading. Adelaide, on the other hand, after her training with Bordogni, saw singing as a hard-won skill that was basically honorable. In her eyes, singing required the perfection of a God-given talent through years of patience and labor; and so, in every sense, it was a worthy pursuit—even though she was obliged to admit that the world tended not to see it so.

Nor did Adelaide seem to fear, as Fanny did, the artist's addiction to excitement. Singing on stage, in Adelaide's experience, required such physical and mental concentration that it was more exhausting than exciting. "I think there is *some* danger in success," she admitted, "and if I do succeed I daresay my head may be turned for a little while, but this excitement will not last long."

In Adelaide's mood, the advantages of a career seemed to outweigh the evils. Her life at Park Place, on those gloomy winter mornings when she had to light the lamp to see her writing paper, seemed lonely and unfulfilling. She longed for fresh experiences and new inspiration. "I feel that all that surrounds me is insufficient to me," she wrote to Count Thun, "and (what I never knew before) that I am no longer sufficient to myself." She ached to possess the rewards of success and to have money, books, and admirers, as Fanny had in her heyday. "I do not look for *happiness* in going on the stage," she told the count, "but I shall see strange and new things—I shall escape from what is painful to me here and I shall earn plenty of that golden trash which supplies one with the best substitutes for happiness."

Above all, a career would give Adelaide independence: the goal that she and Fanny regarded as the greatest desideratum of life. As matters stood, she had no security to protect her in the event of her father's death. With whom, for example, would she live? To be returned to her mother's guardianship would be intolerable, and she had never been close to any of her aunts, other than Dall. "I should be reduced to living in a state of utter dependence," she told the Thuns, "with a person who neither knows, understands nor loves me."

In all these speculations, Adelaide's mind constantly returned to Francis. If he proposed marriage soon, she knew that her worries would be over. If he hesitated too long, and she was forced to choose the opera house, she wondered how her decision would affect their marriage. Her mind roamed back to those earnest talks on the Bohemian hillside. She began to tell herself that Francis scorned empty convention and would never condemn a woman because she had sung professionally. His parents, however, were of a sterner generation. They had openly told her that stage performers were creatures of "falsehood and vanity"—though they tactfully excepted her family. That exception would not extend, she feared, to welcoming a former performer as a daughter-in-law. Nor, if she really thought about it, would Austrian Catholic aristocrats as powerful as the Thuns be likely to accept a non-aristocratic, Protestant Englishwoman as a bride for their son.

Adelaide wondered if she should become a Catholic. She also wondered if she should tell the Thuns that she was descended from a French marquis. According to her mother, her maternal great-grandfather had been the son of the Marquis de Fleury; he had been disowned by his family and obliged to call himself De Camp when he chose to marry a Strasbourg innkeeper's daughter. Over the following months, Adelaide gave the Thuns details of her supposed descent and hinted that she was willing to convert to Catholicism.

Even if she changed her religion and established her aristocratic ancestry, there were still factors weighing against her. She could only hope that the liberalism for which the Thuns were celebrated, plus their obvious affection for her, would tip the scales in her direction. If to those scales was added the weight of a stage career, she knew the balance would tilt against her. She prayed that Francis would make up his mind and ask her to marry him soon, because she could not go on delaying forever.

During these uncertain weeks, Charles refused to give his opinion about her future, and his attitude made her furious. After each of her concerts, as they crisscrossed Europe, he had been asked whether his daughter was about to sing professionally. In Adelaide's words: "his answer was always the same—'it is as my daughter shall decide—it depends wholly on her.'" The answer was pure humbug. Charles knew as well as Adelaide that he was the person who must decide.

In fact Charles was quietly weighing Adelaide's good and bad points. The foremost difficulty, as far as he could see, was her shyness, which made every public appearance an ordeal. She had gained confidence over the past year, but he doubted whether she had gained enough. Another doubt concerned the longevity of her voice. Many mezzo-soprano voices of that time tended to lose their quality early, their owners having reportedly started their training too early, sung too often, and extended their range too far. Giuditta Pasta, one of the finest extended mezzos of the previous decade, had passed her prime by the age of forty. Charles doubted if Adelaide's voice, which was small, would stand up to the rigors of a professional career. But Adelaide thought he was shilly-shallying. "I think what he said about the chance of losing my voice is nonsense," she told the Thuns. "I am a young, strong, and healthy woman."

Most of all, Charles must have been wondering about Francis Thun. Whether he fully accepted Adelaide's belief that Francis might propose, one does not know. At the same time, he was not prepared to risk spoiling her chances of marriage, if chances did exist. It was preferable to wait and see how the wind blew from Tetschen.

Just before her twenty-third birthday, on February 13, 1838, Charles made up his mind. He asked Adelaide casually if she thought she would be happier singing in opera than in her present position. When she replied yes almost unthinkingly, he gave her a kiss and said: "then if you please, my dear, we will consider the matter as settled." In those few casual words, her future was decided. "We are odd people," she commented.

The momentous decision was taken, and for a time Adelaide felt relief. But how could she tell the Thuns? And how could she possibly hint that the next move must be Francis's? To make matters worse, just as she was about to write, a letter arrived from Count Thun, begging her not to take the fatal step. He confided to her that he could not bear to see her "*fallen.*"

Upset by Count Thun's letter, Adelaide composed a reply that the Novellos would have termed one of her "lecturing discourses." Above all else she needed to keep the Thuns' affection, and yet the best defense she could muster was to challenge their prejudices. She argued that a cloistered virtue was not worth having: "you must be *just,*" she told them, "and remember that I am not more worthy of your affection and esteem now because I still possess a reputation that I have not yet been tempted to lose than I shall be when I shall have been tried." To be truly good one must be tempted and withstand temptation, she argued, and the opera would prove a worthy testing ground.

The count and countess replied gently, but Adelaide continued to feel distressed. Her only option, she realized, was to speak to Francis in person, and she thanked heaven that this seemed possible. Charles's doctors were advising another visit to Carlsbad. To Adelaide's joy, it was decided to leave London in July 1838, traveling by way of Bohemia to Italy, the land of operatic opportunity, where Charles would oversee his daughter's professional debut.

A letter from the Thuns thwarted this plan. The countess wrote that they expected to be away from Tetschen in July and August. Adelaide was aghast. She wrote imploringly: "Oh my dear dear friend do not go away without seeing me. Pray do not go before I come—For your sake I look upon Germany as my country and home—*don't* let me go back to feel myself a stranger there." It was fairly clear the Thuns believed it would be wiser to be elsewhere, but eventually their kindness supervened. They invited Adelaide and her father to spend part of July at the castle.

Late in June, Adelaide and Charles set out for Paris, but no sooner did they arrive than Marie Thérèse fell ill, and they were obliged to return to England. Their departure had awakened Marie Thérèse's fears that her husband was deserting her and had reduced her to a "sad state of mind and body." Charles's return improved her health, and after two weeks father and daughter felt secure enough to resume their journey. But as Adelaide said goodbye for a second time, she found herself flooded by a "strange, tumultuous feeling of *agony.*" Instinctively she knew that she would not see her mother alive again.

The travelers made their way as quickly as possible to Tetschen. For the second time in less than a year, they rounded the bend in the Elbe and saw the fairy-tale castle rising beside the river. Adelaide's heart began to beat painfully. How would they receive her? She was not at peace until she alighted from the coach in the spacious courtyard and was enfolded in their arms.

The Thuns welcomed her tenderly; and though she knew it pained them, they did not reproach her for her decision to sing opera. But Adelaide reproached herself. She was on a knife edge, and emotion broke down decorum. Trusting the count's paternal understanding, she seems to have poured out her fears. She loved Francis, and she wished to marry him. It must be arranged at once, or she would be forced to become an opera singer. Looking back later, Adelaide would write: "I never believe I ever spoke so openly to anyone as to him."

The Thuns were very fond of this turbulent, vulnerable girl, but not to the extent of embracing her as a daughter-in-law. As the years would disclose, Count Thun was a proud man, always conscious of his position as head of one of the great families of the Austrian Empire. He placed high demands on his children's marital choices, and many years later he would condemn his own daughter for choosing a man whose social standing was far higher than Adelaide's. At the same time, Count Thun and his wife loved the girl far too much to risk hurting her. Careful to avoid causing her pain, the count seems to have given a slightly devious answer. He told her that he would raise no objections if Francis wished to marry her.

Count Thun's words stilled Adelaide's anxiety. She believed that Francis would certainly ask her, for surely only the fear of crossing his father was holding him back. She waited confidently for the offer. But it did not come. What Adelaide did not know—and would not know for many years—was that the count said nothing to his son one way or the other.

Though Francis seems to have loved Adelaide and to have believed with all his radical soul in the equality of opera singers and aristocrats, he also knew his duty as a son and heir. He did not feel able to ask her without his father's consent; and knowing the obstacles that stood in their way, he did not dare broach the subject with his father. He waited for his father to speak, and his father said nothing. The count "never told him," wrote Adelaide many years later, "as he had me, that he would not object to our marriage." Instead Count Thun kept a forbidding silence: and Francis, the dutiful son, kept silent, also.

Thus the count was able to keep his word to Adelaide and at the same time achieve his object. One must speculate that Count Thun, though a truthful and honorable man, had bargained that Francis would solve his dilemma by doing nothing.

Each morning at the castle, Adelaide rose up in hope, and each evening she went to bed in despair. By an unremitting effort of will, she managed to control her outward self, but inside she was close to collapse. After two weeks, she was obliged to set her heartache aside and bid the Thuns a loving goodbye.

She desperately needed a chance to grieve, but there was no time. Father and daughter were expected immediately at Teplitz, where Charles was to begin the second leg of his spa cure. The season at Teplitz was in full swing, and the town was packed with European nobility. Among them were Count and Countess Chotek and Princess Clary, and they could not have been more welcoming. Their very kindness only served to quicken Adelaide's memory of Francis. She sat moodily in crowded drawing rooms, trying to prize her thoughts away from Tetschen. A presentation to the king of Prussia passed almost unnoticed in her mind.

Teplitz was a stepping stone in Adelaide's career. Charles had astutely timed their arrival to coincide with that of Pauline Garcia, and he was able to persuade the young soprano to sing a duet with Adelaide at a concert at the castle. The importance of singing in public with Maria Malibran's sister was not lost on Adelaide. Since her debut in Brussels the previous December, Pauline had been the subject of constant gossip, some claiming that she had a fine technique but no voice, some that she had a fine voice but no technique, the rest saying that she was far too ugly to be a prima donna. Adelaide was impatient with the tittle-tattle, but she knew that it served as good publicity.

The web of speculation ensured that a capacity audience would attend the concert. The duet from Bellini's *Norma* sung by the two young sopranos earned a storm of applause. Adelaide's success in that concert confirmed her father's judgment as an artistic entrepreneur. The audience of princes, counts, and generals—not to mention the king of Prussia—ensured that Adelaide's name would be circulated throughout fashionable Europe.

Once Charles finished his course of Teplitz waters, the Kembles pressed on by coach to Carlsbad. Adelaide found it sad to drive again into the steep valley and remember the pleasures of the year before. Dessauer was to join them there, and she wondered if she could face him. Worse, she wondered how she would manage at their next stop, Prague. There was talk that the Thun children would be there, and she wondered if Francis would be with them. If he were, how would she face *him*? Adelaide wished she knew what Francis was thinking, and she was desperate for him to send some sign. She and the countess were still corresponding, and though pride did not allow her to speak outright, she managed to make a few indirect appeals. On August 1, from Carlsbad, she wrote Francis a wistful little postscript at the end of a letter to his mother: "I like to fancy that we have been long acquainted," she wrote, "though in point of fact it matters but little—for one sometimes likes and knows some people better in a day than one does others in a year or a life. I am bored to death here!" As a message it barely made sense, but somehow it seemed to convey that she loved him and missed him.

Meanwhile Dessauer had arrived in Carlsbad—but he was not the enchanting Dessauer of the year before. He was distracted and withdrawn, with scarcely a minute to spare for the Kembles. Adelaide was shrewd enough to suspect that Dessauer was jealous of Francis Thun. It had come to her ears that Dessauer was passing on rumors that Adelaide was about to be married, hinting, though he did not say outright, that the bridegroom was Francis. Dessauer's behavior dashed Adelaide's hopes of inviting him to Italy to help with her debut. "It would have been such a consolation," she told the Thuns, "to have seen him there." The thought of the lonely ordeal awaiting her made her "lose courage horribly."

Dessauer gallantly did find time to accompany Adelaide on the piano at two charity concerts at the Bohemian Hall. She sang his "Ouvrez" and songs by Franz Schubert and Saverio Mercadante, an air from *Norma*, and a duet from *Semiramide* in which Dessauer, with his strange little voice, sang the male part. Cheered, perhaps, by their appearance on stage together, Dessauer agreed to accompany the Kembles as far as Prague.

In Prague, Dessauer had further cause to feel jealous. The younger Thuns were in town and—joy of joys—Francis was with them. How one wishes that Adelaide had left an account of their meeting! Whatever they said to one another, it seems to have soothed her—even to have left her with hope. She wrote to Countess Thun: "You cannot imagine the happiness and the *good* that being with them at Prague was to me." She set out for Italy "with a stronger and more hopeful feeling than I was ever blessed with before."

Buoyed up by this hope, Adelaide's mind was at last sufficiently free to notice the beauty of the mountains, and as they drove to Salzburg and Königsee, then to Innsbruck, her imagination caught fire. The lake of Königsee sent her into raptures. "The entrance to it is very fair and inviting," she told the Thuns. "The hills are lower, more undulating, and well wooded, which gives it a softer look, and the water of the palest green—but suddenly by an unexpected turn you become shut in on every side by the highest sternest crags, rising almost perpendicular from the very edge of the lake, so that it seems impossible to land or even stand upon the margin—the color of the water too is changed—it is here of the darkest intensest green. Oh, the most magical water!" She half expected to see a fairy lady with white arms and long green hair rise from the emerald depths.

The tranquility of the mountains and lakes brought calm to Adelaide's heart. "I think it does one good to rest from the sight of men and houses," she told the countess, "and be alone with those awful, mysterious hills." Even at night her newfound poise did not desert her. She was determined to love the Thuns as unselfishly as she could. At bedtime she would undress and read a letter from Tetschen, then say her prayers and get into bed: "thinking of you all, praying for you all, gives me such a sweet sleep and such happy dreams."

Thus Adelaide was at least able to hold on to Francis in her mind. To let go of him completely was neither in her nature nor in her upbringing. Like her mother, once she loved, she was committed until death.

From Innsbruck the Kembles drove high into the mountains. Often the road was so steep that the horses could not pull the weight of the coach, and the passengers had to get out and walk. Panting up the mountainsides, they had no difficulty believing that the Stelvio Pass, through which they were traveling, was the second highest way through the Alps. As they approached the summit, they left behind the wooded valleys and foaming torrents and entered into the bleak, windswept landscape of grey rocks and scant vegetation that marked the really high country. In the near distance, on all sides, towered majestic, snowy peaks that struck the soul with awe. It felt like being on the roof of the world.

They descended into the small spa town of Bormio, which gave Adelaide her first taste of Italy. The accommodation was poorer than on the Austrian side of the pass, but the flavor of life was irresistible. To hear the flowing Italian language was a joy to her ears. As they reached the lower slopes and traveled toward Lake Como, Adelaide's anxiety resurfaced. Ahead lay a demanding test. Charles, in his search for musical contacts, had written to the Italian diva Giuditta Pasta and had received an invitation to visit her villa on the shores of the lake. Adelaide worshipped Pasta as "incomparably the finest singer of the age." The prospect of singing for her filled Adelaide with a mixture of excitement and fear.

In her prime, Pasta had been an operatic Sarah Siddons: a tragic actress of such authority that no other singer could match her. She had achieved her skill against great odds, because one of her legs was shorter than the other, and her untrained voice was mediocre. With great determination she overcame both disadvantages, extending her mezzo-soprano voice until she had "the rare ability to be able to sing contralto as easily as she could sing soprano," and perfecting her stagecraft until her clumsy leg was barely noticeable. There was one fault that she never overcame, and that was a poor sense of pitch, which grew worse as she grew older. Even this, however, was only a minor flaw to those who, like the French novelist Stendhal, were enthralled by her magic.

Adelaide had seen Pasta perform in London the year before, and the memory was vivid as they drove toward Como. In one sense the performance had been a disaster, because by that time Pasta's voice was worn out. In another sense it was a triumph, because her acting moved most of the audience to tears. After the performance, Adelaide heard the condescending voice of a dandy remark, "Oh, poor dear old thing! How stumpy she is! How old she has grown, to be sure! She oughtn't to have come back again." Needless to say, the remarks found no sympathy with Adelaide, who was already "worshipping this great goddess and thanking Heaven for this new revelation of happiness."

At the time of Pasta's death in 1865, Adelaide would write an account of the Kembles' visit to her villa; so fresh were the descriptions that the details had obviously been burned into Adelaide's memory. They arrived on a Sunday morning at the end of August, traveling by boat across the blue waters of the lake and stepping ashore at the villa's jetty. Nearby stood the main house, on the door of which Adelaide knocked shyly. An answer was shouted from within: "Who's there? You can't come in."

Daunted but firm, Adelaide shouted back in Italian, "Foreigners." Pushing open the door, she saw a group of card players headed by a fierce old peasant woman. This was Pasta's mother, who lived with her granddaughter and great-granddaughter in a house within the grounds of the villa. Another moment and, mercifully, the diva entered. She was wearing a dirty dressing gown, but her presence filled the room. "What a grand head it was," wrote Adelaide, "full of nobleness and sweetness."

Madame Pasta greeted her visitors and asked what she could do for them. When she heard that Adelaide wanted to sing opera, she lamented that these days she exercised so little influence with impresarios. "But perhaps for singing I might be of some use," she modestly proposed. Before the

Kembles could quite believe it, they had been invited to stay, and Adelaide had been enrolled as Pasta's pupil.

Showing her guests to their rooms, the diva paused outside the entrance to her own bedroom. The doorway was hung with the cages of song birds. Smiling ruefully, she made a joke at her own expense. "I love to hear them singing in the morning," she said in French, then added, in a comic reference to the jibes of her critics, "the little rascals—they always sing in tune."

For three days Adelaide overcame her nervousness and sang often for her teacher. Together they studied Pasta's greatest roles, some of which had been written for her by two of the most famous operatic composers of the day, Gaetano Donizetti and Vincenzo Bellini. With the conviction of youth, Adelaide did not entirely admire these composers; she was a fan of Rossini and believed that his music had greater merit. While she was probably overjoyed when they rehearsed Rossini's *Semiramide*, she may have been less pleased when they studied Donizetti's *Anna Bolena* or Bellini's *Norma*.

It was the role of the druid priestess Norma that they studied the most carefully. Acknowledged as Pasta's most memorable success, the part was written for her by Bellini in 1831 and was so difficult that at first Pasta doubted she could sing it. Today it is described by one opera historian as the "very acme of the soprano's repertory . . . more challenging than Brünnhilde or Isolde and rarely sung even competently." To sing the part of Norma requires power, stamina, flexibility, variety of tone, theatrical presence, and high musical intelligence. As the role in due course would become Adelaide's finest success—she is still remembered as one of the great Normas of all time—Pasta's talents as a teacher must have been impressive.

As Pasta accompanied Adelaide on the piano in the great aria of the opera, "Casta Diva," she suddenly ceased playing. "You are too sharp, my dear," she commanded in Italian. Adelaide sang the phrase again. Again she was halted. When she had sung it a third time, Adelaide gently touched the notes on the piano as she finished and found herself "in perfect unison." Her teacher, still not satisfied, sang the phrase herself, and to her pupil's astonishment, was a quarter of a tone flat.

On these notes—"the C of the third space with D and E to follow"— Madame Pasta was, according to Adelaide, always flat. It was a fault, Adelaide insisted, that came from an imperfect ear and not from an imperfection in her vocal technique. Pasta's technique, nevertheless, was not to everyone's taste. As aspects of it were possibly passed on to Adelaide, it is worth briefly examining.

In those years singers were eager to extend the voice's ability to express emotion. Madame Pasta was a leader in this musical crusade—possibly, as the uncharitable said, because she wished to disguise inferior qualities of her own voice. Whether this criticism was true or not, Madame Pasta realized the theatrical possibilities implicit in producing emotionally charged timbres at will. Stendhal, while admitting that Pasta's new technique was far from the smooth *bel canto* ideal, marveled at her skill, calling her ability to express emotion "one of the richest veins of musical expression which the artistry of the great *cantatrice* is able to exploit." Since Adelaide would later be praised for her dramatic power, it seems possible that this skill was one that her teacher passed on to her.

Madame Pasta also seems to have passed on to Adelaide her views of musical embellishment. Singers in her tradition were permitted—within accepted guidelines—to add their own decoration to the melodic line to show off their vocal and musical expertise. Composers accepted it, audiences demanded it, and singers exploited it to enhance their fame. The soprano Isabella Colbran once transformed a tune by her husband Rossini by "running through chains of triplets of extraordinary difficulty," giving a "vocal imitation of the most difficult arpeggios of a stringed instrument," before finally "executing a formidable ascending and descending scale of two octaves." It was no wonder that Rossini scarcely recognized his own music. He ended up taking the initiative and composing his own cadenzas—acrobatic flourishes ornamenting the final cadence in an aria—as his only means of keeping the singers of his operas in check.

Pasta was famous for her choice of ornament, always dramatically appropriate and usually restrained. By so choosing, she was responding to a change that was developing in operatic style. As the century advanced, opera was becoming less like a concert and more like an integrated drama. Singers had to act more effectively and to sing louder, because orchestral scores, once merely the singers' accompaniments, were assuming a more dramatic and a louder role. As singers competed with orchestras, embellishment declined. Within a few decades, florid *bel canto* expression would be dead.

In Pasta's time, this trend was discernible but not conspicuous. To such instinctive actresses as Pasta and Adelaide, the movement toward a simpler, more dramatic style—provided it did not go too far—was welcome.

Nearly a century and a half after Adelaide's visit to Lake Como, the present writer, along with Adelaide's great-granddaughter, unpacked a trunk of family papers and came across a fragile manuscript book of music. It contained Adelaide Kemble's cadenzas for twenty or so arias, drawn from her roles in La Sonnambula, Beatrice di Tenda, Lucia di Lammermoor, Norma, Anna Bolena, and a dozen other operas. Now in the British Library, the book is considered a rare source for the study of bel canto ornamentation in its declining years, and the nearest that we can come today to recapturing the art of a singer taught by Giuditta Pasta.

"That time I passed with her seems almost like a dream to me. I sang to her a great deal, and I hope I profited a great deal by all she said upon her art." Thus Adelaide described her lessons with Pasta, on the eve of setting out with Charles for the nearby city of Milan. In Milan the Kembles' days were spent in meeting or contacting agents and patrons, many of them enlisted through Pasta's influence. Milan in 1838 was the operatic center of Europe, "where those desiring engagements meet with the impresario or agents in search of prey." Adelaide called opera the "slave trade," and she came to hate the feeling that she was being bought and sold.

Milan in the first week of September was in the throes of a party. The Emperor Ferdinand I of Austria—the immediate predecessor of the famous Franz Joseph—was to be crowned ruler of northern Italy with Charlemagne's Iron Crown of Lombardy; and every balcony and window was draped with brilliantly colored cloth. For almost a week, splendid processions of priests, officials, and soldiers filled the streets, and almost every night, the sky was lit by displays of fireworks.

Charles and Adelaide brought letters of introduction from Count Thun and Count Chotek to prominent Austrian officials, and on the strength of these introductions the Kembles received invitations to some of the festivities. They were invited to the oath-taking in a great hall of the palace, where the emperor's vassals swore their allegiance. The "magnificent uniforms," wrote Adelaide, "the costumes of the heralds, the priests in their purple and point lace, and the court dresses of the ladies made it a splendid sight." Curious to see the emperor, who was known to be mentally subnormal, subject to epileptic fits and outbursts of insanity, Adelaide was relieved to hear from his courtiers that he loved music, the more florid the better. Two days later, on September 6, Adelaide and her father watched the emperor and his escort ride through the winding streets to Milan's cathedral for the coronation. So great was the hostility of the Milanese to their Austrian overlords that sections of the crowd jeered as the red-and-white-coated soldiers rode by.

Thanks to their letters of introduction, Adelaide was invited to perform at the banquet following the coronation, and at a grand reception given by Princess Metternich, the wife of Ferdinand's chief minister. At the coronation banquet, held in the glittering Hall of the Caryatids, Adelaide sang a highly ornamented cavatina from Pacini's *Niobe*, which brought great pleasure to the feeble-minded emperor. Next evening, when Princess Metternich was the hostess, Adelaide sang again, this time in company with Guiditta Pasta, Clara Novello, and a gifted Italian amateur, Prince Belgioioso. Though Ferdinand gave every sign of reveling in the music, Clara Novello noticed that those with him were nervous. They seemed to be expecting him to fall down in a fit.

Adelaide's singing delighted the Metternichs, and the following day the grateful princess sent Adelaide a handsome bracelet, the usual reward for a professional singer. The princess had not realized that Adelaide would see the gift as an insult to her social status. "I had sung out of good will," Adelaide told Countess Thun, "and was wounded at being paid for it—besides she has no *right* to pay me as I am not a concertsinger." Adelaide would have sent the bracelet back if Charles had not taken her to task for ungraciousness.

Two weeks after the last concerts and banquets, Charles opened the latest copy of *Gallignani's Messenger*, the journal that supplied Europe with English news. A paragraph suddenly captured his eye. It briefly announced the death, on September 3, 1838, of Marie Thérèse De Camp. As neither Charles nor Adelaide had received a letter from England since leaving Prague, they had no way of knowing whether the announcement was true. Charles refused to believe it, even though the journal gave a specific day of death. In high anxiety, he wrote an urgent letter to London to find out if the news was correct.

Adelaide believed the announcement of her mother's death all too readily; she had had a presentiment when they left England that she might never see Marie Thérèse again. She was haunted by the vision of her mother's anguished face as they said goodbye. A flood of harrowing memories engulfed her. She could not turn to her father for comfort, because even in this crisis he shut himself off from her. The Thuns became her emotional lifeline, and without their patient understanding, she might have broken down altogether.

8

Triumph in Italy

Charles could not bring himself to believe the announcement of his wife's death. Only when he visited the post office in Milan and found a letter from England that had lain unclaimed for eight days did he at last accept that it was true. In the letter, his son John announced that Marie Thérèse had died at her cottage in the country, with only himself to comfort her in the last hours. Was it "not awful," wrote Adelaide, "to think of that lonely and deserted deathbed?"

Stricken by sorrow and a growing burden of guilt, father and daughter struggled to regain their composure. Though Adelaide was thankful that her mother "was released from a life in which the only impressions she seemed capable of receiving were those of pain," Charles was unable to accept such consolation. He blamed himself for her lonely death. Under the weight of his remorse, his health gave way. At times he was so weak and in such pain that he could scarcely walk. "I sit and watch him," wrote Adelaide forlornly, "and pray God not to take away from me the only thing left me in this wide world."

Charles's first thought was to return to London, but as common sense returned, he decided to remain in Italy. Adelaide could not stay unchaperoned in Milan, and it would be foolish for her to return to England now that she was about to secure contracts with the major opera houses. It would also be unwise for Charles to leave Italy—his experience and prestige were needed to cope with such shrewd impresarios as Bartolomeo Merelli of La Scala Theatre in Milan and Domenico Barbaia of the San Carlo Theatre in Naples. Unlike Fanny, Adelaide had no Kemble company to protect her. In the cutthroat world of Italian opera, Adelaide would need every particle of help she could find.

On October 16, 1838, the anniversary of her first arrival at the castle in Tetschen, Adelaide signed the contracts her father had negotiated for

< 128 >

her. She was to travel to Trieste to open on December 26 and sing there until March 26 the following year. Then she would return to Milan; during the next twelve months, she would perform for the impresario Merelli, either at La Scala or at his other theatre, the Karntnertortheater in Vienna.

Once the time had come for firm commitment, Adelaide hesitated. As she began to fill in and sign her opera contracts, she grew dizzy. "I could hardly write the words that were dictated to me," she told Countess Thun. "Tetschen with its hills and its waters, its hospitable home and its dear *dear* people came before me, and my head swam round and my heart sank within me as I thought of the happy past and the dark uncertain future." Was there any hope, she implored, of Francis coming to hear her if she sang in Vienna?

In November the Kembles arrived in Venice. Sailing by boat across the lagoon and entering the quiet streets of water, Adelaide could hardly contain herself. Before them lay the home of Othello and Portia, a city so mysterious that it had fired her imagination since childhood. She could not wait to see the great, galleried square with its towers, obelisks, and winged lions, or to enter the golden gloom of St. Mark's Cathedral. But when she entered the fairy-tale church and saw the mosaic walls gleam gold in the candlelight, smelled the incense, and heard the chanted prayers, the sights and sounds seemed muted, because Francis dominated her thoughts. When she returned to the hotel, she took up her pen and wrote a "crazy letter" to Countess Thun. Part of her letter has been lost or destroyed, but enough remains to show how, even at this late hour, she felt impelled to make a last, veiled appeal for Francis to marry her quickly, before she took up the stage career that would forever prevent their marriage.

The surface of Adelaide's letter told what it was proper for her to say; the undercurrent hinted what her pride did not allow her to put into words. She began by saying how much her nature cried out for fulfillment and happiness. Whereas the countess, as a married woman, possessed the love of a husband and children to ensure her fulfillment, Adelaide lacked that type of love and so was obliged to turn to her career for her emotional reward. She then went on to write about her future life. Her father seemed to doubt whether she could withstand the dangers of an operatic career. He wondered if she should turn back. But now that the contracts were signed, it was virtually impossible to cancel them, although, she added hopefully, marriage could cancel a contract. As a postscript she wrote the name that she had so far avoided, but which ran between every line: "Is Francis ill?" she asked.

Countess Thun appears to have deciphered Adelaide's message and to have answered with a parable drawn from her own life. As a young girl, the countess had been ordered by her mother to give up the man she loved, and she recounted the incident to Adelaide, adding that she had lived to be grateful for her mother's intervention. The story sent Adelaide into a passion. "Do you think that mothers or fathers have rights over their children's hearts and souls," she wrote furiously. "Do you think one *human creature* can and should have such a right over another? and though *self* sacrifice is a noble thing *in itself*, don't you think it was a cruel thing to offer up the happiness of the man who loved you to satisfy an opinion or prejudice of your mother's? . . . I thought it *horrible!*" Then, recollecting herself, she added rather miserably: "will you forgive me and give my love to Francis?"

Adelaide's agony of mind continued through November as she struggled to come to terms with her approaching debut. Then, all at once, her indecision was over. In the early hours of Sunday, December 2, 1838, she wrote to the Thuns from her hotel room in Venice. She addressed the letter to the countess, declaring that she could "not go to bed without asking your sympathy in our pleasure." A few hours previously she had made her debut at La Fenice Theatre in the role of Norma and had "succeeded as well as you could wish." The decisive step had been taken, and there was no going back.

The decision to make her debut in Venice, and earlier than planned, had been taken suddenly. Venice was honoring the visit of a young Russian prince and, though the opera season had not yet begun, impresario Gallo of the San Benedetto Opera had decided to stage a special performance of *Norma* in the prince's honor. The San Benedetto Theatre was being refurbished, so a home was quickly found at La Fenice. In the scramble to assemble a cast, Charles had seized the opportunity.

The remainder of the cast was, in Adelaide's view, decidedly second rate. Knowing Charles Kemble's careful preparations at Covent Garden, she was dismayed by the perfunctory run-through that passed for a rehearsal and amazed at the haphazard way in which performers arrived at the rehearsal room. In an amusing letter she described her first rehearsal. Summoned for eleven o'clock, she waited alone for over an hour, until Carcano, the musical director, condescended to arrive. Nearly another hour elapsed before they were joined by "a little fusty woman, with a grey-coloured white petticoat dangling three inches below her gown, holding a thin shivering dog by a dirty pocket-handkerchief." Realizing the woman was Giuditta Saglio, who was to sing Adalgisa, Adelaide politely rose to greet her; but

Signora Saglio ignored the greeting, seized the dog, and disappeared in search of coffee. Adelaide waited another half hour for her to return, during which time the tenor appeared. He was "one of the dirtiest men" Adelaide had ever seen. The tenor was followed by the bass, and to Adelaide's relief, he was clean.

When Signora Saglio returned, the pianist was ready to begin, but the Saglio dog had its own ideas. It "kept up a continuous plaintive howl" as soon as they began to sing, preferring, Adelaide was told, an orchestra to a piano. She was also told that the dog was in delicate health—it had recently borne five puppies, which "it had nursed itself, as if Italian dogs were in the habit of hiring out wet-nurses." Given the chaotic rehearsals, Adelaide wondered how a performance took place at all!

There was nothing makeshift about La Fenice Theatre, which was one of Europe's most splendid opera houses. Holding just fifteen hundred people, it had been rebuilt after a fire the previous year. The name *Fenice* means *phoenix*, and by Adelaide's time the theatre had risen from the ashes of two fires. Resembling a painting by one of the Venetian masters, the theatre and its boxes glittered with blue, cream, and gold, and half-clad goddesses trailed across its painted ceiling. To appear for the first time at a gala in such a magnificent setting was an opportunity to be grasped with both hands. But to sing the fearsomely difficult *Norma* in such circumstances would have tried the most experienced performer. Like Fanny, Adelaide was making her debut in deep water. "You must allow," she told the countess, "that I had double reason to be fearful."

Twice before, *Norma* had been sung at La Fenice, the first time by Pasta, the second by the legendary Maria Malibran. As Adelaide sat with her father in her dressing room, waiting to be called, she was haunted by the specters of her two great predecessors. She was so nervous that when she attempted to warm up her voice by singing a few bars, she could scarcely open her mouth. Sensing that his presence was increasing Adelaide's tension, her father left to take his seat in the audience. At that moment, surrounded by strangers, Adelaide longed for the comfort of Aunt Dall.

Once Adelaide took the stage, her Kemble blood asserted itself. She gained control of her voice, and, though feeble at first, it grew in strength. Her first recitative was applauded, and she took courage. Trembling, she approached her big test: "Casta Diva," the aria in which the druid priestess Norma prays to the moon. One of the most beautiful and difficult pieces in the repertoire, it demanded tight control of tone and rhythm; and because it was sung very early in the performance, before the soprano's voice was warmed by exercise, it was doubly difficult. One moment's lapse of concentration, and Adelaide would have failed. How she blessed Pasta's inspired tutoring.

Adelaide completed the aria to acclaim. The Venetian audience, prepared to endure vocal mediocrity for the sake of a gala, suddenly discovered a new talent. At the end of the act, she was twice called back by prolonged applause. Throughout the opera, her "own single parts were all much applauded," she told the Thuns happily. At the end Charles rushed backstage, bursting with joy, and wept in her arms.

Impresario Gallo was so delighted with Adelaide's performance that he invited her to sing Norma for a dozen nights at his San Benedetto Theatre when it re-opened, and there she continued to draw enthusiastic houses. In the long interval between acts, she was encouraged to sing the showpiece cavatina from Pacini's *Niobe*, which she had already sung so successfully in Milan. It became a popular feature of the performances. On one evening, it was encored five times.

Though her voice would improve over the next three years, it already gave ample signs of quality, with its forcible lower range, firm middle voice, rich top register, and excellent breath control. A few years later an English critic would write: "She can sustain a note in any part of the soprano compass—swell, diminish, and keep it exactly to the same pitch for an incredible space of time." And like her mentor Pasta, Adelaide earned a reputation for tasteful ornament. Describing her performance of Pacini's cavatina, a critic would later praise her complete mastery of embellishment, tempered by a pleasing "severity of judgment" that forbade vulgar excess.

On December 21, 1838, Adelaide and Charles reluctantly said goodbye to Venice and sailed to the port city of Trieste, a town perched on a steep hill overlooking the Adriatic, with the houses running down almost to the water. There Adelaide was astonished to come face to face with her brother John, who had crossed Europe especially to ensure that his father gained the latest medical advice. Since his escapade in Gibraltar, John had redeemed himself in his father's eyes by studying philology at Göttingen University, publishing a brilliant translation of the old English epic *Beowulf*, and marrying the daughter of one of his professors.

John insisted that his father accompany him to Paris, where Dr. Jean Civiale was removing bladder stones with such skill that patients were hastening to him from every corner of Europe. Adelaide listened to her brother's arguments with dismay. She was terrified at the prospect of being left in Italy without her father's backing. She was also fearful of what might happen if her father submitted to the surgeon's knife. Making it her duty to read the doctor's treatise, she was appalled to discover that, by the doctor's own admission, it was "impossible to say whether the operation will be followed or not by death."

John had brought with him his German wife, Natalie, and his aunt Victoire De Camp. Adelaide could stand neither of them. She considered Aunt Victoire—Marie Thérèse's youngest sister—a cross old maid, and her sister-in-law a smug and domineering *hausfrau*. Adelaide was vexed to learn that it was her brother's plan to install her aunt as her guardian while her father went to Paris. She told him plainly that she was "weary to death" of both women.

Disturbed by the discussions of Charles's health, Adelaide was relieved to learn that her debut in Trieste was postponed. She wondered if it would not have been better canceled, for the company at Trieste's opera house was almost as makeshift as the hastily assembled group in Venice. Just before Christmas, during a performance of *Anna Bolena*, the bass had been hissed off the stage, and the company was unable to find a replacement. Not until late January 1839 did the season resume, with Adelaide singing scenes from *Anna Bolena*—presumably scenes not requiring the bass. In February she went on to sing the lead in Donizetti's *Gemma di Vergy*, followed by Bellini's *La Sonnambula*. Now that her nervousness was retreating, Adelaide found that she enjoyed acting. After many years of learning the music of the operas and acting the roles in her head, it was exciting to stand on a stage and impersonate the characters. She felt a thrill of pleasure whenever she looked in the mirror and saw herself in costume.

At the end of February, John and his wife returned to England, leaving Victoire behind with the excuse that she would be valuable as Adelaide's dresser. While John had not given up his efforts to persuade his father to consult the surgeon in Paris, his advice did not prevail. Charles was determined to manage Adelaide's next engagement. In April, in Milan, she was due to perform at La Scala, the finest opera house in Italy—possibly the finest in the world. If she succeeded there, her career would be assured.

Early in March, a few weeks after Adelaide's twenty-fourth birthday, the Kemble party arrived in Milan. Though the city seemed welcoming and familiar, the circumstances of this visit were vastly different from the previous one. Then Adelaide had been a newly discovered amateur, whom an indulgent public had been delighted to fete. This time she was a professional, of whom a high level of competence was taken for granted. If she slipped below that level, she could expect only scorn.

Her first opera was a challenge, for it was to be the premiere at La Scala of *Lucia di Lammermoor*. Written three years earlier by Donizetti, the opera had been highly acclaimed in Naples, London, and Paris. Already famous was the chilling mad scene in the last act, when love-crazed Lucia appears in her bloodstained nightgown, clutching the dagger with which she has just killed her newly wedded husband, and begins to sing eerie versions of melodies heard earlier in the opera. The scene seldom failed to bring spectators to their feet—so long as the soprano could sing and act superbly.

Adelaide was to be partnered by singers of high reputation. The tenor Napoleone Moriani and the baritone Giorgio Ronconi were at the peak of their careers and were renowned for their performances of Donizetti's music. Handsome Moriani was so celebrated for his death scenes that he was nicknamed *il tenore della bella morte*, the singer of beautiful death. If Adelaide had made her debut in Venice in deep water, this was even deeper water, and she was frightened that she might drown.

Moreover, she was joining a company full of tension. The previous few weeks at La Scala had been dogged by illness, and the spate of illnesses attacked the confidence of the whole company. Tempers were short, and changes of cast were frequent. Adelaide was a foreigner, she was inexperienced, and she was shy—the perfect target when tempers blew up. The singers complained that impresario Merelli was rash in engaging a little-known English beginner to sing the lead at the most respected house in Italy. As rehearsals progressed, Adelaide found herself slighted with increasing frequency. When she appealed to Moriani and Roncini for support, neither would raise a finger to help her. They made it obvious that they would rather be singing with one of the Italian sopranos of that season—either Eugenia Tadoleni or Giuseppina Strepponi, a popular singer who was also about to make her debut at La Scala. Strepponi was due to sing in the premiere of Guiseppe Verdi's first opera, *Oberto*. Some years later she would become his wife.

On the opening night, April 1, Adelaide felt ill prepared for the ordeal that lay ahead of her. The auditorium was far bigger than any she had sung in: a vast horseshoe of space, five tiers high, holding thirty-five hundred listeners. She had not had time to learn how to pitch her voice to such a house, and she doubted if her sound would reach its heights and depths. To make matters worse, the boxes in an Italian opera house were buzzing drawing rooms that only ceased their chatter when a particularly stirring scene or popular singer came onstage. For the rest of the time, people flitted like butterflies from one brightly lit box to another, flirting, laughing, and talking. This was especially true of La Scala, the hub of fashionable life in northern Italy.

As she waited to go on stage, Adelaide was so nervous that she could scarcely move. Through sheer force of will she pushed herself on and went through the first two acts almost mechanically, desperately hoping that her voice was reaching the top tiers. Back in her dressing room, exhausted and alone, she tried to pull herself together for the last act. She knew that her success or failure would be determined by how she performed the demanding mad scene.

The interval before the last act lasted more than an hour, so that the spectators could watch a ballet and perform their social duties. Adelaide, dressed in Lucia's bloodstained nightgown, sat in her chair, trying to will herself into calmness. Gradually relaxing, she drifted into sleep, only to awaken to find hands shaking her and voices telling her to hurry onstage. Knowing the consequences of her unplanned nap, she was terrified. A newly awakened singer cannot sing effectively, because the voice remains sluggish for some time after awakening. Adelaide could not possibly manage the vocal intricacies of the mad scene. But she had no choice. She was rushed onstage, where she sang, to quote her own words "about as ill as possible."

Next morning she and her father discussed the setback to her career. Though painfully upset, she was determined not to be beaten. Coached by her father—who had faced many theatrical crises—she spent the next two days studying the score, testing her voice in the theatre, and mentally preparing herself so that she might "*fight* well at night."

On the second night, Adelaide sang well, if not as well as she had hoped. On the third night, just as she was beginning to feel some confidence, supporters of the rival singers Strepponi and Tadoleni set up such a howl that they almost halted the performance. At the sound of the first catcalls, a mixture of anger and resolution took control of her, and Adelaide felt ready to fight to the last breath. Continuing to sing with great presence of mind, she elicited the sympathy of three-quarters of the audience. It was not enough to halt the noise. On the following night, she was booed again.

Meanwhile a rumor reached her that Merelli wanted to be rid of her and was trying to sell her contract to the Florentine impresario Alessandro Lanari. Lanari was said to be holding out for a bargain price. Adelaide had no difficulty believing the rumor. "You have no idea," she told the Thuns, "of the *wickedness* that goes on in the theatre."

In her letters to the Thuns, Adelaide frankly described the misery of those first four nights—"the agony, the sick fear that came over me before going on the stage, and the utter exhaustion and depression at the conclusion." Charles watched in distress, knowing that something must be done to save her career. Realizing that the resentment against her was due in part to the belief that she had come straight to La Scala "from the hands of some English master," Charles joined Merelli in insisting that Adelaide take lessons from Milan's most celebrated maestro, Nicola Vaccai. Adelaide protested that she had already been trained by Bordogni but finally agreed. After a couple of lessons, she had to concede that the sheer fact that she had become Vaccai's pupil had a miraculous effect on the parochial Milanese, who decided that her talent must be "*wonderful* to profit so greatly and quickly from his instruction." This "would make me laugh," she told the Thuns, "if I were not indignant that three years of patience and labour and talent of my dear Bordogni should all go to the credit of five lessons I have had from Vaccai, who teaches me nothing."

Vaccai's influence tipped the scales in her favor. By mid April the catcalls had ceased. Night after night she was applauded generously, and at one performance Adelaide received eighteen encores. Nevertheless, the ordeal of those early performances had taken its toll. When *Lucia* went temporarily into recess—after nearly twenty performances—Adelaide felt that she was close to collapse. "I feel quite exhausted," she informed the Thuns, "and am incapable of any exertion, mental or bodily."

Throughout those weeks, her father was her loyal supporter. Without his experience and instruction, she could not have endured the hostile demonstrations, let alone have improved her stage technique. Although it pained her to see him, ill and anxious, shouldering her burdens, she sent up a prayer of thanks that at least she seemed to be succeeding. "My poor father has been neither well nor happy, as you may imagine," she wrote to the countess, "but *now* is satisfied—oh, if it had not been for him I do not think I *could* have gone through with it—but for his sake I felt I must make an effort, and thank God it has succeeded."

One suspects that she was feigning a confidence she did not really feel. When *Lucia* resumed after its recess, Strepponi was singing the lead. Adelaide had withdrawn "through illness," but whether she was more sick in heart than in body one does not know. In the end Charles took the step of paying Merelli a large sum to cancel the contract. "We should have considered ourselves happy," Adelaide concluded, "in regaining our freedom at any price."

After her failure in Milan, Adelaide was fortunate to pick up an engagement in Padua. She was even luckier to find the terms acceptable, for it was essential that she keep her prima donna status. As she was fond of explaining, the Italian operatic world was so thoroughly disreputable that every care had to be taken for a singer to remain untainted. To be "anything but *first* in the theatre is a terrible fate," she wrote, "not as regards amour propre—but what is more valuable—if one chooses as *first*, one may keep aloof from those one dislikes, but sinking into mediocrity, one becomes the companion of *all*."

In down-at-the-heels Padua, where grass grew high in the cracked streets and belligerent beggars crowded the squares, Adelaide longed for success. She sang the lead in the recently premiered *Elena da Feltre*, by the Italian composer Saverio Mercadante, whose work is remembered today as a bridge between florid Rossinian *bel canto* and the heavier, more dramatic style of Verdi. Though not a masterwork, its robust music caught her fancy. Less florid and more dramatic than the older operas, *Elena da Feltre* gave her ample scope to act and displayed all her talents.

As Adelaide's confidence grew, so did her stage presence. Though in the operas of her era, stage movements normally were subordinated to the physical demands of singing, her own experience and her father's tutoring helped her to strike the right balance. In a few years, critics in England would marvel that Adelaide could act so well, yet sing so exquisitely. As the months passed, she was becoming that rare combination—a first-class singer and a first-class actor.

The conservative Paduans did not share Adelaide's love of *Elena*. They dismissed the opera as dull, until Charles had a flash of inspiration. He persuaded the management to allow Adelaide to sing the florid cavatina from Pacini's *Niobe* during a change of scene. The effect was instantaneous. "Every night," Adelaide wrote, "when the scene changed and the public knew it was coming, I have had to wait nearly five minutes that the shouts of applause might subside a little before I made my appearance."

After rehearsing every day from midday to four o'clock, Adelaide performed the grueling *Elena* at night in the stifling July heat. Some days she ran a fever. "I know not indeed when I shall entirely recover," she wrote, "for they have had no mercy on me, but have made me sing well or ill every night but two when my fever confined me to my bed." One night she was so weak that she fainted after her first aria, but as soon as she recovered, the manager pushed her back onstage. The following day, when she should have been resting, she was obliged to rehearse until late afternoon and then perform in the evening. She did not reach her bed until half-past two in the morning, by which time she was utterly exhausted.

Adelaide was being worked to death, but she had to struggle on, because after the debacle at La Scala she was in no position to argue. When she eventually wrote to the Thuns after several months' silence—a sign in itself of her weakened state—she poured out her grievances. "I have no resources," she wrote, "in this odious southern country where everything is sensation—animal sensation—and where there is nothing either for the heart or intellect." She completed her season at Padua on August 4, by which time Charles was so concerned about her health that he insisted on adjourning to the hill city of Bergamo on the edge of the Alps, where the air was said to be healthier.

At picturesque Bergamo, with its squares and fountains, Adelaide grew so weak that she could not walk without help. She had spells of fainting and spitting blood, and the fear arose that she might have tuberculosis. Even the memory of Francis seemed to grow dim beside this possibility, because in those days tuberculosis was almost a death warrant. She could only pray that it was not so.

Since Adelaide's best chance lay in careful nursing, her aunt and father looked after her day and night. Victoire was a poor nurse—she tended to panic in the face of illness—so it was usually Charles who sat by Adelaide's bedside, sponging her forehead and giving her sips of water, though on some days he himself was almost too ill to leave his own bed. Adelaide was touched by her father's gentle care. In those weeks, many of the old wounds were healed, and many bonds strengthened, though some residual bitterness—the product of those years when Charles failed to defend Adelaide against her mother—would always remain.

With rest, quiet, and the aid of Charles's patient nursing, Adelaide's fever retreated, and the coughing stopped. Hope revived, and they began to believe that she would make a full recovery. As Adelaide grew stronger, she became hungry for news from home, and she reread the sparse letters that had arrived in Italy over the past months. Fanny had written, describing her visit to Pierce's plantations in Georgia, and her brother Henry had announced his engagement to Mary Ann Thackeray, a girl Adelaide knew and liked. Henry Greville wrote with the news that their friend Giovanni di Candia—renamed Mario—was singing successfully at the Paris Opera. Only Anna Jameson disappointed her. Having promised to come to Italy,

Anna sent the excuse that, since Adelaide had Victoire as a chaperone, there was no need for her company. Adelaide replied that, to the contrary, she very much needed Anna. To be shut up from morning to night with her little aunt irritated her nerves and wore out her spirits.

At the end of September, Adelaide felt strong enough to travel to Bologna, a city of brown churches and brick towers soaring crookedly into the sky; she almost expected to see the figure of Dante treading the ancient footways. Discovering that the composer Mercadante lived in Bologna, Charles had decided that Adelaide should study his operas with him, believing that this might help to restore her reputation with the impresarios. Adelaide herself applauded the plan until, reaching the city, she heard stories of the maestro's character. He was said to be so coarse and rude that she doubted if she wanted even one lesson from him. Charles reminded her that, after La Scala, she could not afford to be fastidious. In the end Adelaide took the lessons and was forced to admit that, as a result, she sang *Elena* more perceptively.

In November she prepared to take up an engagement in Mantua, a damp but lively city encircled by swamps and entered by a string of covered wooden bridges. There she endured twelve-hour rehearsals in an unheated theatre and was filled with anxiety in case her illness should return. She was delighted, however, to be singing the role of Elena. Her interpretation, sharpened by study with the composer, was one of the successes of that season, which almost made up for the months of worry and illness.

The past year had changed Adelaide beyond recognition. The shy, gawky girl who had struck attitudes and flung herself into passionate discourses had gone forever: the stresses of La Scala and Padua had made her decisive and self-assured. Physically she had changed, as well. After her illness, she put on much-needed weight. Most important, her attitude toward Francis had changed. She had so concentrated her thoughts on saving her health and career that his image had moved to the side of her mind. For the first time in three years, a large part of her mind was free of him.

Toward the end of the year, Adelaide learned that her brother John's visit to Italy had been as much about money as his father's health. John's only means of support was his editorship of *The British and Foreign Review*, which paid far too little to sustain a married man. Needing income, he came up with a clever scheme. He suggested that Charles should pass on to him the paid position of examiner of plays, thus relieving Charles of the embarrassment of being an absentee examiner and giving John the money he needed. Charles agreed to the transfer and in December 1839 set out for

London to hand over his authority, leaving Adelaide behind, with Victoire as her chaperone. Expecting to be away three months, Charles delayed for close to six, after Queen Victoria commanded four final theatrical performances from him. So absorbed was he in his brief return to the stage that he almost forgot his daughter, waiting patiently in Florence.

Knowing nothing of the queen's command, Adelaide went day after day to the post office, expecting a letter from her father. The letter did not arrive until April, at which time Adelaide had to visit Milan to negotiate contracts for the forthcoming year. She dreaded the task of negotiating without Charles, but it was a measure of her newfound ability that, all on her own, she secured a contract to sing at Palermo in Sicily in August. With considerable pride she showed her father the contract when he returned at last in May.

Freed from the worries of the past year, Adelaide's spirits soared. She, her aunt, and her father went sightseeing along the Mediterranean coast, to Sorrento, Naples, and Genoa. It was the beginning of Adelaide's long love affair with Italy. She adored the brightly colored houses perched on the sides of the cliffs, the pale stone churches with their gaudy saints, the pinks and reds of the oleander blossoms seen against the summer sky. So rapturously did she respond that she felt sure that the De Camps must have Italian blood. Henceforth she began to identify with all things Italian.

While Adelaide was in Genoa, her contract to sing in Palermo was purchased by the powerful impresario Domenico Barbaia, who proposed to employ her at his San Carlo Theatre in Naples. Though she voiced indignation at being the subject of underhanded maneuvering between Naples and Palermo, she was not really angry. San Carlo was one of the most respected opera houses in Europe: splendid to look at—"a symphony in silver," and, according to Stendhal, "the very fount and birthplace of fine singing." To have secured a contract to sing there was a decided coup. San Carlo was also the largest opera theatre in Europe, holding more than thirty-five hundred spectators, as well as a crowd of singers on its immense stage. Adelaide no longer feared vast spaces. Her voice had strengthened since her appearance at La Scala, and when she first stood onstage at San Carlo, she exulted that her voice so easily filled the auditorium.

The operas advertised for her first Neapolitan season were Bellini's *Norma* and *Beatrice di Tenda* and *Otello*, by Rossini. Two German sopranos were vying with Adelaide for the leads, a form of contest by then all too familiar. Madame Marray and Mademoiselle Pixis and their entourages were united in their hostility toward this English interloper. The ensuing maneuvers would have been amusing had they not been so ill-natured and irritating. Francilla Pixis resolved to sing Beatrice that season. Adelaide, by then wise in the ways of rivals, tactfully deferred to her and asked instead for the role of Norma. Pixis, at that point, decided *she* should sing Norma, notwithstanding that *Beatrice di Tenda* was to open five days later.

Adelaide did not mind taking over the role of Beatrice, though it called for constant study. "I learned the whole of that long part in *three* days," she boasted. "I came out in it and had a triumphant success." Her Desdemona in *Otello* was equally triumphant. The aria in which Desdemona placed her love for Otello above her duty to her father was "received with shouts," Adelaide informed Yuza Thun in a letter. Cryptically she added: "how it did make me think of poor Francis!"

When Adelaide eventually captured the part of Norma, she won loud praise. During one performance, her fans broke into wild cheering, too excited to observe etiquette and allow the royal family of Naples to lead the applause. To be cheered at San Carlo was a feather in any singer's cap, for the theatre's audiences were known to be among the most discriminating in Europe. Adelaide never ceased to be thankful that she had regained the ground she had lost at La Scala and had at last fulfilled her father's hopes. "My professional success has been all that we could wish," she wrote proudly, and "as it has been accomplished by honest means (God's good gifts and my own hard labor) I see no reason why it should not continue."

Singing with Adelaide at San Carlo was her former teacher from London, the bass Giovanni Cartagenova. He had used his influence on her behalf ever since her arrival in Italy, and her engagement at San Carlo probably owed something to his efforts. She was grateful to him for a further reason. On those days when her father was too ill to leave his bed, Cartagenova was happy to sit with him.

Adelaide hated to leave her father alone and did everything in her power to amuse him. As Charles passed most of the weary hours in reading, she scoured the city for English books, pouncing on a novel by Sir Walter Scott in a dim Neapolitan bookshop. The daytime heat was scorching, but in the cool of the evening, if she were free, and her father well enough, they would drive to the waterfront and sail in a boat for a refreshing hour to watch the smoking cone of Mt. Vesuvius. Adelaide could scarcely bear to see her father's weakness as he climbed into the boat and wished for his sake that he would go back to London. He "suffers constantly," she wrote, "and God knows has no pleasures, no intellectual resources to divert him from his pain—in England he has friends—the very stones of London are friends to him—People of all classes look pleased and smile at him as he passes, while here he meets with neither forbearance for what he is, nor respect for what he has been."

Adelaide's wish that Charles would return to London was at last granted. Late in 1840, his partial recovery and an enticing letter from Fanny in America persuaded him to go home. Fanny hoped to reach London before the end of the year, and Charles decided that he must be there to meet her. But he insisted that Adelaide should stay in Italy and fulfill her contract, which expired the following April. By that time Charles hoped Adelaide would have signed a subsequent contract to sing at San Carlo during the following year.

Bidding her father farewell, Adelaide thought longingly of home. She pictured Fanny arriving in London in a flurry of excitement, surrounded by children, nursemaids, and baggage, and knew that she must see her sister as soon as humanly possible. A little more than a month later, Adelaide's urge to go home turned into a firm resolve when a letter from John announced that their father lay gravely ill in London. "I have suffered unutterable agony," wrote Adelaide, "thinking how he must have longed for me."

Desperate to reach her father, Adelaide begged to be released from her contract, but her pleas fell on deaf ears. She was forced to spend a miserable Christmas, wondering each day if she would receive a black-edged letter announcing Charles's death. Finally a letter arrived—mercifully lacking a black edge—proclaiming that her father was out of danger. Adelaide was intensely relieved, but she had made up her mind. Refusing to renew her contract, she made plans to return to London the moment she was free.

9

"Like a Boiling Spring"

In the space of three years, Adelaide had made her opera debut, had had her heart broken, then had blossomed. But what of Fanny? Back in 1837, when Fanny said goodbye to Adelaide and her father as they began their journey from London to Carlsbad, she assumed that the family would soon be reunited. But Pierce had other plans. The sisters would not meet again for more than three years.

After Fanny said goodbye to her father and sister, she retired to the seaside town of Crosby, near Liverpool, to await her husband's arrival from America. Stormy weather delayed the ship, and as Fanny waited she had time to consider her lot. Her three years of marriage had been a merry-go-round of quarrels, reconciliations, short periods of calm, and more quarrels. "I am not patient of restraint or submissive to authority," she had told Harriet eight years before, and she had spoken the truth. Most of her quarrels with Pierce were about her liberty and his right to curtail it. "Pierce," she would protest, "upon what ground should you exercise this control over me. . . . Is it because you are more enlightened, more intellectual? You know that is not so." What Fanny increasingly longed for was a marriage where a husband and wife were friends and equals—a type of partnership.

Fanny's idea of marriage stemmed largely from her unusual upbringing. In the world of the theatre, married women were entitled to continue their acting careers, and husbands and wives often formed working partnerships. Before her were the examples of her Aunt Sarah Siddons and her husband-manager William Siddons, and her own parents and grandparents; and in each of these marriages the wife had been an equal, if not dominant, partner. Fanny knew that, in the eyes of the general public, and in the eyes of Pierce in particular, her desire for equality was untenable, but a position of equality seemed the only remedy for her unhappiness.

Fanny still held high hopes of winning ascendancy over Pierce. She

< 143 >

knew the force of her personality and the weakness of his; and she was familiar, thanks to her mother, with the principles of wifely negotiation through tirades. Marie Thérèse had spent her married life using emotional scenes to snare and ambush the love and attention she craved from Fanny's straying father. Fanny seems to have believed that she could win the freedom and equality she demanded from Pierce by similar tactics. They appealed to the combative side of her character and were tactics that suited her theatrical skills.

IN ALLOWING FANNY to visit England without him, Pierce had foolishly hoped that a temporary separation would soften her. Before sailing to bring her home, he appears to have probed her feelings by letter, asking if absence had not strengthened their ties and weakened her urge for independence. Her answer was a qualified no. While admitting that she loved him and was prepared to be dutiful, she also affirmed that she rejoiced in her liberty. As she had been away for almost a year, acting successfully as the guardian of his daughter and the steward of his money—in all but name a totally independent agent—Fanny asked Pierce to acknowledge, at least in principle, her right and ability to live a life of her own. To a modern reader this sounds just, but to Pierce it was heretical. According to his belief, a wife was always subject to her husband's will, and anyone who persisted in holding contrary ideas was plainly wrong.

When Pierce's storm-battered ship finally docked in Liverpool in August 1837, he told Fanny that he had promised to attend a political convention in America and could spare little more than a week in England before returning home with her. There was an excited reunion, during which they realized how much they had missed one another. Stirred by so many months of separation, their sexual passion ran high. Exactly nine months later, their second daughter was born.

Fanny sailed for America reluctantly. She was deeply disappointed that she could not join Charles and Adelaide at Carlsbad, and she had mixed feelings about the life that lay ahead of her at Butler Place. To make matters worse, the voyage across the Atlantic was so rough that she lay on her bunk for most of the thirty-seven days, almost too ill to raise her head. She informed Harriet that she arrived in America more like "a ghost than a living creature."

Pregnant and unwell, Fanny settled down to face the winter in Butler Place. After the liveliness of England, she felt her isolation. Six miles of poor roads—muddy quagmires in winter and sandpits in summer—separated her from Philadelphia, and she had few visitors. Even if the city had been closer and visiting easier, she still may have felt lonely, for few residents in the city—which by then held more than a hundred fifty thousand people—had the leisure to form a social circle. "There is no rich and idle class here," she explained to Harriet. "The persons I should like to cultivate are professionally engaged." They "have no time, and, it seems, but little taste, for social enjoyment." One of the few exceptions was Thomas Sully, the eminent Philadelphia portrait painter. Born in England of actor parents, and a former student of Thomas Lawrence, his background was so like Fanny's that they immediately took to one another, and he painted several portraits of her. "He is a great friend of mine," she told Harriet, "and one of the few people here that I find pleasure in associating with." Alas, Sully was visiting England at the very time Fanny longed for his company.

Through November and December, the contrast between Fanny's English and American lives was sharply brought home to her. "My whole life here," she wrote, "passes in trifling activities, and small recurring avocations." During a typical day, she would supervise the servants, take the dogs for a walk, practice the piano for an hour, and watch little Sarah play. Boredom and frustration were draining her energy at such a rate that she had no inclination for serious study. She picked away at a play she had started to write in England: a successor, she hoped, to *Francis I*, which had done well when it had eventually been published and staged. But inspiration seemed to have deserted her. "I read less, write less, study little, plan no work and accomplish none," she told Harriet: "all things tend to check any utterance of my thoughts, spoken or written; and while in England I could not find time enough to write, I here have no desire to do so."

A little more than a month after arriving home, Fanny received a letter from Anna Jameson, asking permission to stay with the Butlers. Anna's estranged husband was the attorney general of Upper Canada, and Anna had been visiting him in the vain hope of a reconciliation. Though Fanny was sympathetic to her friend's troubles, she responded without much enthusiasm. Once her guest arrived, however, she pulled herself together and put on such a brave front that Anna was impressed. In a gushing letter to her confidante, Ottilie von Goethe (the German poet's daughter-in-law), Anna reported that Fanny Kemble was "brimful of genius, poetry and power and eloquence, yet is an excellent wife, an excellent mother, and an excellent manager of a household." She added that she liked "Pierce Butler very much—more than I expected." Not for a moment did Anna guess that Fanny was concealing her deteriorating marriage under a lively exterior.

One event, unwished for, did arouse Fanny from lethargy. In the first days of 1838, two-year-old Sarah caught scarlet fever. A month later she underwent an operation for an enlarged tonsil. Doctors slid a double-barreled silver tube down her throat, looped the tonsil with a tight wire, and left the apparatus in place for twenty-four hours for the tonsil to rot away. Fanny, who did not trust doctors, looked on with horror. "The medical mode of treatment in this country," she commented, "appears to me frightfully severe." When Sarah recovered quickly, Fanny was intensely relieved but rather surprised.

In the final weeks of pregnancy, Fanny's boredom and frustration blazed into anger. Goaded by cross words from Pierce and unable to bear her home a moment longer, she ran away and ended up staying with Pierce's brother John and his wife in Philadelphia. From there she issued an ultimatum. While Pierce had been kind to her, she said, it had been possible to endure the boredom; but now that he was cross and rude, she was no longer prepared to do so. Instead she would return to England, and she would sell her watch and chain to pay the fare if he refused to pay it for her. She promised to send the baby back to him once it was born.

Pierce, in some alarm, hurried to Philadelphia to bring her home, believing that at least some of her ill-humor was caused by pregnancy. But he was also aware that not all could be blamed on the approaching baby. He was at last beginning to see a pattern to Fanny's outbursts. He said it was as though "a boiling spring" bubbled inside her, reaching its zenith when they were "most together and alone." Every few months the spring would boil over, and Fanny would shout and rage and say she wished to leave him. If the outburst was extreme, she would actually leave home. Gradually, after three or four days, the shouting would subside, and the spring would simmer quietly—until the next time. As far as Pierce could see, there was no basis in fact for Fanny's outbursts. Her talk of loneliness and boredom was nonsense. She lived a life no different from scores of other women of his acquaintance. If they could be happy, why could not she?

As Pierce had half predicted, Fanny's mood brightened. She returned to Butler Place and on May 28, 1838, gave birth to her second child. The baby was born on her sister's third birthday, almost to the hour: "a striking instance of my love of system and regularity," joked Fanny, who could not have been prouder of her new daughter. The little girl was named Frances after her mother, but was usually called Fan, the name by which Fanny had been known in childhood.

Fanny was unwell after the baby's birth, suffering once again from depression. She also suffered from a "painful and exhausting indisposition," which was probably hemorrhoids. To add to her burdens, the weather was hot, Pierce became rheumatic, and little Sarah caught measles. While the outside temperature rose to ninety-four degrees in the shade, Fanny sat at Sarah's bedside in a darkened room, giving soothing answers to the child's feverish flow of questions. So desolate did Fanny feel that she informed Harriet that she was considering severing all ties with absent loved ones, simply to save herself the pain of contrasting her present despair with her past joy.

In her low mood, Fanny agonized over Adelaide's decision to go on the stage, news of which had reached her a month or so before. It was an unwise decision, Fanny felt sure. She enlarged at some length upon her various objections to a public life, which centered, as might have been expected, on her belief in the addictive effect of performing on the performer. Fanny predicted that Adelaide would not be happy. But Fanny's viewpoint was changeable, and writing to Harriet some weeks later, she made a moving profession of faith in Adelaide's ability to succeed. "Her voice haunts me," she wrote, "like something precious that I have lost and go vainly seeking for; other people play and sing her songs, and then, though I seem to listen to them, I hear *her* again, and seem to see again that wonderful human soul which beamed from every part of her fine face as she uttered those powerful sweet spells of love, and pity, and terror. To me, her success seems almost a matter of certainty; for those who can make such appeals to the sympathy of their fellow-beings are pretty sure not to fail."

Troubles had so crowded in on her over the past year that there were probably times when Fanny would gladly have exchanged her life at Butler Place for the chance to stand upon a stage again. But as Pierce's wife, the theatre was barred to her. One consolation for her was the society of people who recognized her worth and were prepared to allow her to be herself. Her thoughts turned to the few friends who had given her mental companionship since she arrived in America.

The circles Fanny frequented in England had accustomed her to the companionship of people possessing intelligence, vivacity, good breeding, and education. They were rare qualities in any society, and Fanny had despaired of finding them in America—until, on her second trip to New York, she met Catharine Sedgwick, a devout spinster with a sharp mind and a sweet, simple manner, who was regarded by many as the best female novelist in America. Responding immediately to Catharine's warmth and insight, Fanny quickly became Catharine's friend, and the friend of

Catharine's lawyer brothers, Theodore and Charles. As her problems threatened to overwhelm her, Fanny longed to see the Sedgwicks and regain her sense of identity.

For once Pierce was sympathetic to Fanny's wishes, because he approved of the patrician Sedgwicks. Of more immediate concern was young Sarah's health. Convalescing from measles, the child needed a seaside holiday; and in the first week in August, the Butlers set out for the popular resort of Rockaway Beach on Long Island, where Fanny fell in love with the "ten miles of hard sparkling sand, and the broad open Atlantic rolling its long waves in one white thunderous cloud." But though she loved the sea and sunshine—becoming as sunburnt as a gypsy—and rejoiced to see the roses return to Sarah's cheeks, Fanny had a catalogue of grievances. She disapproved of the wooden barn of a hotel, whose bedrooms were "furnished barely as well as a common servant's room in England." She detested undressing in a communal female dressing room, and she hated strangers staring at her clinging bathing dress. When, after two weeks, they traveled to New York so that Pierce could consult doctors about his rheumatism, Fanny burst into a tirade against "doctors, leeches and medicine," all of which, she believed, were keeping her from her Sedgwicks. She was not happy until she and the children boarded a Hudson River steamer bound for Albany, on the first leg of their journey to western Massachusetts.

The extended Sedgwick family lived a hundred miles to the west of Boston, in adjacent villages among the rolling Berkshire hills. Catharine owned a house—still standing—in the idyllic village of Stockbridge, and her brother Charles and his family lived in equally idyllic Lenox. It was to Lenox, with its classical wooden houses and steepled church set high on a hill, that Fanny and her children came in the coach from Albany. She had grown to love loyal, upright Charles and his sweet-natured wife Elizabeth, who kept a girls' school called The Hive near the top of Lenox Hill. The Sedgwicks' companionable marriage inspired Fanny with the belief that such a relationship was possible; and their "rich minds and noble hearts" provided that sense of family for which the Kemble girls always longed. What the Thun family was to Adelaide, the Sedgwicks became to Fanny. And just as Adelaide drew strength from the blue hills of Bohemia, Fanny drew strength from this corner of Massachusetts. She never tired of the view from the hilltop at Lenox. Standing at the highest point, she looked down first into a small valley, whose center was studded by a jewel of a lake, ringed by a thicket of trees. Lifting her eyes, Fanny saw the wooded summits of the Berkshires, rising one above the other to the edge of the horizon, topped by the jagged crest of Monument Mountain. In September the mountains were wreathed in swirls of fine white mist: as exquisite a sight as any she believed she could ever see.

The Red Inn at Lenox, home to the Sedgwicks' guests, housed not only Fanny, her daughters, and nursemaid, but also the teenage sisters Mary and Frances Appleton. This was the same Frances Appleton who had visited the Kembles in London and penned a breathless description of a soirée at Park Place. She painted an equally breathless picture of Fanny's life in Lenox. The day at the Red Inn began at nine, when the guests appeared for breakfast, Fanny attired in her dressing gown. After breakfast, Fanny would breast-feed the baby, then change into her riding habit: a black velvet jacket and cap and wide white riding skirt, under which she wore a man's trousers. The costume was deliciously daring, because it was deemed improper for a woman to wear trousers, even under a skirt. Once dressed, Fanny and the Appleton girls would ride or walk with their Sedgwick hosts to sites of natural beauty, which never failed to send them into raptures. In the evening the guests would gather at Charles Sedgwick's house, with Fanny dressed in a short-sleeved, low-necked muslin gown, however cold the weather. Fanny was always eager to sing old ballads and read aloud, and dance wild Spanish *cachuchas*. Fanny herself described the same activities to Anna Jameson more modestly: "We laugh and we talk, sing, play, dance and discuss; we ride, drive, walk, run, scramble, and saunter, and amuse ourselves extremely with little materials."

The circle around the Sedgwicks was socially progressive and quietly radical. Disciples of the celebrated Unitarian minister William Ellery Channing of Boston, they devoted much of their time to the intellectual, social, and moral advancement of their fellow beings. They were especially concerned with the emancipation of slaves and the emancipation of women, seeing—as many other people did—a parallel between the two forms of enslavement. The Sedgwicks' work toward the emancipation of slaves was as personal as it was altruistic. A slave named Mumbet had cared for Catharine and her brothers as children, when their mother lost her reason, and Mumbet had become their much-loved foster mother. However analytical the Sedgwicks' discussions of slavery, their debt to Mumbet was never far from their minds.

The crusade against slavery had begun to snowball in evangelical circles in the North just before Fanny's arrival in America. The year 1831 had witnessed the founding by William L. Garrison of the influential abolitionist journal *The Liberator*, followed shortly thereafter by the Slavery Abolition Society of Massachusetts. But even as antislavery forces were grouping for battle, the slave owners were also gathering strength, for they were selling increasing amounts of cotton to the factories of northern England. The Sedgwicks and their friends, being realists, were not so foolish as to believe that the antislavery cause would win an easy victory. Nor were they unsympathetic to Fanny's position, freely acknowledging that she owed a loyalty to Pierce's slave-owning family. At the same time they did not hesitate to discuss the question openly in her company. It was they who gave Fanny an articulate and vigorous viewpoint on the twin questions of women's rights and slavery.

Among the woods and hills of Lenox, Fanny no sooner regained her sense of well-being than it was snatched away. She received a letter from Emily Fitzhugh, which broke the news that Marie Thérèse had died on September 3. Fanny was shocked, but also surrounded by consoling friends. Writing to Anna Jameson, she exclaimed how fortunate she was to be in Lenox when she received the news, for there, among the Sedgwicks, she was supported by those "whom good fortune has raised up in this strange country to fill for me the place of the kindred and friends from whom I am widely sundered."

When Fanny returned from Lenox to lonely Butler Place, her spirits were at their lowest. "My heart," she wrote, "which certainly has found no home here, forever yearns most painfully after those early ties which it renounced for a residence in a strange country." Depression engulfed her. The disputes with Pierce, which had previously been angry, grew bitter. She accused him of never having been her friend. A marriage without companionship grew empty, she told him. Without companionship, passion waned and perished.

Later Pierce would retell the episode to show himself in a favorable light, but there can be little doubt that he failed to give Fanny the emotional support she needed. Hardened to her moods, he cut himself off from her, traveling increasingly to Philadelphia and staying away for several days at a time. He attempted to justify his absences by saying that she was always more cheerful when he was away.

While Pierce was in Philadelphia, Fanny not only failed to display the cheerfulness his absence was said to provide but was so depressed that she set out on paper the details of her misery. She described the barrenness and boredom of an existence in which her only regular companions were two infants and a nursemaid. She contrasted this with the richness of her life in England, reminding Pierce that she had broken the thread "of all former intimacies, friendships and affections" in order to marry him and stay in America. At the end of the letter, Fanny introduced a new grievance: her need for money. As a married woman, she was financially dependent on her husband, her only income being the small dress allowance Pierce gave her each quarter. If she overspent, she was forced to beg for more, which was humiliating because Pierce did not part with money readily. Having the means within herself—as very few other women had—of earning a substantial income, this financial dependency was particularly detestable to her. "These considerations," she ended her letter bitterly, "and the conviction that though my companionship is no source of pleasure to you, my conduct is frequently of annoyance, induce me to propose that we may henceforth live apart; my discontents will then no longer vex you, nor the restraints to which I am now subject, gall and irritate me."

There were elements of self-dramatization in Fanny's words, but also a deeper earnestness than in her previous letters. Instead of firing off an attention-seeking broadside, she produced an ordered argument. Pierce seems to have noticed the difference and felt that he must make a gesture. He offered Fanny a sweetener. To ease her loneliness, he proposed to take her and the children when he traveled during the coming winter to visit his property in Georgia. He seems to have believed that he was making a wise concession. In fact, he was making one of the unwisest decisions of his life.

10

"Ever Your Own Wife"

In 1836 Pierce's maiden aunt died, and those properties that had been held in trust under the terms of Major Butler's will at last came into his possession. Pierce now owned Butler Place, the adjacent farm, and two rice and cotton plantations on islands off the coast of Georgia—estates that were among the most productive in the region and worked by one of the largest teams of slaves in America. Though he enjoyed being the possessor of vast wealth, Pierce was forced to admit that the plantations were too much for one man to manage. He therefore divided that part of his inheritance with his brother John, and henceforth he or his brother spent part of each winter—when malaria was absent from the marshes—down on the islands, superintending the plantations.

Like most educated and religious English women of her time, Fanny disapproved of slavery. She emphasized that, in a woman of her upbringing, "the absence of such a prejudice would be disgraceful." Even so, she had shown a certain ambivalence in her attitude toward slavery during her earliest years in America. While part of her deplored the keeping of slaves, she had married Pierce probably knowing that a large part of his family's wealth came from slave labor. It was only in the first months of marriage, when she was stung by Pierce's authoritarianism, that her distaste for slave-owners blazed into active hatred. During the quarrels over the preparation of her American *Journal*, she proposed adding a "long and vehement treatise against Negro slavery" to the end of the book. She might have done so if Pierce had not expressly forbidden it, invoking a justification which even Fanny accepted—that it would expose them all to the danger of being torched by pro-slavery fanatics.

A year or so later, when Fanny came to know the Sedgwicks well, she was drawn readily into their discussions about slavery. She had always had the urge to fight for a cause, and antislavery was a cause that stood right on

< 152 >

her doorstep. As her reasoned arguments took shape, Pierce's relatives took fright. Ironically, it was the very church the Butlers attended that strengthened Fanny's stance.

On her marriage, Fanny had been expected to go with Pierce's family to the First Unitarian Church in Philadelphia; to her surprise, its doctrines and its minister, the Reverend William Henry Furness, won her over. Furness was a forthright preacher against slavery, and so was Catharine Sedgwick's friend, the brightest of Boston Unitarian luminaries, William Ellery Channing, whom Fanny met on a visit to Boston. Channing was no red-hot abolitionist but a quiet advocate of the gradual emancipation of slaves, a view he expressed persuasively in his book *Slavery and Emancipation.* Fanny came to view his benign message as irresistible. Under the first flush of Channing's spell, she longed to go to Georgia in the hope of ameliorating the excesses of slavery on the Butler plantations. She developed a vision of black rehabilitation, with herself as the chief rehabilitator. Teaching by exhortation and example, she hoped to live among the enslaved workers and set up a model community. She would pay them wages, teaching them how to save and how to use their leisure. On those slaves who showed aptitude she would confer a "freedom, prosperous to themselves, and safe to the community."

For a time she saw this as the special task to which God had called her. "You do not know how profoundly this subject interests me and engrosses my thoughts," she informed Harriet St. Leger. When a troubled Harriet questioned whether this "doing good" in remote Georgia was a suitable crusade for the mother of a child—and, though Harriet did not say it, for the wife of a slave-owner—Fanny answered passionately: "you must remember *we are slave-owners,* and live by slave labor, and if the question of slavery does not concern us, in God's name whom does it concern?"

In her crusading spirit Fanny begged Pierce to let her accompany him to Georgia on his winter visit in December 1836. He refused, cannily explaining that the accommodation was poor and that the climate was unhealthy for young Sarah. Since the health and safety of her child came first, Fanny had no grounds for argument. In compensation Pierce suggested she should visit her family in England.

On the eve of his seasonal trip to the plantation in November 1838, Pierce viewed the situation differently. Troubled by Fanny's depressed mood, he brushed aside his past excuses and actually proposed that his wife and the children accompany him. Fanny was bewildered by his change of heart, and even more bewildered by the excuse he gave to explain his change of mind. Pierce said that, by seeing slavery at firsthand, Fanny would realize that it was a "benevolent institution." The likelihood that Fanny would change her views was remote, to say the least; nevertheless she jumped at the chance. She was eager to investigate the daily life of the slaves and discover for herself the truth about slavery. In her gratitude she even promised Pierce that she would go with an open mind, "prepared to find many mitigations in the practice to the general injustice and cruelty of the system."

Once the decision was made, Fanny began to fear the months that lay ahead. Pierce warned her that conditions on the plantation would be primitive, and the thought of spending the winter with two small children, seven hundred slaves, and an alligator—as she dryly told Anna Jameson—was anything but reassuring. Also, for reasons best known to himself, Pierce decided to travel, not by the direct sea route, but overland as far as Wilmington, North Carolina. In deciding to travel almost half of the way by land, he was exposing his wife and children to long hours in railway cars, stagecoaches, and river steamers, with many exhausting delays. To Fanny, who was still breast-feeding the baby and still suffering from hemorrhoids, it must have seemed a particularly thoughtless choice.

Five days before Christmas, 1838, the Butler party set out. It comprised Pierce, Fanny, the children, their faithful nursemaid, Margery O'Brien, and a female Butler relative who was traveling with them as far as Charleston. Fanny was apprehensive as they boarded the train, and her apprehension grew as she took her seat. She hated confined and airless spaces, and the fumes from the coal-burning stove that heated the carriage made her short of breath. A dispute with fellow passengers over whether she might open a window left her angry and overwrought. Only when she and the children were re-seated in an unheated and half-empty carriage did she feel well and calm again.

Fortunately, as they approached Baltimore, Fanny's mood lightened. There they boarded a bay steamer to convey them to Portsmouth, Virginia, and Fanny comforted herself in her cramped bunk by reading *Oliver Twist*, silently blessing Mr. Dickens for the pleasure of his story. Despite a dispute with the black stewardess over a lack of clean towels, Fanny was responding to the challenge of the adventure.

Arriving in Portsmouth, Fanny's first sight of slaves awakened her investigating ardor. She recorded their appearance with care. "They were poorly clothed; looked horribly dirty; and had a lazy recklessness in their air and manner," which, she believed, came from a lack of those responsibilities "which are the honorable burden of rational humanity." Fanny's ardor was short-lived. At Portsmouth they stepped aboard another stuffy train to travel through a vast black swamp and endless tracks of pine forest. The countryside seemed to her "like some blasted region lying under an enchanter's hand."

From Weldon in the pine woods—where they halted to change trains and eat a nauseating meal—they traveled until the early hours of the morning, when suddenly they were shaken awake in order to alight and join a stagecoach. It followed roads so rough that the travelers feared at every moment they would be thrown onto the ground. "The horrors of that night's journey," Fanny informed Harriet, "I shall not easily forget . . . I expected every moment that we must be overturned."

After many hours the coach at last halted at Stantonsborough. Both Fanny and the baby were acutely uncomfortable, the baby from hunger and she from an oversupply of milk; for modesty forbade her to breast-feed her child in the presence of strangers. The lack of opportunity to feed the baby was just one of the many miseries of the journey.

The local inn at Stantonsborough—like all the others along the way—was comfortless. When Fanny asked for a tumbler of water in which to wash her teeth and a clean towel on which to dry her hands, she was refused. When she asked for milk, she was served a glass so grimy and milk so sour that she could not drink it. In the rough dining room the food was "so begrimed with smoke, and powdered with cinders and full of unutterable-looking things that I felt as if one should never swallow food again," she told Harriet. She was particularly distressed by the foulness of the meals, because she needed wholesome food and drink to make milk for the baby.

Another day and a sleepless night lay ahead of them. Ten miles outside the township of Waynesborough, they left the stagecoach to join a train—which failed to arrive. After some hours shivering at the primitive siding, the women and children were sent in an abandoned rail truck to a nearby farmhouse. "I don't know that ever in my life I felt so desolate as during that half hour's progress," Fanny recalled. The farmhouse turned out to be a tumble-down shanty, but at least it provided shelter, and its gallant host was amusing: an old colonel who claimed to have fought with George Washington. Fanny enjoyed his flirtations, though she was shocked to discover that the "sable damsels" who served the meal were his own daughters.

Rejoining the train, the party limped into Wilmington, North Carolina, at five in the morning. Fanny snatched a few hours' sleep on a hard mattress on the floor of the hotel. This, she observed acidly, "is a place I could sooner die than live in." It was a pleasure that afternoon to board a seagoing boat and collapse into a clean bunk. On Christmas Day they steamed into the civilization of Charleston Harbor.

Fanny loved Charleston. Unlike the other American cities she had seen, it seemed old. It reminded her of Southampton in England, and the thought of home brought "refreshment and rest" to her spirit. She was less impressed by the city's nightly curfew, signaled by tolling bells, beating drums, and a militia patrol: a precaution, she was told, against an insurrection of the slaves. Her wry response was that "these daily and nightly precautions" were surely "trifling drawbacks upon the manifold blessings of slavery."

At Charleston they boarded another boat and chugged through yellow marshes to Savannah, where they joined a smaller craft that crept along low, reedy swamps. Disembarking at Darien, the tiny mainland port that connected Pierce's island plantations to the outside world, they had only two more sea miles to travel, and the boat from the Butler plantations waited to carry them onward. On December 30, 1838, after ten days of traveling and "considerable suffering and heart-achings," they finally came to rest on the muddy shore of Butler's Island.

At the wharf a crowd of slaves waited to greet the newcomers, jumping, dancing, shouting, laughing, and clapping their hands, and "using the most extravagant and ludicrous gesticulations to express their ecstasy" at their master's return. As the Butlers stepped ashore they were seized, pulled, pushed, carried, dragged, and all but lifted into the air. To Fanny's overwrought spirit, it was a fantastic—and ironic—welcome. Poor creatures, she thought, so this is how they bless their captors!

The Butlers' new home, as Fanny soon discovered, was nothing but an enormous mud bank covering several thousand acres, lying low in the marshy mouth of the Altamaha River. Its surface was crisscrossed by irrigation channels and ditches serving the watery rice fields of the Butler plantation. Fanny could scarcely find dry land to walk on: "a duck, an eel, or a frog," she wrote, "might live here in Paradise." Fanny felt overwhelmed by the eternity of water. Nor had Pierce lied when he said that their house was primitive. It was a "strange, bare, wooden walled sort of shanty" of six poky rooms, which they were obliged to share with the overseer and swarms of centipedes.

Nonetheless, in those first weeks Fanny began to revel in the warm January days, the bright yellow sunlight, the exotic chatter of the slaves, and the trees covered with grey mosses that hung from the branches like disheveled hair. "The strangeness of this existence surprises me afresh every hour," she informed Harriet, but it did not seem to deter her. Having overcome the hardships of the journey, her spirits soared. She was gripped by the prospect of seeing slavery in its true colors, and this emotion carried her along.

Before leaving Philadelphia Fanny had read a book, written in the form of letters, by the English novelist Monk Lewis, describing a visit to the slave plantations of the West Indies. With Lewis's book as her model, she decided to write regularly to Elizabeth Sedgwick, detailing what she had seen and done. When the letters were completed she would fashion them into a journal, though whether her work would see the light of day was another matter. She had no power to order its publication: that was a question that only Pierce could decide.

While Fanny tried to look on slavery with an open mind, she soon formed the conclusion that the degraded condition of the slaves was almost entirely the fault of their white masters. The slaves were so downtrodden that they had lost all will to foster intelligence or self-respect. They "cry aloud," Fanny wrote to Harriet, "for instruction and the means of progress and development."

With the zeal of an investigative reporter, Fanny set out to inspect the slave camp. The first cabin she entered contained five ragged children, aged between five and ten, nursing babies on their laps. "To these hardly human little beings," she addressed herself, "bidding the elder boys and girls kindle the fire, sweep the floor, and expel the poultry." When they ignored her, Fanny started to do it herself, and they began to laugh and imitate her. Believing ardently in what she was doing, she refused to be deterred. She was attempting to teach them self-respect.

Over the following weeks Fanny visited the camp again and again, and made the mothers and children her particular duty. The women were forced to labor from dawn to dark in the rice fields, leaving their newborn babies in the care of older children. Fanny exploded with maternal anger every time she saw these "filthy, wretched, almost naked, always barelegged and barefooted children" and their "negligent, ignorant, wretched mothers, whose apparent indifference to the plight of their offspring, and the utter incapacity to alter it, are the inevitable result of their slavery." It became Fanny's special task to instruct the mothers and older children in the art of mothering.

Fanny enjoyed proving that she was not an aloof lady but an able-bodied woman unafraid of physical work. She enjoyed striding into a slave cabin, flinging open the windows, tucking up her skirts, and seizing a broom to sweep down the walls and floor. She did not mind rolling up her sleeves, donning an apron, and bathing a baby covered with lice. She particularly objected to the practice of swaddling newborn babies in red flannel and covering their heads with suffocating woolen caps. Fanny went around confiscating "sundry refractory baby caps," and she would sit for hours of an evening, cutting and sewing layettes to replace the red flannel bindings. By a combination of stern commands, nagging, and bribing—for she was not above bribing the older children with pennies and the mothers with food—she eventually saw progress.

Heartened by her success with the mothers and babies, she turned her attention to the infirmary. There women lay in rows on the earthen floor like beasts, without even the comfort of a pillow. Some were rheumatic, some malarial, some had miscarried, some were in labor. "I stood in the midst of them," she informed Elizabeth Sedgwick, "perfectly unable to speak, the tears pouring from my eyes." To Emily Fitzhugh she wrote, "I spent three hours and a half there, cleaning with my own hands the filthy room where the sick lay, and washing and dressing poor little nearly new-born Negro babies." She wished with all her heart that she had studied practical nursing instead of such useless subjects as music and dancing. The best Fanny could do was to visit the patients regularly and to nag Pierce for medical supplies and a better building. In the end, by dint of pestering, she won an enlarged and refurnished infirmary.

Inspired by her genuine compassion, the slave women began to unburden themselves to her. Fanny heard a flood of harrowing medical histories: accounts of near-fatal miscarriages, childbirths, and dead and deformed children. Sometimes the women would strip off their clothes and show her the evidence—she had never seen such twisted bodies. Not that Fanny was surprised, for she knew how hard they worked. Though the slaves' daily tasks were lightened during pregnancy and canceled for a month after childbirth, slave women were worked thereafter like "human hoeing machines," without any care for their physical welfare.

News of Fanny's sympathy spread around the island. She was swamped with petitions for food and clothing and lighter duties. "I really never was so busy in all my life as I am here," she wrote to Elizabeth Sedgwick: "I sit at the receipt of custom . . . from morning till night—no time, no place, affords me a respite from my innumerable petitioners; and whether I be asleep or awake, reading, eating or walking—in the kitchen, my bedroom or the parlor, they flock in with urgent entreaties and pitiful stories, and my conscience forbids my ever postponing their business for any other matter; for, with shame and grief of heart I say it, by their unpaid labor I live."

Fanny's nursing of the sick and caring for the children had a precedent: various owners' wives cared for slaves in this way. When she lobbied the overseer to assign lighter work to some of the female slaves, however, she was on shakier ground. This was deemed to be none of her business. Though Fanny had been led to believe that flogging was rare on the Butler estates, she learned that several women had been flogged for seeking her help. When she complained to Pierce, he refused to listen. Having consulted the overseer, he insisted that the slaves' punishment was unrelated to their petitions—which Fanny refused to believe—and that the rules of the plantation must be upheld.

Fanny retorted by speaking feelingly of the "brutal inhumanity of allowing a man to strip and lash a woman." Surely, she insisted, this must "be abhorrent to any manly or humane man." Pierce, however, refused to be drawn and brushed her words aside. All he would allow was that it was "*disagreeable.*" Her husband's reply filled Fanny with doubt. It seemed possible that Pierce was not a humane man.

One of the cruelest practices of slavery was the custom of splitting up and selling away members of the same family, and Fanny had been given to understand that this never took place on the Butler plantations. She was consequently disturbed to be approached one morning by Psyche, the nursery slave, begging to know who owned her. The girl feared that she might be the property of Pierce's departing overseer, who was moving to Alabama. If this were so, Psyche and her children would be forced to go to Alabama and leave behind her husband, Joe, who was owned by Pierce. Making inquiries, Fanny was relieved to learn that the incoming overseer had just bought Psyche, and that the family would be staying at Butler Island.

Early next morning Fanny heard loud voices in the room next to her own. A cry of despair caused her to fling open the door and look inside. There she saw Psyche's husband, Joe, in a frenzy, wringing his hat in his hands and insisting to Pierce "in a voice broken with sobs and almost inarticulate with passion," that he would never leave his wife and children. Pierce, lounging nonchalantly with folded arms, was not in the least moved. He simply told Joe not to "make a fuss about what there was no help for."

Fanny did not ask Pierce what was happening and whether he did, in fact, plan to send Joe away. She was too upset to face his answer. Instead she fled from the room, and with a pounding heart inquired elsewhere. She learned that Pierce wished to present a token of his thanks to the overseer bound for Alabama and that Joe was his gift. In other words, Psyche would have to stay as a slave on the Butler plantation, but her husband would go permanently to Alabama.

The discovery planted a sickening doubt in Fanny's mind. What was Pierce's motive in parting with Joe? If Pierce had decided some time ago to part with Joe so that he could go with Psyche and her children to Alabama, then Pierce was a compassionate man. But what if Pierce had decided to give Joe away *after* Psyche had been rescued from the need to go to Alabama? In that case Pierce was callously splitting up the family for his own convenience. Having observed his arrogance that morning in the office, it was not difficult for Fanny to believe that Pierce may have made a gift of Joe for his own selfish reasons. At the same time she clung to the hope that he had acted generously and selflessly to protect the slave family: "you will easily imagine," she wrote to Elizabeth Sedgwick, "which of the two cases I prefer believing."

Fanny went to Pierce and entreated him "for his own soul's sake, not to commit so great a cruelty" as to send Joe away. She harnessed all her histrionic talents: "how I cried," she told Elizabeth Sedgwick, "and how I adjured, and how all my sense of justice, and of mercy, and of pity for the poor wretch, and of wretchedness at finding myself implicated in such a state of things broke in torrents of words from my lips and tears from my eyes!" She obtained no confession from Pierce about his motive, but his silence seems to have strengthened her fear that he had acted callously. She wrote in her journal that the realization that her own husband could "commit such an act was a new and terrible experience" for her.

Pierce was seemingly unmoved by Fanny's plea, and for the rest of the day he studiously ignored her. Fanny was inconsolable. "I think," she wrote, "for the first time, almost a sense of horrible personal responsibility and implication took hold of my mind, and I felt the weight of unimagined guilt upon my conscience." Her instinct was to disown all her husband's actions as a slave-owner. Thereafter she always proclaimed that she had married Pierce without any knowledge that his family owned slaves.

That night the new overseer came to sit with her in her primitive parlor. Haltingly she asked him what had happened to Joe. To her unspeakable relief, she was told that Joe had been reprieved. The departing overseer did not want to own a slave who was "kicking up a fuss," and had handed him back to Pierce. So, for the moment, Psyche's family was safe.

All the next day Fanny thought of ways of raising money so that she could buy Psyche and her children, thus enabling them to live permanently on the Butler estates. She thought longingly of her days as a well-paid actress, when she had access to large sums. In the evening she confided her plans to the overseer and begged him to sell Psyche and her children to nobody but herself. He replied that she was too late: they were no longer his. He had sold them to Pierce.

At once Fanny ran to Pierce to thank him. She had misjudged him—he was a compassionate man—she was filled with gratitude. But afterward, thinking matters over, her mood altered. Her trust was too far gone to be restored by this one gesture. A few days later she wrote to Emily Fitzhugh: "one may live in the most intimate relations with one's fellow-creatures, and really know nothing about them after all."

The quarrels over Psyche changed Fanny's way of viewing her own past. Compared to owning a slave plantation, a career in the theater seemed a noble way of life, and money derived from acting was infinitely more honorable to her than money "wrung from the unwilling and unrewarded labor of seven hundred wretched slaves." She realized also just how desperately she needed to earn her own money again. All in all, Fanny had been given a powerful incentive to return to her old career.

On Butler's Island the cool breezes of winter were giving way to the sticky heat of summer. Though Pierce, in common with his generation, attributed malaria not to the mosquito but to "the miasma which exhales from the rice fields," he recognized that the fever came in season and that it was unsafe to remain on the island beyond the middle of March. Unwilling to take risks, as February drew to a close, he decided to move Fanny and the children to the cooler and healthier climate of his other plantation.

Their new home was the Hampton Point plantation on St. Simon's Island, a larger and drier island lying fifteen miles downstream, at the place where the Altamaha River joins the sea. On the sandy soil of Hampton Point, Pierce grew the famous sea island cotton, which of recent years had so dramatically fallen in price that his revenue from cotton was now significantly less than his revenue from rice. In other respects, however, Hampton Point was vastly superior to Butler's Island. At Hampton Point Fanny had land on which to ride a horse, amiable neighbors to visit, a better house to live in, and a pretty garden displaying "peach trees in full blossom, tufts of silver narcissus and jonquils, and a quantity of violets and an exquisite myrtle bush."

Fanny's reputation had preceded her; wherever she went she was surrounded by groups of petitioners or by slaves who simply sought the comfort of her presence. At night in her ramshackle sitting room, she held a type of court. Dressed in a short-sleeved, low-necked evening dress, she would sit writing at a rough wooden table covered by a green baize cloth, and a silent audience would sit at her feet. As many as fourteen slaves might congregate, having tiptoed into the room, "their naked feet falling all but inaudibly on the bare boards." They would squat cross-legged in front of the hearth, the bright blaze from the huge pine logs shining on their dark faces. If Fanny asked them what they wanted, they would gravely answer almost in unison that they had come to say "how d'ye do missis," and "then troop out as noiselessly as they entered, like a procession of sable dreams."

Fanny's visitors were mostly the older or feebler slaves, sent from Butler's Island to the cotton fields, where the climate was healthier and the labor was lighter. The plight of these worn-out remnants, "flung by like an old rag, crippled with age and disease," was horrifying to behold, for, being of no commercial value, the slaves' welfare was almost ignored. Within the space of a few days, Fanny heard more than a dozen pathetic life stories. One slave had tried to escape twice to the swamps, and each time as punishment had been strung up to a tree and flogged. Another had miscarried as a result of a flogging and been ill ever since. "To all this I listen," she told Elizabeth Sedgwick: "I, an English woman, the wife of the man who owns these wretches, and I can not say 'that thing shall not be done again.'"

On the evening of February 26, 1839, Fanny was passing on more of the slaves' requests when Pierce interrupted her by shouting, "Why do you believe such trash? don't you know the niggers are all d—d liars?" Thereafter he refused to listen to another word. Pierce was tired, Fanny wrote, "of hearing what he has never heard before, the voice of passionate expostulation and importunate pleading against wrongs that he will not even acknowledge, and for creatures whose common humanity with his own I half think he does not believe." The knowledge of Pierce's heartlessness and her own helplessness sunk corrosively into Fanny's soul.

Her main antidote for despair was the study of nature. "I suppose," she told Elizabeth, "one secret of my being able to suffer as acutely as I do, without being made either ill or absolutely miserable, is the childish excitability of my temperament, and the sort of ecstasy which any beautiful thing gives me." On Butler's Island, with nowhere to walk and ride, Fanny had gained peace of mind by rowing about the waterways in a small boat with the help of a slave called Jack, to whom she insisted on paying a small wage. When she moved to Hampton Point, she brought Jack with her, and her happiest days were spent with him. She admired his shrewdness and his knowledge of wildlife, and she laughed affectionately at his amusing ways and sayings. Once, while they were fishing—with no success—he said to her: "Missis, fishing bery good fun when um fish bite." It was testimony to their easy companionship that they "both burst out laughing as soon as he uttered it."

With Jack as her factotum, Fanny walked or rode each day about St. Simon's Island, drawing strength from the beauty of the landscape: the thickets draped with fragrant wild jasmine, the noble magnolia trees standing in the midst of the cotton, and the carpets and curtains of wildflowers that transformed the island into a garden of Eden in Fanny's eyes.

Fanny's garden of Eden was also a purgatory. She found it impossible to shut her ears when the slave women cried, "Oh, missis, you tell massa for we, he sure do as you say"—but it was equally impossible to listen to them when she knew that she could do nothing to help them. "I must return to the North," she wrote in her journal as depression engulfed her. Without the power to assist the women, "my condition would be almost worse than theirs—condemned to hear and see so much wretchedness without the means of alleviating it, without permission even to represent it for alleviation; this is no place for me, since I was not born among the slaves, and cannot bear to live among them." Yet Fanny knew that "if I should go away, the human sympathy that I have felt for them will certainly never come near them again."

Fanny's attitude toward slavery had hardened. The slaves' condition, she wrote, "does not appear to me, upon further observation of it, to be susceptible of even partial alleviation as long as the fundamental evil, slavery itself remains." In distant Milan, Adelaide reported to the Thuns that Fanny's firsthand "acquaintance with the miserable condition of those miserable Negroes" was making her "trebly" an American abolitionist.

Early in March, Fanny reaching a turning point. She decided to leave Pierce. Without a word to the children or their nursemaid, and certainly with no hint to Pierce, she fled to Butler's Island, in readiness to go to Darien to catch the steamer to Savannah. Pierce, locating her at last, sat through the night trying to persuade her to return to him. Were they "not bound to consider our children more than ourselves?" he seems to have asked her. "And what would our children not lose by being bereft of a guardian's care? What could I do with two little motherless children?" They were compelling questions, because there was no doubt in either of their minds that if they parted, Pierce would keep the children. Fanny later told

Elizabeth Sedgwick that, though her spirit cried out to leave, she could not bring herself to do so. It would have meant abandoning her babies; and for their sakes, she had no alternative but to "remain where they are, and learn this dreary lesson of human suffering to the end."

Soon after Fanny's return to Hampton Point, she heard that Pierce was stricken by fever at Butler's Island. As he was too weak to be moved from his bed, she sailed to and fro each day to nurse him. Her devotion and his gratitude brought about a temporary truce. She even wrung a concession from him. Discovering that the slaves were forbidden to attend their church in Darien more than once a month, Fanny won Pierce's permission to hold voluntary prayer meetings at the Butler house each Sunday. Her sitting room was so crowded that she had difficulty keeping her composure. It "is an extremely solemn thing for me to read the Scriptures aloud to anyone," she told Elizabeth, "and there was something in my relation to the poor people by whom I was surrounded that touched me so deeply, while thus attempting to share with them the best of my possession, that I found it difficult to command my voice, and had to stop several times in order to do so."

Watching the slaves at their devotions made her wonder about Pierce's own standing in the sight of God. At a slave funeral Fanny had been shocked when he refused to kneel with the congregation. She longed to see him sink to his knees, thus giving "his slaves some token of his belief that—at least in the sight of that Master to whom we were addressing our worship—all men are equal." But Pierce remained standing while Fanny and all the others knelt, thus proclaiming his separateness. Slavery, Fanny believed, had poisoned his soul; and she looked with dread on the prospect that little Sarah might one day accept so corrupting an inheritance.

When Pierce recovered his health and returned to Hampton Point, Fanny admitted that she was delighted to have him back. They took companionable rides through the fragrant wilderness: her pleasure springs from the pages of her letters. The sexual bond between them continued to be powerful, and once bitterness retreated, they could still magnetize one another.

Out among the slaves Fanny continued to disseminate ideas, the like of which, she told Elizabeth, "have certainly never before visited their wool-thatched brains." One day a house slave, a bright sixteen-year-old named Aleck, begged her to teach him to read. It was against the law—and against Pierce's own commands—to teach a slave to read or write, but Fanny gave a reading lesson to Aleck nevertheless, and her defiance in teaching him gave her a double thrill. As a wife she was considered by the law to be under Pierce's ownership, and therefore it was her husband who would be charged as a result of her offense. A first offense was lightly fined, a second was heavily fined, and the third time, the offenders went to prison. "What a pity it is," she wrote cheekily, "I can't begin with Aleck's third lesson, because going to prison can't be done by proxy, and that penalty would light upon the right shoulders!" She continued to encourage Aleck to take part in the reading lessons she gave to young Sarah.

The months passed, and the heat was increasing daily. In April 1839, while Aleck confidently recited his letters, the Butlers began packing their trunks for Philadelphia. On the whole Fanny was thankful to be leaving. "I think I have done what I could for them," she wrote to Elizabeth. "I think I have done as well as I could by them; but when the time comes for ending any human relation, who can be without their misgivings? who can be so bold to say, I could have done no more, I could have done no better?"

Back at Butler Place, life had never seemed more humdrum, and Fanny's thoughts kept straying to the marshy waterways of Georgia. To depress her further, a letter awaited her from William Charles Macready, the lessee of the Covent Garden theatre. Before leaving for the plantations, Fanny had sent him *An English Tragedy*, the play she had been writing over the past two years. He replied with uncharacteristic ardor, describing it as one of the best modern plays he had read, "full of truth and power and exquisite beauty." However, he dared not put it on. Fanny had based the plot on a scandal current in London at the time of her visit, featuring adultery, blackmail, and gambling. Macready believed the moralists would hound her play off the stage.

Fanny read his letter with deep disappointment. A letter also awaited her from Adelaide, inviting her to Italy; how Fanny wished she could join her sister! Six of the Sedgwicks were sailing together to Europe, and she longed to go with them. There seemed so little to keep her in America. "My occupations are nothing," she wrote, "my amusements less than nothing. . . . Once a week I go to town, to execute commissions, or return visits, and on Sundays I go to church. . . . I really live almost entirely alone."

The Butlers had been at home only a few weeks when Fanny's restlessness found expression in tears and outbursts. Though she varied her words, the substance of her arguments was almost always the same. First she would tell Pierce how desperately she craved society and intellectual company. "We are not all made up of affections," she would tell him, "we have intellects—and we have passions—and each and all should have their objects and their spheres of action, or the creature is maimed." To this Pierce would retort that surely Fanny had no need of "intellectual converse" when she had "an affectionate husband and two sweet babies." An exasperated Fanny would reply, "You might as well say to a man who told you he had no arms—Oh! no, but you have legs."

Pierce's answer was to retreat. He began to spend nights away from home, explaining that he was in Philadelphia on business. Fanny did not accept his explanation. On the night of the childrens' birthday—May 28, 1839—Fanny's side of the marital bed lay empty, and near it was a written ultimatum. "I have at various times," she began, "made ineffectual struggles to get released from the intolerable life I am leading: you have always prevented my doing so, by urging upon me considerations of your happiness: as I can no longer be deceived by assurances which your actions most plainly contradict, I now request once and for all to be allowed to return to my own country." At the end of the letter she introduced a new strand into the argument. "I will not remain here," she wrote, "to be your housekeeper, your child's nurse, or what you make me, that is still more degrading and revolting."

Her words were cryptic but the implication seems clear enough: she suspected Pierce of sleeping with other women during his absences in Philadelphia, and she especially resented his expecting her to go on sharing his bed. Though hurt and angry, Fanny cannot have been entirely surprised by his possible infidelity, because Pierce had always been a ladies' man. His premarital philanderings had been common gossip in Philadelphia, and just before their wedding, a well-wisher had so warned her father, who had passed the warning on to Fanny. At the time she had scorned the gossip. Now she had reason to remember it.

Pierce was alarmed by the tone of her letter. Though he had learned over the years to ignore her moods, he was aware that the rift between them was more serious than ever. Only the day before, she had threatened to sail to England on the fast steamship the *Great Western* to resume her life on the stage. At the time Pierce had brushed her words aside as mere fantasies, but after reading her letter of May 28, he was not so sure. When, on the following day, she broached the subject of gaining custody of one of the children, he panicked. He decided to seek help from the Sedgwicks.

Elizabeth and Charles Sedgwick had recently been staying at Butler Place, and the marital atmosphere had been so bitter that they had tactfully probed Pierce for an explanation. Grateful for their sympathy and mindful of their influence over Fanny, Pierce had unburdened himself to them. By letter, he unburdened himself further. "She seems resolved to part," he told Elizabeth: "I know not what to do."

In his letter to the Sedgwicks, Pierce described himself as an unlucky victim. He believed—no doubt rightly—that almost nobody in upper-class America would see Fanny's dissatisfaction as rational: in his circle, married women were naturally content with a husband and babies and required no other interests. That a gifted woman could be stifled by domesticity and pine for mental stimulation was far outside his comprehension. On her own admission Fanny adored her children, and Pierce could not believe that she would be happy abandoning them. He maintained that he had done every-thing in his power to make her life comfortable, happy, and contented. As far as he could see, Fanny's life was comparable to that of dozens of happy wives of his acquaintance. Though he admitted that "she must feel very much the seclusion in which we live, and constantly regret the separation from her family and early friends," he could see no solution. He could not live in England; and in any case it was customary for wives to abandon their girlhood homes to live with their husbands. As this was the common lot of women, he could not see why Fanny should "be eternally weeping and be-moaning this as the greatest and only calamity."

The source of her unhappiness lay within herself, he told the Sedg-wicks. He believed Fanny had inherited those "morbid tendencies" of her mother's which had made her father's life so difficult, and that if Fanny did not pull herself together, her "mental derangement" might become perma-nent. The theory of mental derangement seems to have occurred to him only since going to the plantations, and one wonders if it were not equally calculated to explain away her views about abolition.

Elizabeth Sedgwick was inclined to accept Pierce's explanation. She, too, had heard Fanny's stories about her mother. She remembered that Marie Thérèse was said to be eminently rational with outsiders and vio-lently unreasonable within her own family—the very behavior that Pierce described on paper. With reluctance Elizabeth conceded that Fanny must be suffering from a hereditary condition. She advised Pierce to treat his wife as a sick woman. She also wrote to Fanny, entreating her to put herself in Pierce's shoes and to heed his advice. "My poor, dear Fanny," wrote Eliz-abeth, "my precious, almost idolized friend, do let me persuade you that your mind is diseased."

Fanny read Elizabeth's words with distress. What if Pierce and the Sedgwicks were right, and her mother's "morbid tendencies" were capturing her mind? She had always recognized the likeness between herself and her mother. At the same time, she could not believe that her mind was actually diseased. She could, however, accept that she was likely to be unhappy whatever her situation. If this were so, it would be better to be unhappy in America, with her children, than in a far-off country without them. Shaken and half-convinced, Fanny canceled her plans to visit Europe and returned to her housewifely duties in a spirit of self-reproach.

Pierce reinforced her mood with vows of faithfulness and undying love, and a heavy dose of self-justification. His visits to Philadelphia continued, but he prefaced them with an excuse: "If sobs and tears are my welcome when I return to my home," he wrote, "and if I am left to lie alone in my bed while you pass the night on the floor absorbed in grief, it can hardly be expected that I shall find my home a cheerful one, nor can it be wondered at if I should sometimes absent myself from a home where gloom so often prevails . . . Oh! my wife be wise!"

For a time Fanny was wise, or rather she was dutiful, which was Pierce's definition of wifely wisdom. Each agreed to map out a safe territory. While Pierce went to the hot springs in West Virginia in the autumn to treat his rheumatism, Fanny found relief in escaping to the Sedgwicks at Lenox, where drama was enthroned and she was a star again. Fanny Appleton, visiting Lenox again, remembered Fanny Butler's "richly modulated and flexible voice reading nearly all the *Tempest*."

At Butler Place at the end of November, Pierce announced his intention to travel to the plantations for the winter and again proposed to take Fanny with him. One must assume that he only made this rash suggestion because he did not dare to leave his wife behind. Even Fanny was hesitant, having no desire to repeat the long overland journey, but as she did not relish remaining alone at home, she decided to go. Closing up the house in preparation for their departure, she, Pierce, and the children moved into Philadelphia to stay with Pierce's brother John until it was time to leave. Their stay lengthened from days to weeks, because Pierce felt too rheumatic to make the journey.

Fanny hated living with John Butler. The heights of Philadelphia society had never really accepted her, and John's wife, Gabriella, was a living reminder of this rejection. The granddaughter of a famous American diplomat, Gabriella had entree into the best houses—and never let Fanny forget it. To be shut up in the same house with Gabriella for weeks on end was more than Fanny could tolerate. But Pierce refused to reopen Butler Place.

By the New Year of 1840, Fanny was approaching desperation. She longed to take matters into her own hands and rent a house in Philadelphia where she and the children might live comfortably, but Pierce refused to allow her the money. So many of Fanny's problems came down to money. Twice in recent months she had been obliged to pawn her gold chains to raise cash, and twice Pierce had redeemed them, then upbraided her for daring to raise money that way.

One way of obtaining money was to return to the stage, and this plan was never far from Fanny's mind. Another way was to ask her father to return the substantial sum she had earned from her American tour of 1832–1833, and which she had made over to Charles at the time of her marriage. Early in January 1840, Fanny composed a letter to her father, saying that she was obliged to ask for the return of her money because her husband could not afford to house her decently. Shrewdly she handed a copy of the letter to Pierce, with an ultimatum that it was her intention to post the letter to her father if he did not provide her with a house of which she was mistress. Her ultimatum succeeded. Butler Place was immediately reopened; the letter to her father was not sent; and Pierce, abandoning his plan to take Fanny south, set out for Georgia with his brother.

Fanny's first weeks in her own home were depressing; but when the weather improved she stirred herself and invited friends to stay, among them Frances and Mary Appleton and Mary's new Scottish husband, Robert Mackintosh. It was years since the old farmhouse had seen such fun. Guests were sleeping, eating, or bathing in every corner. The Mackintoshes were in the Butlers' bed, Fanny was on a sofa, another friend named Kate Bowie was in the nursery, while Frances Appleton used the spare room. Even Pierce's dressing room was invaded, as Fanny was quick to relate, when she wrote to him at Butler's Island.

Now that Fanny was in a sunnier mood, good-hearted Elizabeth Sedgwick decided to do some marriage-mending. When Pierce had written to her the previous May, he had described his wife in terms so loving that Elizabeth wept as she read the letter. Deciding that Fanny should know what he felt, Elizabeth risked his wrath and sent the letter on.

As Fanny read her husband's tender words, her heart melted. Seizing a pen and paper, she scribbled an impetuous reply. "Oh Pierce," she wrote, "forgive me, my dearest, dearest Pierce, if I have so bitterly cursed your existence. I cannot write any more; I am blinded with crying. Ever, ever your own wife, Fanny."

Her contrition lasted well into the summer of 1840, though there was much to try her. Pierce, back from the plantations, was more rheumatic than ever and seemed unable to make up his mind about anything. First he proposed to revisit the hot springs for his rheumatism and to take her with him. Then he talked of taking the family to England in the autumn. Finally he planned to travel with Fanny and the children to Georgia in the winter, until his brother John, as co-proprietor, forbade it, declaring that Fanny's presence was a source of "distress to herself, annoyance to others, and danger" to the plantations.

John's words were prophetic. Though in past months Fanny had tried to reconcile herself to the role of an obedient wife, she could not obey for very long. In October 1840 she informed Harriet that she had abandoned her personal crusade against slavery, but in November she resumed it. Since her return from Georgia, Fanny had been mixing in abolitionist circles; the formidable Lucretia Mott, leader of the Anti-Slavery Convention of American Women, was becoming her friend. Accordingly Fanny was not surprised to receive a written request to contribute an article to a small book being published in conjunction with a forthcoming antislavery fair in Philadelphia. Though Fanny knew that Pierce would protest, she agreed to write it, as a matter of conscience.

Pierce was horrified when he heard of her proposal. In the course of a heated quarrel he told her that her conduct was a betrayal of "the character, position and interests of her husband." He maintained that he could never again take her to the plantations; in fact, he might not be able to go himself, so strong would be the enmity of their neighbors. Fanny, clinging to her conscience, sent off the article. "This," he later wrote, "was the deepest wound my spirit had as yet received at her hands."

A week later their feud ended when a letter from London announced that Charles Kemble was dying. Thrusting aside their disputes, Pierce booked passage for himself and his family on the steamship *British Queen*, bound for Liverpool. On December 1, 1840, they sailed, with Fanny praying that she would arrive in time to see her father before he died.

11

A Homegrown Prima Donna

Fanny landed in Liverpool to hear the welcome news that her father was still alive. Hurrying by train to London, she discovered, to her immense relief, that he was out of danger; but he was still so weak that she could not see him for several more days. When she did at last stand at his bedside, the reunion was dramatic. Charles lifted his frail arms and declaimed in his resonant Kemble voice that Fanny had brought him back from the grave. From that moment on he improved rapidly, and by March 1841 he was more or less his old self again.

Once her father's illness had ceased to worry her, Fanny set about reestablishing herself in London society. She had been in touch on arrival with such close friends as Anna Jameson, the Egertons, and Emily Fitzhugh. Now she began to call on less intimate friends, such as Samuel Rogers and Sydney Smith, and accepted their invitations to soirées and dinners. To her great joy, almost everyone seemed to remember her. Within a few weeks the loneliness and boredom of Butler Place were almost forgotten, and she was Fanny Kemble again.

One of those who remembered her was Harriet Grote, the wife of the banker and politician George Grote. Reputedly one of the brightest and most eccentric women in London Society, Mrs. Grote was hostess to a wide circle of politicians, writers, and performers, and she took to Fanny as soon as they met at the house of Sydney Smith. Hearing Fanny exclaim, "I have always preserved my liberty, at least the small crumb of it that a woman can own anywhere." Mrs. Grote turned to her and said approvingly, "Then you've struggled for it." With those few words, the friendship was established.

Fanny also met Charles Greville, the brother of Henry Greville and Lord Francis Egerton: a man about town whose "clear good sense, excellent judgment, knowledge of the world, and sense of expediency, combined with

< 171 >

his good temper and friendliness, made him a sort of universal referee." A clerk of the Privy Council under three successive sovereigns, Charles Greville knew everyone of importance, and his daily journal is one of the vital sources of nineteenth-century British history. Though Fanny and Adelaide would always think of Henry as the sweeter, more lovable, brother, Charles's friendship was a gift that both the sisters treasured.

Dinners, balls, the opera—Fanny went out almost every night, and everywhere Pierce was received with honor as her husband. Since he had no firsthand knowledge of his wife's English life, he must have been astonished at the celebrated hostesses who welcomed them. He took to the social round with enthusiasm, rejoicing at the "hearts and houses open to him." Pierce inferred that "an American carries into English society a surer passport than any other foreigner," but he was perhaps mistaken. His passport was his wife, not his nationality.

Late in April 1841 Pierce crossed to Paris to meet Adelaide and Aunt Victoire, who were traveling up by coach from Naples. This was to be Adelaide's first meeting with Pierce, and she was nervous that they might not like each other. When they came face to face, however, she was surprised at how much she warmed to him: "he is gentle and amiable," she informed the Thuns, "and I think seems disposed to be my friend."

When Adelaide reached London, it was Fanny's turn to be surprised. She hardly recognized her sister. The ugly duckling she had seen off to Germany almost four years before had grown into a plump, handsome woman with "something completely foreign in her tone and manner, and even accent." What also amazed Fanny was her sister's uncanny resemblance to their mother. Every expression of Adelaide's face, every inflection of her voice seemed to recall Marie Thérèse. As Fanny put it, Adelaide virtually *was* their mother.

This was not the only change in Adelaide. The girl whom Fanny remembered—and whose memory she treasured—had been a shy, worshipping, unthreatening girl. This newcomer, though sisterly and loving, was a self-assured, self-absorbed performer approaching the peak of a successful European career. When they spoke together, Fanny was only too aware how stupefying her life had been at Butler Place. There were times in Adelaide's presence when Fanny felt like an obscure country cousin. Adelaide is "a thousand times quicker, keener, finer, shrewder and sweeter than I am," Fanny wrote sadly, "and all my mental processes, compared with hers, are slow, coarse and clumsy."

To lose her place as the dominant sister was a blow to Fanny's pride, and she had difficulty in adjusting to it. During the following months her feelings for her sister veered between affection and resentment. Her first response, however, was touchingly generous. Adelaide's singing moved her to tears, and the stern self-discipline that accompanied it filled Fanny with wonder. "How her strength is to resist the demands made upon it by the violent emotions she is perpetually expressing," wrote Fanny, "or how any human throat is to continue pouring out such volumes of sound without rest or respite passes my comprehension."

Faithful Henry Greville wrote from Paris, where he was still British attaché, to enlist his brother's help in launching Adelaide into the fashionable musical world of London, and on May 3, Charles Greville called at the Butlers' house in Clarges Street off Piccadilly to hear Adelaide sing. Fanny was in an adjoining room, writing to Harriet, and she described the scene movingly in her letter. Adelaide "is singing most beautifully," she wrote, "and the passionate words of love, longing, grief and joy burst through the utterance of musical sound, and light up her whole countenance with a perfect blaze of emotion. As for me, the tears stream over my face, and I can hardly prevent myself from sobbing aloud." When small Sarah Butler, upstairs in the nursery, heard her aunt singing in the room below, she asked her mother: "Well, how many angels have you got down there, I should like to know?"

Charles Greville used his social influence on behalf of Adelaide, and three weeks later Fanny reported the outcome to Harriet: "We are lifted off our feet by a perfect torrent of engagements, of visits, of going out and receiving; our house is full from morning to night, of people coming to sing with or listen to my sister." Next evening they were expecting to entertain "nothing under the rank of viscount, Beauforts, Normanbys, Wilton, *illustrissimi tutti quanti*." In two days' time, Adelaide was due to sing at the palace in the presence of the queen.

WHEREAS a month before, Fanny had reveled in a social life that centered on herself, the "musical Maelstrom" which was now revolving around Adelaide began to fray her nerves. People came at all hours of the day to call on Adelaide, and there always seemed to be "a most stupendous row at the pianoforte." The Butler children, infected by the general excitement, rioted around the house "like a couple of little maniacs." Worse, since the rest of the family thrived on the bustle, Fanny's was the lone voice of complaint. As she confided to Harriet: "we are all enveloped in a golden cloud of fashionable hard work, which rather delights my father; which my sister lends herself to, complaining a little of the trouble, fatigue and late hours; but thinking it for the interest of her future public career. . . . As for me, I am rather bewildered by the whirl in which we live, which I find rather a trying contrast to my late solitary existence in America . . . the incessant music wears upon my nerves a great deal."

The summer was shining on Adelaide. Following the concert at the palace, she sang at a morning musicale at Mrs. Grote's, "a monstrous proof," said Mrs. Grote, "of the sympathy and interest that I bear that fine creature." After Mrs. Grote's, Adelaide sang at a morning concert held to aid Polish refugees at Stafford House, the home of Lord Francis Egerton's sister-in-law, the Duchess of Sutherland. Four hundred tickets were sold at exorbitant prices, the performers reputedly the best in London. They were the celebrated French actress Rachel, the Hungarian superstar-pianist Franz Liszt—and Adelaide. For a soprano relatively unknown in London, it was a wonderful launching.

The concert at Stafford House was spectacular. The wide stairs and long galleries were filled with brilliantly dressed groups, and Fanny rejoiced at the sight of sunlight streaming onto the panels and pillars of the magnificent hall. The scene cannot fail to have reminded her of her own triumph ten years before at Bridgewater House. Once her sister began to sing, Fanny was unable to restrain her emotions and gave way to floods of tears. As she stood behind a pillar, struggling to control herself, the French actress Rachel took pity on her and led her to a dressing room to recover. "I am almost beside myself," Fanny told Harriet, "with—everything."

THE CONCERT at Stafford House established Adelaide's London reputation. Fanny reported that her sister "sang beautifully, and looked beautiful, and was extremely admired and praised and petted." The concert also confirmed Adelaide's future plans. She had decided to perform for two or three years in London and thereby save enough for an income of 300 pounds a year, after which she planned to retire to Italy, where she could live as her own mistress. Pining for the sunny, easy land where she had found her identity and independence, she often used Italian phrases and gestures. While some found the affectation pretentious, Adelaide's love of Italy was totally sincere.

Though she worried about her future, Adelaide enjoyed that summer in London. For one thing, it was reassuring to have her family gathered around her. Her father and Aunt Victoire were living at the Butlers' house in Clarges Street, and her brother Henry took leave from his regiment in

Ireland for an extended stay. In the renewed family circle, both sisters were conscious of the gaps caused by death. Adelaide spoke often of Dall, though she seldom mentioned her mother and probably did not much regret her passing. On the other hand, Fanny seemed to remember her mother with an increasing admiration, which is curious given how afraid she was that traits inherited from her mother might be wrecking her own life. In years to come Fanny would declare that, with a better education, Marie Thérèse would have been "one of the most remarkable persons of her time."

Success at Stafford House earned Adelaide an unexpected bonus: an introduction to the astonishing Franz Liszt. The first of the musical super-stars, Lizst's sexual magnetism and musical virtuosity dazzled Europe. He could scarcely set foot on a public stage without provoking frenzied scenes, which led to the coining of the new word, *Lisztomania*. Adelaide could not believe her luck to be chosen to appear on the same platform. Since Liszt and Adelaide both knew the Thuns and Dessauer, these first links were easily forged into friendship.

Within a matter of weeks Liszt invited Adelaide to join him in a German opera company to be formed in London the following summer. More immediately, he proposed taking her with him on a concert tour of the Rhineland, his aim being to raise money for a memorial statue in Bonn to the late Ludwig van Beethoven. Once again Adelaide was scarcely able to believe her luck, and she quickly agreed to the tour, leaving all the arrangements to him. She did, however, ask if she could bring companions. While she would no doubt have taken a chaperone as a matter of course, Liszt's reputation with women made this a matter of necessity.

When Fanny heard of the trip, she proposed herself as the chaperone. Gradually the party was increased to include Pierce, the Butler children, and brother Henry Kemble and his fiancée, Mary Ann Thackeray. To complete the entourage, Mary Ann insisted on bringing her aunt, Miss Cottin, and Adelaide invited a young man named Henry Chorley, who for the past half-dozen years had been her devoted musical admirer. Of humble background and largely self-educated, this shy, red-headed young bachelor was the musical editor of the influential magazine *The Athenaeum* and was said to be the most knowledgeable music critic in London.

In the meantime the Kembles and the Butlers kept up their swift social pace. In June they attended a musical party at Chorley's house in honor of Felix Mendelssohn, where Adelaide sang and Fanny read aloud from *Antony and Cleopatra*. In July the sisters and Pierce visited not only the Egertons and Emily Fitzhugh but also the home in Hertfordshire of Barbarina, Lady Dacre, an aging political hostess and minor playwright who had cultivated Fanny in the days of her theatrical fame and was eager to strengthen the friendship. At Lady Dacre's both sisters gave readings of poetry; Adelaide read aloud from Petrarch in her exquisite Italian, and Fanny followed with a reading of the English translation of Petrarch made by Lady Dacre. Adelaide then read from Wordsworth, whose work she admired, while Fanny read from her favorite, Shakespeare. Those who were present gave high praise to both readers.

In mid-August 1841 the Kemble party sailed to Holland, where Adelaide set out to meet Liszt at the Rhine town of Mainz. With his help, she carefully planned her performances. At some she would be his supporting artist, singing a varied program including such Italian showpieces as her favorite cavatina from *Niobe* and, in deference to her German audiences, songs by Schubert and Beethoven. Thanks to hard study and the Kemble flair, Adelaide had become a wonderfully varied stylist, singing Italian, French, German, and English music with almost equal ease and correctness. One English critic called her the "most universal of her contemporaries." Fanny enthused that her sister comprehended "almost the whole lyrical literature of Europe."

Adelaide planned also to perform on her own in excerpts from her most successful operas: *Norma, Lucia di Lammermoor, Beatrice di Tenda,* and *La Sonnambula.* In addition, there would be complete performances of *Norma,* which she had come to consider her speciality. When Liszt named the towns where they would perform, Adelaide noted with pleasure that they included Mainz, Frankfurt, Baden, Ems, Wiesbaden, Coblenz, Heidelberg, Cologne, Aachen, and Liege. The following day she sent word to the Thuns, feeling sure that in such a comprehensive list there would be at least one town where they could visit her. In a postscript she asked wistfully after Francis. The flame for Francis still burned, fanned, perhaps, by the vibrant masculinity of Franz Liszt.

Once the tour was underway, Fanny's lack of enthusiasm became increasingly apparent. In Adelaide's presence she was frequently depressed and angry, making no attempt to act as chaperone, or even to hide her ill humor. Her behavior was so boorish that outsiders often noticed it. The Kembles' old friend, the novelist William Thackeray—no relation to Henry's fiancée, Mary Ann Thackeray—saw Fanny in Frankfurt. He recorded that she looked as dirty and unkempt "as a housemaid," and was so petulant that she could scarcely speak. Henry Reeve, a well-known journalist, met the Butlers in Belgium and noted Fanny's "intensely overbearing" manner and her open contempt for her husband. One evening Pierce bought her a bouquet of flowers, remarking, "I have been all over the town, my dear, to get this bouquet for you." When "she saw there were no gardenias in it, she sniffed and tossed the bouquet to the back of the fire."

To be shut up with Pierce in coaches and hotel rooms day after day stretched Fanny's nerves almost to the breaking point: every minor dispute developed into a quarrel. To watch Adelaide performing was like a knife in her heart, for there can be little doubt that Fanny was missing her own career painfully. She had come to Europe hoping to escape her troubles in the joy of travel. Instead she felt left behind, resentful, and miserable.

How often, sitting alone at Butler Place, had Fanny let her thoughts stray longingly to Europe! But as she jolted along in coaches or sat idle in inns in the Rhineland, she longed to be back in America. As she steeped herself in castles, mountains, rivers, and sunsets—trying all the while to throw off care—she decided that she saw nothing that she liked so well as Lenox and Stockbridge. Though Fanny acknowledged that her feelings were colored by "the powerful charm of affectionate association, and the halo which happiness throws over any place," she did not apologize for her partiality. In serene, rural Massachusetts she was always sure of admiring and understanding hearts, and at that moment she craved them above all else.

As might have been expected, it was at Adelaide's performances that Fanny's discontent surfaced most visibly. The first concerts at Frankfurt she missed entirely, being held back by the children. When she finally attended a concert in Mainz, she could not restrain her disapproval. Her principal complaint was the old one of her girlhood: that Adelaide sang with a thin voice. She harped on that thinness of voice over the next two years, going so far as to predict that when the time came for her sister to sing at Covent Garden, her sound might not fill the auditorium, even though she knew that Adelaide had filled the much larger San Carlo Theatre in Naples.

Fanny's emotional criticisms were written to friends during the Rhineland tour and the two London seasons that followed it. Forty years later—after Adelaide's death—Fanny chose to publish them in her autobiography. Since then, they have continued to cloud Adelaide's vocal reputation. Many historians have accepted Fanny's verdict and have dismissed Adelaide as a second-rate singer, working on the strange assumption that a sister would be more knowledgeable than a professional music critic.

Fanny's criticisms were based on her feeling that Adelaide had weakened her voice by training it upward beyond its natural range. She argued that the uppermost range of her sister's voice—the "artificial" part—had difficulty filling a large auditorium and was insufficiently powerful to communicate dramatic emotion. She also argued that by training her voice upward, Adelaide had spoiled the quality and intonation of her upper *passagio*: that tricky area of the voice where the high and middle sections join, and where evenness of tone and correctness of pitch are among the hallmarks of the great *bel canto* soprano.

Such serious faults, if they existed, must surely have been noticed by the leading music critics. Henry Chorley, possibly the greatest English critic of singing in the nineteenth century, heard Adelaide often, and his opinion differed vastly from Fanny's. While agreeing that Adelaide's natural voice was "limited," Chorley praised the patience and discipline that had extended it and made it capable of "every possible brilliancy." He vowed that he had never heard more honest singing. Chorley believed that Adelaide's Norma was comparable to Pasta's and preferable to the reigning Italian diva in London, Giulia Grisi.

Chorley admitted that Adelaide had her faults. She was too fond, he said, of drawing out her high notes, and of delivering every syllable of the spoken word with equal emphasis. He believed that these mannerisms would have worn off if Adelaide's career had been longer. Her defects, however, were small compared to her virtues. In his final estimation, made in 1861, Adelaide was the "greatest English singer"—but, he added, "not the best of this century." Who *was* the best of the century he mysteriously did not disclose. Chorley considered Adelaide a "poetical and thoughtful artist, whose name will never be lost so long as the art of dramatic singing is spoken of."

Chorley's praise was echoed by other London critics. Kenney of the London *Times* called her voice a "beautiful soprano, full and clear in its quality and completely under control." The music critic of *Punch* praised her "forcible" tone; her middle voice, he said, was "firm and full, her upper voice, sweet and rich beyond comparison," with perfect intonation. Mrs. C. Baron Wilson, writing in *Our Actresses*, considered Adelaide England's greatest vocalist. Not one reviewer drew attention to a purportedly weak *passagio*, a defect in intonation, or a thin upper register. On this evidence, Fanny's criticisms of Adelaide cannot be taken seriously, even if by chance they were valid in particular performances which she attended. Fanny also disregarded the fact that her sister had managed to shine in major Italian opera houses and hold her own against Italian sopranos. A second-rate singer could not have achieved such success.

The truth of the matter was that, in emotional terms, Fanny was still the nervous girl in her mother's drawing room, being scolded while her sister was praised, and bolstering her own self-confidence by claiming that a histrionic contralto was preferable to a carefully trained soprano. Above all, Fanny was a star performer deprived of her stage. The only way she could come to terms with Adelaide's success was to ensure that it did not eclipse her own.

It was possibly for that reason that Fanny began to urge her sister to give up singing and become an actress. Only then, she said, would Adelaide achieve her true destiny. Fanny readily agreed that her sister had the true Kemble talent for acting; but why, she asked, did it have to be allied to all those trills, scales, and high notes, which, because they required such physical and mental concentration, prevented Adelaide from expressing her full powers as an actress? Her "singing cramps her acting," Fanny wrote. "I cannot help wishing that she would leave the singing part of the business, and take to acting not set to music."

Adelaide returned in triumph to London in October. She had little time, however, to savor her success. Before leaving for Germany, she had negotiated an engagement at Covent Garden to organize and appear in four operas over the following winter and spring. She had already selected the singers, enlarged the orchestra and chorus, commissioned English translations—for all operas were to be sung in English—and insisted on the appointment of her father's friend Julius Benedict as musical director. With less than a month to the opening, a thousand details claimed her attention. There was scarcely time for her to move into the large house in Harley Street that Pierce had leased for his family and relatives.

The current managers of Covent Garden were old connections of the Kembles. Charles Mathews had been at school with the Kemble boys, and his wife, Lucia Elizabeth Vestris, had sung the contralto role in Weber's *Oberon*. Since Charles's time the theatre had passed through five different managements, all of which lost money, and the Mathewses were proving no exception. Clutching at Adelaide as though she were a life raft, they looked to her to save their theatre. As they were paying her the very high salary of one hundred pounds a week, this did not seem likely.

On the opening night, November 2, 1841, in a scene reminiscent of Fanny's debut, the theatre was packed with enthusiasts. When Adelaide came on stage as Norma, the audience rose with a shout, which continued so long that it temporarily halted the performance. If any critic in London had fears about Adelaide's skill, her singing that night must have dispelled

them. Her voice rang out, full and firm, through the theatre, and her enunciation was said to be superb. Her recitatives were described by Anna Jameson as a blend of "tragic declamation allied with musical science." Norma's
famous aria, "Casta Diva," earned deafening applause. As Charles Mathews
led Adelaide forward to take her bow, the spectators stood, shouted,
stamped, and called out the name of Kemble. She was hailed as the home-
grown prima donna with the international reputation.

Adelaide sang Norma three times a week until mid January 1842, and
then once a week until Easter; and for each of her forty-two performances,
the house was packed. On January 12, 1842, she sang in the English premiere of *Elena da Feltre*—renamed *Elena Uberti*—which ran alongside
Norma for two weeks. Though London audiences found the music dull,
Adelaide's depiction of madness drew spectators to the edges of their
seats—even Fanny was riveted. Anna Jameson saw Adelaide's performance
several times and never failed to be astonished by it. To "go mad to music,"
she wrote, "and to preserve in the very tempest and whirlwind of passion,
the vocal effects and harmonious grace of movement, so that all shall be
calculated instinctively" must surely constitute "one of the greatest triumphs"
of operatic art. Without Adelaide's virtuosity, wrote the critic of the *Times*,
the opera would certainly have failed.

In March, *Elena* was replaced by the *Marriage of Figaro*, in which Adelaide played Susanna with a grace and wit that reminded many of her
mother's acting at its finest. Her singing of Mozart's music also received the
highest praise. One of her arias, according to a London critic, was among
the "most exquisite specimens of singing we ever heard on the English
stage."

On April 7, when *La Sonnambula* replaced *Figaro*, Adelaide's Amina
earned glowing reviews also. Anna Jameson, by this time an avid fan, was
especially moved by the "delicacy and consistency" of Adelaide's performance. It was a common complaint that sopranos of the day so loaded their
singing with ornamentation that they obscured Amina's simple character.
Adelaide was particularly careful not to overuse ornamentation. "Her correct taste in making sense and sound assimilate," wrote an admiring critic,
"should be a pattern to our florid singers."

While reputable critics praised Adelaide, Fanny clung to her own
opinion. She told Harriet that Amina's music was too high for her sister's
voice and that Adelaide's performance was disappointing. In her determination to speak her mind regardless of the pain she inflicted, Fanny was
growing more and more like her mother. Fortunately Adelaide was too pre-

occupied to pay much attention, and what she did notice, she treated with tolerance. She guessed that Fanny's criticism sprang from a sense of deprivation. She told the Thuns how it saddened her to think of Fanny "giving up the many pleasures she had been enjoying here" and going back to the "cheerless solitude" of her life in America.

While the Thuns were often in Adelaide's thoughts, their responses to her letters had been disappointing. When she sang in the Rhineland, they failed to visit her, and for a time they ceased to write. Their neglect wounded her deeply. In Frankfurt in September 1841, she wrote to the count: "I have been true to you when it cost me *a great deal* to be so—I have had faith in you when others might have doubted—I have accepted pain and grief from you meekly and without murmur and God knows I have loved you through it all! In what have I been wanting to you? I have loved you better than myself." She concluded with the plea: "write to me." His reply seems to have soothed, but not erased, the pain; and the postscript to her next letter inquired plaintively, "Will you give me some news of Count Francis?"

Adelaide's strong words to Count Thun betrayed her inner struggles. As a star in London, she was attracting suitors and was undecided how to handle them. Foremost among them was the Grevilles' cousin, William John Cavendish-Bentinck-Scott, Marquis of Titchfield, the eldest son of the Duke of Portland. Obviously lovestruck, he came night after night to the theatre and was in raptures over Adelaide's singing. Though forty-one years old, he courted like an ardent adolescent, commissioning artists and sculptors to make busts and portraits of her. Eventually he asked her to marry him.

In the eyes of the world, the marquis was a brilliant match, for since the current duke was old, it could reasonably be supposed that William would soon be Duke of Portland. As such, he would have vast wealth, large estates, a very grand house, and a social position close to the highest in England. He would be sufficiently rich and powerful to demand that his wife—whoever she was—be accepted into the very best society. In addition he had a kind heart, a simple manner, and a deep love of animals—he was said to be one of the best judges of horses in the country. Some things about him, however, were unsettling. He was too ardent: his courtship amounted almost to an obsession. Adelaide could not love on those terms; and she was too much of an idealist to marry any man—even a future duke—if she did not believe she could love him.

The poor marquis took Adelaide's refusal badly. Spurned in love, he retired to the family home of Welbeck Abbey in Nottinghamshire, where he degenerated over the following years into eccentricity. According to his relatives, he began to dress and act oddly: "his trouserings were secured above the ankle by a piece of string, he hid himself beneath a vast coat and on top of his long brown wig he balanced a hat which was two feet tall." He seldom left his bedroom, communicating through a hole in the door, and each day a roasted fowl would be passed to him through the hole.

Less eccentric than the marquis was Edward John Sartoris, a suitor whose quiet devotion was beginning to win Adelaide over. The son of Urban Sartoris, a wealthy Piedmontese banker, and of Matilda Tunno, his Anglo-Italian wife, Edward's background was distinctly European, a fact that rather pleased her. At the same time, he had been given a thoroughly English upbringing, a fact also pleasing to her. Educated at Cambridge University, he had developed a penchant for fox hunting and a longing to enter Parliament. He had recently stood—unsuccessfully—for the Welsh seat of Penryn. He also had an artistic side, which attracted Adelaide. He has "read a great deal—thought a great deal—and has a great love and appreciation of art," she wrote to her friends.

Adelaide was surprised and disappointed to find that not all her friends shared her liking of Edward Sartoris. One who expressed a poor opinion was Theodosia Monson, a loyal and warm-hearted friend of nearly twenty years' standing. As a girl, Theodosia had lived near Heath Farm, and she had come to know most of the Kembles. She had married Lord Monson, been widowed, and in the last year had become Adelaide's chief confidante. It was therefore dismaying when Theodosia pronounced Edward Sartoris boringly nondescript. According to Theodosia, he was "not handsome, not ugly, not fat, not thin, not good, not bad, not pleasant, not unpleasant, in short the only quality about him not negative is that he always has his hands" in his jacket pockets.

Adelaide rejected Theodosia's assessment, but she continued to wonder if she should marry Edward. Francis still ruled her heart, even though she had resigned herself to not seeing him again. At the same time she was well aware that she was twenty-six years old, in a poor state financially, and unlikely to be an opera singer much longer. Her common sense told her that if Edward made her an offer, she would be a fool not to accept it. In April, Edward did make her an offer, defying his disapproving family to do so. He laid at her feet respectability, social position, an independent income and, as heir to his maternal uncle, the prospect of substantial wealth and a grand country house.

Fanny and Adelaide's mother, Marie Thérèse De Camp, was married to Charles Kemble. The daughter of a French flautist, she was on stage from the age of six, and by eighteen had few rivals as a combined dancer, singer, and actress.

Charles Kemble, Fanny and Adelaide's father, as Vincentio in Shakespeare's *Measure for Measure*. Born into the leading family of the British stage, he developed "a fine majestic figure" and a flair for performing dashing roles.

Adelaide Kemble was at her handsomest in the early 1840s at the time of her marriage. Fanny could scarcely believe that her shy and skinny little sister had grown into this confident, statuesque woman.

This best-known portrait of Fanny was lithographed in 1829 from a sketch by Thomas Lawrence. Lawrence had planned a life-size portrait of her but died before he could start it.

Nineteen-year-old Fanny made her debut at the Theatre Royal as Shakespeare's Juliet. Here she performs with Mary Davenport as Juliet's nurse.

The Theatre Royal at Covent Garden filled newcomers with awe. A giant horseshoe of galleries, it held close to three thousand spectators.

Thomas Sully, who painted Fanny in several roles (here as Beatrice), was one of the few Philadelphians with whom Fanny found much in common. (*Pennsylvania Academy of the Fine Arts*)

Adelaide Kemble

In the Character of

NORMA.

Adelaide in Bellini's opera *Norma*. Critics considered her one of the finest Normas of the time.

Short and slightly built, with spaniel eyes and a petulant mouth, Pierce Butler had an easy charm and was used to having his own way. (*Historical Society of Pennsylvania*)

Fanny's children, Sarah and Frances, had a stormy upbringing, and after their parents' divorce, did not see their mother for five years. (*National Portrait Gallery*)

Butler Place on the rural fringes of Philadelphia was regarded by Pierce as his "country seat"—but was dismissed by Fanny as "a second-rate English farm house." (*Historical Society of Pennsylvania*)

Count Franz von Thun-Hohenstein headed one of the powerful families of the Austrian Empire. His son, Francis, was the great love of Adelaide's life. (*Okresní Muzeum Děčín*)

Tetschen Castle on the Elbe River in Bohemia in 1837, as Adelaide first saw it. (*Okresní Muzeum Děčín*)

Intelligent, handsome, and a painter of great promise, Frederic Leighton instantly attracted Adelaide when she met him in 1854 in Rome. (*National Portrait Gallery*)

In 1856 Frederic Leighton lovingly sketched Adelaide in Paris.

At the age of forty-five, Adelaide sat for the well-known photographer Camille Silvy. By now she had run to fat and wore crinolines and draperies to disguise her shape. (*National Portrait Gallery*)

Adelaide's elder son Greville and only daughter May, shown here in adolescence. Greville's tragic death in a riding accident at the age of thirty clouded Adelaide's last years. (*Lyulph Lubbock family*)

Frederic Leighton painted this superb portrait of Adelaide's daughter May when she was fourteen. Dressed for riding, with a red scarf draped across her breast, she stands in a landscape near her Hampshire home, and faces the artist confidently and unself-consciously. (*Kimbell Art Museum*)

Frederic Leighton painted May again in 1875, when she was thirty-two and married. This older May no longer gazes at the artist: her pose is evasive. One wonders if Frederic had transferred his love from mother to daughter and May is attempting to deflect his admiration. (*Leighton House Museum*)

By her sixties, Adelaide had grown so obese that she and Fanny weighed 382 pounds together.

A friend described Fanny in old age as upright, stately, and vigorous. She felt "the throb of life with an intensity far beyond that of younger people." (*New York Public Library*)

Adelaide did not answer immediately. The opera season had come to an end, and she was due to tour Ireland, Scotland, and northern England over the following three months with a company managed by John Calcraft of the Theatre Royal in Dublin. With the help of singers from Covent Garden, she was planning to reproduce the successes of her London season. The Irish baritone Michael Balfe, who had studied with Bordogni, had been invited to sing with her, and she was delighted when he accepted. A gifted composer as well as a talented singer, he added luster to the company.

Adelaide described the tour lightheartedly, likening it to a "traveling menagerie" to be "shown off at the different fairs," but inside she was anything but lighthearted. She kept asking herself if she should forget Francis. At some stage during her tour of Ireland, she wrote to him. It was the first letter she had sent him since leaving Tetschen, and it is a pity that the letter has not survived. Did she hope that by telling him about Edward she would galvanize Francis into making the proposal that he had failed to make four years before? Or did she write to say goodbye? To say goodbye seems the most likely explanation, because when she returned to London at the end of May, she was conspicuously happy. A few days later she announced her engagement to Edward Sartoris.

The news of Adelaide's engagement drew a protest from Theodosia Monson. For months Theodosia had been urging Adelaide to marry "a good man she could esteem and not to marry him from any superabundance of the *belle passion*"; but she "did not mean her to go as far as that." Fortunately, a few weeks later, Theodosia cheered up sufficiently to write to Anna Jameson: "That *man* Sartoris (I hope he is positively that, bye the bye, but I never thought of him as of any particular *sex* even) always has given me the idea of *not* being *otherwise* than a good *moral* sort of thing and may I think make A. happy." Theodosia also wondered, as did many others, what Charles Kemble would say about the engagement.

Charles was not enthusiastic. He was ready to bless the marriage, but he was not ready to consent to an early wedding. Having not really accepted retirement from his theatre, he was about to return as manager to Covent Garden, where, despite large audiences, the Mathewses' season had ended in hopeless debt. As the new lessee and manager, Charles had plans to run an opera season from the coming September until the following April. He was designing it as a vehicle for his daughter's talent; and without Adelaide, the season had not a chance of success. Appealing to his daughter's sense of duty, Charles begged her not to abandon him by marrying and giving up the stage.

Adelaide acknowledged her duty as a daughter, but she was aware that she owed a duty to Edward, as well. He was growing impatient, and he did not want to wait another ten months for her. On the other hand, he could not lead her to the altar until she had abandoned her career, because no gentleman could afford to marry a woman who continued to appear on the professional stage. As Adelaide and Edward discussed their difficulty, a solution emerged, though neither of them liked it, because it seemed slightly devious. They would marry in secret—probably while she was on her tour of Scotland in July—and would announce the fact publicly only after the season was over.

Glad at last to have made a firm decision, Adelaide gave herself up to enjoying the summer. Josef Dessauer arrived in London, and late in June she, the Butlers, and Henry Chorley accompanied him to Mrs. Grote's house near the pretty Buckinghamshire woodland called Burnham Beeches. It turned out to be the happiest of visits, with Dessauer and their hostess competing to make them laugh. Dressed in a coachman's hat and flowing coat and wielding a big stick, eccentric Mrs. Grote stumped about her garden, issuing instructions to her guests like a general drilling troops. At one time she barked her orders through a speaking trumpet. At another, she astonished them by playing the cello, then considered an indelicate instrument for a woman to take between her knees. Dessauer had no idea what to make of her and responded like a naughty child. His imitations of her, done not quite behind her back, sent his fellow guests into fits of barely suppressed laughter.

Back in London, plans were finalized for Charles Kemble's opera season. Advertisements proclaimed it to be the most ambitious program of opera so far attempted at Covent Garden. Fifteen different operas were to be given, and Adelaide was to take the lead in five of them. As so often in the past, Charles basked in the expectation of success and purred with excitement, while his daughters trembled at his optimism and hoped he was not courting disaster.

By late August, with the season fast approaching, an army of scene painters and seamstresses was working overtime. When all was ready, on September 3, Adelaide suddenly became ill, forcing a postponement of a week. The delay lost Charles a week's takings, but he shrugged it off. When Adelaide walked on stage on September 10, and the audience rose to its feet and cheered, Charles believed that the Kemble magic was invincible.

Throughout September, the favorites of the past season were replayed:

Norma, La Sonnambula, and *The Marriage of Figaro.* Charles was whetting the public's appetite for the "novelty of the season," which was due to open on October 1. This was to be *Semiramide,* by Rossini, a blockbuster of an opera, fearsomely difficult to sing, requiring not only a first-class soprano but also a first-class contralto. Adelaide had selected the contralto with care, choosing Mary Shaw, an English singer with whom she had sung successfully at Padua.

Charles had insisted on staging *Semiramide,* because he believed that his daughter would be sensational in it. He proved to be correct. Adelaide was "sublime," wrote the journalist Henry Reeve: no other Semiramide "ever came up to her." The *Theatrical Journal* went further, declaring that "no opera within our recollection ever made so powerful an impression." Though the largest share of credit undoubtedly went to Adelaide, a share went also to Mary Shaw. She, like Adelaide, was one of the very few English-born singers of the nineteenth century to gain a European reputation. The sound and sight of these two Englishwomen shining in the music of Rossini carried audiences and critics to raptures of patriotism.

Later in October Adelaide also sang in Cimarosa's *Il Matrimonio Segreto,* renamed for the English stage *The Secret Marriage.* Chorley gave her high praise, writing that her Carolina was "good enough for any Opera house in Europe." Equal appreciation came from the public, who flocked to her performances. On those nights when Adelaide did not sing, so few came that the season was placed in peril. By late October it was apparent, even to Charles, that the theatre was going bankrupt. In desperation he mounted an expensive production of *The Tempest* to draw audiences on those nights when the opera was not playing, but this only succeeded in hastening bankruptcy. During the final month of his managership, he hardly left his room; but lay upon the sofa hour upon hour, with his eyes closed.

Confined to his sofa bed, Charles sadly invited Alfred Bunn, the manager of the theatre at Drury Lane, to take control as soon as Christmas was over, and to see the season through until its normal close in April. Until Bunn could take over, the performers agreed to form a cooperative, paying the rent and expenses and sharing the receipts among themselves. Adelaide generously sang for no payment for almost a month, finally announcing on December 6 that she was about to retire from professional life in favor of marriage.

On December 23, 1842, Adelaide gave her last professional performance, choosing her favorite role of Norma for her farewell. Anna Jameson was in the audience and has left a moving account. As Adelaide made her entrance, the house rose and thundered out her name. Overcome by the reception, she stood quite still and covered her face with her hands, the tears streaming through her fingers. Her first notes were so choked by weeping that she was obliged to pause to try to regain command of herself. Possessed by the emotion of the occasion, she stopped completely and "fairly gave way." The spectators sat stunned for a moment or two, then began to shout their goodwill and stamp their feet in sympathy.

Adelaide began again, huskily, and by the time she came to "Casta Diva," she was beginning to take control; so much so that at the end she received an encore. By this time totally in command, she proceeded to give one of the most electrifying performances of her life. At the last curtain call, she did not trust herself to make a farewell speech. Choosing a laurel wreath from the flowers strewn at her feet, she pressed it to her lips, gently inclined her head, and silently made her exit.

UNKNOWN TO THE AUDIENCE, unknown even to some of her close friends, Adelaide was a married woman. Five months before, on July 25, 1842, while on her opera tour of Scotland, she had met Edward by arrangement in Glasgow and quietly married him at St. Mary's Episcopal Church—sandwiching the ceremony between performances of *Norma* and *Elena*. She was—as Fanny wistfully attested—"blissfully happy."

Eight months after her farewell performance—on August 15, 1843—Adelaide gave birth to a boy. He was named Greville Edward, after his father and Henry Greville, who stood as his godfather. In the following year Adelaide became pregnant again and gave birth to a daughter. This baby was called Mary Theodosia, after Marie Thérèse and Theodosia Monson, who became the little girl's godmother. Mary Theodosia, however, would soon be known within the family circle simply as May. Adelaide doted on both her children, especially on toddling Greville. He "is very strong," she wrote, "very healthy—very willful and a darling beyond words!"

Adelaide's married happiness was so intense that it radiated as far as Bohemia. She described her husband to Yuza Thun in loving detail. Edward, she wrote, was of middle height and distinguished by:

> Dark hair and dark eyebrows and eyelashes and dark grey eyes—he is very pale and always has a serious face that looks heavy and rather stern till one knows it well when one thinks it only thoughtful and benevolent—

he has a capital forehead and very good teeth and a very kind smile—his voice is gentle and his manner of speaking and manner in general are slow and indolent—he is tolerant and generous and tender hearted in the extreme—he is of a most grateful and affectionate nature—and utterly incapable of malicious or rancorous feeling—I think he is the most humble and modest person I ever knew—his temper is very even and he is *perfectly* easy to live with—to love—to trust and to be happy with.

In the same letter she tried, reluctantly, to describe herself. "I feel that I am grown so old," she said, "and I was so young at Tetschen." Her hopes were fewer than in those past days, "but clearer and stronger." Her temper was more cheerful, and she clung to "simple pleasures and natural affections." Unlike Fanny, Adelaide had never grown to despise her profession, but she had slowly come round to her sister's view that a life set free from incessant performance was healthier and happier. At the same time, Adelaide's nature rebelled at giving up performing. She had practiced faithfully almost every day since childhood, and to give up singing in the presence of an audience would remove a cornerstone of her life. Fortunately, Edward understood her feelings and agreed that, as long as she did not perform for money and selected her listeners from their own circle, there could be no valid objection to her continuing to sing before an audience. In fact, he encouraged her to sing regularly in her own home and in the homes of her friends.

Edward leased an elegant terrace house at 27 Chapel Street, Grosvenor Square, across the road from Hyde Park, and Adelaide spared no pains in arranging the rooms charmingly. She placed the piano in pride of place in the front drawing room and lined the dining room with books, because she "hated a soul-less room." In the back drawing room, where she sat in the morning, she crowded her personal mementos: portraits of her mother, Aunt Dall, Fanny's children, Charles and Henry Greville, Trelawny, Mendelssohn, busts of her father and Fanny and Mario, a view of Tetschen painted by Francis, a plate with the family's heads depicted on it, and a medal from Liszt. This small drawing room was her favorite room in the house, for in it she was not merely Edward's wife but Adelaide Kemble, surrounded by the treasured memorabilia of a proud career.

The Sartorises entertained often and grandly and, thanks to Adelaide, with distinctive flair. She daringly mixed writers and musicians with her fashionable London guests, and she always provided them with theatrical and musical entertainment. She invariably sang, and famous musicians sometimes played. From among her own circle she coaxed amateur actors to try their skills in *tableaux vivants* and charades. Edward became an enthusiastic performer and began to take singing lessons.

As Edward's wife, Adelaide entered a new social class. "Our society is large," she told Yuza, "and what is called very good—but for *intimates* I am not well off." Familiar from her own life with the class above, and artists— "who I suppose rank in the class below"—she found her husband's friends and family an alien breed. "They are extremely rich and very kind to me but they belong to a class of people I never have mixed with—the *rich* landed proprietors of England." They were "full of observances and appearances and conventionalities and etiquettes"—and dull in the extreme. Adelaide felt sure that "I must appear quite as extraordinary to them as they do to me." On her visits with Edward to his Uncle Edward Tunno's country house in Hampshire, she found income was the master key: "everyone who goes there *has* no name and *has* 30,000 a year."

Adelaide had to confess that those visits were often painful. "Fancy," she wrote, "a country house in which I have to wear the finest clothes I have, where there are no flowers—no—*not a single one* in any of the rooms—and where they ask me to sing only when they have people to dinner. . . . I am only a sort of curiosity that they don't feel certain whether to be proud of or ashamed of." She disliked taking the children there, because "they only come into the drawing room once a day for a quarter of an hour, and that by special invitation; and my whole anxiety is to keep them the rest of the time out of sight and hearing—a difficult matter with poor baby who . . . has yet to learn that with some people anything natural amounts to something criminal."

Within a year or two of Adelaide's marriage, Edward's family seemed more sympathetic toward her: "I do believe they like me," she wrote gratefully. She had won over her husband's four brothers, and partly won over Edward Tunno—which was important, since her Edward was Edward Tunno's heir—but her husband's only sister, Eliza, Marquise de l'Aigle, still resented her. A snobbish beauty who had married into the French aristocracy, Eliza seemed to see it as a slur against herself that her brother had married a singer. Adelaide despaired of ever softening her.

In these uneasy circumstances, it was just as well that Adelaide commanded her own exciting circle. She and Edward were frequent guests at Samuel Rogers's brilliant breakfasts, while at the Procters' house, she met the "choice spirits of London society," among them Robert Browning, Charles Dickens, and William Thackeray. The tall, squashed-nosed Thackeray had become almost a brother. She loved his ebullient sense of fun, and he loved her kind heart and her Kemble theatricality.

In those artistic circles in which Adelaide shone, Edward was not fully comfortable. He became tongue-tied and so was nicknamed the "silent Sartoris." Yet it excited him to be on familiar terms with his wife's famous acquaintances, particularly with Felix Mendelssohn, whose reputation in England had reached vast proportions. Mendelssohn liked Edward, inviting him to Germany in 1844, and he liked Adelaide even better. In 1842 and 1845 he dedicated two songs to her: "Schilflied" (Song of the Reeds) and "Frühlingslied" (Spring Song). Presenting her with the manuscripts, Mendelssohn added an affectionate inscription in his distinctive handwriting. Anna Jameson, who heard Adelaide sing "Frühlingslied," said how exquisitely she interpreted it.

Happily married to Edward, Adelaide was achieving a serenity that she had once feared might never be possible. Fanny, on the other hand, was about to enter the stormiest years of her marriage. Just how turbulent Fanny's life was becoming would very soon be revealed.

12

"Submit Your Will to Mine"

Fanny returned from the musical tour of the Rhineland in October 1841 at odds with herself, depressed with life, and imagining walls rising all around her. Back in the tall terrace house that Pierce had rented in Harley Street, she regained the sense that she was someone of importance. On her desk, when she arrived home, lay an invitation from Lord Lansdowne inviting the entire Butler family to spend a week at Bowood House, his country residence in Wiltshire. Agog to visit Bowood, which was noted for its brilliant house parties, she was quick to accept, with Pierce's permission.

Fanny reveled in the grand life, but Pierce felt less satisfaction. While he was flattered to be mixing in high society, he was swimming in the wake of the Kemble sisters, and he did not relish the lesser role. In London, he and Fanny went their own ways. As the weeks passed, his secretiveness awakened Fanny's suspicions. Since their time in Georgia, she had ceased to trust him. Down on the plantation she had seen a side of him that hitherto she had barely glimpsed—an arrogance and callousness that she feared might one day be directed against herself. In Philadelphia, when he spent night after night away from home, she had suspected him of infidelity and had not really believed his protestations of innocence. His behavior in London revived her doubts.

In this mood she began to reevaluate their marriage. The solution to their faltering relationship, so far as she could see, was to stay within the marriage but pursue her own interests: to institute a "partnership, in which, if both partners agree, it is well; but if they do not, neither is bound to yield." By following a life of her own, no longer subject to Pierce's constant veto, she might perhaps regain a measure of the mental stimulation and emotional satisfaction she needed to be happy. Whether Pierce would agree to this arrangement, she doubted. But somehow he must be persuaded to

< 190 >

agree, for such a partnership seemed to offer her only chance of personal happiness.

The recent months, whether in England or Europe, had shown Fanny all too painfully how much she missed her theatrical life. Whenever she watched Adelaide sing in public, she could scarcely contain her longing and envy. Though part of her still hated the negative side of acting, Fanny recognized that performing was necessary for her mental and emotional well-being. She also knew that if she wished to stay married to Pierce, she must give up all hope of a theatrical career, because even if he allowed her a life of her own, he would never allow her a life on the stage. Not that she believed any longer that Pierce had any moral justification for condemning the theatre. To live on money earned from acting was far preferable, in her mind, to living off money derived from slave labor.

If Fanny could no longer act, she could still reach the public. For an audience, she selected the antislavery cause, which had given her more satisfaction than anything—apart from her children—in her seven years of married life. She convinced herself that she could conduct a moderate campaign that would satisfy her need to perform and be active, yet not embarrass Pierce too acutely. She already possessed the ammunition for her new campaign. After returning from Georgia, she had collected the letters she had written to Elizabeth Sedgwick and woven them into a kind of journal. During her last months in America, she had read aloud from that journal to antislavery groups in Philadelphia. So moved were her listeners that glowing reports spread to abolitionists in other cities, including New York.

On returning from the Rhineland, Fanny found a letter awaiting her from Lydia Child, editor of the *National Anti-Slavery Standard*, the New York weekly. Mrs. Child had heard of Fanny's journal and was offering to publish portions of it. While Fanny was delighted by the offer, she knew that Pierce would never forgive her if she exposed the practices of his plantations in a newspaper. At the same time she was reluctant to refuse the invitation, and for days her mind swung back and forth.

She also seems to have grown increasingly disturbed as Adelaide's Covent Garden debut drew closer. To see her sister perform on a stage that Fanny had once regarded as her own must have been almost more than she could bear—in response she mounted her own platform. On November 2, 1841, the night before Adelaide's debut, Fanny wrote to Mrs. Child, refusing to contribute those parts of the journal referring to the plantations, but suggesting a solution. She believed that she could safely offer the account of her journey to Georgia, to which she was happy to add "some observations on the effects of slavery." If this would satisfy Mrs. Child, Fanny would be pleased to send the appropriate extracts and commentary.

Fanny addressed her answer to the *National Anti-Slavery Standard*. Then, in a curious gesture, she handed the letter to Pierce to post. She seems to have believed that only by handling this thorny issue openly and decisively would she win her independence. Pierce, for his part, appeared to accept the letter and made as if to post it. What Fanny did not realize was that, in the moral code in which he had been raised, it was perfectly proper for a husband to keep back a wife's letter. He quietly hid the letter in his desk.

Six weeks later the Butlers set out on their visit to Bowood, taking the children and their American nursemaid with them. The exquisite house, designed by the famous architect Robert Adam, with its classical facade, sweeping staircases, splendid library, and costly art gallery, filled Fanny with delight. "You know this place is celebrated," she told her friends proudly. Though it was midwinter, Fanny and young Sarah fell in love with the park and gardens designed by that prince of landscape gardeners, Capability Brown. When the little girl first looked across the lake and saw the white swans shimmering in the frosty sunshine, she told her mother that this was her idea of paradise.

At Lord Lansdowne's, Charles Greville was a fellow guest, and he and Fanny each wrote a tantalizing picture of that week. She watched Thomas Macaulay, the historian, standing on the hearth rug and talking so torrentially that loquacious old Samuel Rogers, scarcely able to squeeze in a word of his own, became quite piqued. Greville also was delighted to hear talk that was vigorous and wholesome, devoid of politics, gossip, and scandal. There was excellent singing and reciting, too. Thomas Moore, the Irish poet, sang selections from his popular *Irish Melodies*, and Fanny read aloud from *Much Ado About Nothing*. Charles Greville, not an admirer of Fanny on stage, thought her reading was admirable, her voice "equally happy in the humorous and the pathetic parts."

The visit to Bowood restored Fanny's self-confidence. Returning to London happier than she had been for months, she determined to set her life in order. But as the weeks passed, nagging suspicions clouded her mind. Pierce was out from morning to night, seeing she knew not whom and going she knew not where. In an effort to find out, she took to reading her husband's private papers. Searching through his desk, she came upon her unposted letter. The discovery hit her almost like a physical blow. While still in the first flush of rage, she seized her pen and wrote another letter to

Mrs. Child. In the course of it, she offered her the article and explained the delay, making no attempt to spare her husband. Then she went to Pierce and demanded that he read what she had written.

Pierce was thunderstruck. Before his eyes swam a picture of Fanny's article in the abolitionist press, accompanied by her letter denouncing him. "I warned her openly," he later wrote, "that if she sent a letter so derogatory to me, it might lead to our separation." Fanny calmly ignored his threat and sent the letter to the mailbox. Over the next few days, Pierce racked his brain for ways of preventing the impending catastrophe. Then, in a flash of inspiration, he remembered Elizabeth Sedgwick's persuasive powers. Imploring Elizabeth to use her influence, he begged her by letter to persuade Fanny to withdraw the article.

It would be many weeks before Pierce could expect an answer from America, and in the meantime he maintained a semblance of calm, watching the family go about its business. At the end of February, Harriet came to stay, and she and Fanny spent many hours talking. How much Fanny confided in Harriet one does not know—probably not much, since pride prevented her from unburdening herself to her English friends. But Harriet was no fool and could read between the lines. She understood something of what was going on, and her talk seems to have brought comfort.

Once Harriet had gone, Fanny threw herself into preparing for another house party. The Duke of Rutland, an old admirer of the Kembles, had invited the Butlers and Adelaide to stay at his Leicestershire castle for Easter week. Fanny could scarcely wait for Easter to come, and her first sight of the duke's Belvoir Castle was almost as exciting as her first glimpse of Bowood. Built only twenty-five years before, this modern castle, set on a hilltop, was as stately and splendid as Fanny could have wished, and the view it commanded across the Vale of Belvoir—a patchwork of meadows and woods stretching as far as the distant horizon—was one of the loveliest in England. Standing high on the castle battlements, Fanny was moved almost to poetry. The spring winds "swell up as from a sea of woodland, and snatches of bird-caroling and cawing rook-discourse float up to one from nests in the topmost branches of tall trees, far below one's feet," she wrote to Harriet. The guest list was equally splendid and included the Duchess of Richmond and the Duke and Duchess of Bedford. Fanny was overjoyed to be mixing in such exalted company. Proudly she read aloud to her admiring fellow guests in a drawing room hung with red silk and tapestries, and Adelaide sang in the lofty ballroom at the top of the staircase. Everyone adored Adelaide's voice, from the music-loving duke to the servants, who stood in neatly arranged rows on the stairs to hear her sing, and who clapped as loudly as their master.

Fanny was so swept away by the warmth of their reception that on leaving she composed verses, which she offered to the duke. He, in turn, issued orders for the verses to be carved in a stone, which was set on the battlement close to the castle entrance. Forty-one years later, almost to the day, Fanny would visit Belvoir again and present the new duke with concluding verses. Today both poems can be seen on adjoining stones near the great doorway of the castle.

Fanny returned to London on a wave of pleasure, only to find Elizabeth Sedgwick's letter waiting for her. With surprise and shock, Fanny read her friend's strong appeal on Pierce's behalf. It was not advice that she wished to heed, but in the face of Elizabeth's forceful pleading, she felt obliged to assent. On April 1, 1842, Fanny wrote to Lydia Child, withdrawing both her letter and her article. But she did not spare Pierce in the process. In a powerful concluding sentence, she made it clear that she was acting under duress: "however great your contempt may be," she wrote, "for my want of purpose, or your indignation for this proceeding, it cannot possibly exceed my own."

Fanny had bowed to Elizabeth's forceful entreaties, but the effort cost her dearly. Three days later her resentment boiled over, and she ran away from her London home. Having left a farewell note explaining that she was returning to America, she boarded a train for the port of Liverpool. In what was almost a reflex action, Pierce set out in pursuit and managed to intercept her when her train stopped for a time in Birmingham. Since she refused to leave the train, he remained in her carriage and argued with her all the way to Liverpool. There she engaged a room in the Adelphi Hotel, and, while Pierce looked on, ordered the proprietor to obtain her a steamship ticket for a ship sailing to Boston the next day.

All that night, in her room in the hotel, she half-listened to Pierce's pleading. He reasoned with her, pointing out the shame it would cause her family if she publicly abandoned him in England. "I spoke of her father's grief," he wrote later, "and of the mortification as well as distress, her sister and friends must undergo." His argument carried weight, because the last thing Fanny wanted was a public scandal. In the end Pierce offered to go back to America with her at the end of the month if she were still of the same mind. This satisfied her. Next day they drove together to the station and returned to London.

In England, Fanny had taken pains to make it seem that her marriage was reasonably successful. While the facade was not always as convincing as she hoped, she managed to keep up the pretense, even to the extent of partially deceiving her father and sister, who shared the house with her. Her abrupt departure to Liverpool, however, revealed the truth to her family at one blow. The revelation shocked them. While Charles and Adelaide knew that Fanny and Pierce did not always agree, they had had no idea of the extent of the disagreement or the depths of her unhappiness. Charles, as might have been expected, quickly distanced himself from the situation, but Adelaide made no attempt to spare herself and took Fanny's misery to heart.

Fortunately for Fanny, a diversion caught her attention. The Duke of Rutland had described his Easter house party to the youthful Queen Victoria, who, on hearing that Fanny was the wife of a respectable American, suggested that she should be presented at a court drawing room. This was an honor reserved for women in the very highest level of society, and it involved a formal ceremony. While the queen and her husband sat on gilded chairs in the Buckingham Palace drawing room, young women were presented to them one by one, each curtsying low at the queen's feet and kissing the queen's hand. Though affecting nonchalance, Fanny was thrilled to be chosen. She knew that participation in the ceremony would set the seal on her social success.

The official costume for a presentation was a formal dress with a train, and three white ostrich feathers worn in the hair. Determined to cut a dramatic figure, Fanny ordered a splendid gown from Madame Devy, who had made her clothes in the days of her theatrical fame. Cut from white satin and point lace, and trimmed with Roman pearls, it cost ninety-seven pounds—much more than a small shopkeeper could earn in a year. Fanny also hired a splendid set of diamonds. Decked out in her white lace, with the ostrich feathers rising from a diamond necklace worn like a band across her forehead, she must have looked magnificent. The only setback was that she had already overspent her dress allowance and could not pay the bill. She surmised that Pierce would pay it, especially as he was arranging for his own presentation to the queen at an equivalent ceremony for men. What Fanny did not know was that while she was spending money like water, the prices of rice and cotton were falling so fast that Pierce was in serious debt. After one glance at the dressmaker's account, he told her she had to find the money herself.

Hurt and angry that he had not warned her sooner, but drawing on her pride, Fanny vowed that she would pay the bill by her own exertions: "I am determined *my brains* shall pay it," she told Harriet. She began to translate a play by Alexandre Dumas and to sketch a play of her own based on Kotzebue's drama *The Stranger*. The idea came to her while she was brushing her hair in her bedroom, and she snatched up young Sarah's copybook to jot down her thoughts. She also resuscitated the article describing her journey to Georgia, which she had initially promised to Mrs. Child's abolitionist journal, and sold it to the well-known magazine *Bentley's Miscellany*. With the proceeds she paid about half of the dressmaker's bill. She convinced herself that she had a cast-iron excuse for selling the article, because Pierce had told her to find the money herself. But he, of course, did not see her conduct in those simple terms. Not only did he make it amply clear that she had seriously offended him; he angrily reminded her that what she earned was, by law, not her own money but his.

Fanny's determination to write forcefully about slavery had a further consequence. When the lease of their house in Harley Street expired at the end of April 1842, Pierce renewed it for another six months, thereby breaking his promise to return to the United States. The Butlers' rate of spending in London was well beyond their means, and it would have been far more sensible to return home. But now that Fanny had resolved to support abolition publicly, it would seem that Pierce could not risk taking her home. In America she would associate with those formidable abolitionists Lucretia Mott and Lydia Child. It seemed safer to keep Fanny in England until he felt more certain that he could keep her under control.

Fanny made the most of their extended stay in London, renewing friendships and throwing herself into social activities. At the beginning of June, she and Adelaide took part in amateur theatricals at Bridgewater House. The play was *The Hunchback*, by Sheridan Knowles. The author and Fanny were the stars, while Adelaide, Henry Greville, and even Pierce took lesser parts. Rehearsals were at Oatlands, where golden gorse covered the fields like a carpet, and Fanny must have recalled that other spring eleven years before, when she and Augustus Craven acted together in that very house. She had just heard the news of her sister's engagement to Edward Sartoris, and while she rejoiced in it—"as much as I can rejoice in anything"—the sight of her sister's joy also made her wistful and envious. Adelaide was about to enter the kind of marriage Fanny had always wanted for herself. Fanny, however, was also painfully aware of what her sister could be losing if the marriage proved unhappy. "I was surprised," she wrote sadly, "to find how terrible it was to me to see my sister, that woman most dear to me, deliberately leave a path where the sure harvest of her labour is independent fortune, and a not unhonourable distinction, and a powerful hold upon sympathy, admiration, and even kindly regard of her fellow-creatures, while she thus not unworthily ministers to their delight, for a life where, if she does not find happiness, what will atone to her for all this that she will have left?"

On the opening night of *The Hunchback*, Fanny was such a mass of nerves that the chair shook under her as she applied her makeup, and the curl papers in her hair rustled "like a forest cracking and rattling in a storm." But as soon as she stood before the audience, it was as if she had never been away. On the third and final night, as she waited to go on, her thoughts kept straying to four-year-old Fan, who appeared to be coming down with measles. But once on stage, nothing broke her concentration. She was back in harness, and nothing else mattered. She was Fanny Kemble again.

Fanny's success in *The Hunchback*, while uplifting, also left her restless and vulnerable. The tug of the stage had never been so strong, and the knowledge that she might lose her children if she answered it, never more painful. Prey to a host of worries, she felt an increasing suspicion that Pierce was being unfaithful to her. On July 4, those feelings overcame her, and she called a cab and drove off. Pierce saw her leave and supposed that she was going to visit her brother John, who was living in Marie Thérèse's old cottage at Addlestone in Surrey. In fact, Fanny took a train to Kingston, a pretty rural town on the outskirts of London, where she booked into a hotel. Next day she wrote to Pierce requesting money to maintain her until September, when the theatres would reopen and she could go back to her old profession. After a few more days, however, she limped home. As always, the pull of her daughters proved too strong.

Fanny's return to Harley Street lasted only one day, for once she was home, she could think only of escaping again. Fortunately, Adelaide was on her opera tour of Scotland and was urging Fanny to join her; so with Pierce's agreement, Fanny left young Fan in the care of the nursemaid and set out by train for Edinburgh, taking Sarah with her. In a few days' time, Adelaide was due to marry Edward in Glasgow. While there is no evidence that Fanny was at the wedding, it seems more than likely that she made the short journey by train from Edinburgh to Glasgow and stood among the empty pews in St. Mary's Church while Adelaide quietly became Edward's wife.

Fanny hoped for peace of mind in Edinburgh, but she failed to find it. Adelaide's radiant happiness only highlighted her own distress, and, to add to her burdens, her dear Scottish friend Andrew Combe was dying of tuberculosis. The lively man Fanny had once known was reduced to a living skeleton, and she found it hard not to stare at his bony knees rubbing against the thin fabric of his trousers. From Edinburgh, just four days after Adelaide's wedding, Fanny sent Pierce an unhappy letter saying that while she was prepared to return to America with the children, she was not prepared to live with him again.

Pierce retaliated by ordering her to remain in Edinburgh. He then set out to do business in Liverpool, the port to which he shipped his American cotton. Arriving about August 10, he met—either by design or accident— Adelaide and Edward, who were staying there for a week. Though he realized that they were newlyweds, Pierce had no qualms about joining them at their hotel. He had barely settled into the hotel when Fanny arrived to visit her sister.

As Pierce had forbidden Fanny to leave Edinburgh without first informing him, he confronted her with angry accusations. She replied with angry accusations of her own. The bickering continued for the rest of the week, during which time Edward and Adelaide were obliged to abandon their honeymoon and take on the role of peacemakers. One does not know how they viewed this unexpected intrusion. Edward probably took it badly; Adelaide, on the other hand, was sympathetic. Through her patient listening and healing words, a truce of sorts was effected, and on August 17 Fanny and Pierce returned together to London, partially reconciled.

Their reconciliation lasted until the end of October, when the lease expired on the house at Harley Street. Pierce then engaged rooms for his family at a hotel for five weeks, expecting at the end of that time to sail for America. But as the day of sailing drew near, he changed his mind again, arranging to lease a house in nearby Upper Grosvenor Street for another six months. Fanny voiced strong objections to their staying on, but Pierce—with the specter of Fanny's abolitionist campaign looming before him—insisted they remain in London. The upshot was a string of quarrels conducted in their suite at the Clarendon Hotel. Pierce opened hostilities by asserting that their marriage, on its present basis, was over. Arguing that the freedom he allowed Fanny over the past year had failed to make her happy, he demanded that they return to a conventional marriage in which he, as her husband, held supreme authority. Fanny absolutely refused. In her opinion the prime cause of her unhappiness lay in his neglect and unfaithfulness. Calling on him to abandon his "unworthy pursuits and pleasures," she begged him to reinstate their home as a "place of virtue." For

"God's sake," she pleaded, "and for your children's sake, and for your own soul's sake, Pierce! my husband, oh, still my most tenderly beloved, let us be wise before it is too late."

Pierce was perfectly prepared to be wise, but only on his own terms. "The fault has been entirely your own," he wrote. "If you will govern your irritable temper, and if you can consent to submit your will to mine, we may be reconciled and may be happy. I firmly believe that a husband and wife cannot live happily together upon any other terms; and it would be in vain for us to be reunited unless upon a clear understanding of the conditions I propose, and a full determination to abide by them." Reading Pierce's answer, Fanny's mood changed to defiance. "I consider it my duty," she informed him, "*not* to submit my conduct to the government of any other human being." These angry exchanges were conducted entirely by letter, for neither was speaking to the other, even though they continued to occupy the same suite in the hotel.

Late one night, Fanny declared her intention of leaving and rang for the porter to order a cab. Pierce, prepared for a confrontation, was ready with the threat that if she left the hotel "in that disgraceful manner, at that hour of the night," he would take the children to Liverpool the next day and sail on the first steamer for the United States. He warned Fanny that she would never see either of her daughters again. He had no sooner delivered his ultimatum than the porter announced the arrival of the cab. Pierce angrily told him to send it away. Fanny, momentarily crushed, retreated to her room.

Next day her courage returned. She summoned another cab and, calling Pierce's bluff, moved in with Adelaide and Edward at their house in Chapel Street. After years of concealment, the Butlers' marital troubles were suddenly out in the open for all to observe. As Fanny had long feared, London gossips relished the spectacle and were quick to discuss it. Writing in his diary in December 1842, Charles Greville expressed a view that was probably widely held among the Kembles' friends. He did not spare Pierce, calling him a "weak, dawdling, violent-tempered man" who had mismanaged his affairs and had outlived Fanny's respect. Nor did he spare Fanny, acknowledging that his affection and admiration for her were mixed with exasperation. He described her as the "artificer of her own misery" and condemned her lack of tact, judgment, and discretion, especially over the thorny question of American slavery. "She has acted like a Fool," he wrote, and "he is now become a Brute. In consequence she is supremely and hopelessly wretched." Charles Greville noted with sympathy how Fanny lived in terror, afraid that her marriage might completely collapse, "and that then she shall be separated from her children for whom alone she desires to exist." He concluded by doubting whether Fanny could be happy in any marriage: a doubt probably shared by Edward, and perhaps even by Adelaide.

Greville's private, handwritten account omitted one bond that still held the marriage together. This was Fanny's sexual and emotional attachment to her husband. No arrogance on his part, nor pain on hers, could quite sever the bond. From her refuge in Adelaide's house, she sent Pierce a letter that could almost have been written by her mother, so closely did it echo the "bitter joy" of Marie Thérèse's feelings for Charles:

> Having loved you well enough to give you my life, when it was best worth giving, having made you the center of all my hopes of earthly happiness, having never loved any human being as I have loved you, you can never be to me like any other human being, and it is utterly impossible that I should ever regard you with indifference. My whole existence having once had you for its sole object, and all its thoughts, hopes, affections, and passions having, in their full harvest, been yours, as you well know they were, it is utterly impossible that I should forget this—that I should forget that you were once my lover, and are my husband, and the father of my children. . . . I cannot behold you without emotion; my heart still answers to your voice, my blood in my veins to your footsteps; and if this emotion is to be one of perpetual pain, sudden violent, intense, almost intolerable pain, judge how little I am endowed by nature with a temperament fit to endure so severe and incessant a trial.

Pain, rather than happy affection, had bonded Fanny's parents for more than thirty years. As Adelaide put it, their mother's married life "was one of the deepest disappointment, but like a true woman she loved to the very last." It seemed at that moment that Fanny, so like her mother, would follow a similar path.

Late one night Fanny arrived unexpectedly at the house that Pierce and the children were occupying at 26 Upper Grosvenor Street. Arousing the servants from their beds, she insisted on having a room prepared for her and announced her intention of moving in permanently. Next day, to everyone's confusion, she set about organizing "an entirely separate establishment though in the same house." Thereby she had free access to the children but was not obliged to subject herself to the discomfort of meeting her husband. She and Pierce occupied separate apartments and slept, ate, came, and went separately, their solitary exits and entrances provoking much comment.

During these weeks in Upper Grosvenor Street, Fanny veered between defiance and helplessness. She knew that she would be committing emotional suicide if she submitted to Pierce's will, but to lose her children would be equally suicidal. Eventually, in her misery and uncertainty, she proposed a compromise. She promised to obey her husband's wishes "in every respect in which they do not interfere with the dictates of my conscience." While this was not entirely what Pierce wanted, he declared himself satisfied. He did, however, insist that she should seek outside guidance on those issues where her conscience and his own will clashed. Fanny, not to be vanquished, answered that, according to God, her conscience was her own. For days their argument rocked back and forth. Finally she made a further concession, promising "to *endeavor heartily* to do my duty better henceforward." Since both were tired of wrangling, this vague agreement was sufficient to constitute an armistice in the seemingly endless war.

During the tensions, Pierce, not surprisingly, fell ill. Hearing the news in her part of the house, Fanny found the excuse for which her emotions had been waiting. Seizing a scrap of paper, she wrote on it the remorseful words: "Oh, Pierce, I love you dearly; pray let me come and nurse you, and do anything in the world I can for you." According to him her note was the required catalyst, and she returned to his bed, though Fanny remembered the incident less harmoniously. Whatever the exact facts, the Butlers' relationship had undoubtedly improved. In February 1843 Fanny wrote that "for the first time for many a day I am possessing my soul in peace and breathing an atmosphere of affection and happiness." Pierce felt so certain of her obedience that he gave a firm undertaking that they would be sailing to America in less than three months.

As a united couple the Butlers made a long round of farewell visits. They dined with the Procters, Mrs. Grote, and the Dacres, breakfasted with Samuel Rogers, and attended a party at Sydney Smith's so that they could meet Charles Dickens, who was just back from America. They were visited by Trelawny, and they called on Charles Greville, who was stricken with gout and unable to leave his sofa. At Henry Chorley's exotic house in Victoria Square, where the ceilings were painted gold and the walls were hung with crimson silk, Fanny read excerpts from *Much Ado About Nothing* to a circle of friends, Felix Mendelssohn among them, and openly rejoiced at her brief return to stardom.

Fanny and Pierce almost forgot their financial pressures and late in

April staged two farewell parties of their own. On successive nights they entertained about four hundred people with style and extravagance. The food was supplied by a fashionable caterer, and six policemen stood guard outside the entrance to protect the guests and their property. Adelaide sang several arias, Fanny sang several more, and, "upon the whole," Fanny wrote modestly, everyone seemed "tolerably well amused."

A day later Fanny began packing the mounting piles of luggage, helped by Aunt Victoire and Emily Fitzhugh. She dreaded the moment of parting, picturing her own sense of loss and her father's grief, though she knew that her sister would be brave. "I know of no one," she told Harriet, "with more determination and self-control" than Adelaide.

While this was true, the parting on May 2 was almost as disturbing for Adelaide as it was for Fanny. Six months pregnant, Adelaide often felt far from well. While she must have welcomed the peace that Fanny's departure promised to restore, she could only feel anxious as she speculated on her sister's future in America.

13

Caught in a Trap

During the voyage to the United States the sea was rough, and day and night Fanny felt ill in the swaying, creaking cabin. According to her recollection—and she liked to dramatize—she was able to consume only two glasses of calves'-foot jelly and sips of iced water during the entire fifteen days and nights at sea. A respite came at last in Halifax harbor where, as she sat huddled on deck, seemingly too weak to go ashore, the owner of the steamship line recognized her and generously escorted her to his house. After a few hours of Samuel Cunard's hospitality, Fanny felt considerably stronger and convinced herself that she was almost in charge of her life again. A further two days of sailing brought her to the Boston docks, where, on May 20, 1843, she fell thankfully into Elizabeth Sedgwick's arms.

Safely ashore, Fanny felt that her roots lay in America and that she must tend them. Her dearest link with the United States was Aunt Dall, who lay buried in the cemetery at Mt. Auburn, on the outskirts of Boston. Almost immediately Fanny made a pilgrimage to the beautiful burial ground and searched among the trees and winding paths until she found the headstone. Lying on the grass above the grave, she remembered the "perfect lovingness and self-denial" that her aunt gave to those she loved. From her grave, wrote Fanny, Dall's "lovely virtues seemed to call to me to get up and be of good cheer, and strive to forget myself, even as perfectly as she had done." As Dall had been to Fanny, so Fanny vowed to be to Sarah and Fan.

To commune with her aunt gave Fanny that sense of renewal she had been seeking, and her letters to English friends began to echo Dall's serene devotion to duty. To elderly Lady Dacre—who in recent months had become almost like a grandmother to her—Fanny announced that "duty and not happiness is the purpose of life." To Harriet she confided that she was "very sad, but far from out of courage."

< 203 >

Fanny's wish to redirect her life along the paths of duty and tranquillity would have had more chance of success if Pierce had been as wealthy as his social life in London suggested. On both sides of the Atlantic in 1843, trade was depressed, commodities were in glut, and the rice and cotton on which the Butlers' income relied were alarmingly low in price. Pierce's fortune was so depleted that he could not afford to return to live at Butler Place. He was forced to let the house and farm in order to raise income and was obliged to look for a new way of housing his family. Fanny's mind kept returning to those times in London when he had refused to save money by returning home.

At first Fanny hoped that they might rent a house in Philadelphia. She had a particular affection for the city, preferring it to New York because of its "greater air of age," and the tone and texture of its buildings. The brick houses "are not so fiercely red," she wrote, "nor the white facings so glaringly white." She admired the pretty marble bank on Chestnut Street, like a "beautiful little copy of the Parthenon." In such a city she had hopes of enjoying a reasonable social life. "Had I a house of my own in Philadelphia," she informed Harriet, "I should not at all despair of gradually collecting about me a society that would satisfy me perfectly well."

Fanny's hopes were dashed when Pierce decided that, to save the expense of hiring servants, they would not rent a house but live in a boardinghouse. He chose Mrs. McPherson's, a supposedly superior establishment in fashionable South Sixth Street. Catering to the well-to-do and the socially acceptable, the boardinghouse exuded an air of ostentatious gentility that set Fanny's teeth on edge. From the first moment she saw it, she hated it.

If life at Butler Place had been boring, life at Mrs. McPherson's was a hundred times more so. Cut off from a routine of household duties and social engagements and cooped up in one small bedroom, Fanny felt she would go mad. Her hopes for a social life turned out to be fantasies. A few Philadelphia ladies paid calls on her, but she hesitated to encourage further visits, having no private sitting room in which to entertain. The overfurnished public rooms, crowded with fellow boarders, filled her with such distaste that she avoided going into them. And her bedroom was no fit place to receive visitors. She purposely slept on an uncomfortable sofa bed so that her bedroom would seem more like a sitting room by day—which confirms the impression that she and Pierce were no longer sharing a bed—but a bedroom was still a bedroom. Fanny could find no way to disguise the washstand and dressing table, and she had too much delicacy to ask a caller to share her embarrassment.

Fanny had been at the boardinghouse only a few weeks when her gold watch was stolen, along with a gold chain that Harriet had given her as a parting gift. It was the final insult in a series of annoyances. "Of the discomfort and disorder of our mode of life," she wrote to Harriet, "I cannot easily give you a notion, for you know nothing of the sort, and, until now, neither did I. The absence of decent regularity in our habits and the slovenliness of our whole existence is peculiarly trying to me, who have a morbid love of order, system, and regularity, and a positive delight in the decencies and elegancies of civilized life."

The Butlers had no sooner settled into Mrs. McPherson's than a spell of hot weather hit the city. Thermometers registered more than ninety in the shade, and the brick pavements became almost too hot to walk on. Fanny, accustomed to the grass and trees of Butler Place, could not believe how hot it became in the city. Even indoors the temperature was oppressive, and nowhere more so than inside the boxlike bedrooms at Mrs. McPherson's.

By the end of June the children were pale and languid, and their English governess was suffering from the heat. Fanny decided that the family needed a holiday, and, with happy thoughts of sandy beaches and sparkling water, she pleaded with Pierce to take them away—perhaps to Rockaway Beach. Pierce instead insisted that they were far too poor to take a holiday. When Fanny continued pleading, he offered a compromise. Since he was unable to afford a smart hotel in a fashionable resort, he proposed to rent a house in Yellow Springs, about thirty miles west of Philadelphia. A once-thriving health resort, it had fallen from fashion and had become no more than a mineral spring surrounded by a collection of ramshackle farmhouses. These houses were available to summer visitors at a trifling rent.

Fanny described Yellow Springs as a "third-rate watering place," while the wooden farmhouse where she, the children, and the governess stayed was "as comfortless as it is possible to imagine." Yet she was surprisingly content there. The walls might be collapsing and the chairs and sofas broken, but there was space to move, and the sense of being in a place of one's own. The surrounding countryside was undeniably lovely: yellow cornfields, dark-green woods, and orchards dotted with white farmhouses. "I ride, and walk, and fish, and look abroad on the sweet kindly face of Nature, and commune gratefully with my Father in heaven whenever I do so," Fanny informed Harriet happily. "The hours pass swiftly by, and life is going on, and the rapid flight of time is a source of rejoicing to me."

Fanny's favorite excursion was to the open-air pool, a "beautiful deep spring of water, as clear as crystal and almost as cold as ice, surrounded by whitewashed walls," and open at the top to the sky. There, every morning, she and the children took "three breathless dips." Sarah and Fan loved the bracing water as much as their mother and splashed about like a couple of little ducks. The only defect was the presence of their fellow bathers. Fanny disliked sharing her morning bath with other women during the bathing hours for females, which ran from ten to twelve. When, at the start of August, the resort and the baths became crowded, she felt impelled to devise a scheme whereby she and the children could bathe on their own.

They arrived at noon, just as the last women were leaving, and promptly locked themselves inside so that they could swim and dress at their leisure. At about half-past twelve, they sauntered out, passing the impatient crowd of men congregated around the door, whose time of entry was well overdue. Pierce, arriving on a brief visit, was met by the angry pool-keeper, who demanded that Mrs. Butler obey the rules. Pierce passed the order on to Fanny, who refused to listen. In retaliation, Pierce gave her just three hours in which to pack the children's and her own belongings and return to town.

After five more weeks of heat, Fanny gained the welcome respite of a few days at cooler Lenox, and the bonus of a few more days in New York to meet the English actor William Macready, who was on a theatrical tour of America. She and Pierce dined with him on September 30, and Macready recorded in his diary that Fanny spoke admirably, "but quite like a man." Some of her sentiments, he added, so lacked charity that they ought not to have been expressed in the present company. One presumes that she denounced slavery in Pierce's presence.

Soon after the Butlers returned to Philadelphia, Fanny made a startling discovery. For some time she had been in the habit of prying among Pierce's private papers, and on this foray, she came across a packet of sealed letters, which she did not hesitate to open. They were from an unnamed lady, and they suggested, though not conclusively, that Pierce was engaged in a sexual affair. Pain, shock, and anger swept over her as she examined the incriminating pages, for she had no shadow of doubt that he was guilty. Her pain was made worse when she realized that the letters were some years old, and that they referred to a time when she had fondly imagined that she and Pierce were getting on well. Even though Fanny had long suspected her husband of adultery, the sight of the written evidence was deeply wounding. The fact that the letters seemed to prove her right did not ease her hurt.

She immediately wrote to the Sedgwicks, and they were almost as shocked as she, because they had always believed Pierce's vows of innocence. As a family they at once sprang to her aid. Charles Sedgwick's lawyer brother, Theodore, came down from New York to interview Pierce on Fanny's behalf. He found Pierce ill in bed but ready with excuses. Pierce claimed that he had never opened the letters from the mysterious lady and that Fanny had broken the seals to read the contents. He protested his innocence with every appearance of sincerity. As the questioning grew heated, however, he is supposed to have let down his defenses. According to Fanny, "in a moment of unguarded exasperation," he "*repeatedly* acknowledged the fact of his infidelity," adding that the knowledge would do his wife no good, because nothing could legally be proved against him.

As Fanny's rage subsided, she started to review her position. She thought a reconciliation was hopeless, for it would lead only to more neglect, disappointment, and betrayal. She wished to be rid of Pierce and at the same time to keep her children. Whereas until then this had seemed impossible, with the discovery of the letters, it suddenly seemed feasible. Despite Pierce's avowals of innocence, a cloud of suspicion hovered over him; and even if nothing definite could be proved, she would be justified in the eyes of the world in leaving him. With public opinion on Fanny's side, Pierce could scarcely deny her unlimited access to her daughters. She might even be able to win a reasonable financial settlement.

At the beginning of November, on the advice of Theodore Sedgwick, Fanny asked Pierce for a legal separation. Pierce received the request calmly and said that he would not oppose it. He seems to have believed that this was simply another instance of the "boiling spring" of Fanny's emotions, and that her anger would in time subside. He therefore told Theodore Sedgwick that they did not need lawyers or a legal declaration: it was better to keep the separation informal. He suggested that Fanny should engage a separate apartment for herself at Mrs. McPherson's.

At the same time, Pierce was careful to place curbs on her conduct. In return for his agreement to separate, Fanny had to promise never to resume acting, to write nothing of which he did not approve, and to abandon her campaign against slavery. In return, he agreed to give her unrestricted access to the children, and to pay her one-third of his income in monthly installments.

Fanny accepted his proposal, but her acceptance was grudging. She resented having to agree to restrictions that prevented her from pursuing the very activities that, next to her daughters, gave meaning to her life. She confided to the American actress Charlotte Cushman that, if it were not for Pierce's restrictions, she would certainly return to the stage. Most of all, she resented Pierce's arrogance in daring to impose conditions on her while he was brazening out his adultery. What Fanny craved was a clear-cut victory, so that her terms, not his, would prevail. She confided these feelings to Elizabeth Sedgwick, who was about to visit her at Mrs. McPherson's.

Before arriving at the boardinghouse, Elizabeth informed Pierce that "there can no longer be friendship, or even the appearance of it, between us." At the same time, while under the same roof, she was determined to treat him civilly, and since Pierce was eager to avoid a scandal, he responded with matching civility. For the four weeks of Elizabeth's stay, Pierce treated her and Fanny with elaborate courtesy. He even insisted that they share his table in the dining room. When the actor Macready arrived to pay a call, Pierce conducted him upstairs to Fanny's room, and graciously left him with Fanny and a visitor, who was either Elizabeth or Catharine Sedgwick.

Stern Elizabeth was not deceived by Pierce's playacting. The Sedgwicks were on Fanny's side and determined to lend whatever assistance they could. They were so convinced of Pierce's guilt, and so enraged by it, that their enthusiasm rather got the better of them. When Elizabeth heard rumors that Pierce had seduced a maid at Butler Place, she began her own investigation. Theodore Sedgwick also hired agents in London to cross-examine the Butlers' former servants at Harley Street. In January 1844, reports and rumors reached Pierce from both sides of the Atlantic that investigators were examining his sex life, and that gossip concerning his love affairs was proliferating.

Perturbed that his name was being blackened in the eyes of his English friends and relatives, Pierce wrote to Charles Kemble, Adelaide, and Edward, protesting his innocence. Charles, no doubt thinking of his own unhappy marriage, was decidedly more sympathetic to Pierce than to his own daughter, and he was obviously drawing on personal experience when he wrote: "Mutual forbearance is the only remedy to be resorted to in such a case." He concluded his letter with the revealing phrase: "God bless you, my son, I long to hear that you are reconciled to poor Fanny." Poor Marie Thérèse or poor Fanny—they must have seemed almost the same person to Charles. He seemed to be implying that God's blessing was sorely needed for any man married to either of them.

Edward Sartoris replied to Pierce's letter with more caution. Reluctant to pass judgment on either partner, he merely expressed the wish that "a better time may come." Adelaide, who by this time was forceful in her private criticism of Pierce, must have been warned by Edward to be tactful. She refused to write at all, passing on through Edward the excuse that it would be painful for her to enter the dispute. Pierce, however, seems to have felt certain that he was planting goodwill among Fanny's family, and that they would silence the wagging English tongues. What he did not know was that he was about to face wagging tongues nearer home.

A lawyer by training, Pierce knew that if adultery could be proved against him, Fanny would most likely win a divorce and gain custody of the children. And yet in March 1844, in the midst of the gossip and investigations, he allowed himself to become involved in another affair. That month he traveled with a socially prominent Philadelphia couple, the Schotts, to New York. There, in the Astor Hotel late one night, James Schott discovered Pierce and Mrs. Schott together in her bedroom. Pierce attempted an explanation, but it was insufficient to satisfy the suspicious husband. Schott issued a challenge, and the two men met in Maryland on May 15 to exchange pistol shots. Fortunately, their aim was amiss, and the duelists' honor—but not Fanny's—was satisfied without physical injury. Though an attempt was made to hush up the incident, it figured juicily in gossip of the time.

Fanny could not fail to hear about the duel. It can only have added to her sense of injustice and frustration and strengthened her conviction that her husband was a perpetual philanderer. Her response was to fan public opinion in her favor. As a consequence Pierce found all Philadelphia gossiping about his marital and extramarital affairs. It was a heavy blow to his patrician pride. For nine years he had tried to conceal his domestic troubles, even from his relatives, and now the secret was released, with his own wife spreading the details. All hope of mending his marriage or concealing his problems vanished from his mind. Instead, he felt a vindictive anger. Fanny was damaging his public standing in Philadelphia, and he wanted her silenced and punished. He was still in a position to exact revenge. Those "low-bred and vulgar meddlers," the Sedgwicks—whose very name was now anathema to Pierce—had failed to uncover a grain of firm evidence against him.

Proximity to the children was the weapon Pierce chose to control and chastise Fanny. He knew that she would do anything to be near her daughters, and he began to use this knowledge unscrupulously. He had never before called her an unfit parent: rather, he had emphasized her competence as a mother, and even during some of their worst arguments he had spoken generously of her devotion to the children. Now her unfitness became his theme. Arguing that by separating herself from the children she had shown herself an unstable and undutiful parent, he declared that she had forfeited many of her maternal rights.

In the spring of 1844 Pierce announced his intention of giving up his rooms at Mrs. McPherson's at the end of the summer and taking his daughters for three months to the fashionable resort of Newport. He concluded his announcement with a new set of stipulations designed to bring his wife to heel. She was not to be permitted to join them at Newport, nor was she to be given automatic access to Sarah and Fan when they returned to live in Philadelphia. Their new home would be a rented house opposite that of his brother John in Walnut Street, and if Fanny wished to live under the same roof and see her daughters daily, she must agree to a new arrangement, which included two fresh conditions. The first was that she should communicate with no one of whom Pierce disapproved—and the Sedgwicks were first on his list of those prohibited. The second was that she should never discuss their life together or Pierce's household with anyone in America or in England—nor, indeed, mention him in public in other than favorable terms. "If Mrs. Butler considers her duty to her children paramount to all other considerations," wrote Pierce to Fanny's lawyer, "she will have no difficulty in acceding to this proposal; in which case I need scarcely say to you, that I will endeavour to make her residence with her children as comfortable as it can be, whilst her excited state of feeling against me continues."

Fanny saw these conditions as outrageous. To live in his household merely on sufferance, and to lack the support of her friends, would be a fate worse than anything she had so far endured at Pierce's hands. In his determination to show that he was master, he was treating her with that callousness he had shown toward his slaves. On May 5, 1844, she replied by posting him a lawyer's letter rejecting his terms. And yet, as she well knew, if she did not ultimately agree, she would risk losing her daughters.

Meanwhile she found herself the target of further humiliations. On May 28, the day of the children's joint birthday, Sarah and Fan were taken to Butler Place for their birthday party. Fanny was not allowed to join them, because Pierce declared that there was no room in the carriage. She witnessed their departure from the boardinghouse, and, determined not to be beaten, decided to follow on horseback. Later she watched them surreptitiously through the trees as they played in the garden of their old home.

Painfully aware that access to her daughters would soon be restricted, Fanny made the most of what precious time remained. Each morning before breakfast, and each afternoon when lessons were over, she walked with the girls for an hour in the square adjoining Mrs. McPherson's or took them to the nearby market to buy fruit and flowers. When Fan fell and broke her arm in June, the walks were briefly stopped, but once the child recovered, they were resumed. They continued even when riots erupted, and Catholic homes and churches were burned and pillaged. In every way, Fanny noted, it was a miserable time in Philadelphia.

After Sally and Fan went with their father to Newport in August, Fanny's life in Philadelphia became dismal. To fill in the long weeks, she read, walked, studied German, and played the piano. She could no longer ride, because she had just lost her horse Forrester—a bright bay, with black legs, who grinned "with delight, like a dog," when Fanny spoke to him or patted him. The loss distressed her the more because she had only just bought him back, Pierce having arbitrarily sold off the family's horses when they sailed for England. Having repurchased Forrester with the proceeds of a book of poems she had published especially for the purpose, Fanny could not believe her bad luck when he broke his hip and had to be put down.

In the late autumn Pierce and the children returned from Newport and moved into their new house in Walnut Street. Fanny was relieved to have her daughters back with her in Philadelphia, but she was still uncertain what course to follow. She continued to regard her husband's proposals as monstrous. On the other hand, she knew that she could not endure a life separated from her children. To gain time she took rooms in a boarding-house not far from Walnut Street and spent as many hours as possible with the little girls.

By Pierce's latest edict, she was allowed only seven hours a week in the children's company, and even some of those were whittled away. When she tried to augment her visits or perform what she saw as her motherly duties, she was rudely rebuffed by Pierce or by his servants. Once she approached the children in the street and was prevented by their governess from speaking to them. When she attempted to supervise their clothes or correct their manners, she was reproved by Pierce for interfering in matters that no longer concerned her.

During the last weeks of 1844, Fanny felt so desperate that she knew she was close to surrender. Wretched and uncertain, she turned to a friend, the Unitarian minister of her church, the Reverend Dr. William Henry Furness. An abolitionist and a long-standing friend of the Butlers, he was able to sympathize with both sides. Furness was moved by Fanny's distress and offered himself as a mediator. But after representing her interests in a correspondence with Pierce over some weeks, he found that he could only advise one course of action—he begged Fanny to agree to her husband's terms.

At the turn of the year, having rarely seen her daughters in the past four months, Fanny gave in. She agreed to Pierce's terms and prepared to move into the house in Walnut Street. Another three months were to pass, however, before she was allowed to join the children, thanks to the delays orchestrated by Pierce. Before she could set foot in his house, she was forced to sign a written agreement accepting his conditions.

On March 3, 1845, Fanny was permitted to take up residence in Pierce's house. She entered the door with a feeling of dread, and within days found herself in a nightmarish world where she had always to be on her guard. Before leaving London, Pierce had engaged a young and pretty English girl, Amelia Hall, as a governess to the children. At first Fanny had warmed to her, looking on her as an ally. But her opinion of the governess changed drastically.

It seemed to Fanny that Amelia Hall excluded her from all decisions regarding the girls' welfare, and that Pierce upheld Miss Hall's authority. Worse, Fanny found herself insulted or ignored by her husband in Miss Hall's presence, while the governess looked smugly on and appeared to register approval. It leaped to Fanny's mind that the two were conspiring to humiliate her, in which case, she argued, they were probably sleeping together. In her indignation she confided in Adelaide, who was immediately up in arms on her sister's behalf. "To think of it!" cried Adelaide as she relayed part of Fanny's letter to the Thuns, "her children . . . under the care of a heartless governess who teaches them to behave with impertinence and disrespect to her—she is not allowed to choose their clothes or even to take a walk with them! and this, a most devoted mother and a woman of irreproachable character!"

Besides confiding in her sister, Fanny passed her suspicions on by letter to Anna Jameson and Mary Appleton Mackintosh. Adelaide and Mary were so incensed that they took it upon themselves to write to Pierce, begging him to dismiss the governess, though neither went so far as to make an open accusation of sexual misconduct. Anna Jameson spoke less guardedly to her friend Lady Byron—the poet's widow—talking of a "criminal connection" between Mr. Butler and his children's teacher. Lady Byron passed the allegations on to a Dr. Carpenter, who, in turn, passed them on to the Hall family in London.

The gossip, having crossed the Atlantic to England, returned to

Philadelphia by way of a letter written to Amelia Hall by her sister. When the governess showed the letter to Pierce, he was quick to suspect that his wife was the originator of the gossip—and almost as quick to seek retribution. According to his reading of the situation, Fanny had willfully broken her word never to discuss their marriage with outsiders, and even more wickedly, had uttered a malicious slander against an innocent employee. In these abusive exchanges Fanny held her own, keeping cool while Pierce ascended to higher and higher levels of rage. She also covered herself by sending, without his knowledge, a note to Amelia Hall denying that she had endorsed the sexual allegations. This was a skirmish that Fanny seems to have won, but her minor victory served only to make Pierce angrier. How justified Fanny was in her suspicions of sexual misconduct one cannot know, but certainly Amelia Hall's loyalty to her employer was unusually ardent.

While Fanny directed her anger at the governess, some of Pierce's anger fell once more on those "vulgar and obtrusive people," the Sedgwicks. In April 1845, barely one month after Fanny's arrival at Pierce's house in Walnut Street, a letter came to the house from Catharine Sedgwick. Pierce was undecided whether Fanny should receive it, because one of the conditions of her reinstatement was that she would have no communication with any of the Sedgwicks. Finally he decided that Fanny could have her letter, and he entrusted it to a servant to take to her.

Aware that the letter came to her by way of Pierce, Fanny justifiably argued that it was passed on with his consent and assumed that she was entitled to read it. She had barely broken the seal when Pierce confronted her. Why had she not kept her promise and sent the letter back unopened to Miss Sedgwick? "I felt myself completely caught in a trap," wrote Fanny.

The more she struggled, the tighter the trap seemed to close. As the year progressed, the extent of her helplessness dawned on her, and her fury surged upward like a volcano and exploded over Pierce. The children were incapable of coping with the violence of the quarrels. Already depressed and pressured beyond their limits, they reacted visibly, especially ten-year-old Sarah, who was naturally sensitive and temperamental. Pierce decreed that Fanny had lost the respect of her children, and demanded that she cease all communication with Sarah.

The late spring and summer of 1845 were laced with retaliatory incidents. On May 28, the day of the children's birthdays, the exclusive birthday party was repeated, with the same punitive features as in the year before, along with a further harrowing incident. When Fanny was again refused entry to the carriage in which the children and their governess were departing for the party at Butler Place, poor little Fan tried to remain with her mother. Seeing her mother in tears, the child cried out that she wished to travel with Fanny in another carriage. Fanny had not the heart to accept her daughter's offer: she sent the little girl back to take her seat with the others and followed in a hackney by herself.

Fanny knew that Pierce was attempting to drive her out. What was worse, he was succeeding, because she daily felt her strength failing. Since her position was untenable, she began to think of taking matters into her own hands and simply quitting, as Adelaide and others were suggesting. On September 1, when the children had been on holiday for two months without her, she wrote a last letter pleading with Pierce to learn from "the discomfort, disorder and the most serious disadvantages" of the previous six months and to reinstate her to the "rights and position of a mother." She waited each day for a reply, but none came.

Nine days after writing her plea, Fanny wrote again. She had been systematically excluded, she said, from her children, for whose sake alone she had stayed in discomfort and humiliation in Philadelphia. If Pierce at a future day should see fit to restore her to her rightful position as a mother, nothing would prevent her from accepting it. Meanwhile, she informed him, she was returning to London on the advice of her family. After all the commotion, upheavals, and loss of face, he was probably only too glad to see her vanish from his life.

After a quick visit to the Sedgwicks at Lenox, where Fanny seems to have borrowed money for her fare, she went to Boston, and on October 16, 1845, she boarded a ship for England. Though emotionally still not free of Pierce, she would not live with him again.

❧ 14 ❧

Land of Consolation

In the autumn of 1845, Fanny came to live in Charles Kemble's lodgings in Mortimer Street, London. Her spirits were bruised but not broken. From schooldays she had discovered that mental and physical activity could throw off depression and bring a buoyancy that had "nothing to do with happiness or peace or hope." Nevertheless, at times her composure gave way, especially when she thought about her daughters. One night at the Procters' house, she heard a lullaby that had been composed by Adelaide. Her thoughts turned to Sarah and Fan, and she broke into agitated weeping.

Seeking comfort as never before, Fanny clutched at her family. She was dismayed, however, on arriving in London, to find that Adelaide was no longer there. Just as Fanny had set sail from America, Edward Sartoris had whisked his household off to Italy. The timing may well have been deliberate, because Edward was becoming "indifferent" to Fanny and probably thought it wiser to avoid her. Adelaide, for her part, was far from indifferent, and she went to Italy with sad backward glances. She said straight out that, unlike her sister, she would suffer anything to keep her children with her, but this did not prevent her from feeling an overwhelming sympathy. Her thoughts were loyally with Fanny, and her words breathed affection.

With Adelaide away in Italy, Fanny turned to other members of her family, but without much success. Her brother Henry, still with his regiment in Ireland, came only occasionally to England, and though he expressed sympathy, he was unable to be of practical help. Her brother John lived nearer at hand—in Marie Thérèse's old cottage at Addlestone—but he could give no assistance, either. Poor as a church mouse and struggling to provide for his nagging wife and three children, John was in no position to assist anyone.

Fanny's father, who should have been her guardian and companion,

< 215 >

was not very helpful. He was too busy fawning over his landlady who, according to Adelaide, was a "very vulgar low woman whose character is bad and who *drinks* into the bargain." Fanny had arrived in England to find herself expected to lodge with the pair of them, and to enter into "terms of intimacy with this horrid woman." She loathed the arrangement, but she had so little money that she could not afford to move elsewhere.

Aunt Victoire, with whom she might have lived comfortably, had died the previous year, leaving Fanny a modest sum of money that would have eased her poverty if only she had been able to claim it. Alas, as a married woman, Fanny needed her husband's permission before she could accept a bequest of any kind. She wrote to Pierce asking for his permission, and also asking for an allowance on which to live, since she preferred not to be financially dependent on her father. But she received no early response.

As the weeks slipped by, Fanny felt obliged, not only to live off her father, but to badger him into repaying the large amount she had earned on her American tour of 1832–1833. At his insistence, she had made over the money to him at the time of her marriage, and he was entitled to keep the interest, provided he bequeathed the capital back to her on his death. But Fanny was too poor to wait for his death.

Her request was not altogether unreasonable, because Charles was well off. In 1844 he had been invited to read Shakespeare's *Cymbeline* aloud to Queen Victoria, and his success at that reading had spored a mushrooming series of public performances, bringing in twenty guineas at a time. Nevertheless, Fanny's pleas for Charles to return her earnings went disregarded. His refusal to part with a penny of what both sisters believed was, in moral terms, Fanny's money, was an omission for which neither could forgive him for the rest of their lives.

Searching for another source of income, Fanny began to revise some of the poems that she had written recently. The year previously she had published a book of verse in America, but since it reflected her depressed state, it had enjoyed very little success. Even loyal Fanny Appleton had disliked the poems, describing them as "too bitter and morbid for a Christian woman." Fanny's new poems were happier. Henry Chorley liked them so much that he approached the British publishing house of Blackwoods on her behalf. To her intense relief, Blackwoods accepted the manuscript and offered her an advance.

Fanny was especially touched by the way her English friends rallied round, giving her as little time as possible to feel sorry for herself. Harriet had come to the Liverpool docks to meet her ship and had whisked her off to Bannisters to stay with Emily Fitzhugh. Lord and Lady Dacre and Mrs. Grote had insisted on her coming to their country houses and had plied her with clever talk, charming music, and long rides through the countryside. In London, the Greville brothers, the Egertons, the Procters, Samuel Rogers, Anna Jameson, Henry Chorley, and the frail old Berry sisters (who, as Fanny put it, "still hang on the bush") overwhelmed her with help and hospitality. She dined out at one or another of their houses almost every day.

Another acquaintance who offered her sympathy was Caroline Norton, the granddaughter of the Kembles' old companion, the playwright Richard Brinsley Sheridan. Fanny had known Mrs. Norton during the late 1820s, when she and her husband lived close to the Kembles at Westminster and attended the same church at the back of Downing Street. Fanny admired Mrs. Norton's sparkling beauty and poetic talent, calling her a "splendid creature."

Since those prosperous days, Caroline's life had suffered. In June 1836 her husband sued the then prime minister, Lord Melbourne, over a supposedly adulterous relationship with Caroline; and though she and Melbourne were declared innocent, Caroline was cast out of the marital home, losing her children and the right to claim the earnings from her poems. A passionate crusader for women's rights, she knew, firsthand, the plight of a discarded wife and was able to empathize with Fanny's unhappiness

Now that Fanny was distanced from Pierce, she began to see how futile her dreams had been of returning to America to fight for her daughters, for Pierce would never agree to her repossessing them—or even seeing them—no matter how hard she and her family fought. The sense of loss distressed her as she tried to write cheerfully to her girls. It was a happier task to write to her friends in Lenox, where pastoral beauty and virtue still reigned supreme. "My little sketch of Lenox Lake lies always open before me," she told Harriet, "and I look at it very often with yearning eyes." Lenox had become for Fanny what Tetschen had long been for Adelaide— a place of safety to which her mind retreated when reality became too much for her. She needed Lenox because emotionally she was in almost constant pain. Sometimes she passed the whole of a morning sitting on the floor, crying.

In far-off Rome, Adelaide worried about her sister; and it was presumably at Adelaide's urging that Edward wrote in November 1845 offering Fanny a temporary home in the Sartoris household. In view of his indifference to her, it was an astonishingly generous gesture. To Fanny it was a godsend. Having consulted her father, she wrote a thankful assent and began to plan her visit.

She knew that the journey to Rome would not be easy, because social convention decreed that a lady traveling across Europe should have an escort. Her father, who was the obvious choice, made a tentative offer but then withdrew it. In the end, rather than risk further delay, Fanny decided to defy convention and go without an escort, accompanied only by her maid. Her next task was to pick an itinerary. Many roads led to Rome, but in December all were hazardous—some even impassable. How to reach her destination, virtually alone and unprotected, posed a serious problem. Eventually she decided that her safest plan was to travel by ferry to Le Havre and by public coach and train across France to Nevers. There, boarding a coach, she could cross the mountains to Chalon-sur-Saône and catch a steamer down the Saône to Lyons, then down the Rhône to Avignon. For the last stage of her journey she could travel by coach to Marseilles, where she could set sail for Civitavecchia, the port of Rome. The timetable seemed reassuringly simple but, as she was soon to find, her European journey rivaled her trip to Georgia in discomfort and difficulty.

Winter had set in, and snow lay deep along much of her route. The French inns and boats were as uninviting as their American counterparts, though Fanny had to admit the French food was infinitely tastier than anything she ate in America. While it was piquant to be lifted, still sitting in the coach, onto a railway wagon and be pulled behind a locomotive into Paris, it was downright terrifying to be snowbound in a "most horrible cutthroat looking hole" of an inn between Nevers and Chalon. In her own words, she could "have cried for very cowardice." Nevertheless, she braved bleak mountain passes and brigands when she set out next day in a "crazy, dirty, rickety sort of gig" rented from the one-eyed and rapacious landlord.

At Chalon the river Saône was running too high for the safety of steamers, and Fanny was obliged to make one of the most trying coach journeys she had ever made. She quickly revised her opinion of American travel. Why, compared to France it was safe, pleasant, and sanitary. How she missed the American courtesy toward a lady traveling alone! She regretted that she had spoken harshly of her adopted homeland, and from then on, in coaches and boats across Europe, she found herself chauvinistically defending American customs, people, and scenery, not once finding a place to rival her beloved Lenox.

Her journey was not without its pleasures. She savored a succulent perch caught in the river Saône. She encountered an agreeable antiquarian from Lyons, who was eager to show her the sights of that city. At Marseilles she leaped from her carriage and ran down the beach to dabble her fingers in the Mediterranean waves. When she reached Italy she was utterly enchanted by its sun, sky, and gardens. Fanny called it her "land of consolation."

On January 10, 1846, twenty-one days after leaving England, she caught her first glimpse of towering St. Peter's and was suddenly filled with hope. Her feelings overflowed into verse:

> Oh! Rome, tremendous, who, beholding thee,
> Shall not forget the bitterest private grief
> That e'er made havoc of one single life?

One hour later she was among her trunks at the customs house, waiting for the Sartorises' carriage to collect her. Soon she was driving up the steep, slippery streets to the top of the Pincio hill, then stopping at the door of the Sartorises' apartment. Adelaide was watching from a high window and racing downstairs to greet her. At the open door they fell into each other's arms.

Next morning Fanny awakened to a new life. The first sound she heard was the cooing of Adelaide's children, and the first scene that met her eyes was the terrace adjoining her room, ablaze with oleanders and camellias and bathed in winter sunshine. Seeing her standing in her dressing gown at the open window, Edward beckoned her onto the terrace to look at the view. The city was spread out like a map around her. Above her soared the twin towers of the church of Trinità dei Monti; on the opposite horizon pines spread their dark branches against the sky, and below she could see the Spanish Steps, crowded with picturesque Italians hoping to earn a fee by posing for artists. She could see "old men with grizzled beards and hair, and lads with blue-black locks falling all round the most wonderful eyes," and girls in brilliant peasant costumes, with "splendid heads and shoulders, and scarlet jackets, and daggers thrust through the braids of their hair." They lolled beneath Fanny's window, "screaming, shouting, laughing, gesticulating, or dozing like cats with half closed eyes upon the worn stone steps."

Fanny drank in the beauty and basked in the warmth. Adelaide's love enveloped her, and the children enchanted her, especially little blond May. There was also a dark side. Safe with Adelaide, Fanny no longer felt the need to fight off anguish, and the full impact of her loss took hold of her. Adelaide's children revived memories of Sarah and Fan. When she saw the flowering acacias, Fanny was overcome by recollections of her children's spring birthdays, and a "ten-fold agony" pierced her heart. In the following days she suffered headaches, dizzy spells, and fits of black depression.

The Sartorises tried to distract her, and each afternoon they took her sightseeing to a picture gallery, an ancient church, an antique garden, or a splendid fountain. Thanks to their efforts Fanny's headaches and faintness retreated, but many of their activities annoyed or depressed her. Shopping irritated her because the streets seemed always to be jammed with beggars, and the shopkeepers seemed to be dishonest. Social calls bored her because the English residents in Rome had no intellectual conversation. Of all their pastimes, only sightseeing really pleased her. She praised the noble proportions of St. Peter's, enthused over the fountains—she loved to watch running water—and wandered with intense appreciation through the picture galleries.

Sometimes Fanny and Edward rode on horseback out of the city—the happiest diversion of all. The open country known as the Campagna, studded with honeysuckle and wild roses, sprinkled with brown sheep and white dogs, filled her with such delight that she was able to ride across it and forget almost everything. The motion of the horse beneath her, the scents of the flowers, the sounds of the bells on the sheep—all were a joy to her senses.

Carnival week was in February, and on a cloudless St. Valentine's Day—one day after Adelaide's thirty-first birthday—the sisters draped their hats and gowns with white calico, donned pink mesh masks to protect their eyes, and, clutching trays of sugarplums, flowers, and floury dried peas called *confetti*, drove to the street named the Corso to join the merrymakers. In that crowded thoroughfare, soldiers and brass bands marched, and noisy Italians in costume pelted one another with flowers, peas, and sugarplums. "The bright air resounded with acclamations of joyful human voices," wrote Fanny, "and was misty with fine flour, hail and nosegays flying in all directions."

For a time Adelaide and Fanny stood on a balcony and watched the mock battle beneath them. Then, unable to contain themselves a moment longer, they took up their trays of weapons and joined the masked revelers below. Hoarse with laughing, their arms aching from hurling peas, their shawls awry, their faces smeared with flour, their bonnets dented, and their "very stays filled with horrid little confetti," they cavorted like a pair of skittish schoolgirls up and down the crowded Corso. For a few blissful hours, Fanny's cares were gloriously forgotten.

Six weeks later, during Holy Week, Fanny visited the Vatican and was not pleased. Protestant to her marrow, she watched the elaborate Easter rituals with disgust. She did not bother to hide her disapproval when a *monsignore* gained them access, on Good Friday, to a Hospital for Pilgrims, where they were to witness the spectacle of high-born ladies in red aprons washing the feet of poor women. Fanny's sympathies were entirely with the poor women, penned up like sheep in one corner of the room. "I think," she wrote, "that nobody looking at the whole scene with the eye of common sense, would have seen anything but awkwardness, embarrassment, a sort of terrified surprise, fatigue, and shy dismay depicted on the countenances of the poor creatures. . . . I find it difficult to imagine that frame of mind which rejoices in the unsympathizing presence of crowds of strangers at the sacred services of one's religion."

Fanny preferred to seek God away from pomp and ritual. On early mornings she would pass through the streets, stopping to watch the mobile dairy of goats being milked on the Roman doorsteps. She would wander through the Forum and eventually reach the ruins of the Coliseum, that silent arena where so many had died to the cheers of bloodthirsty crowds. There Fanny would sit at the foot of a cross and meditate on those martyrs who had offered up their souls within the Coliseum's walls. From every rift and crevice where an inch of soil could lodge, wildflowers cascaded down the stones, winding over cracked marble seats and around fallen marble columns. Thus the hand of God transformed a great slaughterhouse to a place of beauty, Fanny mused. The sight never failed to fill her with religious awe.

After Easter, Edward Sartoris leased part of a grand villa at Frascati in the nearby Alban Hills, a summer retreat of the nobility. The outside walls of the villa were a patchwork of peeling paint, but the inside walls were exquisitely painted with graceful classical designs. Within those painted walls, Fanny found peace. She would rise early and walk through the neighboring countryside, picking bunches of amber grapes and purple figs, like a greedy bird. On one such morning she met a peasant girl who, noticing her solitariness, called out in Italian: "It is better to be alone than ill accompanied." The comment—so apt to her situation—followed her back to the villa. "God keep her in that mind," wrote Fanny.

Dallying in the villa's garden at noon, Fanny liked to plunge into the cool fountain with the Sartoris children, "their round, rosy limbs shining through the clear water, and their bead-like, glancing eyes bright with delight." In the fragrant dusk she liked to ride with Adelaide along the tree-lined avenues. Adelaide was not a horsewoman, but in her sister's company she improved her skills and began to look forward to their excursions. Every new ride, Adelaide told the Thuns, "brings us on some unexpected view surpassing those we had thought not to be surpassed."

Life was not entirely a procession of pleasant distractions. Both the sisters spent "earnest, silent, *begrimed*, absorbed, drawing hours" out of doors with Edward, who surprised them by his skill as a painter. Art had become Edward's passion, and he spent many hours in Rome taking lessons and haunting artists' studios. In the evenings, on the terrace amid the cypresses or in the long gallery overlooking the flower garden, there were readings aloud from Fanny and songs from Adelaide. How "perfectly all the elements were united, tempered and attuned!" sighed Fanny. In this haven of peace there was no past, no future, simply a healing present.

On the Feast of Ascension, Fanny, the Sartorises, and a Russian companion rode up nearby Mount Cavo on donkeys. They passed through picturesque villages, where the women wore scarlet jackets and head scarves, and the men wore scarlet sashes and brown velvet jackets. After pausing on the plateau where Hannibal was said to have camped on his way to Rome, they climbed the steep slabs of the old Roman road leading to the ancient temple of Jupiter. Halting from time to time to take in the view, their eyes swept across "forest and town, the lakes of Albano and Nemi, the great sunny plain and Rome the glorious." Captivated by the scene and its historical associations, Fanny felt her spirits grow livelier. For the first time in months she forgot her misery and recalled happier times. As she looked out across this scene of ancient splendor, she speculated on the destiny of the New World.

> Here amid these stupendous memories and thoughts, how often do I muse upon the wonderful world beyond the Atlantic! Dowered with a natural wealth unparalleled; the latest born of Time; peopled by the descendants of the freest and wisest nation now on earth; not led through doubtful twilight ages of barbarous savageness and feudal semi-civilization, but born like Pallas from the head of Jove, inheriting the knowledge of all previous times, endowed with the experience of all former nations; whose heroic age boasts but one victory, the victory of Freedom—but one

demigod, Washington. Oh! if wisdom and virtue should yet by times govern the counsels of that people, and at last bring into being the glorious Christian commonwealth!

Accepting the United States as the land of her own and her daughters' future, she prayed that it might throw off the chains of slavery and achieve its glorious destiny. "She had a sort of American patriotism" and "a love for the United States," wrote one of her American friends, "which was totally different to liking." On the one hand, Fanny could stringently criticize her adopted country; on the other hand, she could reveal a heart that throbbed "with American passions."

The expedition to Mount Cavo heralded a happier time for Fanny. Freed from the worst of her depression, she was at last capable of enjoying the guests who streamed to the Sartorises' house. While the English and American residents of Rome usually held themselves aloof, Adelaide and Edward took pleasure in living like Romans and mixing in cosmopolitan society. Whereas at home Edward was the proper English gentleman, in Italy he became the proper European gentleman, often calling himself by the Spanish title of Marchese di Caza Barguiller y Sartoris.

At Frascati that summer, Adelaide and Edward entertained visitors from many nations. Their favorite guests were a Hanoverian diplomat and a Scottish scientist living in Italy. The diplomat was Georg Kestner, the son of Charlotte Kestner, who had been a great love of the German poet Goethe and the inspiration for his heroine in *The Sorrows of Werther*. Kestner had brought copies of Goethe's letters to Charlotte, and several mornings were spent in hearing the letters read aloud. The scientist was a small, elderly Scotswoman named Mary Somerville, whose brilliant expositions of scientific subjects had gained her honors from learned societies across Europe. To Frascati that summer, Mrs. Somerville brought her two daughters, Martha and Mary, and in the marble-floored gallery, Fanny, who still loved to dance, taught the Somerville girls the wild *cachucha*, which she had danced years before at Lenox. Serene and white-haired, Mrs. Somerville looked on through her eyeglasses and pronounced the spectacle "ladylike." Ladylike! marveled Fanny. Why, the *cachucha* was anything *but* ladylike! She was amazed, amused, and a little piqued that Mrs. Somerville should have chosen so tame a word.

Outwardly Fanny was almost her old provocative self, but inwardly she often grieved for Sarah and Fan. Whenever the mail from America arrived, she scanned the numerous letters addressed to her, knowing the authors instantly by their handwriting. A letter in a childish hand was read again and again. Fanny felt weighed down by the injustice of her position. Pierce, the adulterer, had sacrificed nothing, and she, the ill-used wife, had sacrificed everything—even her daughters. The months in Italy had drawn the sisters close, and Adelaide—who described herself as a fat, rosy, happy, uninteresting mother—could scarcely bear to watch her sister's pain. It was "so monstrous and unnatural," fumed Adelaide, "to ask a mother to give up her child." For that child was the "fruit of her entrails, whom she has risked her own life to give birth to. The one thing she has a right to—that is *hers* if any thing is."

Adelaide's concern for Fanny in those months was almost obsessive. One afternoon, in the woods near Tusculum, Adelaide gathered forget-me-nots to send—presumably after pressing and drying them—to the Thuns. But she did not send them. "When I showed them to my sister," she told the count, "she fancied that I had plucked them for her." Adelaide had not the heart to deny Fanny anything that she thought might ease her pain.

By late October the sunny days were over. Thunderstorms rattled the villa, and rain revived the bleached landscape. Sadly the sisters prepared to leave their pleasant country home. Fanny had come to rely on Edward as the guardian she believed to be vital in a male-dominated world: "something kind and dependable belonging to me," she wrote, "—the only thing of the kind that I possess, for my sister is a woman, and you know I am heartily of the opinion we are the weaker sex, and that an efficient male protector is a tower of strength." But Fanny was under no illusion concerning her place in Edward's household: she was a guest, and no more. She had been invited for a year, and that year was nearly over.

Back in Rome Fanny tried to see every sight. For a month, she spent each morning in the Vatican galleries. With Edward and Adelaide she saw the stately entry of the newly elected pope into St. John Lateran. For seven consecutive days she sampled the delights of the Capitol. On December 7, 1846, a wet and gloomy day, she went to drink from the Trevi Fountain, which legend said would bring her back to Rome. Afterward she composed a poem in which she blessed Edward, Adelaide, their children, and the household hearth at which she had warmed herself. Then she took up her wanderer's staff: "let us now depart," she wrote.

Making the long return journey to London in December, Fanny resumed her solitary and uncertain life. Not wishing to live with her father, she moved into rooms of her own in fashionable Orchard Street, even though she knew that she could scarcely afford the rent. The need for money oppressed her at every turn, and she searched her letters each day in the hope of finding a remittance from Pierce. While in Italy she had elicited from him the promise of a thousand dollars a year. It was more than twice the income of a highly skilled tradesman, but it would not be enough to keep her as she wished. Nevertheless she accepted it, believing it was probably the best offer he would make.

At the same time she was aware that any payment depended on Pierce's whims and his current finances. Knowing his capacity for gambling and spending, Fanny felt no confidence that he would remain rich. It would be better, she decided, to hold out for an annuity: an invested sum, guaranteeing her a fixed annual income of a thousand dollars. The money would thus be securely hers, no matter what happened to Pierce, and could go to her children after her death.

Though Pierce was prepared to agree to the annuity in theory, he raised his own objections. Since he would have to mortgage substantial property to buy an annuity large enough to produce an annual income of a thousand dollars, he demanded in return that Fanny resign her dower rights—the legal entitlement she held, as his wife, to one-third of his estate after his death. Fanny agreed; but the negotiations, carried on painstakingly through their lawyers, came to a halt. Though Pierce did sporadically remit money to her—a total of one thousand dollars by the end of January 1847—he kept delaying the purchase of the annuity. Maybe he could not raise the money, maybe he was trying to keep Fanny dependent on him, maybe he just wanted to annoy her—one can only guess.

With shrewd foresight Fanny had kept a travel diary in Italy, and back in London she was ready to flesh it out into a book for the English and American markets. She conferred with Edward Moxon, a publisher recommended to her by Samuel Rogers, and Moxon gave her favorable terms and an immediate payment. Entitled *A Year of Consolation* and dedicated to Edward Sartoris, the book was a quick success. It was lively, forthright, and confident in its opinions—in other words, it reflected Fanny in her more attractive mood. As one reviewer put it, when the book was finished, the reader felt that he had made a friend.

By February 1847, thanks to Moxon's payment and Pierce's remittances, Fanny had gained some financial security. At the same time she could not stop worrying about her future. She was beginning to see only one answer to her insecurity, and that was to return to the professional stage.

She was only too aware of the many obstacles to her return. Could she, at the age of thirty-seven, bear the strain of constantly performing and touring? Could she endure the social indignity associated with acting? Could she cope with all the practical daily problems that Charles and Aunt Dall had previously managed for her? Above all, Fanny asked herself, would Pierce retaliate if she broke his cardinal rule that she never return to the theatre?

Did she, one wonders, have any suspicion that Pierce might be manip-ulating her back to the stage in order to justify divorcing her? For just as Fanny, by threatening to return to acting, was trying to pressure Pierce into buying her an annuity, he may have been seeking moral grounds for a di-vorce by forcing her back into the theatre. Their relationship had become a nightmarish contest of threats and tricks, from which each was determined to emerge as victor.

Having at last made a firm decision to return to the stage, Fanny agreed to appear in a theatre in Manchester. Admitting that her middle-aged face and body were a liability, she allowed Emily Fitzhugh to take her to a dentist to improve her teeth and did not object when Emily applied a bleach of vinegar to her weather-beaten throat and face. She did, however, draw the line when Henry Greville urged her to paint her face and arms with white greasepaint. Fanny said that she certainly did not want to ap-pear "like a whited sepulchre." Otherwise she was touched by her friends' kindness. When Henry insisted on coming to her opening night, she con-fessed that she was pleased to have her courage thus bolstered.

Fanny needed all her courage as she prepared to stand on the profes-sional stage for the first time in thirteen years. On the opening night, Feb-ruary 16, 1847, as she made her entrance as Julia in *The Hunchback*, she was so nervous that she thought she might faint. At the end of the perfor-mance, however, she felt assured that she had done well. She believed that she had earned the bouquets that were heaped at the stage door and the fa-vorable reviews that appeared in the papers next day.

The morning after *The Hunchback* opened, Fanny rose with a cough and a sore throat, rehearsed the role of Juliana in *The Honeymoon*, cor-rected the proofs of her Italian book, wrote to her father, negotiated with theatrical managers about other engagements, received visits, consulted a doctor about her sore throat, and prepared her stage dresses. Though ex-hausted, she was back into the routine of her youth, and it was comforting. She believed that she could endure two years of theatrical touring so long as she continued to augment "the small capital upon which I can contrive to live independently." How to keep her capital secret from Pierce had already been planned. She had decided to invest her earnings in the name of faithful Emily Fitzhugh.

After two weeks in Manchester, Fanny traveled to Birmingham, Liverpool, Bath, and Dublin. As she seated herself in her railroad carriage, she blessed her old hero George Stephenson for perfecting the steam train, thus enabling her to move swiftly from city to city. For the next year, along with her long-suffering maid, she crisscrossed the British Isles, playing Lady Macbeth, Lady Teazle, Juliet, Julia, and Juliana, and drawing audiences of varying sizes.

Colorful stories began to circulate about Fanny's style of acting. At Manchester she was reported to have included a southern plantation song in *School for Scandal*, some saying with dramatic effect, others saying with disastrous results. As her tour went on, Fanny's popularity declined, and her peak income of forty pounds a week slowly dwindled by more than half.

Between her engagements in the theatre, Fanny sandwiched in visits to nearby friends: to Lord and Lady Dacre; to the Egertons, who were now Lord and Lady Ellesmere; to Harriet and her companion Dorothy Wilson; to Mrs. Grote; to her brother Henry in Ireland; and to a new favorite named Jane Mitchell, who, along with Theodosia Monson, was hosting a "widows' house party" in Scotland. Fanny was invited to the house party as an honorary widow.

Resting briefly in April 1847, she submitted to surgery for the hemorrhoids that had troubled her since Fan's birth. The operation was painful, and the aftermath debilitating. On May 13, when she was still almost too weak to stand, she generously obliged Henry Greville by appearing in London at the St. James's Theatre in a performance of *Hernani* to raise money for the victims of the Irish famine. She played the heroine, and playing opposite her was none other than Augustus Craven. What a shock it was to act with him again, and what a sorry pair of stage lovers they made. No longer the dashing youth of Fanny's memories, Augustus was now a grey-haired diplomat without money or ambition, and she was a grey-haired, cast-off wife. Did they regret the past? An answer can be found in the reminiscences of their joint friend, witty Montstuart Grant Duff. He wrote that Fanny was "as glad, in after life, that he had not become her husband as he must have been that she was not his wife."

Following her success in *Hernani*, Fanny agreed to play in a gala performance of Shakespeare to raise funds to maintain the Bard's birthplace. The gala was held at Covent Garden, and Fanny was so overcome by memories as she stepped onto the stage that at first she could barely speak. She had chosen the death scene of Katherine of Aragon, Henry VIII's discarded wife, and both she and the audience must have seen the parallels to her own situation. No wonder that her words took wing, and the spectators shouted and clapped for more. But Fanny could not face a curtain call. Instead, she clutched her skirt and fled the stage.

Fanny had been spreading the word privately that she was ambitious to perform again in the main London theatres. She was even prepared to act with William Charles Macready, although in the back of her mind she had doubts. She knew that as well as being the brightest star of the British stage, he was a tyrant in the theatre, ambitious, ruthless, and uncontrollably bad-tempered. She also knew that he hated her father, having parted with the Kemble company after a bitter quarrel. Aware of these obstacles, she was of two minds when James Maddox, the manager of the Princess Theatre in London, offered to negotiate a contract for Fanny to appear with Macready.

She would have been even more hesitant had she known that Macready had witnessed her performance in *Hernani* and thought it abysmal. "*She is ignorant of the very first rudiments of her art,*" he wrote severely in his diary. "She is affected, monotonous, without a real impulse—never in the feeling of her character, never true in look, attitude or tone. She can never be an actress." In light of this extreme opinion, it seemed unlikely that Macready would ever agree to Maddox's proposition. Yet six months later he signed a contract to appear with Fanny in a season of Shakespeare at the Princess Theatre.

As soon as the rehearsals began, in February 1848, Fanny knew that she had made a mistake. Macready was one of the new breed of "natural" actors who scorned majestic declamation, spoke blank verse as if it were prose, and saturated themselves with the emotions of a role. When he was called on to play a violent character, he believed he had to become one. Once, when playing Othello, he had almost smothered his Desdemona. As Fanny was to play Desdemona, she was not looking forward to the death scene.

To make matters worse, she had recently jammed her little finger in a carriage door, and it remained fragile. She was afraid that Macready might accidentally rebreak it in one of his stage rages. Seeking advice from Harriet, Fanny told her that in *Macbeth*, "he pinched me black and blue, and almost tore the point lace from my head. I am sure my little finger will be rebroken, and as for that smothering in bed, 'Heaven have mercy upon me!' as poor Desdemona says."

The daily conflict was aggravated by their contrasting approaches to their art. The mannered utterances and gestures that Fanny had learned from her father filled Macready with disgust. "There is nothing genuine in her, poor woman!" he wrote in his diary. "I have never seen anyone so bad, so unnatural, so affected, so conceited." Fanny, for her part, considered Macready's natural approach to blank verse appalling, and she described how he "growls and prowls, and roams and foams, about the stage, like a tiger in his cage, so that I never know which side of me he means to be, and keeps up a perpetual snarling and grumbling like the aforesaid tiger, so that I never feel sure that he *has done* and that it is my turn to speak."

As the opening night drew near, personal accusations sped back and forth between them. Macready called Fanny vain, demanding, and overbearing. She called him boorish, tyrannical, and self-seeking. He was piqued when the playbills gave her name equal prominence with his own. She was offended when he moved into the best dressing room.

The prospect of actors of such contrary styles appearing together on the same stage sparked public interest. When the season opened on February 28, theatregoers flocked to see whether the two could perform together successfully. On the whole, the opinion was that they could. The performances, though so different, were equally valid: a verdict with which Fanny and Macready, in their better moments, seemed partially to agree. She was forced to admit that Macready's tragic characterizations were frequently striking. And he conceded that her Desdemona was a "very correct and forcible conception," though he added: "if she would give herself up to the study of execution, she might yet become a fine actress."

One critic who had no doubts as to who was the superior actor was Charles Kemble. He came many times to watch his daughter and sat with his stick beside him, knocking it loudly on the ground when Fanny's acting particularly pleased him. On February 23, after a performance of *Henry VIII*, Macready wrote in his diary: "C. Kemble in the stalls knocked so loud and so often with his stick—often almost *alone*—that people called *Turn him out!*"

Fanny was tired of dealing with unsympathetic actors and grasping managers. On the other hand, she was not tired of the theatre and the money it earned. She needed another vehicle for acting, and for some time she had had a plan in mind. She had long considered that the only respectable way to act in public was to read a play aloud. She also considered that this might well be the best way, because, in its simplicity and sparseness, to read a play aloud encouraged the imagination to fill in the blank spaces. As a child, she had heard Mrs. Siddons read the witches' scene from *Macbeth*, and she had never forgotten the experience. The witches came alive through the simple power of her aunt's voice and Shakespeare's words.

Fanny's father was reading aloud professionally, skillfully reducing each of Shakespeare's plays to two hours in length, acting all the roles himself, and transporting his hearers into a convincing Shakespearean world. It was mainly fear of trespassing on her father's livelihood that restrained Fanny from giving public readings of her own. At the end of 1847, realizing that Charles was too deaf to read aloud much longer, she decided to move into his terrain.

Fanny gave her first professional reading late in March 1848 at the Highgate Institute in the outer suburbs of London. There was nothing theatrical about the setting. She sat at a plain desk, in a simple dark gown, close to two candelabra: a lady reading aloud to her friends. And so it was to be at all her performances. Theatrical magic came solely from her voice, which portrayed an entire cast of characters and conveyed her hearers to Venice, Verona, or the "vasty fields of France." After a reading of *The Winter's Tale* at Brighton, one listener wrote: "How exquisite! how sublimely accented! I never, till then, believed human mind, or human voice, capable of so much expression."

Charles presented Fanny with his printed texts, complete with cuts and dynamics, and from that nucleus she built up a repertoire of twenty-four Shakespearean plays. Though Fanny did not yet realize it, she was launched on an exciting career. Bookings poured in six months in advance, and she engaged John Mitchell of the St. James's Theatre as her agent and moved her performances to the Willis Rooms in London. She made money, and that in itself was pleasing, practically and psychologically. In fact Fanny's prospects in England were so rosy that she unwisely postponed the trip to America that she had planned for the early summer.

All was not well in Philadelphia, where Pierce was again taking up arms. If, by returning to the stage, Fanny had hoped to shame him into adequately providing for her, her hope was thwarted. He paid her no further money after February 1847, when she began acting, and negotiations over the annuity came to an end. At Pierce's command, the children ceased to write to her. "The other day," wrote a distressed Adelaide, "she got a letter written in secret by her eldest girl telling her that her own letters to them were suppressed by their father, who had forbidden *her* to write to her mother, while the other poor little child, who is too young to be trusted with her father's bad secrets, is allowed to write letter after letter (which letters are never *sent*) and getting no answer, to think that her poor heart-broken mother has forgotten her."

While divorce was almost unobtainable in England, in Pennsylvania it could be gained after two years on the grounds of willful desertion. For the Butlers, those two years had already expired. In Philadelphia Pierce was preparing his case for a divorce. Though his suit was to be based on desertion, Fanny's return to the stage was the obvious catalyst: "the consummation," he called it, "of a sad career of error." Fanny's letter to her children, placing the blame for her resumption of acting on Pierce's refusal to pay her a quarterly allowance, was the final straw.

In March 1848, two and a half years after the alleged desertion, Pierce formally filed for divorce in the Philadelphia Court of Common Pleas. The legal summons did not reach Fanny in England until April 24, and it commanded her to appear in court on June 5. The sudden shock of the summons and the short time allowed for the voyage across the ocean threw her into confusion. In the space of a week she canceled her engagements, wrote to her lawyers, and booked passage on the steamship *Hibernia*. Writing to Elizabeth Sedgwick as she waited for her ship, Fanny said that she did not care about the divorce itself, but she did care about being "publicly branded as a woman who has deserted her most sacred duties." Most of all, she cared about her daughters. Somehow she had to fight Pierce and win back her precious girls.

🌿 15 🌿

Thunderclouds

While Fanny's emotional troubles were so dramatic and public that they were soon to fill newspaper columns on both sides of the Atlantic, Adelaide's emotional troubles were not for the public to see. Likewise, while Fanny was capable of conducting her battles as if they were a form of theatre, Adelaide sought privacy.

Fanny certainly knew of Adelaide's emotional wounds. It so happened that at the end of 1845, just before Fanny left London for her long stay in Rome, she had called on Anna Jameson. From Anna she heard a snippet of gossip so sensational that it sent Fanny reeling. It must have been with feelings of dread that she realized that it was now her duty, as soon as she reached Rome, to pass on the snippet to Adelaide. The subject of the gossip was the man whom Adelaide loved—Francis Thun.

The fact that the news came from Anna Jameson was enough in itself to distress Adelaide. Seven years previously, Anna had met Count Thun and his family through a friend who had married a German baroness and gone to live at an estate near Tetschen. Thereafter Anna, a natural busybody, had cast herself in the role of Francis Thun's informant, and had seen fit to pass on to him intimate details of Adelaide's life.

Count Thun had grown so alarmed by the influx of tittle-tattle from Anna in the months following Adelaide's marriage that he had written to Adelaide to put her on her guard. At first Adelaide had been disinclined to believe him, but as time went on she began to see just how mischievous Anna was. "I am *utterly* and *entirely* come round to your views about Mrs. Jameson; and see very little of her," Adelaide wrote to the count in 1844. "She has never quite forgiven my throwing away my laurel wreath for a home, and no doubt thought it would have been much prettier to have let my disappointment with regard to your son have devastated my whole exis-

< 232 >

tence." It was the united opinion of Adelaide and Count Thun that Anna resented Adelaide's happy marriage.

Anna Jameson, in her eagerness to meddle, appears also to have drawn a startling inference from a best-selling novel called *Consuelo* by George Sand, the French female author. Sand's novel centered on a humbly born soprano named Consuelo, who visited a castle in Bohemia and fell in love with the handsome son of the count. The heroine was reputedly modeled on Sand's beloved friend Pauline Garcia; but the parallels to Adelaide's life were easily recognized by anyone who knew her history. Those who, like Anna Jameson, knew that George Sand was close to Dessauer and therefore had access to the details of Adelaide's love affair felt little doubt that the novel contained—in part at least—a portrait of Adelaide. Inevitably people talked about it. Today such gossip would be seen as part of the normal merry-go-round of show business, but to Adelaide, married to a man who worshipped respectability in an era of respectability, the public inference that she had fallen in love with Francis was embarrassing and even harmful.

These incidents, annoying in themselves, were only a curtain-raiser to the bombshell that Anna passed on to Fanny in her London drawing room in December 1845—the astonishing allegation that Francis Thun had fathered an illegitimate daughter and was planning to marry the mother, a low-born, uneducated servant who worked as a maid at the Tetschen castle.

When Adelaide heard the allegation the following year in Rome, she felt her life had suddenly been turned upside down. If the rumor was true, it meant that the man she had loved, the man who had rejected her, had been enticed away by a common servant. As pain and shock swept over her, Adelaide had difficulty retaining her footing, but her respect for Francis cushioned the force. In one sense the news did not entirely surprise her: their love for one another had been based on their shared idealism. Francis had always been egalitarian, and she revered him for it. In proposing to marry this woman—so lowly that, in all her years at the castle, Count Thun had scarcely spoken a word to her—he was showing the courage of his convictions.

These thoughts comforted Adelaide as in deep anxiety she awaited the next letter from Tetschen. Only from the Thuns' own lips would she believe such a story. But Yuza's letter, when it came, left her no wiser. Yuza could not bring herself to reveal the shocking truth, and while she spoke eloquently of the family's pain and grief, she gave no indication of the source of the grief. Admittedly the countess had died two years previously, deeply mourned by her family, but Adelaide did not think that Yuza was speaking of her mother.

On April 23, 1846, unable to bear the uncertainty a day longer, Adelaide wrote bluntly to Count Thun: "I hear that Francis is going to be married—is this true? I hear moreover that this marriage makes you all wretched—is this true? Oh dear Thun what would I give to be near you, to comfort you. . . . You will hardly guess what was the nature of the emotion I felt at hearing of this—I thanked God that Francis had courage to make good a false step in his life . . . dear friend will you hate me for saying this?"

In her letters in the following months, when the truth of the news had been confirmed to her, she continued to write with the same compassion: "My dear, dear Thun, the woman has been faithful to him for many, many years and has borne him a child! These are strong strong holds upon the heart of an honest man. I do beseech you to think of the agony he must have endured between so many and various duties and be merciful to him."

Count Thun-Hohenstein, to give him his formal title, could not quite view his son's infatuation and social disgrace in this generous light. His family was one of the most aristocratic and wealthy in Austria. His second son, Friedrich, a year younger than Francis, was a rising politician who in 1850 was to become president of the German Diet in Frankfurt, asserting himself as an opponent of the young Bismarck, and a little later was to hold two of the highest diplomatic posts in Europe. The count's third son, Leopold, was also rising, and before long would begin an influential term of eleven years as Austrian minister for education and religion.

To such a proud family, a social scandal enveloping the eldest son was like acid in the eye. Count Thun could not hide his anger as he answered Adelaide's pleas. His oldest son's folly was so acute that Thun expressed the hope, with some sarcasm, that Francis would remain blind to his own personal folly. "God grant that this blindness may continue long," he told Adelaide, "for should the band fall once from his eyes and he see the unworthiness of the person to whom he has yoked himself he would doubly feel *how* unhappy he has made me and his whole family, how he has blasted my finest dearest hopes, and proudest expectations."

Implicit in the count's letter was the regret that Adelaide was not his daughter-in-law. Calling her his "own dear child," he declared that nobody loved and valued her more than he; and he added his opinion that no husband could be other than happy "with my own dearest Adelaide at his side." When he came to sign his name, he wrote above the signature: "one who to the end of his life will be attached to you with the warmest fatherly love." Though Adelaide did not yet know the count's true part in Francis's rejection of her, one wonders if she sensed the underlying guilt in his regret. For if Count Thun had only permitted and encouraged Francis to wed Adelaide, Francis would not have been free to take up with his mother's maid. The count had reaped a bitter harvest.

What troubled Adelaide as much as her own wounded pride was Francis's welfare. She had heard that he was still unmarried and living at the castle, and that his baby daughter and her servant mother had been sent away, out of sight. Adelaide longed to advise and comfort him, but each time she raised her pen to write, her courage failed. Instead she sent messages through the count and Yuza. While she applauded Francis's principles, she urged him to think carefully before taking up a burden he might not be able to carry. She begged him to write to her, or allow her to write to him. But no letter or message came in reply. Later she heard that he had married the mother of his child.

The months that Adelaide and Fanny spent together in Rome during 1846 were outwardly tranquil—a round of picture galleries, parties, and country excursions—but inwardly they were dominated by their private griefs. For a time Adelaide forgot some of her own turmoil in comforting her sister, but when Fanny left for London in December 1846 to resume her career on the stage, Adelaide found it increasingly difficult to keep her mind off Francis. When Edward departed six months later for London in an abortive attempt to win a seat in the House of Commons, Adelaide was left entirely alone with her memories. She mentally relived each moment of those precious weeks at Tetschen and felt her love and pain blaze anew. There was no way that she could stifle thoughts of what might have been.

Edward had rented the villa at Frascati for a second summer, and there Adelaide sank thankfully into country life and the duties of motherhood. Most of her time was devoted to the children. She described her son, Greville, aged four, as her "dear companion," and her daughter, May, a year younger, as her "charming plaything." On the surface Adelaide appeared motherly and serene, but her private thoughts leaped across the Alps to the Bohemian castle.

On Edward's return to Italy in the autumn of 1847, Adelaide's private world, with its blend of family coziness and personal hurt, began to disintegrate. For the first time, a barrier descended between husband and wife. How much Edward knew about Francis Thun cannot be known, but it seems likely that he knew much more than Adelaide supposed. Though on the surface she remained loving, she had ceased, emotionally, to be exclusively her husband's, and he cannot fail to have noticed.

Adelaide herself refused to acknowledge any gap between her and her husband. Instead she attributed Edward's emotional retreat to the grief he felt at Felix Mendelssohn's sudden death. The composer had died in Germany in November 1847 at the early age of thirty-eight, and the news speedily reached Rome, where Adelaide heard the announcement "casually in a whole room full of people." She almost fainted from the shock, and so she was not surprised that Edward also took the news so badly. As she explained to the Thuns, her husband did not give his allegiance easily, and he had worshipped Mendelssohn from the moment they met. Fanny seemed to endorse Adelaide's opinion that grief was making Edward withdraw into himself. "For a person who has permitted intellectual refinement to become almost a narrow fastidiousness," wrote Fanny, "and whose sympathies are of the exclusive kind that none but special and rarely gifted persons can excite them, the loss of such a friend as Mendelssohn must be incalculable; and I am grieved to the heart for Edward." Observant and sympathetic as this diagnosis is, there seems little doubt that the living Francis Thun rather than the dead Felix Mendelssohn was driving the wedge between husband and wife.

The first months of 1848 were among the unhappiest Adelaide had known since girlhood. Edward was emotionally cut off from her, Francis's marriage was tormenting her, and Fanny was causing alarm, for reports of her impending divorce had arrived in Rome. Hearing that Fanny was about to leave for America to foil the divorce, Adelaide expedited her own plans to return to England, preparing to travel by the fastest route in the hope she could meet Fanny before her sailing day. But at that very moment, riots and revolutions broke out across Europe; whereupon Edward insisted, for Adelaide's safety, that she go by sea, even though the journey was slower. As it happened, Adelaide missed Fanny altogether, arriving in England a day or two after her sister sailed from Liverpool.

The widespread unrest in Europe inflicted further worries on Adelaide and Edward. Most of the Sartorises' family fortune was invested in France, which was in the grip of the revolution. Without regard for his personal safety, Edward hurried from Rome to Paris to save what he could for himself, his brothers, and sister. The riots had spread from Sicily all the way to Prague and Vienna, and many of their friends and some of Edward's relatives were exposed to danger. In Prague the younger Thuns were victims, and Leopold Thun, at heart a Czech nationalist, was imprisoned by the rebels and fearful for his life. Even Francis fled from the mobs clamoring to overthrow the old regime. Surely, wrote Adelaide, "his marriage would have forever bound the *people* to him." One can be sure that she feared for Francis's safety just as keenly as she feared for her husband's.

Before the return of the Sartorises to London, faithful Henry Greville had arranged on their behalf the lease of a house in fashionable Eaton Place; but when Edward arrived home from France, he knew that he could barely afford the price, so considerable were his losses. Nevertheless out of adversity came some relief. Edward's disapproving sister, Eliza de l'Aigle, was so grateful for her brother's efforts to save her fortune that for the first time she became positively tender toward his wife. "I have had few prouder moments in my life," wrote Adelaide, "than when she told me that she thought her brother had done well to marry me, and *thanked* me for his happiness."

Now that the two women were closer, Adelaide was able to confide something of her own supposed descent from the French Marquis de Fleury, who, according to her mother, had changed his name to De Camp when he abandoned his heritage in order to marry a Strasbourg innkeeper's daughter. Adelaide explained at length the noble but doubtful pedigree that the De Camps held so dear. To her relief, her sister-in-law took the claim seriously and consulted her husband's uncle, Victor de l'Aigle. To Adelaide's surprise and relief, the elderly aristocrat declared that he vaguely recollected the marquis whom Adelaide claimed as her great-grandfather, and he seemed to accept the legitimacy of Adelaide's ancestry. Henceforth Adelaide could face the de l'Aigles on a firmer footing.

By the last months of 1848, Adelaide was so unnerved that she was ripe for illness. When she finally took to her bed at Christmastime, the doctors diagnosed inflammation of the alimentary canal and congestion of the liver, a condition that can only have been aggravated by her obesity. At thirty-two, her face was still lovely, with its expressive dark eyes, smooth dark hair, and majestic Roman nose, but her mother's genes had ballooned her body. Though Adelaide made the most of her height, wore flowing gowns, and diverted attention from her girth with graceful theatrical gestures, observers could not help but notice her bulk. When the art critic John Ruskin and his young wife Effie dined with the Sartorises at Lansdowne House in London in 1848, he sat next to Adelaide and declared her a "very clever woman"; but Effie, who sat opposite, wrote bluntly that she was "fat and covered in old point lace."

Another who observed her size was the glamorous Polish composer-pianist Frederic Chopin, who had first known Adelaide in Paris several years before. When he met her again in London in the summer of 1848, he could scarcely believe she was the same woman. Her stoutness, he said, had quite destroyed her beauty: "only her head has remained like a cameo."

Chopin, who met Adelaide often in the course of that summer, came to treasure her friendship. He needed friends, because he was depressed by the parting from his mistress, George Sand—the author of *Consuelo*—and by the tuberculosis of which he would die in little over a year. London's lionization left Chopin exhausted; it was with relief that he retreated to the peace and comfort of Adelaide's house. As he told his family in Poland, she had many virtues. Not only did she have a first-class brain, but she had managed to acquire a wealthy husband: "She has been taken up by the whole of London society and is received everywhere, while everyone comes to her house." He felt quite at home with her, he told his mother: "she knows of all my little private faults from our common friends—Dessauer and Liszt for example. I have often chatted with her and it seemed as though I were talking to someone who knew you, although in fact she only knows the rooms we occupied in the Thuns' house at Tetschen." The castle at Tetschen was of course the vital link: both Adelaide and Chopin had experienced the Thuns' generous Bohemian hospitality.

Chopin was pleased to have Adelaide's house as the setting for his first public concert in London. On the afternoon of June 23, 1848, a hundred and fifty guests crowded onto elegant chairs in Adelaide's large drawing room at Eaton Place and listened to Chopin play. Adelaide's old friend Mario, who had become a highly fashionable tenor, also sang three groups of songs. Tickets, one guinea each, were sold out the day before the performance: the money was for Chopin, who was in financial need. The maestro was ill, and his spirits were subdued, but he played superbly. At least one observer in the crowded room, however, noted his "death-like appearance," and contrasted it with Mario, who looked "extremely handsome in his velvet coat."

In October 1849, the year following Chopin's recital, Edward moved his household out of London. He sublet 99 Eaton Place and took a three-year lease on Knuston Hall, not far from Wellingborough in Northamptonshire, where his brother had an estate. It was a fine mansion built of pale stone, set atop a steep hill, with farm buildings standing beside it. The farmyard contained stables, cow and poultry yards, a lambs' pen, dovecotes, a hay loft, a dairy, and a brewery. The accompanying land included a park of twenty-seven acres, four acres of fish ponds, an extensive garden, and shooting and fishing rights. Adelaide called it "our little country place," and loved its splendid view over rolling fields and woods.

Though the rents that came to Edward from France were severely curtailed, and the move was prompted largely by the need for economy, the family managed to live in remarkable style. Edward kept expensive horses in the stables and took up hunting and shooting with the same dedication he had once lavished on his painting. When not at field sports he entertained, and his brothers and sister were frequent visitors, as were several of Adelaide's family. On census night, March 30, 1851, Edward disclosed that his household contained his brother-in-law Captain Henry Kemble and his sister-in-law Frances, as well as a dozen servants, including a Swiss nurse, a German lady's maid, an Irish groom, and three stable boys.

In Northamptonshire, Adelaide recovered her health and, for a time, some of her happiness. The tranquillity of the country soothed her. She took long walks in the adjoining woods, walking sometimes five or six miles a day: breathing in the scent of the damp leaves, picking bluebells in the spring and mushrooms in the autumn. She discovered the joy of gardening, planting rose bushes and herbaceous borders and attempting to tame the overgrown shrubbery. As she settled into country life, the specter of Francis Thun began to fade, and she and Edward softened toward one another. At the start of 1850 Adelaide became pregnant again; but in the spring, while staying with Lady Southampton for the hunting, she found herself miscarrying. Being too shy to admit it and longing for her own bed, she summoned a carriage and was jolted for twelve miles over rough roads to the railway station. She reached home more dead than alive. In the following days she lay seriously ill in her bedroom at Knuston Hall. When, in the early spring, she was able to leave her bed and sit beneath the budding chestnut trees in the garden, she felt, in her own words, "like a hurt beast."

To cheer herself up, Adelaide threw herself into activity. She spent as much time as possible with the children, and was keen to organize treats and excursions. On Christmas Eve, 1851, she hosted a children's party; and while the Sartoris children and fifteen small neighbors were romping around the Christmas tree, Edward arrived home from hunting with a broken collar bone. Adelaide was forced to abandon the party and attend to him. It was one of the many items of domestic news that she relayed to far-off Bohemia.

Adelaide also began teaching her children and loved the task. Though only seven and five, they sped ahead in French, Italian, and history. Little May was a true Kemble—willful and energetic and, according to Adelaide, "more like *me*"—but Greville was lazy like his father. In fact the laziness of father and son was becoming a family byword. Adelaide once complained that Greville seemed so indolent that she could "only suppose his father must have been in a *crise* of *ennui* when he was engendered." Fanny declared, during the riots of 1848, that Edward was so lazy that he would not save himself "unless people are massacred in the streets, and, moreover, in the identical street in which he lives." Adelaide and Fanny openly laughed about the laziness because, as Marie Thérèse's daughters, they had been brought up to believe that sloth was self-defeating and that constant self-improvement was essential to a good life. Those who did not follow those principles were at best misguided and, at worst, deserving of mockery, in the sisters' view.

Though Edward tended to live for pleasure, Adelaide tried to use her days profitably. She sang, to quote her own words, "as if I were going to return to my profession—and then sometimes ask myself for whom and why I take all this trouble!" Now that the children were growing up, she was increasingly aware of the void left in her life by the loss of her career. There were times when Adelaide longed desperately to stand on a stage again. How satisfying it would be, she sighed to the Thuns, to sing regularly to an audience of friends, but she was lucky to spend even a couple of weeks in London. When she did stay in London, she made the most of her opportunities: singing at soirées, dining with Pauline Garcia—by that time a famous diva and married to the impresario Louis Viardot—and attending concerts at Vauxhall Pleasure Gardens with her affectionate old friend William Thackeray. To keep hold of her musical identity and to sing to selected audiences was foremost in Adelaide's mind when she stayed in town. Thackeray heard her sing one night at Mrs. Procter's, where a singer named Gagiotti was also performing. Thackeray disliked Gagiotti and was jubilant at the way Adelaide outshone her. Of Adelaide's performance, Thackeray wrote:

> She was passionate, she was enthusiastic, she was sublime, she was tender—there was one note which she kept so long, that I protest I had time to think about my affairs, to have a little nap, and to wake much refreshed, whilst it was going on still—at another overcome by almost unutterable tenderness she piped so low it's a wonder one could hear her at all—in a word she was *mirobolante*, the most artless affected good-natured absurd clever creature possible—when she had crushed Gagiotti who stood by the piano hating her and paying her the most profound compli-

ments—she tripped off on my arm to the cab waiting. I like that absurd kind creature.

A visit to London had one drawback—Charles Kemble lived there. From what Adelaide could learn, he was now besotted with a Miss Glynn, "an actress at one of the minor theatres; a woman who has been in the streets, and who keeps him from his friends and prevents him from taking a decent lodging where his old acquaintances would come round him, and where his daughters could look after and take care of him—it is quite *deplorable!*" Charles was also to be deplored because he would not give Fanny one penny of the money she had made over to him at the time of her marriage, and which was rightfully hers, in Adelaide's mind. When Adelaide found that Charles had been borrowing illegally against the money, she was stonily unforgiving. Though she condemned his behavior, she was forced to marvel at his energy, for he was well into his seventies, gnarled with rheumatism and almost stone deaf, yet he pursued his love affair with the zeal of a boy. He "will die," Adelaide wrote gloomily, "with us close at hand in the next street, and that horrid woman by his pillow."

While her father was happy in his own way, the thunderclouds seemed to be gathering around Fanny again. Fighting the proposed divorce, she was caught in such a web of misery that there seemed no way out. At first she fought Pierce's divorce suit with all her strength, believing that, if she were divorced, she stood to lose her children, her financial support, her social position, and possibly even her children's inheritance—for, like all Philadelphia, she confidently expected Pierce's remarriage. "He is perpetrating this wickedness for a sum of 80,000 pounds left by a brother of his, lately, to Pierce Butler's *male heir*," wrote Adelaide, quoting a rumor Fanny had passed on to her; "he has devised this admirable mode of getting rid of her and enabling himself to contract another marriage which may provide him with a boy who is to secure to him for 21 years at least the control of this large fortune." The rumor that Pierce was about to remarry so that he could lay his hands on an inheritance proved untrue, but it was disturbing because at first it was believed.

Since Fanny's only defense was to prove that her husband's cruelty had driven her out of the marital home, she marshaled her evidence in a written account—one of the saddest she ever penned. Walking the fine line between describing Pierce's faithlessness and callousness, on the one hand, and saving his reputation for the sake of the children, on the other, she put together her account. On her lawyers' advice Fanny submitted it to the court in November 1848. To her dismay, the *Narrative*—as her account came to be called—was ruled inadmissible evidence. It was not, however, inadmissible to the newspapers. The *New York Evening Post* managed to get hold of a copy, and Fanny saw details of her marriage, together with transcripts of some of her letters to Pierce, made public property. Though the sympathy of the public was welcome, no amount of sympathy made up for her loss of dignity.

The first hearing of the case in the Philadelphia Court of Common Pleas produced no judgment, and a trial by jury was set down for April 1849—a date that was later changed to October 1849. Pierce was clearly annoyed by the delay, because at first he had been confident of blasting Fanny quickly and easily out of his life. The prospect of Fanny in front of a jury made him uneasy—and with reason, because Fanny was more than capable of swaying her listeners. Adelaide confidently told the Thuns that her sister would win the case if it went before a jury.

As the trial drew closer, Pierce began to show signs of nervousness. On the Sedgwicks' advice, Fanny had retained for her defense Rufus Choate, an eminent advocate from Boston. Not to be outdone, Pierce engaged George M. Dallas, the vice president of the United States—it was permissible at that time for a vice president to appear as an advocate. Pierce also retained Daniel Webster, the most renowned lawyer in America: he said that he engaged Webster largely to prevent Fanny from employing him.

Unexpectedly Pierce lifted his embargo on Fanny's access to Sarah and Fan, who were pupils at a boarding school near Philadelphia. Seeming to need to escape from the tension, he made an unexpected trip to Georgia. At this point, Fanny's advisers, sensing that she might gain an advantage, urged her to negotiate. And Fanny—though her instinct was never to submit—did as they suggested. In this more hopeful climate, negotiations went so smoothly that, before the trial date, a solution had been hammered out. In return for her dower rights, Fanny was to be allowed a yearly visit of two months with Sarah and Fan and uninterrupted communication with them throughout the year. She was also to receive a lifelong income of fifteen hundred dollars a year, the income to be passed on to her daughters after her death. If she agreed to these conditions, she was to cease to contest the divorce, which would then be awarded by default, with no stain on either character.

While Fanny always fought to win, she had not wanted a tug of war over the girls, nor did she wish to wash her dirty linen in open court. Though she disliked the idea of being a divorced woman—and liked even less the loss of social standing that divorce would inevitably bring—she welcomed independence. She was about to turn forty, and with every passing year she relished her own identity more and more. So she withdrew her opposition, and on September 22, 1849, she became a free woman.

By the time she was divorced, Fanny hated Pierce with such fervor that for the rest of her life she could scarcely bear to hear his name mentioned. If, as one suspects, she took after her mother and derived satisfaction from a ceaseless marital contest, then her lifelong rage is understandable. She continued to argue with him in her mind, and Pierce, in that sense, remained her husband. Some years later Anne Procter, who had known Fanny for most of her life, offered a shrewd observation that was supported by another old friend of the Kemble family, the Reverend William Harness. Both thought that Fanny had adored Pierce, and "was frightfully jealous, and bitterly wounded by his neglect." Hell, said Mrs. Procter, had no fury like a woman scorned. "At this moment," she continued, "Fanny carries about in her work basket a piece of her wedding gown." Mrs. Procter was sure that in carrying this memento, Fanny unconsciously announced that she still loved Pierce. This observation may well have been true.

Pierce, for his part, did not readily forgive, either. He had been so stung by the newspaper publication of Fanny's *Narrative* that he could not wait to publish his own side of the story. Urged on by friends, he composed and circulated privately a much longer and less discreet version of events, called *Mr. Butler's Statement.* An extraordinarily candid document, it contained many of the letters that had passed between them; and, since both sides accepted the contents of the letters, they come down to us blessedly intact.

Fanny was not in the least ashamed of what she had written. And Pierce, since he was sure that she would stand convicted by her own words, had no motive to doctor the evidence her letters provided. As he said in his opening paragraph, Fanny had always held the peculiar belief that marriage should be companionship on equal terms and always "unequivocally refused . . . the customary and pledged acquiescence of a wife to marital control." No one, he argued, "who is not morally or intellectually astray can fail to see the heedlessness and falsity of the pretension." That future generations would interpret the letters so differently is something Pierce could not have foreseen.

The ordeal of the divorce drained Fanny emotionally and financially. Some time before legal negotiations were completed, she was forced by lack

of money to commence her stage readings in America, using the same formula she had already established in England. Thanks to the notoriety of
the divorce, her theatres and halls were packed. She was received with acclaim in New York, Philadelphia, Boston, and a string of lesser places, as
her readings took hold of the public imagination. The critic of the *Spring-
field Republican* described a performance in Boston so vividly that even now
the review captures the flavor of those evenings. One can almost hear the
scrape of the chairs and the dying buzz of conversation as Fanny walked
onto the stage and sat down at her reading desk:

> Presently Mrs. Butler took her place behind the desk. She was elegantly
> dressed, as if for a ball, wearing a rich silk with short sleeves and low
> neck. . . . Bowing with infinite grace she put back with her hand her dark
> and glossy hair (which was dressed with elegant plainness,) and with
> slightly affected emotion said, "I have the honor to read the Merchant of
> Venice." Then taking her seat and just reading the list of characters, she
> entered at once upon the play. And now, how shall I describe the beauty,
> the power, and the genius displayed by this woman, by which for two en-
> tire hours, with a short intermission in the middle, she kept her large
> audience bound in almost breathless silence, interrupted only by sponta-
> neous outbreaks of applause, which it was impossible to restrain. I could
> not have believed before that a single human voice was able, by the sim-
> ple reading of a play, to produce such an effect.

At almost every reading Fanny received the same glowing response. If
fault was found, it was with the coarseness of some of her male portrayals
and the staginess of her declamation: to a newer generation, her acting
style sounded affected and dated. A few years later in England, the young
Henry Irving—soon to be as great an actor in his own way as the Kembles—complained that Fanny introduced *Hamlet* as "Ham-a-lette by Will-
y-am Shak-es-peare." Nevertheless, this staginess—learned from her
father—continued to have wide appeal during the Victorian era. With the
skill of a timeless artist, Fanny used her technique well into the eighteen-
sixties, even though public taste was running against it.

Young Frances Appleton was still an avid Kemble fan, and throughout
February 1849 she attended the readings in Boston, accompanied by her
husband, the poet Henry Wadsworth Longfellow. They were enthralled by
Fanny's declamation. After a recital, Longfellow would write in his diary:
"What glorious reading," or, "sublimely read," or, "What nights these
are!—with Shakespeare and such a reader." At the final reading at Har-

vard, on March 2, Longfellow—a Harvard professor and soon to become one of the most popular poets in the English-speaking world—led Fanny onto the stage. At supper afterward he read a poem he had composed for the occasion.

> O precious evenings! all too swiftly sped!
> Leaving us heirs to ample heritages
> Of all the best thoughts of the greatest sages,
> And giving tongue unto the silent dead!
> How our hearts glowed and trembled as she read,
> Interpreting by tones the wondrous pages
> Of the great poet who foreruns the ages,
> Anticipating all that shall be said!

Almost a year later, when engaged to read for the Mercantile Library Association of Boston, Fanny opened her performance with Longfellow's stirring poem "The Building of the Ship." Longfellow himself was in the audience, and he was almost overcome by the way she stood on the platform, "book in hand, trembling, palpitating and weeping, and giving every word its true weight and emphasis."

To keep the dignity of her married state, and at the same time to proclaim herself free of a husband, Fanny began to call herself Mrs. Fanny Kemble. As Mrs. Kemble she earned large sums of money. The press calculated that she took in up to three hundred dollars a performance, and she sometimes earned more than twelve hundred dollars a week. In her public-spirited way, she donated part of her earnings to charity. On one evening in New York, reading without a fee for the St. George's Society for Indigent Englishmen, she raised so much money that the grateful governors presented her with a replica of their badge, a gold St. George and the dragon hanging from a ruby cross. Fanny adored her St. George and often wore it on stage, pinned like the Order of the Garter to a sash across her breast. Years later Henry Greville would tell an amusing story of how two men in the audience speculated on the origin of her badge: "It must be an order bestowed by a foreign potentate," argued one. "I tell you it isn't," said the other, "She was never *ordered* abroad or at home by anybody."

By the start of 1849, Fanny had made enough money to buy a modest house in her beloved western Massachusetts. It was a picturesque wooden cottage with a tiny tower, standing beside a pretty stretch of wild woodland, less than a mile outside the village of Lenox—just where the track led off toward Stockbridge. A previous owner had named it The Perch. The house no longer stands, and the woodland has vanished, but a bronze plaque on a roadside boulder marks the site, and the road is still called Kemble Street.

Fanny quickly became Lenox's most conspicuous resident. Her eccentric ways spawned many local stories, some of which were affectionate, some critical, and several of which she repeated herself. One personal habit that shocked her neighbors was her custom of wearing trousers. Fanny had always liked men's clothes, and in her youth she had worn men's hats, waistcoats, and even trousers for riding, though she usually wore a skirt over them. A fellow Philadelphian, who met her one day on horseback, described her costume: "A green cloth riding habit, with rolling collar and open in front, under it, a *man's* waistcoat with rolling collar, yellow and gilt buttons, a calico shirt collar and breast, blue striped and turned over and a black silk cravat tied sailor fashion, with a man's hat and a veil." Her riding outfits had been considered becoming, if peculiar, and just within the bounds of propriety.

At Lenox, Fanny ignored her increasing weight—to say nothing of the rules of propriety—and started to wear loose trousers, minus the skirt. Convinced that they were the most suitable clothes for walking, riding, and fishing, she shrugged off letters to the local paper complaining that she was corrupting the youth of Lenox. At the same time, she had no wish to offend her neighbors, because she loved Lenox and Stockbridge and the surrounding lakes and mountains more than anywhere else on earth. Fanny sang the praises of the villages to all who would listen. It is partly thanks to her that the district became a popular holiday resort and artistic center—and remains so to this day. Each year hundreds of Americans come to Lenox for the Tanglewood Music Festival.

Fanny summed up her feelings for Lenox when she wrote that it had afforded her the "happiest days I have ever known in this land of transplantation." She also claimed that Lenox was where she had enjoyed the society of "some of the sweetest and noblest men and women I have ever known."

The summer of 1850 was especially stimulating for Fanny because it provided so much intelligent company. A swarm of writers was visiting the area, including the novelist Herman Melville, the poet James Russell Lowell, and that autocrat of the breakfast table, Oliver Wendell Holmes. Best of all, the novelist Nathaniel Hawthorne had just moved into the little red house near the lake. When Fanny, mounted on her wild black horse, came calling on Hawthorne, she would scoop small Julian Hawthorne up onto her saddle and carry him off for a ride. Later she would bring him back with the cry: "Take Julian the Apostate!" Though Fanny liked small boys, they seldom liked her: she usually scared the wits out of them. Theodore Sedgwick, Catharine's nephew, remembered how, as a little boy, he opened the front door to a woman who had "an air of great importance," grandly dressed in a long black veil and flourishing a parasol. She greeted the terrified child: "You are an ugly boy. You look like your father. Go tell him Fanny Kemble is here."

During that summer, Fanny agreed to give her first public reading in Lenox. At Charles Sedgwick's invitation, she consented to give a benefit performance for the Lenox public library, and she later read aloud to raise money for the clock tower of the Congregational church. Fanny loved this stately church on the hill overlooking the town; she wished to be buried in its churchyard, which looked out over deep valleys and distant blue hills. "I will not rise to trouble anyone if they will but let me sleep there," she wrote. "I will ask only to be permitted, once in a while, to raise my head, and look out upon this glorious scene."

Later, Fanny read in adjacent Stockbridge, where her chosen work was *The Merry Wives of Windsor*, a play in which her tone and manner were sometimes described as masculine and coarse. When Fanny came on stage she made the defiant announcement: "Ladies and Gentlemen, I have been met in my robing room by the clergymen of your town, and they have requested me not to read *The Merry Wives of Windsor*. Ladies and Gentlemen, I have been met in my robing room by a committee of the schoolteachers of your town and requested not to read *The Merry Wives of Windsor*. Ladies and Gentlemen, I have the honor to present to you this evening, Shakespeare's immortal play, *The Merry Wives of Windsor*." This brave speech made it clear to many in Stockbridge why her marriage to Pierce Butler was not harmonious.

Though outwardly Fanny seemed happier, her emotional wounds still smarted. She continued to pine for her daughters. As the summer progressed, her thoughts turned hopefully to the two months of annual holiday that Pierce had agreed to grant her with her girls. Alas, he was to break his word, both in 1850 and in the future. Fanny was not permitted to see her daughters for another five years, and only when Sarah turned twenty-one and was free from her father's control did the first reunion take place.

Fanny did not attempt to fight Pierce's embargo: she was too afraid of the reprisals that might be inflicted on her children. And there may also have been another reason for her silence. In the autumn of the previous year, when Pierce had been anxious to court her goodwill, he had allowed

Sarah and Fan a brief holiday at The Perch. One can safely say that it must have been a difficult reunion, for the children's memories of their mother must have been painful. Trapped in the middle of their parents' tug of war, they had spent nightmarish years obediently taking sides, called on to support their father one moment and their mother the next. After Fanny's departure, they had been fed stories of her misdeeds by Miss Hall and her successors, and most of all by their father. By the autumn of 1849 they could scarcely have known if Fanny was the loving mother of their distant childhood or some monster who bore her name.

It seems more than possible that when Fanny fell on them with gusts of motherly affection, she found herself repelled by a silent wall of mistrust. In those circumstances—fearing that she might do more harm than good by her efforts—she may well have decided to wait until the girls were mature enough to relate to her as rational adults. If this were so, what courage the decision must have taken.

16

Leighton's Madonna

When Adelaide's third and last child, Algernon Charles Frederick Sartoris, was born on August 1, 1851, her husband's interest in his family miraculously revived. He ceased to be obsessed with the fox and the hounds and suddenly became a doting father. It was so endearing, Adelaide wrote joyfully, "to see that grave man unbending to his small baby." She hoped that thereafter they might all live happily together as a family.

They might have lived happily—or so one is tempted to think—had not Francis Thun still been at the heart of Adelaide's thoughts. Months before the baby's birth, she received word that Count Thun and Yuza were coming to England. After reading the letter, Adelaide ran to Edward's room where she "could scarcely find a voice with which to tell him the good news." She had not been so happy for years.

No sooner had Adelaide's excitement subsided than she felt uncertainty and doubt. She wondered if the Thuns would still love her when they saw that she was older, fatter, and certainly more care-worn than the fresh-faced girl they had last seen in Bohemia. She wondered if she would still love them when she saw them as real people, and not simply as the rulers of that fantasy world to which she retreated when reality became too much for her. It was possible that in the cold light of everyday life, the friendship would founder, because each would find the other disappointing.

One month after her confinement, the Thuns crossed the Channel to England and traveled by train to the station at Wellingborough. Adelaide was listening for the carriage that was to bring them on to Knuston Hall, and at the sound of its wheels, she ran excitedly to the door. Once the greetings were over, it was as though they had never been parted. Count Thun was as tender a father as she had remembered, and when he took her baby in his arms, she glowed with happiness. Yuza was the calm and sensitive sister she had recollected. From being "a most dear part of a most dear

< 249 >

time of my life," she told Yuza, "I now regard you as a real, warm, living friend."

At the same time it was not altogether a harmonious reunion for Count Thun. He must often have reminded himself that, but for his principles, Adelaide might have become his daughter-in-law. He seems to have anxiously asked her several times if she were happy. She told him that she would be happy if only she could be "reasonable." What she meant, but could not put into words, was that her happiness depended on her feeling an overwhelming and requited love for somebody. She had once felt it for Francis, and for a time she had felt it for her husband. But now she felt it for no man, and the memory of Francis was troubling her again. The count seemed to sense her meaning, and her answer cannot have brought him comfort.

Adelaide's excitement in the presence of the Thuns betrayed only too clearly her continuing preoccupation with Francis. It was not surprising, therefore, that Edward suddenly announced that he was about to visit his uncle in Hampshire and demanded that his family go with him. For once in their marriage, Adelaide refused his request. She explained that she had not seen her friends for thirteen years, and she might not see them again; adding the gentle ultimatum that her own plans "*must depend entirely*" on the Thuns' proposed itinerary in England. Since she never asked favors of her husband, Adelaide believed that he owed her this one. Edward, in turn, drew the conclusion that the Thuns had a higher priority in her life than he. In the following years he would invent a string of excuses to prevent her from visiting Tetschen.

No one could fairly blame Edward for jealousy, because throughout the Thuns' visit, Francis was foremost in Adelaide's thoughts. Her excitement increased when she realized that there was a prospect of his coming to England to join his father and sister. On the one hand she ached to meet him; on the other, she recognized that it would be wiser if he did not come. "I dare say," she wrote with a sense of resignation, "it would on the whole be pleasanter to him not to see me again." Mercifully her confused emotions were not put to the test, for Francis traveled no further west than Paris.

The Thuns returned to Tetschen, and soon afterward a letter arrived from Francis, his first direct communication in thirteen years. When his letter arrived, Adelaide vaguely hoped that his long-delayed words might prove to be a panacea. But instead of soothing her, they made her feel worse. The letter does not survive, but Adelaide told Count Thun that it "gave me intense pain—it hurt me in a thousand ways—but perhaps this was not his fault—I hardly know what words of his would not hurt me." In her fluctuations of mood, swinging from love to resentment, she could not be satisfied by his words, even if he had sent her a succession of fifty letters.

Meanwhile her attentions and affections were diverted. In the spring of 1852, baby Algy became seriously ill, and only careful nursing saved his life. At the same time, Charles Kemble and his disreputable girlfriend added to Adelaide's distress. She could not look at her father without "mingled commiseration and disgust that makes me quite ill for the rest of the day. . . . Good God, what an end!" Charles was frequently fighting with Fanny, who had returned from America and was living with him. The "violent rages he gets into with both my sister and myself," Adelaide told Count Thun, "are really frightful and pitiable to behold—it makes me absolutely dread to go near him."

To the scandal of her father was added the disgrace of her younger brother. Henry had never married, though for a time he had been engaged to "dull, plain, commonplace" Mary Ann Thackeray, who had traveled in Germany with the Kemble party in 1842. Mary Ann had been eager to marry him, even though her father—the wealthy provost of King's College, Cambridge—threatened to disinherit her if she did so. Since Henry's interest was largely financial, his ardor cooled, and only after her father's death did he renew his suit. For a while they courted, and his hopes ran high, for Mary Ann had inherited great wealth. Eventually, however, she took her leave, thus giving him a taste of his own medicine. Years later Fanny would tell the story to the American novelist Henry James, who would harvest it in his novel *Washington Square*.

Disturbing details began to emerge about Henry's past. It seemed that while soldiering in Ireland, he had formed a liaison with a woman who had borne him a son and then, in a fit of insanity, tried to kill herself. Eventually she emigrated to Philadelphia, leaving the infant in Henry's charge. At the beginning of 1852 an unrepentant Henry told the story to his horrified sisters, adding that he was arranging to have the child adopted into a Protestant household.

Though outraged by Henry's behavior, the sisters' first concern was for the welfare of the little boy. Fanny agreed to take him, generously undertaking to pay all expenses. Little Harry—as he was called—was then rescued from Dublin: a three-year-old ragamuffin, covered with dirt and skilled in tantrums. When scrubbed up and calmed down, he quickly won Fanny's affection. No sooner had he settled down than his father sprang a second surprise. There existed another illegitimate child called Janey.

Quashing her fury, Adelaide took charge but was less pleased with the result. She found the "poor little puss" affected and artful. Rather than have Janey live with them, Adelaide sent her to board with a family in Fulham.

What Edward Sartoris thought of the behavior of Adelaide's father and brother can safely be inferred. He was never devoted to the Kembles as a family, preferring to cling to his own respectable relatives. Faced with these scandals, he decided to take flight. In 1852, with his lease of Knuston Hall about to expire, he announced his intention of taking his family to Rome in the autumn. Normally Adelaide disliked his sudden ultimatums, but this time she willingly fell in with his plans, even adding her own. In the course of the journey from England to Italy, she hoped that she might at last seize the chance to visit the Thuns in Tetschen.

Her hopes were dashed by baby Algy's illness. As Edward hastened to point out, a long, roundabout journey with so delicate a child was out of the question. Not deterred by his objection, Adelaide began to think that she might use the new network of railways and go to Tetschen alone—except, of course, for her maid—before she joined the family in Italy. She would visit the Thuns, however, only on the condition that Edward positively agreed. He did not agree. If she had been Fanny, she would have gone her own way, but being Adelaide, she obeyed. For some weeks she fretted at the lost opportunity, until she brought herself at last to a "state of resignation."

Not enamored with his wife's relatives, Edward cannot have been pleased when Fanny joined the Sartorises in Italy the following year. Nor could her state of mind have lessened his displeasure. Fanny was on the verge of a psychological collapse. Longing for her daughters and embittered by the injustice of her divorce, she found every day a struggle. In some of her depressed moods she even wondered if she might be losing her senses. It was then a common belief that some menopausal women went insane, and though only forty-two, Fanny seems to have believed that her menopause was imminent. She confided to Harriet that she feared she might be going mad.

Fanny began to adopt rigid, even bizarre, rules for everyday living. She wore her gowns in strict rotation, a special dress for each day of the week, and she wore them regardless of their suitability. Some days she trailed through the dusty Pamphili Gardens in a delicate silk ball gown, while on others she paid a simple social call in a shimmering red and gold evening dress. "How do you suppose I could have lived my life," she would say, "if I had not lived by rule, if I had not made laws for myself and kept to them." Fanny was beyond caring what other people might say or think of her. By the same token, she gave little thought to the hurt she might inflict on others. Like her mother, she spoke her mind regardless of circumstances, justifying her pronouncements as "the truth."

A minor writer, Mrs. Lynn Linton, has left a memorable description of Fanny riding roughshod over those she disliked. Though inflated by ill feelings and maybe by jealousy, Mrs. Linton's words paint a picture that is echoed in other journals and letters of the time:

> The deep voice and stage-stateliness of her manner, the assumption of supremacy, and the really cruel strength of this lady, crushed me flat. The way at which she leveled her black eyes at me, and calmly put her foot on me, was an experience never to be forgotten. The pitiless brutality of her contradictions, her scathing sarcasm, her contemptuous taunts, knowing that I was unable to answer her, the way in which she used her mature powers to wound and hurt my even then immature nature gave me a shuddering horror of her, such as I fancy a man would feel for one who had flayed him in the market place.

Other observers insisted that Fanny was capable of "infinite solicitude" and often regretted having caused pain by words uttered in the heat of the moment. But Fanny's victims seldom saw her behavior in that light. The novelist William Thackeray was one who found Fanny abrasive, although he also acknowledged her admirable character and intellect. He said that, in the course of their long acquaintance, he had learned to love Adelaide and to "admire but not to endure Fanny."

Adelaide was as aware of her sister's shortcomings as she was of their unhappy cause. She looked for remedies, and to jolly Fanny along she used to recite a nursery rhyme:

> The Dragon of Wantley, round as a butt,
> Full of fire from top to toe,
> Cock of the walk, to the village I strut,
> And scare them all wherever I go.

Far from taking offense, Fanny would quote the verse against herself. She also liked to quote a description of George Sand—"unamiable, very emphatic, very dictatorial"—and laughingly agreed that it applied equally to herself.

Adelaide, in contrast, remained calm and sweet-natured even when sunk in depression. And in Italy she believed that she had much to depress her. Everyone seemed to have let her down—father, brother, and—most of all—her husband. Edward, to whom she longed to turn for comfort, stood at a distance, his emotions shut off from her. To the faithful Thuns she opened up her heart:

> I have felt so depressed and sad that many of the delights of this wonderful place have been greatly lost to me . . . I should be happy but I *cannot.* . . . I have at last begun to give up all hopes of being happy—life seems to me every day more and more unlike what it should or might be—and I can-not look my disappointment courageously in the face—neither can I, now that the true Gods have left me, do as I see so many others do, take up with idols and worship them—I can never fill up the waste and desolate places with the miserable aims and mean ambitions that seem to stand so many other people instead of happiness—and I feel more hopeless and helpless than you could well imagine—Meanwhile the outward life has been noisy and dissipated enough—I receive twice a week and sing a great deal, and what with going out of an evening and seeing people at home I do not know when I have had five minutes alone with my husband.

Had Adelaide been like her mother and sister, she would have tried to extract sympathy and affection from Edward through tantrums and tirades, but being Adelaide, she withdrew into herself. To Count Thun she again wrote longingly, "I want to see you *very* much. You are the only person upon whom I have counted who has not betrayed me—and my thoughts turn to you instinctively with unwavering love and trust whenever my mind is troubled or my heart heavy."

Few who met the Sartorises and Fanny on their summer trips to Sor-rento and Amalfi or in their winter apartment in Rome could have guessed the inner sadness of the three of them. It was common knowledge that the Sartorises gave some of the liveliest parties in Italy, and that their guest list read like a cross between the *Almanach de Gotha* and an artistic *Who's Who.*

One prominent member of Adelaide's Roman salon was William Thackeray, as large, bespectacled, and amusing as ever, and by then the very famous author of *Vanity Fair.* He was keeping house in a lofty apart-ment above a pastry cook's and felt tugged in two directions: trying, on the one hand, to finish his latest novel, and on the other, to care for his shy teenage daughters, Annie and Minnie. Attempting to be mother and father to his girls—his insane wife was shut up in an asylum—he was constantly thankful for the Sartorises' kindness. Mrs. Sartoris "is all good nature," he wrote appreciatively, and of gruff and morose Edward, he commented: "there was never such a kind creature with such a scowling countenance."

Other visitors to the salon were the poets Robert and Elizabeth Barrett Browning. Sixteen-year-old Annie Thackeray described these visitors minutely in her diary. "I think Mrs. Browning is the greatest woman I ever saw in all my life," wrote Annie. "She is very small, she is brown, with dark eyes and dead brown hair; she has white teeth, and a low, curious voice." Robert Browning "is dark, with a frank open countenance, long hair streaked with grey; he opens his mouth wide when he speaks."

Fanny and Adelaide had known Robert Browning for years, having met him often at the houses of Bryan Procter and Henry Chorley. His wife was a newer acquaintance, though the sisters had heard many times of her romantic elopement with her husband to Italy. Adelaide admired Browning as "a precious man . . . simple and sincere . . . full of originality and power." But her admiration did not prevent her from making fun of some of his and his wife's more obscure writings. She quipped, after the Brownings' son was born, that there were now not one, or two, but "three incomprehensibles."

In the early months of 1854, the Brownings and the Sartorises exchanged many visits. Even four-year-old Penini Browning loved to call on Mrs. Sartoris, and practiced his scales in the hope that he would sing just like her. Shy, serious Elizabeth took surprisingly well to Fanny. "What a voice," she exclaimed, "what eyes, what eyelids full of utterance." She summed Fanny up with more appreciation and charity than was usually accorded by visitors. "Somewhat inelastic," she wrote, "and unpliant to the age, attached to the old modes of thought and conventions, but noble in quality and defects; I like her much." While Fanny was considered "a very noble creature indeed," Adelaide was genuinely loved for being "genial and generous." Her milk, wrote Elizabeth, "has had time to stand and turn to cream in her happy family relations, which poor Fanny Kemble's has not."

Adelaide welcomed to her salon a group of English and American young people who described themselves as a "most jovial crew." Among them was Harriet Hosmer—Hatty for short—a tomboyish sculptor who had been educated at Elizabeth Sedgwick's school at Lenox. Hatty adored Fanny and thought Adelaide was an angel. There "is only one woman like her that I know, in point of goodness," she wrote, "and that is Mrs. Sedg-wick."

Prominent in this group was an aspiring artist and writer called Hamilton Aïdé. The son of an Armenian father and an aristocratic English mother, Aïdé had been, until recently, a captain in the British army, but he had resigned his commission in favor of the arts, and he radiated an air of gentlemanly bohemianism. Another member was the Honorable Richard Lyons, the shy secretary to the British legation in Florence. Though reserved with strangers, Lyons worshipped Adelaide and threw off his shyness in her presence, becoming funny, dry, and jolly. He was famous among the crew members for his imitations of Fanny, especially of Fanny in the act of rebuking a terrified young waiter. He would fling back his head in the Kemble fashion and declaim in Fanny's imperious accents: "I asked for *water*, boy: you bring me *beer*!" Adelaide "loved her following of young people," wrote one friend, "and was good and helpful to them all in turn." Even when she encountered stupidity, she preferred, rather than to upset the young man or woman who expressed it, to register her distaste "in witty but kindly words." Believing that the young needed the wise influence of the old, Adelaide did her best to integrate them into her circle. As a skilled hostess, she soon had them chatting with Thackeray or the Brownings, and even with such European guests as the Duke of Sermoneta or witty Jean Jacques Ampère from the French Institute.

On Sundays and Wednesdays Adelaide held her soirées, providing music, readings, *tableaux vivants*, and charades by way of entertainment. The performers were her friends and family, not least among them Edward. Deep down, the silent Sartoris was almost as much of a thespian as his wife, and he increasingly took pride in his well-trained bass voice. But Adelaide was the star. Dressed in a shimmering, flowing tea gown, she looked majestic and sang exquisitely.

In Rome Adelaide's drawing room, with its large windows, grand piano, and swinging lamps, was arranged like a sumptuous stage set. Annie Thackeray, describing her first visit there, caught the aura of theatricality that always surrounded her hostess:

> There was a big Roman drawing room with a great window to the west and the colours of the room were not unlike sunset colours. There was a long piano with a bowl of flowers on it in the centre of the room; there were soft carpets to tread upon; a beautiful little boy in a white dress, with yellow locks all ashine from the light of the window, was perched upon a

low chair looking up at his mother, who with her arm round him stood by the chair, so that their two heads were on a level. She was dressed (I can see her still) in a sort of grey satin robe, and her beautiful proud head was turned toward the child.

While Adelaide reigned like a queen, Fanny remained aloof, except for uttering the occasional forceful remark. Annie Thackeray remembered that the Sartorises' drawing room had fireplaces with huge logs, and that Fanny sat beside the fire, alone and withdrawn, steadily and silently stitching at her needlework while the brilliant company came and went. Annie stood in awe of Fanny and noted with trepidation the extremes of her moods. Sometimes, in a burst of energy, Fanny would take the Thackeray girls driving, shouting to the driver, "Go to the devil!" and out they would hurl through the cobbled streets in the Campagna, with Fanny singing at the top of her voice.

Fanny's high moods were rare, however, and her low ones were frequent. She was fond of saying that "it was a very hard and difficult hour of her life," when she "needed all her courage to endure her daily portion of suffering." The friends who came to call brought her little pleasure. "We have not a very agreeable society here this winter," she said, "but then I am hard to please." Charles Dickens, seeing the sisters together, wrote that they often avoided each other while part of the same group.

On these strange terms Fanny took part in Adelaide's picnics into the Italian countryside. Often three carriages of revelers set out, complete with champagne and food hampers. On these "exquisite excursions," as the Brownings called them, the tea kettle would be placed on the open fire, and the energetic would set out to walk along rural paths, while frail Elizabeth rested, with her faithful husband beside her. Fanny once remarked that Browning was the only man she had ever known who behaved like a Christian to his wife. Another picnic guest who preferred to rest was John Gibson Lockhart, an eminent Scottish journalist who was slowly dying. Adelaide took care to make him comfortable: his illness seemed in tune with her inner melancholy.

Although deeply unhappy, Adelaide had the precious gift of containing her feelings rather than spreading them far and wide. Aïdé remembered walking beside her *chaise à porteur* as they climbed a hill on their way to Ostia and hearing her say, "I have suffered so much myself from unkindness and neglect, that it makes me lenient to anyone who is kind." Little May Sartoris would long remember a middle-aged woman, with a white cap tied under her chin, running out of a Roman villa and "holding out both her hands with cordial warmth and excitement." It was George Sand greeting her Consuelo. What she and Adelaide said to one another is not recorded, but it would seem that their warmth continued for many years. Though Adelaide was at pains to keep her love for Francis Thun discreetly secret, she may well have been flattered that Sand had seemingly harvested at least some of her heartache in the cause of art.

On these excursions the company of one friend particularly charmed Adelaide. An exuberant young painter, he was English by birth and European by education, having studied in Italy, Germany, and France. He was also well-mannered, handsome, artistically brilliant, a fluent linguist, and reputedly the best waltzer in Rome. He performed so many things so capably that his friends nicknamed him the Admirable Crichton and elected him unofficial leader of the "jovial crew." His real name was Frederic Leighton, he was twenty-three years old, and Edward had met and admired him several years before in Paris.

Adelaide and Frederic were drawn to one another by a powerful dovetailing of needs. She was the dazzling mentor he had been craving, and he was the exciting companion she needed to lighten her depression and ease her loneliness. In her fragile state, she clung to him for survival, and he responded without reservation. During the Roman winter of 1854, they fell in love.

Frederic was so bowled over by Adelaide's talents that there was little about her that he did not adore. Seen through his eyes, she was the world's greatest living soprano, a hostess of remarkable talent, and "a true painter in her sense of beauty of composition, in her great feeling for art." He was captivated by her physical features to a degree that ordinary observers must have considered quite absurd. He informed his sister that she had a "large aquiline nose and the most beautiful mouth in the world, a most harmonious head . . . artistically speaking, her head and shoulders are the finest I ever saw with the exception only of Dante's." He conceded rather crossly that "many people think her barely good-looking, because she has no complexion, very little hair, and is excessively stout. *You*," he told his sister firmly, "will be more discriminating."

What Adelaide did not desire, being moral and idealistic, was a sexual affair, and Frederic seems to have obliged her. His sexual instincts are said to have been either slight or carefully controlled: to this day his sex life—if he had one—remains a mystery. Certainly no friend in gossipy Rome thought that he and Adelaide were anything but platonically attached. A mutual friend, Lord Fordwich, wrote perceptively that Leighton was "insep-arable from Mrs. Sartoris (without scandal)." Even Edward seems to have shown no suspicion. In fact he liked Frederic and helped to promote his ca-reer. The large difference in their ages possibly lulled his anxieties, for Fred-eric was almost young enough to have been Adelaide's son. Edward may also have assumed that with Francis Thun still foremost in Adelaide's emo-tional life there was no room for Frederic Leighton—or for anyone else.

So, with Edward's concurrence, Adelaide adopted a high-souled role as the muse and mentor of Frederic Leighton. She saw herself as his mother but more often as his sister. Often in his company she called herself Sister Adelaide or Sister Ad—Ad being the affectionate diminutive by which she was known to her husband and Henry Greville. Frederic, himself, she nick-named Fay: just as she had affectionately given the nickname Gay to her son Greville, and the nickname May to her daughter Mary. Thus she ele-vated Frederic to the same degree of intimacy she shared with her family. "I have no sunlight without or within that at all mitigates my loss in your de-parture—dear Fay—my dear companion," she wrote to him five years after they had first met. "I miss you very sadly—even here where nothing that surrounds me is in any way associated with you." By this time he had be-come an essential part of her life.

During those early months of their friendship in Rome, Frederic was constantly at Adelaide's side. He became the manager of her charades and the painter of scenery for her *tableaux*. He began to take piano and vocal lessons, and in no time he was the *primo tenore* at her musical recitals. To prove his devotion he painted as a surprise a portrait of baby Algy. It was not one of his finest portraits, he told his mother, but it pleased "them." In-deed, to please *them*, or more accurately, *her*, had so occupied Frederic's life that his physician father, on reading his letters at home in Bath, England, became worried. He would have been even more worried had he known that, by the middle of 1854, his son was virtually alone with Adelaide and her children, for Fanny had returned to London to resume her readings, and Edward, on "the most sudden caprice," had sailed to Constantinople.

During that sweet Italian summer, Adelaide left Rome and traveled to Bagni di Lucca, a group of spa towns nestled in a pretty river valley, high in the mountains behind the walled city of Lucca. It was a favorite summer re-treat of the English, and they had made the area their own, building an En-glish church and even setting up an English circulating library. While Adelaide conceded with a tinge of regret that the spa towns were thronged with her own countrymen, many of whom were not to her taste, she also pointed out that the natural scenery was magnificent. One could roam the chestnut forests and hear nothing but the cry of the cicada and the song of the rushing river; or one could climb to the high meadows and picnic on a carpet of wildflowers. There was room to wander, and to dream, and to be alone in the wilderness.

Harriet Hosmer and Hamilton Aïdé were already there, and eventually Frederic joined the party, though his rooms were discreetly separate from those of his patroness. Aware of his mother's increasing displeasure at his intimacy with Adelaide, Frederic had been preparing his defenses for some time. His mother was worried about the outbreaks of cholera in Italy, but he reassured her that Bagni di Lucca was the healthiest of places. And if he did become ill, he wrote, "I have in Mrs. Sartoris that genuine friend, and, especially *woman friend* that in such a case would leave nothing undone for you, the best of mothers. . . . In the friendship of that admirable woman I am rich for life." Less tactfully he also admitted, "It would be a blank day to me in which I did not see her; God bless her! for my dearest friend—I warm my very soul in the glow of her sisterly affection and kindness."

The summer in Bagni sealed the couple's attachment. They walked, sang, and read aloud together, and their pastimes were innocent and peaceful. One Sunday Hatty Hosmer, Fay, and Aïdé sat on the terrace of the Sartorises' villa while Adelaide read them a sermon by Fanny's American hero and friend, the Reverend Dr. Channing. On other Sundays, almost as an act of charity, they called on Gioacchino Rossini at his lodgings, not a stone's throw from the villa's door.

Adelaide had long wanted to know the gifted composer and wished she might have known him in his prime. The melancholy, irritable old man she met for the first time in 1854 lived in a dim room, ministered to by his wife, three doctors, and assorted shabby hangers-on. "He has not opened a book, nor read anything—not even a newspaper for years," she wrote sadly, "and his mind from constantly preying on itself and receiving no proper food or wholesome exercise is almost in a state of insanity. He takes interest in nothing. Will not talk or hear about music. Says that he is the most miserable of God's creatures."

To Adelaide's pleasure, Rossini brightened up when the talk moved to Charles Kemble, and he recalled with enthusiasm her father's Hamlet. He even brought himself to ask which works she had been singing recently. When she said, "Rossini," he sighed ruefully and said with a flash of his old humor, "Don't sing him; he is out of date."

So intensely did Frederic enjoy his days at Bagni that he could scarcely tear himself away. Writing to his mother on September 20, 1854, from Florence, where he had just arrived, he tried to tame her disapproval by describing his attendance on Adelaide as the action of a good Samaritan. He explained that the Sartorises had received grave news, the husband had instantly been recalled to England, and so his own presence was needed to comfort and distract Adelaide and to help her son Greville, whose tutor had also been called away.

In his efforts to reassure his mother, Frederic was rather bending the truth. He was lying about Edward's sudden journey, which had actually begun several months before, but Frederic was truthful in writing that Adelaide had recently received bad news. Both Charles and Henry Kemble had fallen seriously ill. Charles, who was in his seventy-ninth year, was to die in London that November; and the exasperation that the two sisters had long felt with him suddenly vanished.

While the death of Adelaide's father was not a surprise, the collapse of her brother was a profound shock. Henry, who had been disabled for the past two years with rheumatism, had grown so deranged that he was committed to a private asylum at Hillingdon, near London. William Thackeray, visiting him there, reported that Henry was disoriented but happy, believing he was living in a fashionable country house, and boasting of his prowess with women and horses.

To Adelaide, the news of her beloved brother's madness struck at her "very roots." Without Frederic she could not have coped: he was the rock to which she clung. Many years later, remembering that time, she wrote to him: "My dear Fay, you are right to think I shall remember our Italian days—all, all the lovely sights you mention I shall remember until memory itself departs: and lovelier than all, the true and tender friendship so steadfast, so unfailing, and that was a joy to me when suffering prevented my getting joy out of anything else."

What Frederic did not seem to tell his mother, nor Adelaide tell her friends, was that she left Bagni and joined him for a time in Florence. According to her testimony, they were together in Florence for ten days, and the time passed "very quickly." What happened in that city and why they kept it secret one cannot really know, but her visit would seem to have had a sentimental importance. Nine years later to the day, she would write reminding him of the anniversary.

Late in October 1854 Edward returned from London, met his family in Bagni, and escorted them back to Rome. There Adelaide and Frederic were still inseparable; he was preparing to paint a half-portrait of her and a portrait of May. To his former art master in Frankfurt he confided, "Mrs. Sartoris is my dearest friend, and the noblest, cleverest woman I have ever met." To his mother he wrote, "I look upon her as an angel, *ni plus ni moins* and I feel terrified at the idea of how much more exacting she has made me for the future choice of a wife, by showing one what opposite excellences a woman may unite in herself."

Their Roman idyll was to end in the new year. Restless Edward was ready to move back to London, and Adelaide was expected to follow him. Frederic, too, had pressing engagements to fulfill. His earliest masterpiece, *Cimabue's Madonna*, was finished and was ready for shipment to London, where Queen Victoria would buy it on sight. In mid year he left for London and the start of his rise to fame.

Adelaide's return to London in June 1855 gave her a sense of "unspeakable sorrow." Her father's death and her brother's insanity were almost more than she could bear. Hastening to visit Henry at Mr. Stilwell's asylum in Hillingdon, she found him "thank God, happy and peaceful—he knows me, and his great delight is to make me sing to him almost all the time I am there." She was less diligent in visiting Fanny, who was forthright in her observation: "She has been here nearly three weeks and I have seen her once."

In her unhappiness Adelaide clung to Frederic, who was quick to arrange a meeting with his family in England. Frederic's sister Augusta observed this new friend of her brother's carefully, and has left a striking pen portrait. "She is very stout," Augusta wrote, "very high coloured, and has little hair. But the shape of her mouth is very fine, the modulations of her voice in speaking are exquisite. She is a creature who can never age, and before whose attractions those of younger and prettier women must always pale." Augusta also noticed how protective Adelaide was of Frederic. "She seems very fond of him," wrote Augusta reassuringly, "as she might be of a younger brother."

While in London, Adelaide saw her twelve-year-old son Greville off to boarding school in Brighton. She hated parting from him and had fears for his well-being, but she hoped for the best. "He is a manly little fellow in spite of his home education," she wrote, "he rides capitally, and swims like a fish, so I hope he may be able to hold his own." Adelaide had no trouble whatsoever in believing that her husband could hold his own. He made all the decisions for the family, and he stood no interference. Edward's decision was that they should go to live in Paris, since it would be nearer to his investments and nearer to his sister, who lived at the de l'Aigles' country estate, about fifty miles north of Paris. To that estate he now made a long visit, taking Adelaide with him.

Adelaide had always loved the de l'Aigle house, which stood on a cleared hill at Francport in the midst of the vast, mysterious forest of Compiègne. Of a summer's morning, she could look out of her bedroom window onto a "great ocean of forest, drenched in deep dews, steeped in warm sunshine, swaying in the fresh morning sweetness." In autumn the view was even more magical: a medley of "emerald mosses and the red-gold of fallen beech leaves—the whole air filled with delicious autumn savours, musky gusts of wild woodland odor, and the bitter fragrance of bruised leaves."

Adelaide was on better terms than ever with her sister-in-law, Eliza de L'Aigle, whom she had come to regard as "one of the most beautiful women it is possible to see." They read novels, gossiped together, and confided in one another like real sisters—or better, maybe, than real sisters, for, as Adelaide knew, Fanny disliked gossip and frivolous novels and did not always confide. Adelaide was well aware that to be accepted as a confidante by her sister-in-law was socially no small prize, for the French emperor was a frequent guest at the de L'Aigles' house during the stag-hunting season, when the court moved to the nearby palace at Compiègne. For an actor's daughter—even a Kemble's daughter—Adelaide had come a long way.

In November 1855, the Sartorises moved to an apartment in Paris at 15 Rue de l' Arcade, and soon their household was like Rome over again. The jovial crew flocked to her salon, as did her older friends. The Thackerays were there, and the Brownings, and Lyons and Aïdé and Harriet Hosmer. Referring to Adelaide in a letter, Robert Browning wrote: "She sings and talks and looks and *is* just as of old and *so* good that is." Soon Frederic joined her, and so did Henry Greville and Theodosia Monson. Adelaide also renewed her connection with white-haired Mrs. Forster, by that time almost blind, with whom she had lived as a timid young girl while studying with Bordogni. She even seems to have repaired her friendship with Anna Jameson.

To create a dashing setting for her parties, Adelaide furnished the Paris apartment with Italian color and dressed herself in flowing silk gowns, to which she sometimes added a pair of turquoise eyeglasses. Once more she assembled artists, authors, musicians, and a string of cosmopolitan titles in her drawing room. She entertained all the distinguished English travelers to Paris: her only criterion was that they must be "agreeable." Writers seemed to proliferate that season. Alfred Tennyson was there and also John Ruskin, Thomas Carlyle, and Charles Dickens.

In return Adelaide was invited to the most convivial houses in Paris. She told Henry Greville about an evening she spent at the home of Pauline Garcia Viardot, where Charles Dickens, his wife, and George Sand were her fellow guests. It was wonderful, she said, to see Dickens and George Sand conversing at close quarters. Afterward Dickens told her that he was astonished at Sand's quiet manners and small, dumpy person, having always imagined her as resembling a sort of "glorified monthly nurse."

In Paris, Adelaide again met Rossini, much healthier than he had been at Bagni di Lucca. She discovered his interest in the music of Weber; and it would seem to have been in her drawing room in Paris that Rossini first heard Weber's "Mermaids' Song," which Adelaide sang often in memory of Aunt Dall. Annie Thackeray heard the lilting melody floating from an inner room, and it moved her ever afterward. Aïdé heard it too, and he remembered that Rossini, who had once seen Weber as an arch-rival, "expressed natural and unreserved admiration" for his former competitor, "and said how much he should have wished to know Weber personally."

Adelaide's evenings were becoming celebrated even in soirée-thronged Paris, and with good reason, for her gatherings had magic. "She liked an atmosphere peaceful yet glowing, and vibrating with her emotion," wrote Annie Thackeray. "She liked to see charming faces, young and gay, handsome and sympathetic. . . . She was a born artist in daily life as well as in music."

In Paris Adelaide introduced her dearest Fay Leighton to Henry Greville, and he was soon Henry's dearest Fay Leighton, as well. Henry demanded equal rights over Frederic and appointed Sister Ad and himself as joint guardians of the young man, a sort of cozy threesome. Having acquired a portrait of Frederic, he wrote, "I have hung you and Ad up side by side in sweet companionship in my dressing room, so that I can see you both the first thing on waking." So strongly did the guardians take their duty, that on one occasion, when a letter from the absent Frederic failed to arrive, Henry and Adelaide fell into a panic over his safety. "I never slept all night," Henry told him, "and of course had worked myself, with her assistance, into a wretched state of anxiety about you."

Whereas Adelaide wrote to Frederic with distance and decorum, Henry's flamboyant letters pulsated with homosexual hints and throbbed with bantering ardor. Frederic was addressed as his dearest Fay, his Fay of

Fays, or Italian style, his dearest Bimbo, to which he signed himself, "your old and loving Babbo." To make his tastes even clearer, he dropped the hint that some young ladies and a Signor Cigala had called, but that Cigala had not earned his favor because he "never made love to me." At the same time a genuinely paternal affection ran through Henry Greville's letters, and one cannot doubt his sincerity when he exclaimed, "I wish you were my son, Fay!" Whether Fay responded with more than filial devotion it is impossible to know. Affectionately, but with propriety, he referred to Henry as "one of the kindest and best men possible" and a "second father."

Adelaide herself seemed to suspect no harm in the association and actively promoted it, for it provided comfort in Henry's loneliness, and it furthered Frederic's career. That there may have been what Adelaide would call moral danger in the men's relationship never appeared to trouble her. Maybe she was too innocent, or maybe she trusted Henry, or maybe she assumed that Frederic, as someone who could be visibly drawn to women, would be uninterested. As time went on, and tiffs abounded, she did advise Fay how to handle his Babbo. "I am glad," she wrote perceptively, "you mean to write a little gossip to Henry—he is not a man of sentiment, he is not a man of thought, he is not an artist, but he has something of a woman's futility that lives upon little things." He also "has a woman's affection" and "loves you nearly as much as I do, only perhaps he don't know *how* to love as well." At the same time she advised Frederic never to consider sharing a home with Henry.

The Sartorises stayed in France until the spring, when they returned to London. But Edward's fondness for Paris had not been satisfied, and he soon took a three-year lease on an apartment in the Rue Royale, which Adelaide hastily converted into another handsome home. Annie Thackeray remembered her "lovely bric-a-brac and tapestries and cabinets" and a "glowing shaded lamp, the first I had ever seen, reflected from one glass to another." She also remembered Adelaide's unusual octagonal dining room, with its round table and pink wax candles, which were lighted for her delightful and intimate dinner parties. For the following three years, the Sartoris family floated between Paris and London.

While still in Paris, Edward took a lease on a large red-brick house in the English countryside. Called Westbury House, it was near Winchester and barely two miles from the mansion of his Uncle Edward Tunno at Warnford. Though Adelaide liked the house and furnished it grandly— hanging the drawing room with red velvet—its proximity to Edward's relatives did not please her. As a dutiful heir, Edward spent much time in the company of the Tunnos, and he expected Adelaide to be always at his side. In self-defense Adelaide set up her own society. Her frequent house parties attracted Frederic, who often came to stay, and Hamilton Aïdé, who lived with his English mother at nearby Lyndhurst in the New Forest.

Fortunately Edward by that time had warmed to fussy little Aïdé, the guest who in Rome had irritated him unbearably. In an unprecedented thawing, Edward even consented to act in the amateur theatricals that Aïdé organized at Lyndhurst. Indeed, thanks to Aïdé, in the following years Lyndhurst became almost a second home to Adelaide and to Frederic, who began to decorate the Lyndhurst church with frescoes of the Wise and Foolish Virgins. While Frederic was at his painting, Adelaide went often to stay in the house in the woods belonging to Aïdé's mother.

Edward's softening opinion of Aïdé came as a relief, for, as Adelaide said, "it is a great comfort to be no longer obliged to keep him in the coal scuttle." Not that Edward was at home very often to notice who was hiding in the coal scuttle. Between hunting and shooting, he spent no more than one day a week at his country house, and even then his thoughts were mostly following the horses and the hounds. When he was at home, he demanded first place in Adelaide's life, regardless of any inconvenience it might cause her; and she—maybe remembering Fanny's ill-fated struggles—dutifully gave priority to him. Henry Greville, who hated to see Adelaide neglected and put upon, wished that she would be a little less dutiful and a little more protective of herself.

Adelaide's life was not simply a succession of parties. Describing her domestic routine, she told Count Thun: "I keep accounts, settle cook's books every week, teach my children every day, and find *an interest* in carpet work. I am another creature . . . dear Thun I am grown so old." The Thuns, as ever, were in her thoughts. But though she often crossed the English Channel on her journeys to the continent, she did not reach Tetschen. Each time Edward found or contrived arguments against such a visit, and even Henry Greville—who was always unhappy about her yearnings for Francis—begged her to forego the journey.

But Adelaide's hopes of reaching Tetschen persisted, and she made tentative plans to travel there by train in the autumn of 1856. Then Edward fell ill while visiting Ireland in August, and Adelaide, who had remained in England to settle their son Greville into Eton College, was instantly called to his side. Once more the hoped-for visit to Tetschen was abandoned.

Not to be defeated, in the new year Adelaide began to plan again, but the disappointment was repeated. Now "as formerly," she told the count, "when the bad hours come, and life seems utterly hideous and odious to me, I think of *you* and feel that if I could only see you, but *only see you*, that peace and steadiness and strength would return to me."

Outwardly cheerful and gracious, Adelaide suffered often from gloom as the year 1857 progressed. Her brother Henry contributed to her mood. He "is without a gleam of reason," she reported from Paris: "I went to England to see him a few days ago, but though he knew me, my presence gave him no pleasure, and they had to speak to him repeatedly to induce him to bid me goodbye—he is very weak and thank God cannot last long—the news of his death will be the most welcome tidings I can get of him—but it is sad to have to say this of all that one has most loved in childhood."

While Adelaide waited for Henry to die—which he did later in the year—she received news of another death. Her elder brother, John, who had been working in Germany as an archaeologist, had journeyed to Dublin to address the Royal Irish Academy. There in March 1857 he caught pneumonia. Adelaide in Paris received warning of his imminent death, but even as she hastened to him he was gone: "a man full of health and strength in the entire vigor of mind and body, not fifty years old."

She was all too aware that she should become responsible for John's three destitute children. As their mother was irresponsible, Adelaide saw little hope for their future unless she herself acted decisively. The eldest child, Gertrude, aged twenty, had inherited the De Camp voice and wished to be a concert soprano. Adelaide at once enlisted the aid of old friends— the critic Henry Chorley, the composer John Hullah, and that finest of vocal teachers, Manuel Garcia, the younger. They gave Gertrude such help that when she made her debut in Handel's *Messiah* some months later, she did so "quite remarkably," according to Adelaide. Gertrude would secure her future in 1859 by marrying the noted English baritone and Garcia's former pupil, Charles Santley.

John's son, Henry, wished to be a soldier, so Adelaide and Fanny bought him a commission and sent him off to India. The younger girl, Mildred, of no special talent, was sent to study languages with a view to teaching, and Adelaide employed her three times a week to instruct May in German. Mildred's humble, loving nature quickly won admirers, and Adelaide was not surprised when she married the Reverend Charles Donne, the son of her father's closest friend, William Bodham Donne.

To guide her brother's children toward a promising future pleased Adelaide. Nevertheless she often found the past more powerful than the future. Suddenly, in the late summer of 1857, word came that Count Thun and Yuza were preparing to travel to England and—terror of terrors and joy of joys—Francis was definitely coming with them.

Once again Adelaide was thrown into an agony of indecision. Should she see him or should she not? With difficulty she decided that she should not, but then she vacillated: "how *I do wish I* could come!" she wrote to Yuza. Deciding it would be best if she stayed in Paris, Adelaide resolved to send Edward in her place to receive the Thuns in England. But then she changed her mind. She decided to return to England, to see, if not Francis, then his father and sister.

At the beginning of September, Adelaide and the children—without Edward—moved into a quiet house at Bonchurch on the Isle of Wight and invited Count Thun and Yuza to stay with them. For an idyllic week, flooded with autumn sunshine, the children bathed in the calm sea, while the adults walked along the coastal paths and talked of Francis's imminent arrival. Yuza urged Adelaide to see her brother. She firmly believed that only by meeting in person would they lay to rest the painful ghosts that tormented them both.

The two women pondered over the most fitting way of arranging the meeting and were relieved to arrive at a tactful solution. Despite the disgrace of his marriage, Francis had risen to be minister for fine arts and president of a prominent society for promoting the arts in Bohemia. As he was visiting London partly to tour art galleries, what could be more appropriate than for Adelaide to meet him on the neutral ground of a London gallery. On September 16, 1857, Adelaide set out by train to London to keep the appointment. What courage the journey must have taken. And yet the long-awaited coming together was serene and placid.

Reporting to an anxious Yuza by letter, Adelaide explained that she "spent the evening of that day with Francis and all the morning of the next, looking at Turner's pictures, and buying small presents with him for his wife and children." Dear Yuza, she exclaimed, "you cannot think how strange it was to be drinking tea together, two sad middle aged people having parted in youth so many years ago! Poor poor dear Francis! I am very glad I went to town—I had one moment of hesitation about it—and of painful dread of some misapprehension on his part—but he seemed so really pleased to see me and so comforted by the little time we spent together, that I feel sure I did what was best."

To Fanny in America Adelaide wrote a more intimate letter, revealing a vital piece of information, which must have taken her breath away when

Francis first imparted it in London. The information was almost twenty years old, but it was no less immediate to Adelaide, because it revealed at last the true circumstances of Francis's rejection of her. "Francis Thun has been in England," she wrote to her sister, "and I saw him after a separation of nearly twenty years—He drank tea with me, and, weary elderly folk, we talked over the strange chances of our lives and the story of our youth—He gave me up because his father never told him, as he had me, that he would not object to our marriage, and it was not till some years after, when he had already a child by his present wife, that his father *for the first time*, mistaking the cause of his extreme dejection said to him 'If you still care for her so, marry her.' And then it was too late—and he could but right the woman he had wronged."

So the truth about the count's strange mixture of caution, cunning, and diplomacy in the days of her courtship was known at last. This revelation, made by Francis during their quiet conversation in London, cannot have failed to shake Adelaide's composure. But it did not weaken her faith in Count Thun. The episode had happened long ago, and she still trusted him.

On seeing Francis again, Adelaide realized that she had made an emotional journey in those twenty years since they last had met. The meaning of the journey was finally clear to her—the son had slowly been supplanted by the father as the real object of her affection. Count Thun, Adelaide told Yuza, "is the only person who never hurts me in any mood."

17

A Fierce and Furious Conflict

In May 1856 Fanny's elder daughter, Sarah Butler, was to turn twenty-one and gain her legal independence. This was the day that Fanny had lived for all through the past six years, because Sarah would now be free of Pierce's control and mature enough, Fanny hoped, to respond to her mother like an adult. In readiness, Fanny crossed the Atlantic to Boston, traveled to Philadelphia, and at the appointed time, removed both girls from their boardinghouse for a two-month holiday in Lenox. To Fanny's intense annoyance, Pierce arrived and insisted on seeing his daughters, making what was inevitably a time of tension considerably more tense.

Fanny hoped to build a true and loving relationship with her grownup girls, but with so much drama in the past, it would have taken a mother more skilled than herself to manage the transition. Though Fanny loved her daughters, she was a perpetual apprentice in human relationships, and, furthermore, Sarah and Fan had had such a turbulent childhood that it was a wonder they could trust anyone. When news of the ups and downs of their reunion reached London, Adelaide wrote sadly to a friend: "it is a painful business—a strong feeling of duty on my niece's side, and a strong mother's yearning on my sister's, draws them together, but they do not agree." To Fanny herself Adelaide wrote affectionately and wisely: "You put me in mind in your relations with your child, of my mother with my father—buying the bitter joy of his presence with such storms of suffering—and only at peace when away from him and full of sad longing—God bless you my dear! and comfort your poor heart."

Though Fanny often longed for Europe in the following three years, she remained in America so that she could be close to her girls. Now that she had her daughters, and the Sedgwicks, and the income from her public readings, her mood was noticeably lighter. She also had the excitement of traveling west on the new railways to perform in cities that a short time be-

< 270 >

fore had been only wilderness. Fanny's readings brought her status, satisfaction, and a sense of security, which was just as well, because Pierce's promised annuity had vanished. His ill-advised gambling in stocks and shares was common knowledge, and forewarned by public talk, Fanny was not surprised when the news broke of his impending insolvency. Nevertheless she was vexed. Her daughters, who should have been among the wealthiest girls in the land, might in future have to look to her for an income on which to live.

Pierce's financial crash proved not so devastating to him, because his half interest in the two plantations was protected by family trusts. His debts forced him, however, to sell 429 slaves—men, women, and children—in order to raise money for his creditors. The sale, held on March 1 and 2, 1859, and said to be the most valuable sale of slaves in American history, attracted intense interest across the South. The hotels of Savannah were crowded for a week beforehand with "profane and bearish" buyers, who made daily excursions to the Savannah racecourse to inspect the human merchandise.

At the racecourse, the slaves were displayed like cattle in the drafty stables and carriage sheds. Most had been born and raised on the Butler plantations and had never set foot outside them. Stunned by the change in their fortunes, they huddled together in the bare sheds, clutching their bundles of brightly colored clothing and tin bowls of beans and rice. As they sat gazing mournfully into space, their bodies rocked to and fro restlessly. Only the infants showed signs of normality. While the slave-dealers and plantation owners sauntered through the sheds, prodding the slaves' legs and arms and forcing open their mouths to inspect their teeth, a few of the adventurous infants climbed up the would-be buyers' legs and clung there like crabs.

The opening day of the sale dawned stormy, and rain pelted through the open sides of the grandstand where the auction was to take place. Each slave was forced to stand on a block at the end of the room, to be inspected closely by all eyes. One woman covered herself with a large shawl, which produced indignant cries of "Ain't she sound? Pull off her rags and let us see her." The auctioneer patiently explained that he had no desire to palm off an "inferior article." The truth—as recorded by a Northern reporter—was that she had given birth to a baby only fifteen days before and "was entitled to the slight indulgence of a blanket, to keep from herself and child the chill air and driving rain." Since Pierce had stipulated that families should not be broken up, she, her husband, their three-year-old daughter, and tiny baby were sold together for the purchase price of $2,500.

Before the bidding started, Pierce moved among the slaves, greeting and being greeted, and the Northern reporters were amazed at how genuinely he was hailed. As a farewell present he gave to each slave the sum of one dollar divided into four shiny coins. He could afford to be generous, for the sale earned a record sum of $303,850, enabling Pierce to pay off his creditors and still retain a sizable bonus for himself.

Thus passed out of the Butler hands most of the slaves whom Fanny had vividly depicted in her journal—Psyche and her children among them. To what homes they went Fanny did not know. She thought of them and grieved for them long after they had vanished.

Fanny celebrated her reunion with her daughters by inviting them, at a time of their choice, to tour Europe with her as their guide. To her disappointment, neither showed an eagerness to travel, because their world, not unnaturally, focused on Philadelphia. Eventually, just before her twenty-first birthday, Fan did agree to travel, and Sarah's refusal soon made sense. Sarah, handsome and clever, with a slender, animated figure and long chestnut hair, had fallen in love with a physician, Dr. Owen Wister, a member of a prominent Philadelphia family. They were married early in 1859, just before Fanny and Fan sailed for Europe.

The European tour was happier than Fanny had dared to hope. They visited Paris to buy clothes—"I am now reduced to a shopping machine," Fanny wrote plaintively—and Fan made an excursion to the Scottish Highlands. Adelaide, who could be so motherly with young people, exerted all her charms and skills to make her niece feel welcome. "I should be so grieved," she told Fanny, "if the child couldn't love me." Greville Sartoris took Fan horseback riding, while his sister May, who adored animals, introduced her to her bulldogs. It was not always smooth sailing between mother and daughter, but the Sartorises tried to calm the waters.

Back in America later that year, Fanny learned that her elder daughter was pregnant. Sarah's son, born in July 1860, was Fanny's first grandchild and a balm for her maternal wounds. Named Owen after his father—but called Dan within the family—he grew up to become a popular American novelist and an admirer of his grandmother, whom he later described as a "tempestuous spirit" who was both "noble and magnanimous."

Fanny continued her reading tours, and between-times at Lenox she carved out a new life for herself. She kept up a rapid flurry of letters, her lifeline to England and Europe, and by the early 1860s she counted Adelaide's ever-present friend, Frederic Leighton, among her correspondents. When Frederic sent over a collection of his paintings for public display and sale in Boston in 1861, he enlisted Fanny's help; and he also sent a drawing of Westbury House as a gift. Fanny told him in return the details of her life amid the changing seasons at Lenox: of the rainbow colors of the leaves in autumn, of finding shy, wild gentians in the spring woods, of the bristling trees and the intense cold of winter in the Berkshires.

Though Fanny would never approach the close relationship with Frederic that her sister had achieved, she did receive a type of immortality at his hands. On a visit to London, she was invited to pose, with a suitably "dramatic expression of wickedness," for his picture of Jezebel, the powerful and evil biblical queen. Sly Henry Greville had proposed her as the model, a suggestion that Frederic gallantly brushed aside, until Fanny herself jumped at the chance. When the picture was completed, she exulted in the stout, menacing figure that scowled from the canvas, wearing her face.

Meantime in America, her spirits flagged. The periods of isolation at Lenox, at first so seductive, began to pall. Missing the excitement of her old fast-paced existence, she described herself as "intolerably lonely." Longing for English news, especially news of Adelaide, she lamented that nobody had "an idea how *banished* I feel." Though Fanny complained of Adelaide's "bitter silence," which left her "ignorant as death does," there was no real sign of estrangement between the sisters. Adelaide in fact corresponded more frequently than her sister was willing to admit, writing amusingly and affectionately, expressing joy at the "happier state of things between Sarah and yourself," and enthusing over the baby.

Fanny was increasingly worried about the future of the United States, of which she viewed herself as an honorary citizen. Perturbed by the rift between the Northern and Southern states, she observed a great nation being stretched almost to breaking point. She sympathized, of course, with the antislavery North, and at first she wished that the South would secede, concluding that the North would be happier and better off on its own. But once the war began, she supported President Lincoln and his refusal to allow any state to secede, even though she sensed that the war might have alarming effects on her own family. In May 1861 she wrote to Henry Greville: "We shall have a fierce and furious conflict now, for both sides are rabid."

Already the war was dividing Fanny's family. Fan, always her father's girl, was for the South, while Sarah, though not entirely Fanny's ally, was for the North. It was Fan's headstrong zeal that made her join her father and a female friend on a foolhardy trip to Georgia just as hostilities were beginning. Gossips said that Pierce was planning to enlist in the Confederate army, but fresh rumors hinted that he was a spy, agent, or financier for the Confederacy. In August 1861, he was arrested at his Philadelphia boardinghouse and taken to detention at Port Lafayette, at the entrance to New York Harbor. Fanny thought that the charge against him—that he was providing or financing arms or other help for the South—was very likely to be true. She also believed that even if the charge were unfounded, Pierce would refuse to give an oath of allegiance to the North and would be interned for the duration of the war. In the event, Fanny's hopeful prediction proved to be false. The charge was not proved, and some weeks later Pierce took his oath of allegiance and was set free.

By autumn of 1861 the flagpole at nearly every Berkshire farmhouse flew the stars and stripes, and villages began to bid farewell to their young men. By wintertime, Fanny felt increasingly nervous, for she heard rumors of war between England and the North, and every particle of her revolted at such a prospect. Through the following months she bombarded the Greville brothers with her written accounts of the North's strength and the South's weakness. She knew that both men were highly placed in England, and she saw them, almost certainly, as the first link in her campaign of persuasion to deter England from backing the wrong side.

As the war went on, Fanny's American reading tours dried up. She needed fresh audiences, and she longed to see fresh faces. Always restless, her thoughts turned to the far side of the Atlantic. In the middle of 1862, she set sail for Europe, soon to be joined by her daughter Fan.

Fanny longed to explore Switzerland—the country, so she believed, of her ancestry. Though Adelaide had admitted privately to Henry Greville that her grandfather, George De Camp, had been a flute player in the Viennese imperial court orchestra, Fanny clung to a more respectable version of the family history. She claimed that George De Camp had been a captain in the French revolutionary army, meeting and marrying her grandmother, a Swiss farmer's daughter, during the French invasion of Switzerland. The awkward fact that the French had invaded Switzerland in the 1790s and that Fanny's mother had been born in Vienna in 1774 in no way destroyed her belief. She presented as evidence the fact that the De Camps belonged in London to the Swiss Protestant church. What she did not realize was that Swiss Reformed was virtually the only Protestant congregation allowed to worship in Vienna at the time of her mother's birth: the family's Swiss connection was almost certainly a Viennese connection. Fanny's other evidence was even hazier, but it was exactly that haze that allowed her the personal certainty that her maternal ancestry was Swiss.

Throughout the summer, she and Fan sampled the finest scenery in Switzerland. They sailed on the clear waters of Swiss lakes, climbed lush slopes beneath the highest peaks, and drove to see the awe-inspiring glaciers. When the weather in Switzerland broke, mother and daughter returned to England, retreating to a cottage standing at the gates of Adelaide's country house.

On visits to London, Fanny found that the American war pervaded the conversation at most dinner tables. The hostile feeling toward the North that was common in the circles she frequented almost tore her apart. She was so apt to cry when the war was discussed that her friends tried to avoid any mention of it. But Fanny refused to be silenced. Somehow England's attitude had to be set right, and its belief in the heroic South cut down to size. Ten years before, Fanny had refused to join half a million English women in signing a manifesto calling on the women of America to ameliorate and then banish slavery. She had said then that the English manifesto was impertinent and patronizing: she did not approve of England's interfering in the affairs of another people. Now the circumstances had altered, and she was prepared to risk impertinence and fight with any weapon at hand. As it happened, she had a weapon, the vivid journal she had kept on Pierce's Georgia plantation. Over the years she had given private readings from it and had entertained thoughts of publishing it, but she had feared Pierce's reprisals. Now she swiftly edited the manuscript and offered it to the house of Longman, which published it in May 1863 under the title *Journal of a Residence on a Georgian Plantation in 1838–1839*.

Did Fanny's journal help to change British attitudes, as she had hoped? The book was probably too late; moreover, only a few English reviewers noticed it. Even without its help, public sympathy in the British Isles was turning toward the North. But one cannot be sure that her book had no effect, for it was powerful and penetrating, and in the English circles in which she moved, it may well have convinced wavering readers.

Fanny at first planned to publish her book only in England, but she was persuaded to offer the rights to the popular publishers Harper and Brothers of New York. The American edition, coming out in July 1863, just after the great Northern victories, won a wide readership in the Northern states, even though, as Fanny anticipated, a squeamish few carped at the impropriety of some of her descriptions. In the pages of *Harper's Monthly* and the *Atlantic Monthly*, Fanny's journal was praised as a "noble service, nobly done." A "sadder book," one reviewer added, "the human hand never wrote." Her book's superb passages of prose are deservedly part of America's literary heritage and still to be found in anthologies.

The book did not find favor with Fanny's younger daughter, who resented its message. The slave plantation was virtually a way of life, and Fan believed in many of its values. When the war was over, ignoring the pleas of her family and friends, Fan went with Pierce to the Butler plantations, still held in family trust. What they found was pitiable. Through nature, neglect, and marauding troops, little was left undestroyed. Through two succeeding winters, she and her father worked to restore the rice and cotton fields, hiring such black labor as was willing to work with energy.

In the winter of 1866–1867, father and daughter stayed as usual at the plantations. In the spring, Fan returned to Philadelphia. Her father, staying in the swampy region later than was safe, went down with a fatal attack of what was probably malaria. Alone in his short last illness, he died in August 1867 at the age of fifty-six. He lies in a lonely grave in the town of Darien.

Fanny was in England when she heard the news. She also was alone, for Sarah and her grandson had just left her. As might have been expected, she was prostrated, though not precisely with grief. The death revived bitter memories. Her daughters, however, were genuinely grief-stricken. Highly strung Sarah was so distraught that she seems, for a time, to have actually lost her memory. Adelaide, who was easily caught up in emotional whirlpools, confided to a friend: "I feel very anxious and uneasy about and for them all."

Adelaide tried hard to lighten Fanny's distress. It was one of those rare times in her life when she felt unburdened by troubles, and she wanted Fanny to share her buoyancy. The meeting with Francis had replaced fantasy with reality, thereby bringing her peace, and Frederic Leighton's exciting company had banished her loneliness. At last Adelaide was free to open her whole heart to her family and friends, and she found the experience rewarding. To add to her contentment, Edward's income had been restored, the children were flourishing, and the family had resumed its London life in a tall terrace house in her favorite street, Park Place.

Since her home was now the center of her life, Adelaide spared no pains to make the house at 9 Park Place dramatic and beautiful. She furnished the drawing room with "high carved cabinets, and worked silken tapestries on the walls, and a great golden carved glass." Annie Thackeray remembered her standing beside the glass, splendid in a velvet brocade dress, "not unlike a picture by Tintoretto." The regality of the drawing room and its hostess made a strong impression on the young girl.

The Sartorises entertained their friends—and were in turn entertained—frequently and lavishly. Not long before Pierce Butler's death, Adelaide described just one week's activities: "last Wednesday we had two parties, at Lady Downshire and Lady Stanley's—and on Thursday the Duchess of Cleveland—Friday Mrs. Mildmay—Saturday Lady Margaret Beaumont. Monday (yesterday) a regular Beargarden here with more people than the house would hold—I thought it simply odious, but I believe as people could neither get in nor get out, I may consider it a success. We have *three* parties for tonight—one, a ball—and a dinner tomorrow."

Sometimes, in the midst of the parties, Adelaide's energy flagged, and she wondered why she bothered. The answer was Edward, "who certainly likes the thing that is called Society." The answer was also May—now out of the schoolroom and a blossoming young woman—who loved balls and parties and young men: pleasures her mother would certainly not deny her. But these days Adelaide herself preferred intimate dinner parties. Her dining room was too small for a crowd, and she usually selected only eight guests. "An intimate little dinner" might include Frederic Leighton, Henry Greville, the historian James Froude, and the Anglo-Italian politician Sir James Lacaita; or maybe Corsair Trelawny—as outrageous as ever—or Aïdé, or even the widowed Robert Browning, whose long poem *The Ring and the Book* had increased his already substantial fame in the English-speaking world.

In a year or so there would be an estrangement with Browning. While the deeper reasons are obscure, the trivial reason was a tiff over the supposed friendship between Henry Greville and a minor composer of ballads named Virginia Gabriel. Miss Gabriel seems to have called herself an intimate friend of Henry's, Adelaide seems to have denied it angrily, and Browning seems to have refused to take her side. The estrangement was evidently still current in 1874, when Adelaide wrote wistfully about the old Italian days and "old good Browning." Usually, however, she did not hold grudges long, as witnessed by her reconciliation with Anna Jameson.

Of her way of life as she turned fifty, Adelaide was occasionally regretful. One evening she confided to Annie Thackeray: "I have everything a woman could wish for, my friends and my home, my husband and my children, and yet sometimes a wild longing comes over me to be back, if only for an hour, on the stage again, and living once more as I did in those early adventurous times." But to perform professionally now, as she was quick to admit, would not have been to her taste. Styles of singing had changed so much. The louder and heavier singing of Verdi's operas, which had become the dominant fashion, went against so much she believed in. Adelaide had been educated in the light and agile style of bel canto singing, and she called the new style "screaming." Describing a performance of Il Trovatore that she had recently seen, she said that the singers bawled until the veins in their throats swelled to bursting: the sound was "hideous." May did not share her mother's distaste for Verdi and sang his music at soirées and concerts. Fanny, as might have been expected, also liked the heavier Verdian style, finding it dramatic and exciting.

Adelaide's yearning to perform found its outlet at her soirées and charity concerts. She trained, and even drilled, her friends and family to surprising heights. She had been "drumming" Edward and Frederic "in the bass and tenor parts of some pieces of Mendelssohn's Elijah and St. Paul," she reported one January. A program for a concert in aid of schools for the poor included a trio from Donna del Lago, by Rossini, for Edward, Frederic, and herself, and a duet from Marino Faliero, by Donizetti, for Edward and a Mr. Smith. There was also a quintet from Semiramide for Frederic, Smith, Edward, Adelaide, and a new friend, Jeannie Senior, who was soon to be the first female inspector of pauper schools. The fact that Frederic and Edward could manage such technically demanding music shows how extraordinarily hard they must have trained.

Amateur music was fun, but Adelaide longed for the technique of professionals. In March 1867 she was delighted to play host to Clara Schumann, celebrated pianist-widow of the great composer. At a select gathering in the Sartoris drawing room, Madame Schumann and Joseph Joachim, possibly the most famous violinist in Europe, played Mozart, Bach, Spohr, and a great deal of Schumann. The "Abendlied," by Schumann, wrote Adelaide, "was quite enchanting and that we had over again, it was so exquisite." Lord Redesdale, known for his travels to the Orient, often attended her soirées, and he described her hospitality as "perfection." Adelaide was no longer young, he wrote, "but so witty, so full of pleasant memories, and one of the best leaders of talk I ever knew. Of an evening she would be surrounded by such men as Charles Dickens, Matthew Arnold, Leighton, while Charles Halle would sit down at the piano and accompany Joachim or Madame Norma Neruda." Adelaide had a saying at this time that summed up her artistic philosophy. "Now to love a thing sincerely is an act of grace," she would say, "but to love the best sincerely is a state of grace."

By this time Edward's tedious years as a dutiful heir were at an end. On the death of his Uncle Edward Tunno in 1863, he had inherited substantial wealth, a fine estate, and the country house of Warnford Park. Adelaide was delighted to have the inheritance. She loved that part of Hampshire, with its "fine breezy down, and lovely lanes all overgrown with clematis and honeysuckle, and charming villages nestled in the trees." As she told the Thuns in a burst of enthusiasm, "the accession of wealth is a matter of very little importance to me, but the country life with all its simple pleasures and most attaching duties has been a blessing for which I cannot be grateful enough." Edward, she continued, "for the first time in his life has an occupation—looking after his estate interests and amuses him, and the being continually in the air and taking a great deal of exercise is excellent for him—I have never seen him so cheerful in all the years we have been married."

Standing at the edge of the historic village of Warnford on the road to Winchester, Warnford Park was a splendid country house, surrounded by terraces, gardens, and spacious parkland. "The mansion stood among the broad spreading trees," one visitor remembered, "and there was ceaseless cawing from the rooks overhead." There was also a deep, wide lake with "fringes of logwood, growing crimson tinted and waving against the banks." Warnford Park was a very stately place.

The visitor to Warnford today finds only scattered clues to this bygone stateliness. The lake is there, but the house has gone, and so has local memory of the Tunnos and Sartorises. The only memorial is in the ancient stone church, standing close to the gates of the overgrown park. On the wall of the church is a tablet to the memory of Edward Rose Tunno. Just visible, too, are the remains of a rose garden, which was once Adelaide's pleasure and pride. Annie Thackeray remembered her standing by a hedge of roses and saying in her passionate way "how dear to her was each plant and flowering shrub, how growing things spoke to her more intensely as time went on, and how Nature came to mean more and more, and the life of cities less and less."

During her four years as mistress of Warnford Park, Adelaide took her duties seriously. Inspired by her friend Jeannie Senior, she visited the poor and sick on the estate, and she and May ran a school for poor children, giving a large portion of their time and energy to their work. Increasingly May was Adelaide's right hand, and her mother found her a never-failing source of strength. She was so "healthy, happy, reasonable, affectionate, and help-ful" that Adelaide sometimes wondered "whether I really did bring her into the world."

There were those who might have argued that May was only too obvi-ously her mother's daughter. The theatrical Kemble manner had descended to May; those who were unused to theatrical ways were apt to misunder-stand and mock her, and even those who did understand were apt to find her amusing. Thackeray—a loyal admirer of all the Kembles—once told a friend that "there must always be a little comedy in any intimacy in that quarter."

According to gossip circulating at the time, the novelist E. F. Benson used some of May's more affected mannerisms when he created the heroine of his popular Lucia novels. The likeness may seem far-fetched, because May was a well-educated, socially secure woman of great charm, and Lucia was an outrageously funny social and intellectual climber. But May's grand-daughter, Adelaide Lubbock, admitted privately that there was some truth in the likeness. She said that Adelaide and May Sartoris centered their lives around "a devotion to sensibility," and it was this that Benson made fun of in his character Lucia.

It was certainly true that Adelaide believed in the cult of sensibility. She took intense delight in the beauties of nature and art, using them as a counterbalance to the pain that life inflicted on her. As Annie Thackeray observed, Adelaide was adept at "stirring and stimulating one's sleepy makeshift soul" toward the wonders of the world. "It was as if Mrs. Sartoris could at will compel the sound and the sense and the colour into that which she was interested, so that we were all for the time, and indeed for a lifetime since, illumined by her."

Fanny, on the other hand, took the opposite route and stirred and stimulated by taking pleasure in denouncing the flaws in those things that were acknowledged to be beautiful. As one friend put it: "Nature had so formed her that she was ever more aware of the one fault something beauti-ful might have than of all the beauties that made it what it was."

On the broad, stone terrace of Warnford Park, during one of her fre-quent house parties, Adelaide's only major literary project was born. A number of the jovial crew were present, and they were busy discussing de-tails of a visit that Adelaide and Frederic had made to the de l'Aigle house at Francport. During their visit, Adelaide and Frederic had agreed to sing together at a confirmation service in the village church. Plans were almost canceled when, a few days before the service, Frederic was called back to

London. Rather than disappoint the villagers, he sped back to France, just for one day, so as not to miss the ceremony.

As guests sitting on the terrace discussed Frederic's kindness, they found themselves helping their hostess make up a story. It dealt with the interplay among a group of friends—many of them drawn from life—who had gathered for a French country house party. Fanny, though she had never been to Francport, was there in the guise of Ursula Hamilton, a professional contralto who hated the stage but still longed to sing on it. The composer Dassauer was there as a character called Dessaix, because his quaint ways and sayings lent color to the story. And Frederic was there as the hero. Adelaide made him the exuberant painter and linguist Kiowski, who, like his real-life counterpart, returned to sing at the service in the village church.

Jotted down on scraps of paper, the story was read back to the Warnford guests the following day, who then began adding and subtracting words as their inspiration moved them. Current jokes were grafted into the written conversation, and Adelaide added some of her insights into human nature. In little more than a week, the manuscript of *A Week in a French Country House* was ready, although it would be several more months before it was sent to George Smith, the proprietor of *Cornhill Magazine*, in the hope that he would publish it. To Adelaide's surprise, Smith not only accepted the story for his magazine but also published it as a separate book. Adelaide's prose was not as powerful or fluent as Fanny's, but it had its own vitality and charm, and the book ran into two editions. Adelaide was pleased to think of it as a legacy "of value to the children when I am gone—the singing will be forgotten—how can it be otherwise."

While Adelaide had long accepted that her career on the stage was over, Fanny refused to consider such a retirement. She was still a successful actress, rejoicing in the skills she displayed and reading to enthusiastic audiences. So reluctant was she to abandon her reading tours that she kept on performing in public until her sixtieth year. The novelist Louisa May Alcott, hearing her perform in Boston in 1868, called her "a whole stock company in herself." Miss Alcott went on to wonder how "a short, stout red woman *could* look so like a queen in her purple velvet and point lace." Afterward, at supper, Miss Alcott observed Fanny at close quarters and described her face and its changing mood: "It was a study to watch her face," she wrote, "so full of varying expression was it—always strong, always sweet, then proud and fierce as she sniffed at nobodies who passed about her."

Though age had not changed Fanny's attitude to nobodies, it had changed her attitude to her daughters. Without announcing as much, she admired Fan's independence. Even after the death of her father, Fan would travel south to the Butler plantations every winter, as determined and individualistic in her own way as her mother had been thirty years before. While antislavery had been Fanny's crusade, restoring the Butler plantations had become Fan's. It was little wonder that, twenty years after Fanny's journal was published, Fan would publish her own sequel called *Ten Years on a Georgia Plantation Since the War*. Significantly, she made no mention of her mother's book. She was trying, without saying so, to eradicate her mother's message and to justify and defend the South.

Though Fan's pen was no match for her mother's, she could write pleasingly. She described how she resurrected the ravaged plantation, and in so working, found self-fulfillment. In her eyes, the degraded plantation owners, struggling to survive, deserved more sympathy than the former slaves, so often idle since the war. To read and compare the stories by mother and daughter is a fascinating exercise.

Strong-willed and combative like her mother, Fan enjoyed imposing order on chaos. She spent her summers at her childhood home of Butler Place, putting it in order. Fanny, making an emotional visit there after nearly thirty years, was amazed at all the changes. The dilapidated house had been "patched, and darned, and bolstered, and propped, and well-aired, dried, and warmed." Sleeping in the room where Sarah and Fan were born, she spent a surprisingly peaceful and contented week in what had once been her "purgatory."

Despite her strong strand of Kemble independence, Fan found reason to remark in her book on "the good old law of female submission to the husband's will." Clearly, in this sphere, she was her father's daughter, not her mother's. In 1869 she found her lord and master in the shape of a young Englishman, the Honorable James Wentworth Leigh, the younger brother of Lord Leigh of Stoneleigh Abbey, Warwickshire. A sweet-natured, sporty young vicar and Southern sympathizer—nicknamed Jimbo for the role he once played in a Cambridge minstrel show—he had visited St. Simon's Island with a group of friends and been captivated by its "fair queen." The following year in England, he asked her to marry him.

The marriage was celebrated at St. Thomas's, Portman Square, in June 1871, with a friend of the bridegroom, the composer Arthur Sullivan, playing the organ. When the young couple set up house in James's parish of

Stoneleigh, Fanny felt sure that this was the type of marriage she herself would have liked to have made, and she rejoiced that Fan now had entree through her husband into English aristocratic life. Ironically Fan's thoughts still roamed toward the plantations, and her muscularly Christian husband longed to save the souls of liberated slaves. Two years after their marriage, the Leighs returned to live on St. Simon's Island.

To abandon an aristocratic life in England for hard work on a plantation in Georgia seemed the height of absurdity to Fanny. Proud of the girl, she applauded her courage and resolution, but she did not approve of her daughter's struggle to save the Butler plantations, nor understand her willingness to forsake her English home. To Fanny this was the opposite of good feeling and good sense.

Fanny admired James Leigh, with his practical bent and his decided way, as she put it, with "rough souls." That he was considered by one of her friends to have the "intellect and manners of a boy of seven" in no way lessened her affection for or admiration of him. Fanny appears to have had pleasant relations with both her sons-in-law. Their goodwill was needed to provide a soft buffer between her strong self and her strong daughters, because her overriding wish by then was to live in harmony with her girls. She who had often been so tactless and overbearing was schooling herself to show tact and patience in their presence.

Every few years Fanny returned to England and then crossed the Atlantic again, drawn by what she termed her two magnets—her daughters. In 1870 the Wisters reversed the process, coming to Europe and settling for several years in Rome, he in search of a cure for his poor health, she to become belle of the American expatriate community. Fanny for a time joined them and became part of their family.

It was in Rome, at the end of 1872, that Sarah and Fanny met Henry James, a sharp-eyed, twenty-nine-year-old bachelor novelist from a distinguished family of the American East Coast, who was intoxicated by Europe and fascinated by its effect on expatriate Americans. He was well aware of the Kemble glamour, having heard talk of Fanny since childhood. Once, as a young boy, driving in a carriage with his parents, he had passed a striking woman on horseback. "Why, it's Fanny Kemble," he remembered being told. Later he had been taken to a house to hear her read; and later still, as a young man, he had taken himself to hear her renditions of some of Shakespeare's plays. Fanny had remained vivid in his memory, and he desired to know her in person.

At the start of the relationship, young Henry James was Sarah's beau. At their first meeting, Sarah, who did not believe in wasting time, "nailed" him for a walk in the Colonna gardens, where she talked at him "uninterruptedly, learnedly, and even cleverly for two whole hours." From then on they were frequently together in a platonic but emotionally adventurous way. Within a few months, however, he grew weary of her, and he began to call her a "beautiful Bore." He told his family that "on the whole I don't at all regret that I am not Dr. Wister."

Henry James's friendship with Fanny proved more enduring. She fascinated him from their first meeting, and he declared that her "splendid handsomeness of eye, nostril and mouth" were the "best things in the room." Her conversation bewitched him, touching as it did on the great American and English personalities of half a century. Her brilliance as a storyteller enthralled him, and her trenchant tongue, stripping away hypocrisy and frippery to expose the bare bones of truth, made him applaud her. Her energy, her frankness, her overflowing theatricality, and her towering knowledge of Shakespeare—and a thousand other topics—never ceased to delight him. Most people, he said, had only surface, but Fanny had only depth. She displayed all those aristocratic, cosmopolitan qualities of which he stood in awe, and which he longed to possess. He called her his "sublime Fanny," and his "terrific Kemble"; and for the rest of her life he was her faithful cavalier. What Frederic Leighton was to Adelaide, Henry James became to Fanny.

In 1873 Fanny returned with the Wisters to America and immediately faced the problem of where she was to live. Her enthusiasm for Lenox had lessened, and years earlier she had made over the ownership of The Perch to her daughters, who, in turn, had sold it. Realizing that the time had come to find another home, Fanny looked tentatively at Butler Place and its farm dwellings but doubted, in view of her bitter memories, if she could ever be happy there. Finally, she decided to move into York Farm, the farmhouse that stood opposite her old home at Butler Place. As Butler Place was then used by the Wisters and in summer by the Leighs, her own children and grandchildren surrounded her. At York Farm she felt a peace of mind she had not thought possible.

Everywhere she was encircled by memories of her stormy marriage, but they were mellowed by the happy present. Across the road she could hear her grandson practicing his piano. Along the way she could hear the cries of her newest grandchild, Alice Dudley Leigh, born at Butler Place during a thunderstorm in July 1874, and duly christened at the local church by her own father. Writing to Harriet St. Leger, Fanny thanked a merciful Providence, "which has led me back to this place, under circumstances of so much content and peaceful satisfaction."

18

Ghosts

Adelaide's years at Warnford Park were among her happiest. Planting her rose garden, writing her novel, tending her children, and entertaining her friends, she felt a contentment that often amazed her. How was it, she wondered, that the passionate girl who had loved Francis Thun had grown into so sedate a matron?

The one cloud was her eldest son, Greville, whose lifestyle sometimes gave her cause for anxiety. His career had followed a fairly predictable path. After leaving Eton, he had gone to Germany to study languages before joining the regiment of the 11th Hussars. From the army he gravitated, like his cousin Maitland Sartoris, to the diplomatic service, and he was stationed at the British embassy in Vienna. Irresistibly attractive to women, Greville was always falling in love: Adelaide hoped that there was safety in numbers. Fortunately, she was a close friend of Georgiana Bloomfield, the ambassador's wife, who was a relative by marriage of Edward's. Thanks to Lady Bloomfield, Adelaide was able indirectly to keep an eye on her boy, though she wished that there were more opportunities to see him face to face. When the Bloomfields invited the Sartorises to visit Vienna, Adelaide accepted without hesitation, even though Edward refused to go with her. When he said truculently, "I don't see how you will ever manage that journey alone," she replied, with all the determination of her sister: "I am going."

Her decision to travel to Vienna had to be postponed for some months because Edward decided to sell Warnford Park and buy a smaller house. Though Adelaide had come to love the stately old house and had made it beautiful, she was less dismayed by his decision than she might have been. She had set her heart on living twenty miles away in an airy, out-of-the-way corner of Hampshire. Flat and sandy, bordering on the Hamble River and Southampton Water, the village of Warsash reminded her of a prosper-

< 286 >

ous part of Holland and seemed a most desirable place to live. The air exuded a "vigorous salt savour," which she believed would give "health to one's bones." Edward agreed with her and proceeded to buy a rambling farmhouse just outside the village, with an orchard and garden of several acres running down to the water. The view from the house was stunning. Adelaide could stand at the windows and look out across Southampton Water to the far shore, where the leaves of the New Forest stood out in dark green prominence against the foreground of blue sea.

The Sartorises had plans for renovating the farmhouse, which they renamed Warsash House, but no sooner had Edward bought the house than Adelaide became ill. She discovered a lump on her forehead, which her doctor insisted on removing at once. The operation, performed under chloroform, met unforeseen difficulties, and afterward the wound became infected. For some days Adelaide ran a high fever and suffered a swollen face. Convalescing in London, she summoned her will to be ready for the journey to Austria. She was determined not to be prevented, because this was to be a kind of pilgrimage. As well as visiting Greville in Vienna, she planned to go to Tetschen, and—if she dared—to call on Francis in Prague. Since their last meeting, she had been seized by a need to see his family, and to judge for herself the truth about his marriage.

In October 1867, having settled her younger boy, Algy, at the Rugby School, she, Edward, and May traveled by train to Munich, where Greville met them at the railway station. Overjoyed to see her older boy once more, Adelaide was delighted to discover that she was also about to meet an old friend. This was Franz Liszt, who by chance was staying at their hotel. It was her first sight of him for more than twenty years. She found him as captivating as ever, his radiance undimmed either by age or by his new office—for he wore the austere robe of an abbé of the Franciscan order. They spent an affectionate evening together, recalling their concerts on the Rhine and discussing their many friends.

When they arrived in Vienna two days later, Adelaide had her second surprise. Dessauer was waiting for them at the embassy. His appearance was a shock. "I had left him forty years old," she wrote poignantly, "and found him again snow white and blind." But the warmth of his welcome was reassuringly youthful, and he declared he was still her faithful follower. His childlike pleasure when she sang his songs was very moving.

Lord and Lady Bloomfield went out of their way to entertain their guests. There was a ball for May, visits to picture galleries for Edward, and concerts, operas, and gypsy music for Adelaide. Among the operas was

Gluck's *Iphigenia in Aulis*, which, according to Adelaide, was receiving its first performance in Vienna for sixty years. (Did she know, one wonders, that her great uncle De Camp had been ballet master at its very first performance in Vienna at the imperial court theatre, when the composer himself had directed it?) There was also a visit to the king of Hanover, who was eager for news of her brothers, having known John in Germany and Henry at Angelo's fencing school in London. To please the king, who was almost completely blind, Adelaide sang an anthem by Handel, several songs by Schubert, a song of Dessauer's, and her own setting of Shelley's poem "Goodnight." This last song affected him "quite strangely—he burst into tears and begged to have it over again."

After a week in Vienna it was time for Adelaide and May to resume their journey alone. On November 2 they boarded a train for Bohemia, intending first to visit Francis in Prague and then to go on to Tetschen. Edward was left behind with the Bloomfields. Whether he realized the full purpose of their journey one does not know: probably not, because one cannot imagine that he would have agreed, had he known that they were going to visit Francis.

As the train neared Prague, Adelaide became very nervous and was thankful for May's company to provide a buffer between herself and her feelings. Francis may also have needed a buffer, because when he came to their hotel next morning, he brought his three daughters with him. For several hours they walked about the narrow streets of the old town, Adelaide and May chatting politely to the shy Thun girls, and Francis walking nervously by their side. At two o'clock Adelaide accompanied him back to his house to dine and at last met the woman who had caused his disgrace. "Saw his wife," she wrote cryptically in her diary—then added the Italian exclamation: "Ohimè!" The word revealed the depth of her dismay.

After dinner Adelaide was relieved to escape for an hour and stroll with Francis in a park overlooking the city. Free of his wife's presence, he was able to talk at last like an old friend: Adelaide recorded in her diary that their walk was *lovely*. It was an anticlimax to be obliged to return to the house for the evening to drink tea and listen to music. As they sat together, his three daughters—"all very nice"—played the piano, and his three sons looked on attentively and shed their charm on Adelaide. His wife, by contrast, could not conceal her hostility.

As a maid in the Tetschen castle, Francis's wife was likely to have known of her husband's attachment to Adelaide, so perhaps her hostility was understandable. Yet even without such knowledge, she would probably have been unwelcoming, so resentful did she seem of her husband's and children's lives. According to Adelaide's sad description, she was a "poor common vehement creature," who was "*overflowing* with misery and angry bitterness uncontrolled." Francis and his children, Adelaide continued unhappily, "take no notice and seem used to it."

Adelaide managed to retain her self-possession, but she was deeply disturbed by the visit. What a terrible price Francis had paid for his chivalry: she pitied him with all her heart. Yet she would not have been human had she not also thought what a fool he had been to reject her in the first place. As for his wife, Adelaide pitied her also, for she was exposed "to the judgment of her children so superior to herself."

Drained emotionally by the happenings of the previous day, Adelaide found it a relief next morning to set out by train with May for Tetschen. Countless times she had imagined the journey in her mind: how different it was proving in reality. Yet there were touches that vividly brought back the past. At one of the railway stations, Count Chotek, eighty-five years old, waited in the snow for more than an hour for a glimpse of Adelaide's face. As the train made its brief halt, he was lifted up to her carriage to kiss her.

When the train came toward the bend in the Elbe River, and she saw the castle rising from its rock beside the water, the sense of unreality increased. So much had changed in thirty years. In 1838 there had been no railway, but now the line ran between the road and the river, and a station stood on the riverbank, just across from the castle. In past years the river had been crossed slowly by ferry; now it was spanned by an impressive bridge. Count Thun and Yuza were waiting at the station, and having warmly welcomed their guests, drove with them in a horse-drawn carriage across the bridge and up to the castle gates. With each moment the years slipped away, and Adelaide felt that she was twenty-two again, the same age as her daughter, who sat beside her.

During that week Adelaide inhabited a strange world "peopled with ghosts—ghosts of former hopes—former pleasures—former pains. Ghosts of those lost—ghosts of those changed." Yet she would "not have missed those days for all the world." In some ways it was as though she had never been away. She slept in her old room, and in the evenings sang the count's favorite songs, just as she had thirty years before. The day before she was due to leave, she had the curious experience of welcoming Francis back to his old home, when he arrived by train with his eldest daughter, Marie. It was the first time that any of his children had set foot in the castle, and the girl's presence was permitted only because Adelaide begged it.

On the following day at the Tetschen railway station, May, Adelaide, Francis, and his daughter boarded the train for Prague. The train had come from Dresden, and Edward was already aboard, ready to join his wife and daughter for the journey back to England. Did Francis remain unobtrusively in another carriage; or was Adelaide obliged to introduce her husband to the man she had long wanted as her husband? How one wishes there was a way of knowing!

On the way home, the Sartorises halted in Paris, where Adelaide's overstretched nerves at last found relief in normal activity. She dined with Richard Lyons, now resplendent Lord Lyons, the British ambassador. He made her laugh, which did her good. Best of all, Frederic Leighton, who was on his way home from Greece, joined them. She was overjoyed to see him.

Back in England, Adelaide threw herself into efforts to make Warsash House her own creation. Her mood soared as she studied the architect's drawings and chose colors and patterns for the furnishings. When her fifty-third birthday came, in February 1868, she declared it was the happiest birthday of her life. Algy gave her a jade bottle, May a blue delft vase, Edward a silver dish, and Frederic gave her his own drawing of St. Jerome with a very disdainful lion. She spent her birthday morning in consultation with the architect over the forthcoming renovations. Normally she disliked her birthday, but on this day—with ghosts laid to rest—she felt unusually light-hearted.

While Adelaide busied herself supervising the builders and other workmen at Warsash, Edward, as usual, pursued his own life. He had decided to stand for a Welsh seat in the House of Commons: not for Penryn, for which he had stood in 1841, but for Carmarthenshire, where he owned the estate called Llanennech Park. Adelaide was delighted at his renewed ambition to sit in Parliament, for "the curse of life has been having too much money and nothing to do." She had long regretted "a nature so nobly endowed, given over to nothing better than pleasure seeking." Supporting his choice of William Gladstone's Liberal Party with all her heart, she declared that she was "ultra-liberal," for had she not been called in her youth the Demon of Revolt? May, though no demon, was a liberal, too, and on polling day at the nearby town of Fareham, she went to the booth—not to vote, for women were not yet enfranchised—but to offer support for her father's party. Proudly she took with her her little black bulldog, decked out in a large blue bow, "in token of his liberal sympathies." When Edward was returned to Parliament in December 1868 as the member for Carmarthenshire, Adelaide called it a day of "serious happiness." Thereafter he and May—though seldom Adelaide—spent part of each year at his house in Wales.

Adelaide's strenuous activities at Warsash seemed to bring on illness. She often complained of a pain in her side, and she was fatter than ever. By August 1869 her health was causing so much worry that there was no other course but to undertake a spa cure. Adelaide had rather hoped to visit Carlsbad, but her doctor insisted on Vichy, a fashionable spa in central France, where the waters were said to be beneficial to the liver. When faithful Frederic agreed to accompany her, Adelaide was delighted, because there was no person she would rather have had as a traveling companion.

Their attachment had in no way diminished with time, and Frederic's frequent absences abroad had not harmed it: if anything their feelings for one another were firmer. Her friends were his, and his were hers. At parties he usually followed her like a shadow. His exotic Kensington house and studio—crammed with Old Masters, Persian pottery, and oriental textiles— bore the stamp of her decorative flair. At his splendid annual musical soirée, it was her friends who performed, and it was she who took pride of place. A few of her circle looked mildly askance. Her nephew-in-law Charles Santley recorded with a frown that once at a party her petticoat fell down, and that Frederic tactfully picked it up and hid it in his hat. But mostly her own set did not judge her. It had grown used to her ways.

Tongues did wag among the artists, many of whom resented the social status Adelaide's friendship had conferred on Frederic. Some claimed that she had tied him so firmly to her platonic apron strings that he was power- less to seek a wife. The rancorous said that Adelaide and Frederic were lovers, and that she ate him up alive. One called her Sartoria the Fat and described her as a mountain of rolling fat with spitfire eyes. One wonders if she heard the gossip, but if she did, her conscience was clear. She was not, in her own mind, preventing Frederic from marrying—on the contrary, she was encouraging him to find a wife.

One evening at Warnford at the end of 1865, they discussed his possi- ble marriage. They also discussed his undefined "vice"—one presumes he was sleeping with prostitutes. "I am *very* glad you are trying to help yourself in real earnest," she wrote. "I am sure it must be difficult, but I am sure that if once you chose to look honestly at the subject instead of going blindly on, the ugliness of vice would repel you." Begging Frederic to think con- structively of marriage, Adelaide chided him for building fantasies against which every woman he met seemed hopelessly inadequate. Later she tried her hand at matchmaking and recommended several girls. One was Aïdé's cousin Dolly Tennant, another was a girl called Pinkie. Of each of them she wrote plaintively, "Oh Fay, wouldn't she do?"

At Vichy in August 1869, the hotel was comfortable, and the surrounding hills, with their vines and fruit trees, were as pretty as a picture-postcard. Adelaide, however, would have been restless and unhappy if it had not been for Frederic's company. On doctor's orders, she rose at six and strolled to the springs, where she walked and drank for most of the morning: the dullest of routines. Vichy, however, was fashionable enough to attract fascinating people, and Adelaide was delighted to meet the poet Algernon Swinburne and the explorer Richard Burton, who arrived together. Burton, the most romantic traveler of his time, had just come from Brazil to take the health cure before moving on to Damascus. His young companion Swinburne had recently sprung to notoriety for his brilliant but "immoral" poetry.

Adelaide found them an extraordinary pair: scar-faced Burton, "so strong and swarthy and with eyes like coals—very handsome," and the little red-haired poet, with his high-pitched voice and fluttering hands. She could not imagine what they had in common and little dreamed that their shared interest was sexual deviation. Perhaps she sensed something improper, because she is said to have reproved their ribald talk.

Soon the two men were joined by Burton's spirited wife Isabel, who disapproved of Swinburne and could scarcely hide her dislike. But despite the obvious tensions, Vichy seems to have proved a tonic for all of them. Isabel later remembered Frederic's brilliant conversation, Swinburne's dramatic recitations, and Adelaide's exquisite voice, though she mistakenly called her a contralto. Swinburne was enchanted by Adelaide's rendering of Shelley's "Dirge from Ginevra," which she had set to her own music. It was worth "playing the pretty to the old lady"—Swinburne wrote cheekily—so that Adelaide would continue to sing to him by the hour. Why, he exclaimed, her voice still sounded like a girl's! He was less taken by her appearance, which was certainly not a girl's. He wrote rather unkindly: "they have sent her here to get down her fat."

Swinburne could be cheeky about Adelaide, but in later years his memory was reverent. At the time of Frederic's death, in January 1896, he wistfully recalled their days together at the resort. Fired by his memories, he dashed off a moving elegy called "An Evening at Vichy." In Swinburne's imagination, Frederic and Adelaide, long parted by death, were reunited in heaven; and her voice, "divine as a bird's at dawn," was singing to him again, as it had sung on those magical evenings in France.

When Frederic was obliged to return to England early, Adelaide missed him. She pictured him wandering through the garden of Warsash House, sniffing the scent of the roses, and sitting down with May to a "nice, nice, English tea with sweet cream and good cake." As her doctor had put her on a strict diet, this last thought gave her particular pleasure.

Was Frederic attracted to May, and did Adelaide see her daughter as a likely wife for him? At least one of Frederic's biographers has suggested the possibility. The mind is drawn, in a curious parallel, to that other painter and lover of Kemble women, Thomas Lawrence, who adored the untouch-able Sarah Siddons and courted her daughters as substitutes.

Frederic painted two superb portraits of May. The first, painted during her adolescence, showed a dark-haired girl dressed for riding, with a plumed black hat and red scarf draped across her breast. The second, to be seen today in Leighton House, was painted when she was in her thirties. Dressed in a sophisticated red gown, she sits soulfully in a studio. Unlike her younger self, the older May does not gaze unself-consciously toward the artists. She looks sideways: her pose evasive. One wonders if she is repelling unwanted admiration.

If Frederic did court May, he was doomed to be disappointed. At the age of twenty-six, May was about to fall in love. Her choice was Henry Evans-Gordon, the son of Major General Charles Evans-Gordon, the gov-ernor of the Royal Military Hospital in the neighboring town of Netley. Henry was a young man of twenty-nine who was worth about a thousand pounds a year, meaning that he was well-off rather than rich. Adelaide re-joiced in her daughter's choice, for a "more worldly marriage" might have taken her far from them, and that loss Adelaide could not have borne eas-ily. Henry was "clever and lovable," a raconteur, a political thinker, and "accomplished in music and painting." As Adelaide quickly discovered, he could sing competently, and he was soon rehearsing for her musical evenings.

The couple were married quietly on April 19, 1871, at the village church at Warsash, with Adelaide's friend Jeannie Senior almost the only outsider present. When they honeymooned in Scotland, May wrote to her mother every day. The married pair returned to live in a cottage owned by Edward alongside Warsash House.

May's wedding was like calm sunshine after a sudden storm. In the previous November of 1870, Adelaide had received an emotional thunderclap: Francis Thun was dead. "Bewildering voices out of my youth cry out his name in my ears, and the tears of a girl of twenty are pouring out of my eyes," she declaimed as she pored over Yuza's letter: "whatever pain he gave me in return is buried with him evermore." Her immediate impulse was to hurry to Prague "for the chance of looking on Francis's face once more." Reason, however, thwarted the impulse. "I should have come too late," she told Yuza, "and if I had not, she who disputed him to me in life, might perhaps have disputed him to me in death." Besides, she had no need to look on his face: it had been enshrined in her imagination for the last twenty-three years and would be with her until the day she died.

Adelaide was wise for another reason not to attempt the journey to Prague. Edward would surely have forbidden it. He hated her absences from home at any time, and he would certainly have withheld his consent for this particular errand. To give Edward his due, he was not entirely inventing the excuses he habitually put forward when Adelaide proposed to leave him by himself. He was so busy that he genuinely believed he could not spare her. Business and politics were combining to give him a new sense of purpose, which Adelaide was at pains not to discourage. He had recently acquired large holdings in Wisconsin in the United States, and their management occupied whatever time he could spare from Parliament. Late in 1872 he decided to visit America, taking his younger son, Algy, with him, for he planned to make the boy his American agent.

Adelaide gave every support to this plan, for Algy had long been a worry to her. Schooldays at Rugby, private tutors, and her own efforts at teaching had not succeeded in giving him a sound education, and she was fearful for his future. She knew only too well that it was difficult to find lucrative employment for a younger son, particularly one with not much aptitude for overcoming obstacles.

While she was actively in favor of the trip to America, Adelaide dreaded the prospect of spending so many months on her own. She so fretted that she became ill, and the cure, in her doctor's wise opinion, was to take a diverting holiday. Adelaide was in a quandary, however, about where she should go and with whom she should stay. Luckily the question was answered by faithful Frederic Leighton. Edward and Algy sailed in October 1872 for America, and she and Frederic left almost immediately for Italy.

Adelaide's feelings on her departure from home were mixed. While part of her was aflame with thoughts of her beloved Italy—she could almost smell the sweet scents of the Campagna—she was downcast at losing her family and nervous when she thought of the final leg of her journey. She had resolved to defy Edward once again and go to Tetschen. On this stage of the trip, she did not think it proper to take Frederic. So she would be traveling with only her maid for company, and she was afraid that she might not be capable of managing the journey.

Sensing her anxiety, Frederic did his best to soothe her. Adelaide observed how artificially enthusiastic he seemed to be as they traveled by train across Europe. She realized he was attempting to raise her spirits, but his good-natured enthusiasm grated on her nerves. She especially disliked his strange habit of kneeling in the railway carriage in order to look out the window, with one knee "upon each seat—so repulsive and like a frog." Another time, when they passed a field of pumpkins, she wrote to May that he cried out affectedly, "Pump*keens* ha ha!" But "I am a beast to mention it," she continued, "and he is an angel and no mistake—neither one's father— nor one's mother—and certainly not one's husband or one's brother could take half the tender care of one that he does of me."

Frederic traveled with her to Venice and possibly accompanied her down the coast of Italy and across the Straits of Messina to Palermo. Adelaide told the Thuns that they were planning to visit Sicily, though she discreetly withheld Frederic's name and spoke vaguely of traveling with "people." She and Frederic finally ended in Rome, where they renewed acquaintance with some of his fellow artists, among them Giovanni Costa, to whom Adelaide had warmed on her previous visit. After Frederic left her, with only her maid for company, she boarded a train for Munich, and then for Tetschen, arriving at the castle in a state of exhaustion after twenty-four hours of continuous travel.

Much as she had dreaded it, Adelaide knew that this visit to the Thuns was imperative, because Count Thun was eighty-six and ailing: it was almost certainly her last chance to see him alive. He spent most of the winter confined to his bed, obsessively pondering the sad events of the past years. The troubles since Francis's death—squabbles over the succession, for he had debarred Francis's sons from inheriting the lands or the title— had almost destroyed him.

When Adelaide reached the castle, she knew that she had been wise to come. She found her precious friend pathetically frail but gentle and loving as ever. She sat by his bed, sang to him, and watched his melancholy face light up with pleasure. "I was so touched at the delight he shows at seeing me," she wrote to Frederic, who by then was her confidant in all matters concerning the Thuns. "Yesterday evening when I bade him goodnight he took hold of my hands and said to me, 'when I feel that I am dying I shall send for you and you will come.'" Promising that she would obey, Adelaide left Tetschen with a feeling of foreboding, believing that the summons would not be long in coming.

Back in London a little more than a month later, Adelaide tore open Yuza's black-edged letter. Her beloved Thun was dead, and there had been no time to summon her. Though she had expected his death, her grief was sharp, for a cornerstone of her life had gone. "With your father's death I lost a great love," she told Yuza. "I have felt cold in the world ever since." For more than thirty years she had sent the count a greeting on his birthday, October 3, which was also Yuza's birthday. Henceforth, though she still sent greetings to Yuza, it would be a day of sadness for her. "The pain and desolation of the loss of him," she told Yuza two years later, "are constant with me."

Within a month of the count's death, Henry Greville was also dead. His loss was the more immediate, because when Adelaide visited London she saw him nearly every day, and he often came to stay with her at Warsash. He was her chief male confidant, closer to her than most of her family. She had shared music, amusement, and gossip with him for more than forty years and had drawn countless times on his loyalty and sympathy. Adelaide called his loss "quite irreparable—one that is felt every day and all day long—my parents loved him, and my children loved him, and he belonged literally to the whole of my life."

Grieving the death of two such friends, Adelaide lived through the first ten months of the following year in frequent depression and loneliness, for her children's lives had taken them far from her. Algy was still in America, and May and her husband had moved into a rambling house called Prestons, in the village of Ightham in Kent. Greville was busy nearby with his latest love affair. Three years previously, Greville had abandoned his career in diplomacy, explaining he had only remained in it to please his father. He returned to England but accepted no other employment, and at thirty he was drifting. Adelaide was fearful that he would end up another indolent Sartoris.

Early in the evening of October 14, 1873, Adelaide was in her drawing room at Warsash when Edward entered with a telegram. It came from the house where Greville was staying. It said simply, "Greville has hurt himself and wants you to come—come as soon as possible." It was followed almost immediately by another telegram, which advised, "Take a special train if possible." The second telegram, and its tone of urgency, gave Adelaide the true message.

In an agony of fear Adelaide and Edward scanned the train timetables. Greville was at Wadhurst in East Sussex, and to travel there from Warsash meant going through London. The next scheduled train left at one in the morning, and Edward and Adelaide caught it. They arrived at London's Charing Cross Station at the dismal hour of four-thirty, and as a special train was not procurable, they waited for the regular train at six. Adelaide would never forget those hours spent in the station waiting room. She kept wondering if she would arrive in time to see her son alive.

Reaching Wadhurst station they were relieved to find that their worst fears were not realized. Greville was living, but he was gravely ill. He had been jumping a low fence on horseback when his horse had stumbled. He was thrown to the ground, and the horse, in rising, had kicked him in the head. The skull was fractured, and some of his brain had emerged from his head, but he was conscious. He recognized his parents when they entered his sickroom and stood by his bed.

The woman of Greville's then-current affection was Madame Jesusa de Murrieta, a Spanish Roman Catholic, and in this same house lived also her husband and brothers-in-law, who, strange as it may seem, appear to have been almost as fond of Greville as she. Adelaide had met Madame de Murrieta once before and hated her for thus engrossing her son Greville in a web of alienating improprieties. But in the face of tragedy she and Edward put aside their distaste and were grateful for her kindness. The lady herself behaved faultlessly, nursing Greville and supporting Adelaide, as hour after hour the young man fought for his life.

During the following six days, while "the poor child's youth and health and strength protested against the cruel, cruel end," Edward, Adelaide, and the de Murrieta family kept vigil beside the bed, waiting for the dreaded "brain fever"—the symptom of infection—which would signal the end. The symptom did not come, and Adelaide wrote that "sometimes we were all quite cheerful with renewed hope."

Greville knew nothing of his own condition, believing that he had suffered only a slight concussion. He was lucid, felt little pain, was delighted to have his parents with him, and even more delighted that his mistress and his mother quickly became such friends. His "eyes filled with tears of joy," wrote Adelaide, "when he saw us standing by his bedside with our arms around each other." He was "very happy during that last week." On the seventh day, when they almost felt safe, "a large quantity of the brain came away, and his strength suddenly ran down."

At once Madame de Murrieta implored permission to send for a priest. If "she had asked for my life," declared Adelaide, "she should have had it and welcome—and so upon his death bed my beloved was baptized into the Romish church, and received the extreme unction." At half-past four on the morning of October 23, "with his hand fast locked in mine my beloved peacefully breathed his last."

Adelaide, unlike her sister, felt kindly toward the Catholic faith and had even considered converting to Catholicism in the days when she had hoped to marry Francis. Greville's conversion gave her comfort. She wrote to friends to scotch the rumors that it had happened under duress. Of the tender care offered by the de Murrietas she could not say enough. Jesusa de Murrieta would be as a daughter to her for the rest of her life. Adelaide blessed her for giving Greville a greater happiness "than any since his childhood."

Adelaide could feel thankful that Greville had not lived to see that happiness fade away, for "I do not see how such a love could bring anything but trouble and sorrow in the future both to him and to her, so I can thank God that He has taken him in time." Thus she tried to comfort herself. But really there was no comfort. Greville's death was a shock from which Adelaide could not recover.

19

"Like the End of Some Reign"

After Greville's death Adelaide shut herself up at Warsash House. To Fanny she wrote: "Of myself dear, there is nothing to tell—Edward and I are still here alone—we walk together and drive together—and we take our sadness out—and bring it back home again—and it lies down with us and rises again with us—and so we are fit company and indeed the only company for each other." In America Fanny set down her sympathy for her sister's plight: "Her grief is unspeakable, and I sit and cry and lament here over her sorrow, helpless to comfort her, and longing only that I were with her to express my infinite pity for her misery, as no words, written or spoken can do."

At Warsash, Adelaide saw almost none of her old friends, though, of course, she made exceptions for May and her babies, and for Frederic, who cut short a trip to Damascus in order to return to comfort her. On most days she was alone. She would sit for hours, looking out onto the calming waters of the estuary, or she would wander in her garden among her roses, or sail her boat through the twilight calm of Southampton Water.

Adelaide thought often about those she loved who had died, and often they seemed more alive to her than the living. Having so many friends older than herself, she had become accustomed to hearing of one death after another. The recent death toll had been dispiritingly long: fourteen dead in the last two years, and soon Dessauer's name would be added, along with that of dear Jeannie Senior. Even without her son's death, the loss of so many friends was a recipe for wretchedness.

Greville was constantly in Adelaide's thoughts. As she explained, he had been part of her being: "we were proud to each other—and we hurt each other—and we loved each other in the same passionate way—and I feel withered up for want of the face that I shall see no more." At the same time Adelaide reproached herself for feeling so unhappy when there were

< 299 >

"so many blessings yet left to me." Edward, in his awkward and silent way, was especially loving; and he was, she knew, just as devastated.

On some days cheerful letters came from her son Algy, on whom so many of her remaining hopes were centered. His letters were almost certainly read over and over. Simple, loving, handsome, and funny, Algy reminded Adelaide of her favorite brother, Henry. How fervently she must have hoped that he did not share Henry's mental instability. Happily for her, she was not aware of Algy's incipient alcoholism, and she died before it became apparent.

Algy, in her eyes, was doing well. He liked America, and he had fallen in love with an American girl. On the trans-Atlantic crossing he had met Ellen Grant—popularly known as Nelly—the daughter of Ulysses S. Grant, the president of the United States. President Grant and Edward Sartoris exchanged letters, and permission was given by the president for Algy to marry his eighteen-year-old daughter.

Of all the Americans living at that time, Ulysses Grant was probably the most famous. A brave and quietly intelligent leader, he had been commander-in-chief of the victorious Union army during the Civil War and was then in his second term as a Republican president. Grant was noted for his simple charm, and some of that quality had passed down to his daughter. In every one of Algy's letters, Adelaide read instances of Nelly's sweetness, and she had already grown to love her. While Adelaide wished that her son had chosen an English girl, whose background she either knew or could ascertain, she readily gave the marriage her blessing. Algy's wedding would take place only seven months after Greville's death. Since Edward and Adelaide were in deep mourning and did not appear at social occasions, they felt obliged to refuse the president's invitation to travel to Washington for the wedding.

This did not mean that Adelaide was not eager for news of the preparations, which had already whipped up a storm of reportage in the American newspapers. A marriage in the White House was a rare event. Nelly was hailed by some reporters as the "American princess," and it was assumed that the Sartoris family was highly connected in England: the papers described the young bridegroom as the heir to a "considerable estate." Weeks before the ceremony, no one was in any doubt that this was to be an event of national focus. The marriage was to be attended by more reigning ministers and high officials than perhaps any other wedding that could be recalled in Washington.

On the morning of May 21, 1874, two hundred guests assembled beneath the lighted chandeliers in the East Room of the White House to watch proceedings that were ostensibly private—but as carefully choreographed as any royal wedding. The East Room had been decorated with snow-white flowers; they spilled from urns, twined up architraves, and formed into a huge wedding bell, under which the young couple were to stand as they exchanged vows.

As eleven o'clock chimed on the White House clocks, the Marine Band struck up the "Wedding March" and Algy entered, escorted by the bride's older brother, Lieutenant Frederick Grant. Immediately afterward a procession of eight bridesmaids entered the room, nearly all from the most powerful families in the United States: daughters of the secretary of state, an admiral, two senators, the surgeon general, and General Sherman. Behind the bridesmaids walked the president, and beside him walked Nelly, dressed in old lace.

When at last the marriage register came to be signed, an Anglo-American pact seemed appropriate, so there stepped forward as official witnesses the American secretary of state, Mr. Fish, and the British minister in Washington, Sir Edward Thornton. How Adelaide wished that Greville could have been there; of all the family, he would have best done justice to the occasion. After his years with ambassadors, he understood the niceties of protocol and would have represented his family and country with decorum. The pomp seemed a touch wasted on poor, dear Algy.

There was one other member of the bridegroom's family who should have been there but was notably absent. This was Fanny, who was living in Philadelphia and could easily have made the journey. But though she was a fervent supporter of General Grant's army, she did not like the man himself. Indeed, she spoke out so forcefully against the match to her daughter Fan, that Fan, a Southern sympathizer, found herself in the curious position of defending a victor of the Civil War as she tried to take Algy's side. Later Fanny distanced herself as far as possible from the proceedings. When Harriet asked her excitedly for details of the wedding, she replied with tight lips: "I can tell you nothing—of my nephew's marriage to Miss Grant."

When Nelly and Algy arrived in England on their honeymoon, they stayed in the Sartorises' cottage next to Warsash House. Adelaide was delighted that she could see them every day, and she took at once to her daughter-in-law. She found that Nelly was warm and unaffected; and while suffering from a poor education, the girl was instinctively musical and artistic. Adelaide was taken aback, however, by Nelly's splendid clothes and by the array of wedding presents. The presents alone were said to have cost the huge sum of twelve thousand pounds: "it is very good to be a President's daughter," Adelaide dryly remarked.

In October 1874 the Sartorises decided to take a long holiday, and they traveled with Algy and Nelly, who was expecting a child, to Italy. The young people loved the excitement and color of Venice, but Edward and Adelaide were less enthusiastic. Venice at the start of winter was "as beautiful and almost as comfortable as living in a soap bubble," wrote Adelaide. They had been there only a couple of weeks when Edward caught influenza and developed lumbago, and Adelaide was obliged to nurse him in cold, damp hotel rooms, which appeared never to have been heated. When she ordered a fire to be lit in their sitting room, they had to flee to the bedroom to escape the smoke, which refused to pass up the chimney. It was a relief to leave Italy before Christmas and return to the warmth and convenience of Warsash House.

Adelaide had decided against spending the winter in London, and Edward for once agreed with her, saying that he had no heart for jollity. He had left Parliament, having lost his seat in the swing against Gladstone's Liberal Party in the 1874 election. Adelaide dreaded his return to idleness. "Your father had every resource that a highly cultivated intellect could give him," she told May, "but the least little banker's clerk who drudged at his desk till four in the day was happier than he until he got into Parliament and had an *obliged* duty to perform." Edward puttered about Warsash House, spending most of the day with his easel and paints—"his chief resource," Adelaide called them.

In July, May came to her parents for the birth of her third girl, Margaret. This delighted Adelaide, who missed her daughter now that she had gone to live in Kent. "My darling," she told May, "I don't think you can measure the length and breadth and depth of satisfaction your letters give me." She loved to hear every detail of the lives of her children and grandchildren. Better still, she loved to have them around her. Adelaide adored seeing Edward "walking gravely about the garden paths with a little one in each hand," and she was delighted when the children gave him the name of Kla Kla and her the name of Gran. Frederic, who had become like an uncle to May's children, loved to spoil the little girls with gifts and outings. In 1875, and on each New Year's Day thereafter, he treated them to a box at the pantomime in London, an annual ritual in which Algy's children were eventually included as well.

Adelaide never ceased to feel a quiet gratitude for the loyalty and homage that continued to flow to her from Frederic. He was perhaps the most famous living artist in England, and art lovers flocked to view his large, vivid canvases, with their white-limbed heroes and heroines of classical mythology. Long ago elected to the Royal Academy, in 1878 he would become its president and receive a knighthood. But he still treasured his homely visits to Warsash and still answered to the name of Fay, as if he were the same young and unknown painter she had befriended in Rome a quarter of a century before.

Gradually Adelaide began to throw off grief and see more people. Aïdé, Lord Lyons, and Annie Thackeray were among the guests at Warsash during that summer of 1875. In September, Algy and Nelly returned from America, bringing with them their two-month-old son. For the first time since Greville's death, Adelaide began to feel a semblance of happiness. But a few months later, Algy's baby came down with scarlet fever, and Adelaide was filled with fear because at the time she was minding May's three infants; thankfully, they escaped infection. The little boy survived, only to die of convulsions in the spring of 1876.

As the third anniversary of Greville's death approached, Adelaide could no longer bear to stay at Warsash or even in London. The Park Place house had been exchanged for a larger one in Kensington—big enough for May and her family to live with them in London—but that winter, at Adelaide's wish, the London house was left unoccupied. Instead, after a stay at Francport, she and Edward traveled to Italy, hoping for an end to tragic memories.

Rome that year worked a miracle. Husband and wife became happier than they thought they ever would be again and felt themselves transformed. The weather was perfect, and the almond trees were blossoming on the Pincio. They took an apartment in the Via Gregoriana, where Edward painted for three hours every morning in his studio; otherwise they were out incessantly, renewing old acquaintances and making new. Aïdé was there, and the artist Giovanni Costa, and the old duke of Sermoneta. Adelaide renewed her acquaintance with the American sculptor William Wetmore Story, whom she had known less amicably in 1855 but now came to like. She often talked with the well-known composer and vocal teacher Francesco Paolo Tosti, who, she said, "sings like a Neapolitan Angel who hasn't been able to get rid of the patois." And she read each morning to a young English invalid named Harding, who fell in love with her: when she left her spectacles in his sickroom, he returned them with a love poem. Most exciting of all, she gave three long lessons to the Italian actress Madame Ristori, coaching her in the English-language roles of Lady Mac-

beth and Mary Queen of Scots. It was deeply satisfying to teach such a celebrated performer, who was at the height of her career and fresh from successes in New York and Paris. With so much visiting, there was scarcely a
dull minute, especially as Adelaide and Aïdé liked to go to bric-a-brac auc-
tions. Aïdé, however, had grown so finicky and affected that all her family
had begun laughing at him. But they had to agree that he was a generous
companion and escort.

Back in England in the summer of 1877, Algy and Nelly came to live
again in the Warsash cottage, bringing their new son, a strong baby of three
months, named Algernon Edward. Following on their heels came President
and Mrs. Grant. Adelaide liked the president immensely: a "sensible simple
unaffected man—never talking except about things he understands, and
then talking well." She was less impressed by Mrs. Grant, who was "full of
pretension."

That winter Adelaide and Edward set out again for Rome, eager for a
milder climate and cheerful society. Adelaide also had another reason for
the trip. Since Henry Greville's death, she had taken up the cause of his old
friend, the tenor Mario. The once feted singer was poor and alone, for the
soprano Giulia Grisi—his partner on and off the stage for thirty-odd
years—had died in 1869. Three of their six daughters were also dead, his
voice was gone, and "after having had at one time an enormous fortune and
after being adored by the whole civilized world," wrote Adelaide, he was a
pauper. It "breaks my heart," she said, "to see my old friend whom I knew at
25—young, beautiful, charming and prosperous, at 70 wanting both food
and fire." She doubted whether "there ever lived a tenderer heart" than
Mario's.

Adelaide and a band of friends in London raised money to buy Mario
an annuity. In Italy the Sartorises made a point of renting an apartment in
a house Mario owned on Via del Corso. It was not really comfortable, but at
least they had a roof over their heads at a time when Rome was crowded
with visitors come to attend the king's funeral. The funeral procession
passed under their windows, playing airs from Norma: Adelaide was much
moved.

Mario lived on the ground floor of the building, the Sartorises on the
upper, so they saw him nearly every day. His modest and childlike simplicity touched their hearts, along with "his sweet smile and his lovely kind
eyes." He adored spicy gossip and improper jokes. When Algy and Nelly
came to join them, Adelaide was heartily relieved that her daughter-in-law
understood no Italian.

Adelaide thought that this Roman holiday was not quite as pleasant as the last one. She lacked energy, and her lethargy—noticeable in one who was usually so spirited—became increasingly apparent as 1878 progressed. She was also losing weight, and not by her own design. Slowly she faded to a moderate and then to an emaciated shape. By the early months of 1879, it was clear that she was seriously ill. Though she did not know it, she was suffering from diabetes.

Notwithstanding her illness, Adelaide tried to carry on. At Warsash House she tended her flowers, sailed her boat, and entertained a few guests. In April 1879 she gained another grandchild when Nelly Sartoris gave birth in London to a daughter named Vivien May. A month later, while Algy, Nelly, and the children were living at Warsash, Fanny arrived on a visit, bringing with her young Henry James, with his novelist's eye. His sharp, almost acidic, account of the visit, so full of pungent flavor, is worth quoting in full:

> There was no one there but Mrs. Kemble and the family—i.e. Mrs. Sartoris and her taciturn husband (the perfect ideal of the ill-mannered Englishman who improves—somewhat—on acquaintance) and the blowsy young Algernon and his wife. But Mrs. Sartoris is the most agreeable woman (literally) in England, and one of the most remarkable it is possible to see. She is extremely nice to me, "appreciates" my productions etc. and we get on preposterously well. One might have worse fortune than to sit and talk with Mrs. Kemble and her together, for the talk of each is first rate, and each is such a distinguished "personality." Mrs. S. has not the magnificent integrity of my sublime Fanny—but she plays round her sister's rugged *méfiance* like a musical thunderstorm. Meanwhile poor little Nelly Grant sits speechless on the sofa, understanding neither head nor tail of such a high discourse and exciting one's compassion for her incongruous lot in life.

Before making the visit, Henry James observed to his mother that Fanny and Adelaide "don't love each other and I may possibly have some fresh sensations as a peacemaker." He was exaggerating, but certainly in those last years all was not harmonious between the sisters. Fanny's daughter and son-in-law, Fan and James Leigh, had returned to live in England, and Fanny had been staying with them or living by herself in London for almost two years. In that time she and Adelaide were not often in one another's company.

Part of the rift between the sisters probably came from Fanny's daughters, who often felt coldly toward their aunt. Again it was Henry James—confident of his own ability to mix with and observe the English upper classes—who offered an explanation. He described Fan as "hating her position in England, detesting the English, alluding to it invidiously five times a minute, and rubbing it unmercifully into her good natured husband." Her sister Sarah shared these attitudes and smarted because Fan's relatives called her "an apothecary's wife." Seen through the eyes of Fanny's daughters, Adelaide and her aristocratic and artistic circles must have epitomized almost everything in England that made them feel uneasy—though Fan was to make her permanent home in England and appears eventually to have become acclimatized as the wife of the dean of an English cathedral.

Despite the quarrels and silences, nothing could interrupt for long the basic love of Fanny and Adelaide for each other. They were cut from the same cloth: both agreed that no one spoke as much sense as they themselves did. To Annie Thackeray, Adelaide said: "it always seems to me that no one I ever talk to seems able to say anything clearly and to the point, except myself and my sister Fanny. When she speaks I know exactly what she means and wants to say; when other people speak, I have to find out what they mean, and even then I am not certain that they know it themselves."

Years before, Fanny had described her relationship with Adelaide in almost the same way. "Our mode of perceiving and being affected by things," she wrote, "is often identical and our impressions frequently so similar and so simultaneous, that we both often utter precisely the same words upon a subject, so that it might seem as if one of us might save the other the trouble of speaking."

In June 1879, when Adelaide's strength was fast ebbing, Sir Frederic Leighton gave a small party for her. He arranged it with tender and anxious care, guessing it might be the last she would ever attend. He invited Edward, May and her husband, Algy and Nelly, plus Adelaide's artist friends, Giovanni Costa and Val Prinsep. Tosti, who was by then living in London, came especially to sing her favorite songs. Throwing aside weakness, which by then was painfully apparent, Adelaide lit up like a candle and for a few hours was herself again.

On June 28, when she was very weak, Adelaide wrote to dear Fay what was possibly her last letter. Intense pride in his achievements shone through its pages, but she also voiced criticism of the pace at which he lived. "You know your life has always seemed to me over hurried, over worried, over crowded, and split into too many threads," she told him. "It seems to me that good work can really only come out of calm—and strength out of rest, not fever. Do see if you can simplify your life some-how." Sensing that she was dying, she was more anxious than ever to pro-tect and guide him. She ended her letter with the poignant phrase: "I am so tired."

A fortnight later, as Adelaide lay gravely ill, her doctors diagnosed congestion of the liver, but even then there were some intervals of slight improvement. Occasionally she was carried downstairs from her bed to sit in front of her conservatory. Early in August she lapsed into a coma, from which she did not wake. On August 6 she died. "The end was without suf-fering," wrote May to Yuza Thun: "when I look at her beautiful peaceful face, my sorrow is almost turned into joy."

Though she died at Warsash, Adelaide by her own wish was buried in the village of Ightham, close to May's home of Prestons, and in the church-yard where Greville's body had been brought for burial from nearby Wad-hurst. She had often thought "of his peaceful grave and the dear bones at rest within it." Near to those dear bones was where she wished to lie. She wanted a simple funeral, and if a stone were to be placed above her, she wanted a small and simple one. She had composed a poem when Greville died, which explained her attitude to gravestones:

> Lay no stone above
> My lonely head.
> Lay no stifling tombstone there;
> The flowers will spring up thick and fair;
> The violets love
> The early dead.

Above Greville's grave she had planted ivy and a cotoneaster tree.

Adelaide's funeral, in the Norman church of St. Peter at Ightham, was as simple as she could have wished. Only a dozen or so close relatives and friends accompanied the flower-covered coffin to its resting place beside the bell tower. Edward, May, and Henry Evans-Gordon, Algy and Nelly, and Frederic were the chief mourners, along with eighty-year-old Anne Procter, who had known Adelaide since childhood, and who loved her like a sister. Never, wrote Mrs. Procter, "was anyone taken to her grave by more loving hearts."

Fanny was in Switzerland when she heard the news of her sister's death. "I alone am left," she mourned, "I am so sad that I can hardly bear myself."

Fanny survived another fourteen years, outliving most of her contemporaries. Though at times she felt very much alone, her life was not without its compensations. As Annie Thackeray noted, Fanny retained "the power of making new friends, of being loved by them, of loving them." Not least among her new acquaintances was Frances Cobbe, an antivivisectionist, suffragist, and champion of battered wives. They had first met through Harriet St. Leger—now, alas, dead, too. Fanny sometimes laughed at Miss Cobbe, and often disagreed with her, but she still had a profound respect for her intellect and purpose. One point where they strongly differed was on female suffrage, which Fanny did not support. Education, she considered, was an essential prerequisite for a voter. First educate the people—the women included—she said, and then award them the right to vote. To allow the uneducated of either sex to vote was, to Fanny's mind, a formula for disaster.

Annie Thackeray, who had become Annie Ritchie—for at forty she had married her much younger cousin—remembered how Fanny in old age received guests in her drawing room. Dressed in a black silk dress and lace cap, she sat alongside a cage of mockingbirds and held her tapestry on her lap. She was stately, upright, and "ruddy and brown of complexion, almost to the very last." She was also "mobile and expressive in feature, reproachful, mocking, and humourous, heroic and uplifted in turn." This was "no old woman," declared Annie, but one who felt "the throb of life with an intensity far beyond younger people." Sometimes she was vehement, and sometimes she was "tender with a tenderness such as is very rare."

Tenderness was almost a keynote of Fanny's last years. "Out of this stress of feeling," wrote Annie Ritchie, "out of this passionate rebellion against fate, she grew to the tender, noble and spirited maturity of her later days." Many of Fanny's letters were radiant with concern for her friends, relatives, and servants. When she took on her travels a Swiss maid from London, she thought of the maid's needs and halted for days at a lakeside Swiss hotel so that this young girl, who had not been home for five years, could visit her parents. When Fanny visited young relatives, she tried to see herself as they might see her, and to modify her behavior accordingly. When she began to journey about Europe with a nephew, she at first wondered how he would cope with what she called her "abrupt and brusque manner and quick, sudden, strong transitions of feeling." She was glad to be able to report that "we get on very well together."

When Fanny stopped her readings, she turned to writing her memoirs. The idea had germinated when Harriet returned her old letters to her. From their fading pages, some written as long as forty-five years before, Fanny relived her early life and felt moved to reconstruct it in a series of rambling articles for the *Atlantic Monthly*. So her books of reminiscence were born: *Recollections of a Girlhood*, in two volumes in 1876; *Records of Later Life*, in three volumes in 1882; and *Further Records*, in two volumes in 1890. "She wrote exactly as she talked," noted one admiring reader, "observing, asserting, complaining, confiding, contradicting, crying out and bounding off, always effectually communicating." The books won a large and affectionate readership; and inscribed copies can occasionally be found in antiquarian bookshops in England and in the United States. Readers discovered a highly civilized and compassionate observer: savoring sermons and musical evenings with discernment, familiar with the best books, discoursing on the weather and the human race, and describing everything she saw in a polished and vivacious prose that has probably not been surpassed by any other leading actress of the English-speaking world.

Fanny had her dislikes, foremost of which were the innkeepers of Switzerland and "their fervent zeal for making money." They snatched a little of the gloss off the mountains, wildflowers, and the "tiny blessed blossoms that creep to the very feet of the terrible glaciers." Fanny came to dislike London and its noise and thick fogs—at eleven o'clock on some mornings she had to write her letters by gaslight. But her imagination was vigorous, and she was instantly carried to new and distant worlds by books, conversation, and the slowly mellowing memories of her past life.

Young relatives and friends often visited her. Gertrude Santley—her brother John's daughter—and Adelaide's daughter May both called on her at regular intervals. One year May invited Fanny to spend Christmas with the Evans-Gordons; in the party were Nelly, Algy, and their children, and Edward Sartoris, who lived on until 1888. May's three little girls, Catherine, Jean, and Margaret, acted scenes from *The School for Scandal*, *The Rivals*, and *Twelfth Night* and showed decided talent. Fanny was delighted with their performances. Two of them, she said, had the makings of real actresses.

Among her relatives, the chief object of her affection was her ward Harry Kemble, her brother Henry's boy. Harry was a credit to his upbringing in almost every way. His only fault, in Fanny's eyes, was that he had insisted on leaving his secure position in the Privy Council office and venturing onto the stage. "I like him very much," said Fanny. "He is very affectionate and kind to me, and his Kemble face and voice, which are both like his father's and my father's, are dear and pleasant to me." Harry was sometimes a dutiful escort on her European trips: so, too, was Henry James.

Punctually on the first of June, nearly every year, Fanny went to Switzerland; punctually on the first of September she returned to London. In the interval she roamed as far and as high as she could, usually in the company of one or other of the young men. Few could imagine, said Henry James, what fun she could be on those trips to the Alps, flinging herself "on the pianos of mountain inns, joking, punning, botanizing, encouraging the lowly and abasing the proud, making stupidity everywhere gape (that was almost her mission in life), and startling, infallibly, all primness and propriety."

Henry James was also her escort in London. He took her to the theatre, where she shouted and wept so loudly that her "sobs resounded through the place." He still worshipped her: she was "the first woman in London," he wrote, and "one of the consolations" of his life. He preferred her to her daughters, whose charm had waned for him with the passing years. Poor Sarah Wister, harried by disappointment, had lost her bloom: Henry James called hers a "tragic nature." Fan, though she had retained "a certain charm of honesty and freshness," could not, in his mind, hold a candle to her sublime mother.

Fanny's third cavalier was Hamilton Aïdé, a friend inherited from Adelaide. He escorted her about London, and his attentive ways almost won her heart, though he was no match, in her mind, for Henry James. Fanny also relied on her daughter Fan as an escort, though mother and daughter did not always agree. When Fanny began her second book of autobiography, Fan turned on her like a terrier, fearing what she might say about Pierce Butler. Ultimately Fanny heeded her daughter's fears and obediently omitted Pierce's name from the text of this and her later books of reminiscence.

Fanny could not afford to alienate Fan, for she desired the comfort and security of her home, and most of all she wished to be near young Alice Leigh, her favorite grandchild. On the eve of the little girl's first English Christmas, at Alverston Manor near Stratford-on-Avon, Fanny decorated the nursery Christmas tree in person, helped by Henry James. Thanks to the generosity of her daughter and son-in-law, Fanny was able to make Alverston Manor her part-time home. The Leighs also welcomed her to Gloucester Place in London, when James Leigh became vicar of the fashionable parish of St. Mary's, Bryanston Square.

A new relationship was slowly established between Fanny and Fan. After a furious outbreak of temper during a trip to Paris, Fanny decided it would be wiser to defer to her strong-willed daughter. Henceforth the relationship was dutiful and "affectionately indifferent." They avoided contro-versy and spoke only on such bland topics as servants and clothes. Fanny, who "detested banalities, preferring silence to the commonplace," saw this form of communication as "one of the most tragical consequences of life," though she must have known that she was, at least in part, to blame. On these terms, there was peace; and Fanny had to offer peace, if she were to be allowed to live out the rest of her days in the Leighs' London house.

On one crucial topic, Fanny did not bow to Fan. When in England in 1879 Fan gave birth to a short-lived son, she insisted on naming him Pierce Butler Leigh. Fanny resented the name so strongly that she refused to come to the christening ceremony and declared the name a bad omen. Fanny still held such painful memories of her husband that she did not wish to speak his name or hear it spoken.

At nearly seventy, Fanny was still capable of walking in the Swiss Alps, singing at the top of her lungs. The Swiss guides used to call her "the lady who goes singing through the mountains." At almost eighty, on one of her last visits to Switzerland, she was carried up the steep tracks in a sedan chair borne by six men, who, physically exhausted by her great weight, had to be replaced every half hour. Fanny adored these excursions but said that she sometimes felt guilty when she heard her bearers huffing and puffing. When it became impossible for her to inspect and savor her beloved moun-tains, even in a chair, she was heartbroken. She would sit tearfully on the balconies of high alpine hotels and gaze for hours at her "paradise lost."

At almost eighty Fanny published her first novel, *Far Away and Long Ago*, a story set in her beloved American Berkshires. It reflected a mind that seemed barely touched by age. By eighty-three, however, the effects of her years were all too noticeable. She was reduced to traveling outdoors in a wheelchair, and her eyesight was too dim to read more than a page or two of print. Sometimes she had difficulty seeing the cards for her nightly game of Patience. Henry James noticed that she resented the little losses of aging far more than she resented the greater ones. He found her "very touching in her infirmity." He said that she conveyed a "wonderful air of smoldering embers under ashes."

Fanny's daily needs were cared for by her maid Ellen, whose devotion over the years was absolute. Ellen had been Fanny's maid in the early 1870s and had left to marry her Italian man-servant, Luigi Brianzoni, going to live with him in Italy. Fanny had traveled to Stresa on the Italian Lakes espe-cially to attend the christening of their son.

In the late 1880s, when Fanny needed extra care, Ellen left her family and returned to her mistress. The personal sacrifice did not go unnoticed by Fanny, who rewarded Ellen generously: in the opinion of her Sarah and Fan, far too generously. But Ellen was indispensable to Fanny, especially since her daughters often spent time on the other shore of the Atlantic.

It so happened that in January 1893 Sarah and Fan were both in America. It was Ellen, therefore, who tended her mistress in her last illness. She chafed Fanny's hands and fed her spoons of water through the night. She helped her to the sofa and back again to bed. Beside the bed on the night of January 15, while Ellen was removing her dressing gown, Fanny fell into her arms. She died without a cry or a struggle. Her soul, said Ellen, went straight to God. Fanny would have liked that phrase, for her religious faith had remained deep and invincible throughout her life.

Fanny had once wished to lie in American soil in the churchyard on the hill at Lenox, but to take her across the ocean, even if this had still been her wish, was clearly impractical. Instead, in London, on a "soft, kind, balmy day," Fanny was buried beside her father in Kensal Green Cemetery. Apart from Ellen—who stood at the graveside "with a very white face and her hands full of flowers"—the saddest mourner was Henry James, who, though scarcely able to walk from gout, insisted on attending the funeral. He stood among the crowd of onlookers and the piles of flowers and thought how much he would miss his "sublime Fanny."

He had looked at her earlier in her coffin and thought how like Adelaide she seemed. The two sisters haunted his mind all that day. How remarkable they had been: so forceful, so noble, so faithful, so talented. The world had lost not only two great artists, but a type of indomitable woman it would not see again. He wrote to Sarah Wister in the evening: "I am conscious of a strange bareness and a kind of evening chill, as it were, in the air, as if some great object that had filled it for long had left an emptiness—from displacement—to all the senses." Fanny's passing seemed to him "like the end of some reign or the fall of some empire."

Acknowledgments

MY TASK in writing this book would have been impossible but for the many people and libraries who have lent me or guided me to letters, manuscripts, and other information. My foremost acknowledgment is to the late Adelaide Lubbock and her family. To her son and daughter-in-law, Lord and Lady Avebury; to her cousin, Mrs. Juliet Daniel; and to her grandson, the Honorable Lyulph Lubbock, I owe a deep debt of thanks.

Many libraries have helped me. I acknowledge in particular the kind assistance of the Folger Library, the Huntington Library and Art Collections, the Harvard Theatre Collection at the Pusey Library at Harvard University, the Lenox Library Association of Western Massachusetts, the National Library of Scotland, the British Library, the London Library, the University of Nottingham Library, and the Library of the Garrick Club, London. The archivists of the Royal Opera House Covent Garden, Museo Teatrale Alla Scala, Gran Teatro La Fenice, and Teatro di San Carlo all gave me useful information.

The kindness and help of my publisher, Mr. Ivan Dee, and of my literary agent, Mr. Michael Shaw, must not go unacknowledged. Nor must I forget to mention the generous interest of Sir Donald Sinden, Mr. Roger Kimball, Mrs. Elizabeth van Rompaey, and Professor and Mrs. Hellmut Wohl. Mention must be made of Miss Jill Fairlie, and of Professor S. C. McCulloch, both of whom performed valuable searching and photocopying for me in the U.S. Lastly I speak with gratitude of the patience, support, and practical help of my husband, Geoffrey Blainey, and my daughter, Anna Blainey.

< 313 >

Notes

THE FOLLOWING ABBREVIATIONS have been used for sources in the Notes:

AJ. Frances Anne Butler, *Journal*, 2 vols., London, 1835.

AK. Adelaide Kemble (after her marriage, Adelaide Sartoris).

AWFCH. Adelaide Sartoris, *A Week in a French Country House*, London, 1903.

Consol. Frances Anne Butler, *A Year of Consolation*, 2 vols., New York, 1847.

DNB. *The Dictionary of National Biography*, Oxford, England, 1968.

FK. Frances Anne Kemble, known as Fanny Kemble (after her marriage, Fanny Butler, and after her divorce, Fanny Kemble again).

Folger. Manuscript letters in the Folger Shakespeare Library, Washington, D.C.

FR. Frances Anne Kemble, *Further Records*, New York, 1891.

Garrick Club. Manuscripts and newspaper cuttings belonging to the Garrick Club, London.

GDO. *The New Grove Dictionary of Opera*, ed. Stanley Sadie, London, 1992.

Hunt. Manuscript letters in the Huntington Library and Art Gallery, San Marino, California.

JRGP. Frances Anne Kemble, *Journal of a Residence on a Georgian Plantation in 1838–9*, New York, 1863.

LA. Lubbock Archives. Letters from Adelaide Kemble to members of her family, written from 1835 to 1879. These and the Leighton and Thun letters were passed down to Adelaide Kemble's great-granddaughter, Adelaide Lubbock, and are now in a private collection.

Leighton. Letters from Adelaide Kemble to Frederic Leighton, written from 1858 to 1879.

LL. Letters and newspaper cuttings belonging to the Lenox Library Association, Lenox, Massachusetts.

MBS. Pierce Butler, *Mr. Butler's Statement*, Philadelphia, 1850.

Nar. "Pierce Butler vs. Frances Anne Butler; Libel for Divorce, with Answer and Exhibits," also known as "Mrs. Butler's Narrative," published in the *New York Evening Post*, December 2 and 4, 1848.

ROG. Frances Anne Kemble, *Records of a Girlhood*, New York, 1879.

ROLL. Frances Anne Kemble, *Records of Later Life*, London, 1882.

Scot. Manuscript letters in the National Library of Scotland, Edinburgh.

Thun. Letters between Adelaide Kemble and the family of Count Thun-Hohenstein, written from 1837 to 1879. These were passed down to Adelaide Kemble's great-granddaughter and are now in a private collection.

< 315 >

CHAPTER 1. GOD ALMIGHTY'S NOBILITY.

Adelaide's Birth and Talma, ROG, 25. **The Great Kembles,** Leigh Hunt, *The Autobiography of Leigh Hunt,* ed. J. E. Morpurgo (London, 1948), 137; AWFCH, xx. **Roger and Sarah Kemble,** James Boaden, *Memoirs of the Life of John Philip Kemble* (London, 1825), I, 4–9; Yvonne Ffrench, *Mrs. Siddons* (London, 1936), 1–7; DNB, X, 1268–1289; The Blessed John Kemble is now Saint John Kemble, having been canonized in 1970. **John Philip Kemble and Sarah Siddons,** Ffrench, *Mrs. Siddons,* 14–16, 33, 57–59, 163; Roger Manvell, *Sarah Siddons* (London, 1970), 24–25; DNB, X, 1260–1266, and XV, 111, 195–202. **Charles Kemble,** Jane Williamson, *Charles Kemble: Man of the Theatre* (Lincoln, Nebr., 1970), 4, 12–25; Boaden, *John Philip Kemble,* 48–49, 122; Hunt, *Autobiography,* 133; DNB, X, 1266–1267. **Marie Thérèse De Camp's background and early life,** DNB, X, 1253–1255; Henry Greville, *Leaves from the Diary of Henry Greville,* ed. Viscountess Enfield (London, 1883–1905), III, 183–184; Michael Kelly, *Reminiscences* (Oxford, England, 1975), 129, 258; Garrick Club, Smith's original letters, XI, 110; ROG, 2–7; Hunt, *Autobiography,* 122; French being her first language, Marie Thérèse generally used the full French form of her Christian name but sometimes also called herself Maria Theresa. **Marie Thérèse's love for Charles,** Thun, AK–Countess Thun, Dec. 21, 1838. **Charles Kemble's early married life,** ROG, 2–8; Thun, AK–Countess Thun, Dec. 21, 1838; Garrick Club, Smith's original letters, XI, 110; Manvell, *Sarah Siddons,* 5–7; Greville, *Diary,* I, 42; Claire Tomalin, *The Invisible Woman* (London, 1991), 14–15, 25. **Burning and rebuilding of Covent Garden and Old Price Riots,** Boaden, *John Philip Kemble,* XI, 453–474, 499–516; *The Annual Register,* L, 1808, 106; Linda Kelly, *The Kemble Era* (New York, 1980) 174–179; R. Michaelis-Jena and W. Mersen, eds., *A Lady Travels* (London, 1988), 168–181. **Fanny's early years,** ROG, 8–18, 256, 305. **Date of Adelaide's birth,** extract from baptismal register of St. James's Church, Paddington, London; ROG, 274; LA, AK–G. Bloomfield, Feb. 26, n.y. **Aunt Dall,** ROG, 18–20, **Fanny's first French school,** ROG, 26–31. **Craven Hill,** ROG, 30–39. **Marie Thérèse's retirement,** DNB, X, 1267. **Fanny's unhappiness,** ROG, 42–44, 311. **Fanny acting in the nursery,** ROG, 10-11. **Mrs. Siddons's last performance,** Charles and Fanny both maintain that Fanny saw Mrs. Siddons in her last performance as Lady Randolph (ROG, 17, and Charles Greville, *The Greville Memoirs, 1814–1860,* ed. Lytton Strachey and Roger Fulford [London, 1938], I, 376–377). Since the date of the performance was June 9, 1819, the Kembles were living not at Covent Garden Chambers (as Fanny says in ROG, 17) but at Craven Hill. Marie Thérèse made her farewell performance on the same night, as Lady Julia in *Personation.* The plays presumably followed one another, so it seems likely that Fanny saw both performances.

CHAPTER 2. LITTLE DEVIL OF A KEMBLE.

Mrs. Rowden's school, ROG, 45–73; Esther Meynell, *English Spinster: A Portrait* (London, 1939), 85, 161; Muriel Jaeger, *Before Victoria* (London, 1967), 158–159. **Fanny's religiousness,** ROLL, I, 40; ROG, 50, 163, 169–170. **Acting in Andromaque,** ROG, 69–70. **Charles Kemble's visits,** ROG, 64. **Fanny's appearance,** ROG, 1, 82, 85; FR, 114–115. **Fanny's appraisal of her mother,** ROG, 2, 5. **At Weybridge,** ROG, 75–82, 387. **Smallpox,** ROG, 82–83, 136; two of Fanny's previous biographers make no mention of her attack of smallpox. **Fanny's reclusiveness and antipathy to marriage,**

ROG, 112; ROG, 135–136. **The Fitzhughs,** ROG, 83, 270–271. **Harriet St. Leger,** ROG, 90–94, 101–103, 273; J. C. Furnas, *Fanny Kemble: Leading Lady of the Nineteenth-Century Stage* (New York, 1982), 35. **Good society's attitude toward Kembles,** ROG, 455. **The Montagu household and Anna Jameson,** ROG, 122, 125–128, 353; Clara Thomas, *Love and Work Enough* (London, 1967), 36, 38–43; E. F. Benson, *As We Were* (London, 1938), 42–44. **Adelaide's education,** LA, AK–FK, Aug. 21, 1837 (Adelaide speaks of her mother's singing teacher); AWFCH, xxviii; ROG, 86, 311; A. Sartoris, "Recollections of Joseph Heywood," *Cornhill Magazine,* X (October 1864), 692; Thun, AK–Countess Thun, Feb. 1, 1838. **Charles Kemble and Covent Garden Theatre,** Williamson, *Charles Kemble,* Ch. 3; ROG, passim. **Weber and Oberon,** ROG, 95–101; John Warrack, *Carl Maria von Weber* (London, 1968), 233, 316–338; James Robinson Planche, *Recollections and Reflections* (London, 1872), 56–58; Thun, AK–Y. Thun, Sept. 1, 1840. **Charles Kemble's debts, Mrs. Kemble's illness,** ROG, 107–108, 117–118, 133, 226; Williamson, *Charles Kemble,* 183–184. **Francis I,** ROG, 104, 114–117. **John Mitchell Kemble's success and decline,** ROG, 109–110, 122, 137, 180, 183.

CHAPTER 3. "HEAVEN SMILES ON YOU, MY CHILD."

Fanny's arguments for and against acting, ROG, 135–136, 138, 191–192, 194, 218, 220–223, 225–226, 247, 287, 396, 432; ROLL, I, 79–80; FR, 12 fn.; Tomalin, *Invisible Woman,* Ch. 2, esp. 17–18; Tomalin's discussion of the status of actors is excellent, and I am indebted to it; Martha Vicinus, ed., *A Widening Sphere: Changing Roles of Victorian Women* (Bloomington, Ind., 1980), Ch. 5. **Mrs. Harry Siddons and Edinburgh,** ROG, 141–144; Scot., FK–George Combe, Jan. 30, 1832; DNB, XVIII, 194; George Combe married Mrs. Siddons's daughter Cecilia in 1833. **Fanny's preparation and debut,** ROG, 136, 186–194, 196–197, 217–222, 225–226, 234, 259; Furnas, *Fanny Kemble,* 51–52. **Fanny's earnings and Charles's debt,** ROG, 226, 335; Fanny says in ROG, 226, that she was paid thirty guineas a week, but receipts for the 1829–1830 season show that she was paid five pounds a performance, as was Charles Kemble himself—see Williamson, *Charles Kemble,* 184–193, esp. 192–193 fn.; Dorothy Marshall, *Fanny Kemble* (London, 1977), 34. **Adelaide at the theatre,** ROG, 341. **Kembles' life of luxury,** ROG, 226, 232–233, 463. **Fanny as a lioness,** ROG, 224, 242, 247, 267, 291, 363, 415. **Harriet's visit,** ROG, 317–323. **Fanny's fear of failure,** ROG, 245–246, 360–361. **Discussion of Fanny's stage roles:** From 1829–1834, FK played Belvidera in Otway's *Venice Preserved,* Euphrasia in Murphy's *The Grecian Daughter,* Mrs. Beverley in Moore's *The Gamester,* Isabella in Southerne's *The Fatal Marriage,* Lady Townly in Vanbrugh's *The Provoked Husband.* Mrs. Oakley in Colman's *The Jealous Wife,* Mrs. Haller in Kotzebue's *The Stranger,* Callisa in Rowe's *The Fair Penitent.* Camiola in Massinger's *The Maid of Honour,* and the Shakespearean heroines Juliet, Portia, Constance, Beatrice, Katharine of Aragon, and Lady Macbeth. These were all Mrs. Siddons's former roles. FK also played Lady Teazle in *The School for Scandal,* Bianca in Milman's *Fazio,* Julia in Knowles's *The Hunchback,* Katharine in Egerton's *Katharine of Cleves,* and Louisa of Savoy and then Francoise de Foix in her own play, *Francis I.* (*Francis I* was published by John Murray in 1832 to coincide with the stage production.) ROG, 191–192, 225–226, 234–237, 245–247, 288, 395, 458; Mrs. C. Baron Wilson, *Our Actresses; Or Glances at Stage Favourites* (London, 1844), I, 294; Marshall, *Fanny Kemble,* 76; *Greville Memoirs,* I, 326, 377; Manvell, *Sarah Siddons,* 82. Williamson, *Charles Kemble,* 186–196.

CHAPTER 4. "EVERYTHING IS WINTER."

Fanny's ambivalence toward acting, Anna Jameson, *Visits and Sketches at Home and Abroad* (London, 1835), 84, 85; ROG, 236, 247; FR, 12 fn. **Tour of Scotland and Ireland,** ROG, 261–262, 272–273, 288–292. **George Stephenson and Huskisson's death,** ROG, 280–284, 298–299. **At Heaton Hall,** ROG, 295, 300–303, 396, 497; DNB, VI, 571–572, and VIII, 606. Lord Francis Egerton was called Lord Francis Leveson-Gower until 1833, when he took the name of Egerton; likewise his father was Marquis of Stafford until 1833 when he became Duke of Sutherland. To avoid confusion, I have used their later titles from 1831 onward. **Fanny's attitude to society,** ROG, 455. **John Mitchell Kemble,** ROG, 179, 183, 243, 294–295, 326, 334, 335–336, 359–360, 363, 405. John had a fortunate escape; in December 1831, one of Torrijos's British supporters was executed by the Spanish government. **At Oatlands,** ROG, 374–376, 402–405; 467–468. **Bridgewater House theatricals,** ROG, 396, 406–407, 410, 417–423, 468. **Fanny's past courtship and Thomas Lawrence,** ROG, 207–217, 227–230, 237; Manvell, *Sarah Siddons*, Ch. 6. **Augustus Craven,** Charles Mayne Young, *A Memoir* (London, 1871), 120; ROG, 294, 418–423, 432, 436, 439, 470, 533; Thun AK–Y. Thun, Sept. 1, 1840; DNB, I, 508–509; V, 42–43, XXII, 504–505. **Adelaide's future,** ROG, 274–275, 284, 462, 502. **Charles Kemble's illness and debt,** ROG, 336, 458–485, 470, 511, 517, esp. 463, 470, 473; W. M. Thackeray, *The Letters and Private Papers of William Makepeace Thackeray,* ed. Gordon N. Ray (Cambridge, Mass., 1945–1946), I, 177; Williamson, *Charles Kemble,* 202. **Harriet farewells Fanny,** ROG, 290, 525–526. **Departure,** ROG, 521–522, 525, 531; AJ, I, 1.

CHAPTER 5. A GENTEEL SLAVE-OWNER.

Arrival and impressions of New York, ROG, 534–535; AJ, I, 41–48, 202–204, 256–257. **Kembles' reception in America,** AJ, I, 111–116; Dorothea Bobbe, *Fanny Kemble* (New York, 1931), 71 (quote from Hone); ROG, 536, 541–543. **In Washington,** AJ, I, 116–136; Furnas, *Fanny Kemble,* 119–120. **In Boston,** ROG, 573–578; AJ, I, 174–215; Furnas, *Fanny Kemble,* 125–126. **Touring,** ROG, 552–553, 555, 563, 567–568, 573–574; AJ, I, 201; II, 131, 139–141, 145–146. **Dall as a chaperone,** AJ, I, 225–228, 256–257 fn. **Fanny's manner,** Ffrench, *Mrs. Siddons,* 188; A. T. Ritchie, *Chapters from Some Unwritten Memoirs* (New York, 1895), 193, 198–199; FR, 12 fn. **Mr. Biddle,** AJ, I, 249; II, 66. **Pierce Butler,** AJ, I, 192, 200, 209; Furnas, *Fanny Kemble,* 120–123. Pierce was the Christian name of the 8th Earl of Ormonde (died 1539) and was thereafter used by a number of his descendants and their relatives; see DNB, III, 502, 518, 524–525, 531. Fanny was amused in 1843 when a Philadelphia admirer insisted on calling her the Duchess of Ormond; see ROLL, III, 46. **Idyllic American scenery,** AJ, II, 89–90. **Courtship,** AJ, II, 76–77, 90–91, 175–177, 183, 192–195; ROG, 590. **Trelawny and Pierce,** ROG, 581–585; AJ, II, 267, 283, 230–287; William St. Clair, *Trelawny* (London, 1977), 146–150; Scot., FK–George Combe, June 27, 1833, and Park Place, n.d. 1837; ROG, 498; Elizabeth Mavor, ed., *Fanny Kemble, The American Journals* (London, 1990), 110. **Fanny complains of overwork,** ROG, 586–588; **Dall's deathbed and Fanny's wedding,** Scot., FD–George Combe, April 11, n.y., and April 17, n.y.; ROG, 588–590; Marshall, *Fanny Kemble,* 104; Furnas, *Fanny Kemble,*

121–122, 140, 143–146; Fanny Kemble Wister, ed., *Fanny, the American Kemble: Her Journals and Unpublished Letters* (Tallahassee, Fla., 1972), 139; LA, AK–H. St. Leger, March 9, 1837. **At Butler Place,** ROLL, I, 14, 18, 24, 35, 40–44; MBS, 74; AJ, I, 259. **The American Journal,** Furnas, *Fanny Kemble,* 160–164; LL, cutting from *Southern Messenger,* May 1835; Greville, *Memoirs,* III, 203. **Sarah Butler's birth,** F. A. Kemble, *Far Away and Long Ago* (New York, 1889), 304; ROLL, I, 41; **Fanny leaves home,** MBS, 22–24; ROLL, I, 41.

CHAPTER 6. AN ENCHANTED BOHEMIAN CASTLE.

Adelaide's adoration of Fanny, Thun, AK–Countess Thun, Feb. 1, 1838. **Fanny's jealousy of Adelaide's voice,** ROG, 341, 480; ROLL, I, 163; II, 171, 122, 293–294. **Adelaide's nature,** ROG, 321; A. Tennyson, *Lord Tennyson: A Memoir by His Son* (London, 1897), I, 82; Thackeray, *Letters,* I, 207. **Adelaide's studies in Paris,** ROG, 276, 462; Thackeray, *Letters,* I, 173; Thun, AK–Y. Thun, March 15, 1858, and AK–Countess Thun Milan, n.d.; Henry Chorley, *Thirty Years' Musical Recollections* (New York, 1984), I, 213; B. Coffin, *Historical Vocal Pedagogy Classics* (Lanham, Md., 1989), 14–30; V. A. Field, *Foundations of the Singer's Art* (New York, 1977), 57; John Rosselli, *Singers of Italian Opera* (Cambridge, England, 1992), 143 GDO, I, 546; Paul Johnson, *The Birth of the Modern* (New York, 1991), 609; Anna Jameson, *Memoirs and Essays on Art, Literature and Social Morals* (London, 1846), 374. Mrs. Jameson is incorrect in saying AK was originally a contralto, see ROLL, II, 293; Rupert Christiansen, *Prima Donna* (London, 1984), 64, 71; Bruno Cagli and Mauro Bucarelli, *La Casa Di Rossini: Catalogo Del Museo* (Modena, 1989), 64–65; AWFCH, xxix. **Adelaide's relationship with her mother,** Thun, AK–Countess Thun, Dec. 21, 1838, and AK–Countess Thun, n.d.; LA, AK–FK, Thursday 17, n.m., 1858; LA, AK–Harriet St. Leger, Nov. 14, 1836. **Adelaide's public debut,** Thun, AK–Y. Thun, Sept. 21, 1840; *The Morning Post,* May 14, 1835 (Review); LA, AK–Harriet St. Leger; *The Lyre: A Musical and Theatrical Register,* Dec. 20, 1841. **Henry Greville, Mario, and Trelawny,** ROLL, I, 74; ROG, 303, 497, 436, 582; Elizabeth Forbes, *Mario and Grisi* (London, 1985), 12–17; Thun, AK–Y. Thun, Dec. 1, 1837; Jan. 14, 1839; and Feb. 17, 1873; St. Clair, *Trelawny,* 156; LA, AK–Harriet St. Leger, Nov. 14, 1836. **Fanny in London,** ROLL, I, 74–81, 96–109, 110–111; II, 139; LA, AK–Harriet St. Leger, March 9, 1837; F. A. Longfellow, *Mrs. Longfellow: Selected Letters and Journals of Fanny Appleton Longfellow* (1817–1861), ed. Edward Wagenknecht (New York, 1956), 41–42; Hesketh Pearson, *Smith of Smiths* (London, 1948), 34, 188–190, 292–293; Williamson, *Charles Kemble,* 221–228. **To and in Carlsbad, Prague, and Teplitz,** ROG, 320, 393; ROLL, I, 94; AJ, I, 232; LA, AK–FK, Aug. 21, 1837; LA, AK–M. T. Kemble, Nov. 19, 1837; AWFCH, xxvii; LA, AK–FK, Park Place, Dec. 21, 1837. **Desssauer,** AWFCH, xxvii, 45. Dessaix is a portrait of Dessauer. Richard Wagner, *My Life,* trans. Andrew Gray (New York, 1992), 213. **The Thuns,** Thun, AK–Y Thun, Mar. 15, 1858; LA, AK–FK, Dec. 21, 1837; Thun, AK–Y. Thun, Sept. 26, 1839, and Oct. 16, 1838, and Mar. 15, 1858; Hanna Slavickova, *Schloss Decin* (Decin, 1991), 10–23; Maynard Solomon, *Mozart* (New York, 1995), 272, 419; Thun, AK–Countess Thun, Dec. 4, 1837, and Feb. 1, 1838; Herbert Weinstock, *Chopin: The Man and His Music* (New York, 1949), 85.

CHAPTER 7. THE GIRL IN THE BLACK CASSOCK DRESS.

To and in Leipzig, Thun, AK–Countess Thun, Nov. 8, 1837, and Dec. 21, 1838; ROG, 96; ROLL, II, 50; Avril Mackenzie-Grieve, *Clara Novello 1818–1908* (London, 1955), 50–54; Clara Novello, *Reminiscences,* ed. Valeria Gigliucci (London, 1940), 63; Eric Werner, *Mendelssohn,* trans. Dika Newlin (London, 1963), 312–331. **Garcia family,** Thun, AK–Countess Thun, Dec. 4, 1837, and AK–Countess Thun, Dec. 1, 1837; Christiansen, *Prima Donna,* 72–83; Howard Bushnell, *Maria Malibran: A Biography of the Singer* (Philadelphia, 1979), 223–225. **Adelaide decides to sing professionally,** Thun, AK–Countess Thun, Feb. 1, 1838; ROLL, I, 162; LA, AK–FK, Dec. 21, n.y. **The Thuns to be elsewhere,** Thun, AK–Countess Thun, June 15, 1838. **Marie Thérèse's illness,** Thun, AK–Countess Thun, Sept. 21, 1838. **At Tetschen,** LA, AK–FK, Thursday 17, n.y. **In Tepliz and Carlsbad,** Thun, AK–Countess Thun, July 1838, July 24 and August 1, 1838. **Adelaide studies with Pasta,** Stendhal, *The Life of Rossini,* trans. Richard N. Coe (London, 1985), Ch. 35; Christiansen, *Prima Donna,* 63–69; A. Sartoris, *Past Hours,* ed. May E. Gordon (London, 1880), I, 205–217; A. Sartoris, *Cornhill,* XII (1865), 704–707; Michael Scott, *Maria Meneghini Callas* (London, 1991), 87, 186 (quote concerning Colbran); Thun, AK–Countess Thun, Sept. 21, 1838. **The Kemble Cadenze,** Howard Mayer Brown and Stanley Sadie, eds., *Performance Practice—Music After 1600* (London, 1989), 427, 435 fn., 446, contains a discussion of the Kemble cadenze. **In Milan,** AK–Countess Thun, Sept. 21 and 22, Oct. 16, 1838.

CHAPTER 8. TRIUMPH IN ITALY.

The need to be at the top, ROG, 136; Thun, AK–Y. Thun, July 25, 1839. **Adelaide's crazy letter,** Thun, AK–Countess Thun, Venice, n.d., and Dec. 21, 1838. **Adelaide's operatic debut,** Thun, AK–Countess Thun, Dec. 2, 1838; R. Turnbull, *The Opera Gazeteer* (London, 1988), 159–160; AWFCH, xxx. Annie Thackeray Ritchie says the rehearsal was in Trieste, but Gallo, the conductor, indicates that it was in Venice— see cast list from Gran Teatro La Fenice, Venice. Christiansen, *Prima Donna,* 67; *London Punch,* Nov. 6, 1841; Mrs. Wilson, *Our Actresses,* II, 256–258. **In Trieste,** Thun, AK–Countess Thun, Jan 14 and Feb. 23, 1839; Herbert Weinstock, *Rossini* (New York, 1987), 230, 460; Jameson, *Memoirs and Essays,* 80. Mrs. Jameson says that AK had difficulty with a rival *prima donna* in Trieste, but AK herself does not mention it in her letters—rather she says she had "brilliant success." Biographical account of AK in Italian by H. R. Beard supplied by the Archives of Teatro alla Scala. **At La Scala,** Turnbull, *The Opera Gazeteer,* 141–142; Thun, AK–Countess Thun, Milan n.d.; cast list from Museo Teatrale Alla Scala; Mary Jane Phillips-Matz, *Verdi* (Oxford, 1993), 88–89; *The Lyre,* Aug. 14 and 30, 1841. **In Padua,** Thun, AK–Countess Thun, July 25 and Sept. 26, 1839; Mrs. Wilson, *Our Actresses,* II, 257. In Padua, Adelaide also sang in *La Marescialla d'Ancre* by Alessandro Nini. **In Bologna,** Thun, AK–Y. Thun, Oct. 3 and Nov. 8, 1839; Jameson, *Memoirs and Essays,* 82. **Charles Kemble's London farewell,** Williamson, *Charles Kemble,* 230–231. **In Mantua and Milan,** Thun, AK–Y. Thun, Apr. 6, 1840; H. R. Beard; ROLL, II, 10–11; Phillips-Matz, *Verdi,* 97. In Mantua, Adelaide also sang in *Lucia di Lammermoor* and *Inez de Castro* by Fabio Marchetti. **At Naples and San Carlo,** Turnbull, *The Opera Gazeteer,* 146–148; Thun, AK–Y. Thun, Apr. 6 and Sept. 1, 1840, and Jan. 17, 1841; ROLL, II, 68; Herbert Weinstock, *Vincenzo Bellini* (London,

1971), 129; *The Lyre*, December 1841, 20; cast list from the Archives of Teatro di San Carlo, Naples.

CHAPTER 9. "LIKE A BOILING SPRING."

Fanny's ideal of marriage, MBS, 9–11; ROG, 135; AWFCH, xxi. **At Butler Place,** ROLL, I, 43–44, 115, 125–126, 134, 140, 142, 149, 151–153, 156, 162–163; Thomas, *Love and Work Enough*, 122; MBS, 26–27. **The Sedgwick family and Lenox,** FR, 35, 195; ROLL, I, 164–166, 259, 168–169; II, 101–102; Longfellow, *Selected Letters and Journals*, 52–53; Catharine Maria Sedgwick, *The Power of Her Sympathy: The Autobiographical Journal of Catharine Maria Sedgwick*, ed. Mary Kelly (Boston, 1933), 125; Constance Wright, *Fanny Kemble and the Lovely Land* (New York, 1972), 18–19, 51–53. **Fanny's bereavement,** ROLL, I, 168–169; MBS, 45–46; **Fanny's depression and departure for Georgia,** MBS, 27–36.

CHAPTER 10. "EVER YOUR OWN WIFE."

Fanny's early antislavery, ROLL, I, 26–27, 35, 46–49, 66–67; JRGP, 15, 104; Wright, *Fanny Kemble and the Lovely Land*, 20–23, 53–56. **To and in Georgia,** ROLL, I, 170–218, 228; Furnas, *Fanny Kemble*, 198–203. **Arrival and first weeks at Butler's Island,** ROLL, I, 216–226; JRGP, 16–19. **Fanny visits slave cabins,** JRGP, 30–32, 63–64, 107–108, 121–122, 158. **Infirmary,** JRGP, 32–35, 37–40, 82–83, 122; ROLL, I, 218–219; Anne Firor Scott, *The Southern Lady: From Pedestal to Politics, 1830–1930* (Chicago, 1970), 28–30, 36, 49. **Petitioners at Butler's Island and Pierce's reaction,** JRGP, 49–50, 73–74, 79–80, 123–125. **Psyche,** JRGP, 97–106. **St. Simon's Island,** JRGP, 157–165. **Fanny in her sitting room,** JRGP, 175–177. **Petitioners at St. Simon's Island and Pierce's reaction,** JRGP, 163–165, 170–172, 177–179, 182, 187–192. **Fanny seeks relief in nature,** JRGP, 48–49, 177, 184, 250, 262–263, 277. **Jack,** JRGP, 126, 217, 221–222; ROLL, I, 238. **Fanny's depression,** JRGP, 171–172, 178, 193; Thun, AK–Countess Thun, Milan, 1839. **Fanny runs away,** MBS, 29–30, 32–39; JRGP, 174. **Fanny holds church services,** JRGP, 217, 220–221, 251–252. **Fanny's view of Pierce and God,** JRGP, 112–116. **Temporary reconciliation,** JRGP, 134, 237, 240–244; MBS, 69. **Fanny teaches Alec to Read,** JRGP, 117, 230–231. **Fanny leaves Georgia,** JRGP, 259–260, 283. **An English Tragedy,** MBS, 19–20; J. C. Trewin, ed., *The Journal of William Charles Macready* (London, 1967), 128–129; ROLL, I, 281. **Fanny's discontent, Pierce's reaction, and the Sedgwicks,** MBS, 31–56; Longfellow, *Selected Letters and Journals*, 60; Scot, FK–Cecilia Combe, June 17, 1840; ROLL, I, 234, 276–278; II, 1–44. **Lucretia Mott,** ROLL, I, 48–49; MBS, 14–15; B. G. Hersh, *The Slavery of Sex* (Urbana, Ill., 1978), 13–16.

CHAPTER 11. A HOMEGROWN PRIMA DONNA.

Fanny arrives in London, ROLL, II, 44, 47–66; MBS, 58–59; Scot, FK–Cecilia Combe, July 1841. **Adelaide in London,** ROLL, II, 72–76, 95–96, 108, 170; Scot., FK–Cecilia Combe, July 1841; Jameson, *Memoirs and Essays*, 93; Anna Jameson, *Letters and Friendships, 1812–1860*, ed. Mrs. Steuart Erskine (London, 1915), 193; Thun,

AK–Countess Thun, Aug. 13, 1841. **Lady Dacre,** ROG, 345–349; ROLL, II, 106–113. **Liszt and Rhine tour,** Henry James, *The Notebooks of Henry James*, ed. F. O. Mathiessen and K. B. Murdoch (Oxford, England, 1947), I, 12; Alan Walker, *Franz Liszt: The Virtuoso Years, 1811–1847* (London, 1983), I, 365; Scot., FK–George Combe, Aug. 6 and Nov. 8, 1839; Thun, AK–Countess Thun, Aug. 20, 1841; *The Lyre,* December 1841; ROLL, II, 113–137, 211; Thackeray, *Letters*, II, 38; Augustus Hare, *The Story of My Life* (London, 1900), V, 359–361; Wister, *Fanny: The American Kemble*, 174–175. **Fanny's criticism of Adelaide's singing,** ROLL, II, 123–125, 133–134, 171–172, 179, 226, 293–295; Chorley, *Thirty Years' Musical Recollections*, I, 213–215; Mrs. Wilson, *Our Actresses*, II, 256–258; Harold Rosenthal, *Two Centuries of Opera at Covent Garden* (London, 1958), 54; *London Punch,* Nov. 6, 1841. Fanny also considered Adelaide's voice inferior to Clara Novello's (see ROLL, II, 293). Here she may have had support since Clara was widely considered England's best concert-singer. Adelaide, having greater dramatic talent, was generally acknowledged the better opera singer. **Return to London,** ROLL, II 138–148, 174–178, 185–187, 209–210, 217, 232. **Edward Sartoris and other suitors,** Thun, AK–Count Thun, Sept. 13, 1841, AK–Y. Thun, Nov. 15, 1844; *London Weekly Telegraph,* issue 149 (1994), 39 (obituary of Lady Victoria Wemyss); Elizabeth Archer, *A Brief Biography of William John Cavendish Bentinck-Scott, 5th Duke of Portland (1800–1879)* (Nottingham, 1998); Sartoris family tree in possession of the Lubbock family. Thackeray, *Letters*, I, cxliv, says that in 1883, E. J. Sartoris's estates were worth 4,988 pounds annually. **Theodosia Monson,** ROG, 90–91, 397, 400; *Anna Jameson, Letters and Friendships,* 200. **Adelaide's opera tour,** AK–Count Thun, Apr. 15, 1842; "Opera at the Theatre Royal," *Glasgow Argus,* July 25 and 28, 1842. Adelaide's Glasgow reviews were as glowing as her London reviews. GDO, I, 286–287. Fanny maintained, in ROLL, II, 224, that Adelaide's manager was "Mr. Calcott . . . the son of the composer," presumably meaning the son of John Wall Calcott, the composer of glees. In fact Adelaide's manager was John William Calcraft, whose real name was Cole (see *The Journal of William Charles Macready,* 7). **Adelaide's engagement to Edward and the two Covent Garden seasons,** Mrs. Wilson, *Our Actresses,* II, 256–261; *The Lyre,* Nov. 8, 1841; Jameson, *Essays and Memoirs,* 92–121; Anna Jameson, *Letters and Friendships,* 200; George Vandenhoff, *Dramatic Reminiscences,* ed. H. S. Carlton (London, 1860), 115; *The Theatrical Journal,* Nov. 6, 1841; ROLL, II, 224; ROLL, II, 36, 252–256, 264–265, 276–278, 295; Williamson, *Charles Kemble,* 232–235; Augustus Hare, *The Story of My Life,* V, 360; Harold Rosenthal, *Two Centuries of Opera at Covent Garden,* 57; Thun, AK–Y. Thun, July 25, 1839, and May 13, 1843; Christiansen, *Prima Donna,* 228; Folger, Mrs. Grote–FK, June 1842. **Adelaide's marriage,** extract from the parish register for Glasgow City Parish (St. Mary's Episcopal Chapel). The wedding was not entirely secret, since the *Glasgow Argus* for Aug. 4, 1842, carried a brief report of the marriage in which Edward is called Count Sartoris. Although her official farewell performance was on Dec. 23, 1842, Adelaide sang at her benefit on Jan. 3, 1843, performing scenes from *Norma* and *Der Freischutz;* see ROLL, II, 281. **Adelaide's early married years,** Thun, AK–Y. Thun, Nov. 15, 1844, and AK–Count Thun, Sept. 5, n.y.; Thackeray, *Letters,* II, 109–110, 559; Jameson, *Essays and Memoirs,* 403 fn.; manuscripts of Mendelssohn's songs formerly in the possession of the Lubbock family. The songs are published in *Six Songs,* Opus 71.

CHAPTER 12. "SUBMIT YOUR WILL TO MINE."

Bowood, Belvoir, and the presentation to the queen, ROLL, II, 140–158, 185–187, 209–211, 215–219; *Greville Memoirs*, IV, 436. Fanny and *The National Anti-Slavery Standard*, MBS, 15–18; ROLL, II, 216. Raising money, ROLL, II, 234–235, 245–248. Bridgewater House theatricals, ROLL, II, 252–256; Fanny's attitude to Adelaide's engagement and retirement, ROLL, II, 248, 258, 264. In Liverpool and Kingston, and quarrels over money, MBS, 59–63; ROLL, II, 220, 224–225, 235–236. Quarrels at the Clarendon Hotel, MBS, 63–79; *Greville Memoirs*, V, 61–63. Marie Thérèse's attachment to her husband, Thun, AK–Countess Thun, Dec. 21, 1838. Marital wrangling, MBS, 79–90. Butlers' possible reconciliation, MBS, 91; Nar, Dec. 2, 1848; Marshall, *Fanny Kemble*, 179. Leaving London, ROLL, II, 286–291; Elizabeth Barret Browning, *Elizabeth Barret to Miss Mitford*, ed. Betty Miller (London, 1954), 179 (Henry Chorley); ROLL, III, 2–5.

CHAPTER 13. CAUGHT IN A TRAP.

Fanny's voyage and visit to Dall's grave, ROLL, III, 7–10. Lady Dacre, ROLL, III, 1, 12, 21. Fanny now often addressed Lady Dacre as "Dearest Granny." Philadelphia, AJ, I, 173–174. Mrs. McPherson's boardinghouse, ROLL, III, 10–11, 38–39; Furnas, 276. Yellow Springs, ROLL, III, 15–25, 30–32; MBS, 93–95. The Butlers entertain Macready, ROLL, III, 42–43; *Journal of William Charles Macready*, 204–205. Pierce's alleged infidelity, Nar, Dec. 2, 1848; MBS, 97–99, 114–116; Wister, *Fanny: The American Kemble*, 185–193. Conditions of separation, MBS, 99–100. Fanny wishes to return to the stage, *Journal of William Charles Macready*, 209. Fanny lives separately at McPherson's, ROLL, III, 50–58. The Sedgwicks collect evidence, MBS, 101–118. Pierce slandered, MBS, 119–123. Fanny's family writes to Pierce, MBS, 122–123. The Schott Affair, Furnas, *Fanny Kemble*, 274–275. The Horse Forrester, ROLL, I, 279–280; ROLL, III, 58. New conditions and Reverend Furness, MBS, 125, 130–139; Nar, Dec. 2 and 4, 1848. Fanny's curtailed visiting rights, MBS, 130–133; Nar, Dec. 4, 1848. Sartoris and Greville letters to Pierce, MBS, 141–143. The written agreement, MBS, 146–149. Miss Hall, MBS, 157–167; Nar, Dec. 4, 1848; Thun, AK–Count Thun, June 15, 1845. The Sedgwick Letter, Nar, Dec. 4, 1848; MBS, 153–156. Sarah becomes temperamental, Scot, FK–C. Combe, Nov. 18, 1839; MBS, 168–169. Last months in Philadelphia, MBS, 170–187; Nar, Dec. 4, 1848.

CHAPTER 14. LAND OF CONSOLATION.

Fanny's state of mind, ROLL, III, 114, 132–133, 137. John and Henry Kemble, ROLL, III, 150–153. Charles Kemble, Thun, AK–Count Thun, Oct. 3, 1847. Charles' relationship with his landlady is described by Adelaide; Fanny gives no mention of it in ROLL. Fanny's money problems, Nar, Dec. 4, 1848. Poems, Longfellow, *Selected Letters and Journals*, 111; ROLL, III, 88. Fanny's social life and nervous state, ROLL, III, 112; Wister, *Fanny: The American Kemble*, 195–196. Route to Rome, ROLL, III, 113–117; Consol, I, 2–59. In Italy, ROLL, III, 123–140; Consol, passim; Spanish Steps, I, 67; Holy Week, I, 114–131; Coliseum, II, 29–30; Frascati, II, 59–62; Mt. Cavo, II, 84; F. Kaplan, *Henry James: The Imagination of Genius* (London, 1992), 356: Thun, AK–Count

Thun, Aug. 8, 1846, and July 1847; ROLL, III, 365. **Edward's Spanish title,** biographical account of AK by H. R. Beard. **Adelaide's attitude to motherly love,** Leighton, AK–F. Leighton, Mar. 5, 1878. **Fanny's opinion of Edward Sartoris,** ROLL, II, 262. **Fanny's maintenance and annuity,** Nar, Dec. 4, 1848. **A year of consolation,** ROLL, III, 145–146; *Douglas Jerrold's Shilling Magazine,* V (1847), 474. **Fanny's resumption of career,** ROLL, III, 141–142, 148–149, 156, 160–180, esp. 164; E. W. Barnes, *The Lady of Fashion* (New York, 1954), 246. **Hernani,** Montstuart Grant Duff, *Notes from a Diary: London, 1896–1901* (London, 1905), I, 33; ROLL, III, 180–181; Furnas, *Fanny Kemble,* 307. **Macready,** ROLL, III, 261, 375–399; *Journal of William Charles Macready,* 207–209, 241–242, 248–249; Alan S. Downer, *The Eminent Tragedian William Charles Macready* (Cambridge, Mass., 1966), 283–285. **Fanny's readings,** ROLL, III, 206, 227–228, 414–415; Edward Fitzball, *Thirty Five Years of a Dramatic Author's Life* (London, 1859), II, 330. **Divorce,** Thun, AK–Y. Thun, Oct. 3, 1847; MBS, 187–188; Wister, *Fanny: The American Kemble,* 200–201.

CHAPTER 15. THUNDERCLOUDS.

Anna Jameson, the Thuns, and Consuelo, ROLL, III, 104; AWFCH, xxxi; Gordon S. Haight, *George Eliot* (Oxford, England, 1968), 148–149; AK–Count Thun, n.d., 1845; George Sand, *Consuelo,* trans. Fayette Robinson (Philadelphia, 1851); Curtis Cate, *George Sand* (Boston, 1975), Ch. 31, esp. 517. Although Adelaide's connection with *Consuelo* was discussed at the time by her friends, it seems forgotten today. Adelaide is not mentioned in Cate's biography, though he does wonder why Sand set the story in Bohemia, a place she had never visited. **Francis's marriage,** Thun, AK–Count Thun, Apr. 3, Aug. 8, and Oct. 3, 1846, and AK–Y. Thun, Jan. 14, 1847, and Count Thun–AK, Jan. 27, 1847. **At Frascati,** Thun, AK–Count Thun, July 1847; ROLL, III, 262–263, 309. **Mendelssohn's death,** ROLL, II, 242–243; Thun, AK–Count Thun, January 1849. **Edward's loss of money,** Thun, AK–Count Thun, January 1849 and Oct. 4, 1850; H. Greville, *Diary,* II, 183. **Chopin,** F. Chopin, *The Selected Correspondence of Fryderyk Chopin,* trans. and ed. Arthur Hedley (London, 1952), 331–335; E. Forbes, *Mario and Grisi,* 98–99. **Knuston,** Jean Long, *Knuston Hall; A Northamptonshire Saga* (Northhants, 1989), 8–11; Thun, AK–Y. Thun, October 1849, October 1850, and Jan. 21, 1852; AK–Count Thun, October 1849 and October 1850; ROLL, III, 219; LA, AK–FK, Sept. 24, 1858; H. Greville, *Diary,* I, 346, 355; Thackeray, *Letters,* II, 558–559. **Charles's girlfriend,** Thun, AK–Count Thun, Oct 14, 1850. **Fanny's divorce,** Thun, AK–Count Thun, January and October 1849; Nar; MBS, 1–8; Longfellow, *Selected Letters and Journals,* 148–149; LL, letter from A. Procter, n.d.; Wister, *Fanny: The American Kemble,* 202–206. **Fanny's reading tours,** LL, newspaper cuttings; Ellen Terry, *The Story of My Life* (London, 1982), 113; FR, 173–175, 299–301: Longfellow, *Selected Letters and Journals,* 49, 150, 166; Samuel Longfellow, *The Life of Henry Wadsworth Longfellow, with Extracts from His Journals and Correspondence* (Ann Arbor, 1968), II, 142, 145, 172. **Lenox,** FR, 194–195; LL, newspaper cuttings; F. A. Kemble and F. A. Butler Leigh, *Principles and Privilege,* ed. Dana D. Nelson (Ann Arbor, 1995), I; Randall Stewart, *Nathaniel Hawthorne* (New Haven, 1948), 106–108; typescript reminiscences by Theodore Sedgwick in possession of Mrs. Alice Wohl; FR, 186–187.

CHAPTER 16. LEIGHTON'S MADONNA.

Algy's birth and the Thuns' visit, Thun, AK–Count Thun, Sept. 5, n.y. (1851), and Oct. 3–4, 1852, and AK–Y. Thun, Mar. 12, 1851, and Jan. 21, 1852. **Charles's and Henry's scandals,** Thun, AK–Count Thun, Oct. 3–4, 1852, and AK–Count Thun, Apr. 7, 1853; Scot, FK–C. Combe, Jan. 9 and 27, Apr. 4 and 17, 1852; Leighton, AK–F. Leighton, Aug. 30, 1860; Leon Edel, *Henry James* (London, 1977), I, 557. **Trip to Italy,** Thun, AK–Count Thun, Oct. 3–4, 1852. **Fanny in Rome,** Folger, FK–H. St. Leger, Nov. 18, 1849; Thackeray, *Letters,* III, 340, 584; IV, 430, 438; FR, 298; A. T. Ritchie, *Chapters from Some Unwritten Memoirs* (New York, 1895), Ch. 11; A. Hare, *The Story of My Life,* VI, 310; Marshall, *Fanny Kemble,* 83 (quote from Mrs. Linton); AWFCH, **Adelaide's unhappiness,** Thun, AK–Count Thun, April 7, 1853. **Society in Rome,** Robert Browning, *The Life and Letters of Robert Browning,* ed. Mrs. Sutherland Orr (London, 1891), 199–200, 248; Robert Browning, *New Letters of Robert Browning,* ed. W. C. de Vane and K. L. Knickerbocker (London, 1951), 67, 74–75; E. B. Browning, *Letters to Her Sister,* ed. L. Huxley (London, 1931), 197–202; Leighton, AK–F. Leighton, Aug. 14, 1858; Lord Newton, *Lord Lyons: A Record of British Diplomacy* (London, 1913), II, 422–423; Leighton, AK–F. Leighton, Aug. 14, 1858; A. T. Ritchie, *Records of Tennyson, Ruskin, Browning* (New York, 1892), 152–155; Harriet Hosmer, *Letters and Memories* (New York, 1913), 23, 26, 32–33, 41, 52; FR, 159–160, 301–311; LA, AK–G. Bloomfield, Jan. 7, 1868; AWFCH, xxxvi–xxxviii, xli; Henry James, *Letters,* ed. Leon Edel (Cambridge, Mass., 1975), II, 199. **Leighton,** Mrs. Russell Barrington, *The Life and Letters and Works of Frederic Leighton* (London, 1906), I, 124–128, 145–149, 165–169, 176–178, 181–184, 193–194, 233, 310; Leonee and Richard Ormond, *Lord Leighton* (New Haven, 1975), 20–25; Leighton, AK–F. Leighton, Aug. 14, 1858; Mar. 27, 1859; Oct. 1, 1862; Nov. 8, 1872; A. Sartoris, *Cornhill Magazine,* IX (April 1864), 436–439. **Bagni di Lucca,** AK–Charles Kemble, July 7, 1854, bMS Thr 357(58), Harvard Theatre Collection, Pusey Library, Harvard University, (quotation describing Rossini); Betty Miller, *Robert Browning* (London, 1958), 159–162. **Charles's and Henry's illnesses,** Williamson, *Charles Kemble,* 239; Thackeray, *Letters,* III, 393; Hosmer, *Letters and Memories,* 532; Thun, AK–Count Thun, Oct. 27, 1855. **In Paris,** H. Greville, *Diary,* II, 298; Hosmer, *Letters and Memories,* 59; AWFCH, 147 and xxv–xxvi; Leighton, AK–F. Leighton, Oct. 13, 1858; Ritchie, *Chapters from Some Unwritten Memoirs,* 200–201; Thun, AK–Count Thun, Oct. 3, 1856. **Henry Greville and Leighton,** Barrington, *Frederick Leighton,* I, 28, 253–268, 282; Ormond, *Lord Leighton,* 36–37; Leighton, AK–F. Leighton, Feb. 18, 1859. **At Westbury House,** Thun, AK–Count Thun, Oct. 3, n.y. (1856), and July 11, 1857; LA, AK–FK, November 1860 and n.d.; Leighton, AK–F. Leighton, Mar. 31, 1859; FR, 343; AWFCH, xliii. **John Kemble's and Henry Kemble's deaths,** LA, AK–FK, Thursday 17 (1857); Thun, AK–Count Thun, July 2, 1857; H. Greville, *Diary,* III, 23. **Adelaide meets Francis Thun,** Thun, AK–Y. Thun, September 1857; AK–FK, Thursday 17 (1857).

CHAPTER 17. A FIERCE AND FURIOUS CONFICT.

Fanny's relationship with her daughters, LA, AK–FK, Thursday 17 (1857); Thun, AK–Count Thun, July 11, 1857, and Mar. 15, 1858. **Pierce's insolvency,** Furnas, *Fanny Kemble,* 375. **Butler slave auction,** London *Times,* Apr. 12, 1859. **Fan in En-**

gland, LA, AK–FK, September 1858; FR, 346. **Owen Wister,** FR, 326, 338; Darwin Payne, *Owen Wister* (Dallas, Tex., 1958), 8–12. **At Lenox,** Barrington, *Frederic Leighton,* II, 68–82; LA, AK–FK, Nov. 29, 1860, and Feb. 10, 1861; FR, 174–175. **Jezebel,** ROLL, II, 92–93. **Fanny's attitude toward war,** FR, 330–331, 335–336; H. Greville, *Diary,* III, 331–333, 351, 364, 373–374, 386, 407; IV, 10–12, 25, 30, 39–40, 81–85; ROLL, I, 259–262. **Pierce's arrest,** FR, 335–336; Furnas, *Fanny Kemble,* 380–382. **Switzerland,** ROG, 2; FR, 287ff. **Fanny's Plantation Journal,** FR, 190; Ritchie, *Chapters from Some Unwritten Memoirs,* 189; LL, newspaper cuttings. **Pierce's death,** LA, AK–G. Bloomfield, Tuesday 15 (1867). **Adelaide's longing for the stage,** AWFCH, xxxv. **Adelaide's social and musical life,** A. Sartoris, *Cornhill Magazine,* XII (1865), 707; LA, AK–G. Bloomfield, n.d. and Jan. 7, Mar. 16, Apr. 2, and July 4, 1867, and July 7, n.y.; Lord Redesdale, *Memories* (London, 1916), 516–517; AWFCH, xlvii. **Adelaide's quarrel with Browning,** Ormond, *Lord Leighton,* 70; Leighton, AK–F. Leighton, Oct. 31 (1874). **Warnford,** W. Page, ed., *The Victoria History of Hampshire and the Isle of Wight* (London, 1908), 268; Thun, AK–Y. Thun, Oct. 3, 1864; AWFCH, xvii, xix; LA, AK–G. Bloomfield, 23, n.y.; Leighton, AK–F. Leighton, July 28, 1866; Kaplan, *Henry James,* 355; A. T. Ritchie, *Chapters from Some Unwritten Memoirs,* 199–200. **A Week in a French Country House,** AWFCH, xv–xvii; LA, AK–G. Bloomfield, Mar. 16, 1867. **Reading tours,** Louisa May Alcott, *Life, Letters and Journals,* ed. Ednah D Cheney (New York, 1995), 136. **Fan on the plantation, at Butler Place, and married,** FR, 346–347; Kemble and Butler Leigh, *Principles and Privilege,* xvi–xix, xxx ff; Furnas, *Fanny Kemble,* 410. **James Leigh,** FR, 195; James, *Letters,* II, 147. **Henry James,** Henry James, *Temple Bar Magazine,* April 1893, 517–522; James, *Letters,* I, 316–318, 322; II, 211, 225; Edel, *Henry James,* I, 367, 556–558; F. Kaplan, *Henry James,* 143–144, 355–356. **At Butler Place,** FR, 21, 29–31, 35–36, 38.

CHAPTER 18. GHOSTS.

Greville Sartoris, Thun, AK–Y. Thun, Oct. 3, 1864; LA, AK–G. Bloomfield, Feb. 26, n.y., Mar. 11, n.y.; Aug. 14, 1867. **Warsash,** LA, AK–G. Bloomfield, June 15, Aug. 6 and 27, 1867; Thun, AK–Count Thun, Nov. 26, 1868. **To Tetschen and Vienna,** Thun, handwritten diary of AK: LA, AK–G. Bloomfield, Aug. 6, n.y.; Tetschen, n.d.; Paris, 9th, n.y. **Adelaide's birthday,** LA, AK–G. Bloomfield, Feb. 26, n.y. **Edward in Parliament,** Thun, AK–Count Thun, Nov. 24, 1867. **Adelaide's ill health,** FR, 363. **Leighton and Vichy,** Ormond, *Lord Leighton,* 69–71; Leighton, AK–F. Leighton, Aug. 23, n.y.; Dec. 4, 1865; Sept. 12, 1875; LA, AK–May Sartoris, Friday 6, n.y.; Philip Henderson, *Swinburne* (London, 1974), 153. Swinburne's elegy is entitled *An Evening at Vichy;* Christopher Newell, *The Art of Lord Leighton* (London, 1990), 84. **May's marriage,** Thun, AK–Y. Thun, Feb. 25 and Apr. 27, 1871; Oct. 3, 1873; W. G. Elliott, *IN My Anecdotage* (London, 1925), 115. **Francis's death,** Thun, AK–Y. Thun, Nov. 29, Dec. 4, 1870. **Algy to America,** Thun, AK–Y. Thun, Sept. 1, 1872. **To Italy,** Thun, AK–Count Thun, Oct. 3, 1872; LT, AK–May Evans-Gordon, n.d. **Tetschen,** LT, AK–F. Leighton, Dec. 3, 1872. **Count Thun's death,** Thun, AK–Y. Thun, Jan. 21, Oct. 3, 1873, and Oct. 3, 1875. **Henry Greville's death,** Thun, AK–Y. Thun, Feb. 17, 1873. **Greville Sartoris's death,** Thun, AK–Count Thun, Oct. 3, 1870, and AK–Y. Thun, Oct. 30, 1873, and Jan. 18, 1874.

CHAPTER 19. "LIKE THE END OF SOME REIGN."

Adelaide's grief, LA, AK–FK, Jan. 14 (1874); Thun, AK–Y. Thun, July 22, 1874; FR, 353; Ormond, *Lord Leighton*, 72. **Algy's marriage,** FR, 11, 353; Thun, AK–Y. Thun, Jan. 18, 1874; Leighton, AK–F. Leighton, Jan. 11 (1874); Furnas, 412; *New York Times*, May 22, 1874. **Venice,** Leighton, AK–F. Leighton, Oct. 31 (1874). **At Warsash,** LA, AK–May Evans-Gordon, June 30, (1875); Leighton, AK–F. Leighton, Jan. 24, 1877; Thun, AK–Y. Thun, Jan. 18, Oct. 3, 1876. **At Rome,** Leighton, AK–F. Leighton, January 1877. **President Grant,** Thun, AK–Y. Thun, Oct. 3, 1877. **Rome and Mario,** Thun, AK–Y. Thun, Jan. 18, 1878; Forbes, *Mario and Grisi*, 211–212; FR, 244–245. **Henry James at Warsash,** James, *Letters*, II, 147–148, 231–234; Ritchie, *Chapters from Some Unwritten Memoirs*, 199; ROLL, II, 170. **Adelaide's last months,** Ormond, *Lord Leighton*, 72; Leighton, AK–F. Leighton, June 18, 1879; Thun, May Evans-Gordon–Y. Thun, Aug. 9, 1879; LA, AK–May Evans-Gordon, Nov. 25 (1877); Folger, Anne Procter–FK, Aug. 9, 1879; **Adelaide's funeral,** Folger, Anne Procter–FK, Aug. 17, 1879; information kindly supplied me by the Reverend J. H. B. Talbot, rector of St. Mary's Church Ightham. **Fanny's last years,** Ritchie, *Chapters from Some Unwritten Memoirs*, 191–192, 195–197, 203–205; FR, 224, 225, 243, 249, 233, 266, 269,272, 275–277, 364; James, *Letters*, II, 147, 211, 225, 232–234, 241, 310; III, 211–213, 399–402; James, *Temple Bar Magazine*, April 1893, 522–523; Hunt, FK–Polly, Sunday 26, n.y., and FK–Blanch, 1887; Furnas, *Fanny Kemble*, 442–443; Kemble and Butler Leigh, *Principles and Privilege*, xviii–xix; Folger, Ellen Brianzoni–Frances Cobbe, Jan. 19, 1893.

Index

< 329 >

A NOTE ON THE AUTHOR

Ann Blainey, who lives in East Melbourne, Australia, has published two literary biographies, *The Farthing Poet* (about Richard Hengist Horne) and *Immortal Boy* (a portrait of Leigh Hunt). Ms. Blainey studied English and history at the University of Melbourne and soon after began writing biography. She is a member of the National Council of Opera Australia, the nation's main opera company, and an elected member of the governing council of the University of Melbourne.